The Great Mail Order Bazaar

THE GREAT MAIL ORDER BAZAAR

by Irvin Molotsky

TIMBRE BOOKS

Arbor House   New York

Manufactured in the United States of America

10 9 8 7 6 5 4 3 2 1

Library of Congress Cataloging in Publication Data

Molotsky, Irvin.
   The great mail order bazaar.

   1. Mail-order business—Directories.   2. Catalogs,
Commercial—Directories.   I. Title.
HF5466.M59   1986   381′.14′0294   85-16489
ISBN 0-87795-641-3

Design by Laura Hough

To Iris

❖ Acknowledgments

This book was written with a Kaypro II computer on which I used two software programs mastered by my wife, Iris. They were the Perfect Filer program, for compiling and keeping track of the questionnaires that I sent to upwards of 5,000 mail-order companies, and the Perfect Writer program, for putting everything together. The people at Kaypro and at Perfect Filer and Perfect Writer were very helpful when I ran into problems and Iris or I phoned them for assistance. My family and I entered the computer age in our home with this book and there is no turning back.

My whole family was part of this enterprise. When it became clear that the undertaking was much bigger than anyone could have expected, their tolerance was extraordinary. Besides handling the computer end, Iris joined our daughters, Michele and Ellen, and my mother-in-law, Blanche Madley, in stuffing, stamping, and addressing envelopes. They also helped out in the tasting of sample foods, particularly my younger daughter, Ellen, who became quite adept at it. Our letter carriers were tolerant as well. There were some days when the mail would include perhaps fifty catalogues, which certainly doubled the burden on our block, but I never heard anything but a cheery word from the nice people who work for the Postal Service.

❖ Contents

Introduction   **xiii**

   Buying by Mail Order   **xv**
   The Law   **xvi**

1. The Big Selection   **1**

   Department Stores and Mail-Order
     Giants   **1**
   Country and General Stores   **4**
   Sale and Surplus Goods   **5**

2. Food and Drink   **7**

   Gourmet, Ethnic, and Special
     Foods   **8**
   Meat, Fish, and Seafood   **18**
   Cheese   **22**
   Fruit and Nuts   **25**
   Grains and Vegetables, Natural and
     Freeze-Dried Foods   **28**
   Baked Goods, Sweets, and Snacks   **32**
   Coffee, Tea, Condiments, and Pre-
     serves   **40**
   Herbs and Spices   **42**
   Wine and Liquor   **45**

3. Food Companions   **46**

   Cookware and Dinnerware   **47**

   Wine- and Beer-Making Supplies   **52**
   Cheese-Making Supplies   **54**
   Cookbooks   **55**

4. Clothing and Accessories   **56**

   Specialty Department Stores   **57**
   Men's and Women's Clothing   **58**
   Casual and Sports Clothing, Western Wear,
     Printed T-Shirts, and Team
     Jackets   **64**
   Work Clothes and Uniforms   **68**
   Women's Clothing   **69**
   Men's Clothing   **74**
   Furs   **76**
   Hosiery, Lingerie, Underwear, and Lounge
     Wear   **76**
   Shoes and Other Footwear   **78**
   Gloves and Scarves   **81**
   Luggage, Handbags, Briefcases, Canes and
     Umbrellas, Travel Clocks   **82**
   Belts, Buckles, and Buttons, Uniform
     Insignia   **83**
   Jewelry, Watches, Diamonds, and
     Gems   **83**
   Wigs   **85**
   Hats   **85**

5. Parents and Children   86

    *For Mothers and Mothers-to-Be and for
        Fathers, Too*   86
    For Children   87

6. For the Home   94

    Furniture and Furnishings   95
    Clocks and Clock-Making Kits   105
    Bedding, Linens, and Towels   103
    Lamps and Lighting Fixtures   106
    Wall Coverings and Curtains   108
    Floor Coverings   109
    *Closet Accessories and Storage
        Trunks*   110
    Hardware for the Home   110
    *Wood Stoves, Solar Devices, Insulating
        Materials, Heaters, Windmills and
        Armageddon Supplies*   113
    Hot Tubs and Saunas   115
    *Building and Architectural
        Supplies*   116

7. Collectibles and Decorations   117

    Antiques   118
    *Cloissoné, Lacquerware, Paperweights,
        and Collector's Plates*   119
    Music Boxes   120
    Sculpture   121
    *Paintings, Prints, Posters, Maps, and
        Decorative Printed Matter*   121
    *Movie and Fan Posters and
        Pictures*   125
    Signs, Insignia, and Militaria   126
    *Railroadiana and Firehouse
        Memorabilia*   127
    *Coins, Stamps, Sports Memorabilia, and
        Postcards*   127
    Fossils, Shells, and Minerals   128
    Collectible Junque   128
    Flags   128

    Floral and Fruit Decorations   129
    *Accessories for Collectibles and
        Decorations*   129

8. Marvelous Machines   131

    *Audio and Video Equipment, Computers,
        Electronics, Appliances, and Gad-
        gets*   132
    *Cameras and Optics, Photographic Sup-
        plies, and Photofinishing*   138
    *Telephones and Telephone Equip-
        ment*   140
    *Fire and Burglar Alarms, Security Equip-
        ment*   140

9. Marvelous Machine Accompani-
    ments   141

    *Records, Audio Tapes, and Compact
        Disks*   142
    Films and Video Tapes   147
    Computer Software and Books   149

10. Driving, Riding, and Flying
    Machines   150

    Automotive Needs   151
    Bicycles and Motorcycles   159
    Aviation   160

11. The Great Outdoors   162

    Sporting Goods   164
    Boating and Fishing Supplies   165
    Camping Equipment   169
    Army and Navy Goods   173
    Birding and Wildlife Supplies   174

12. For the Garden   176

    Seeds and Plants   177
    Garden Tools, Equipment, and

Furniture **194**
Beekeeping Supplies **197**

13. **For Horses and Other Pets** **199**
Pet Supplies **200**
*Horse Supplies and Riding
Equipment* **201**

14. **Crafts and Hobbies** **203**
General Craft Supplies **204**
*Needlecrafts, Weaving, and Textile
Dyeing, Fabrics and Yarn* **206**
Art Supplies **212**
*Calligraphy, Bookbinding, Paper-Making,
and Art Preservation* **214**
Ceramics and Sculpture Supplies **215**
Woodworking Tools and Lumber **216**
*Basket-Making, Caning, and Furniture
Webbing* **218**
*Plans and Patterns for Do-It-
Yourselfers* **219**
*Model and Hobby Kits and
Supplies* **219**
*Tools and Equipment for Craftspeople,
Tinkerers, and Do-It-
Yourselfers* **221**
Crafts to Buy **224**

15. **The Performing Arts** **231**
Musical Instruments **231**
Music Books and Fan Accessories **238**
*Dance and Theater Supplies and
Costumes* **239**

16. *Amusements and Vices* **241**
Games and Toys **242**
Fireworks **243**
Novelty Items and Gag Gadgets **244**
Novelty Rubber Stamps **245**
Erotica and Far-Out Amusements **245**
Tobacco and Smoking Equipment **246**

17. **Religious and Spiritual
Needs** **248**
Religious Articles and Books **249**
*Occult, Meditation, Self-Help,
Astrology* **250**

18. **Health Care and Beauty
Aids** **252**
*Vitamins, Herbs, and Health
Guides* **253**
Cosmetics and Perfume **255**
*Medical Supplies and Physical
Aids* **256**
*Eyeglasses and Hearing Aids, Eye and Ear
Protectors* **258**
*Supplies and Services for the Physically
and Visually Handicapped* **258**

19. **Stationery and Business and Social
Needs** **260**
Stationery and Office Supplies **260**
Wedding Stationery and Supplies **264**
Party Supplies **264**
Office Furnishings and Equipment **265**
*Clip Art, Printing, and Promotional
Services* **265**
Promotional Gifts and Premiums **266**

20. **Reading Matter** **268**
General Booksellers **269**
*Out-of-Print and Used Books and Modern
First Editions* **272**
*Rare and Finely Printed Books,
Juvenalia* **274**
Art and Illustrated Books **277**
Poetry, Literature, Mysteries **277**
*Books on Business and Technol-
ogy* **278**
*Selected University, Scholarly, and Small
Presses* **278**

Government Publications   **286**
*Foreign Books, Foreign Language and
    Culture, Travel Guides*   **287**
Magazines   **288**
Comics   **289**

21. Gifts   **290**
    Fine and Unusual Gifts   **290**
    Gifts for Nature Lovers   **298**
    *Museum, Botanic Garden, and Public
        Radio Gift Catalogues*   **299**

❖ Introduction

Why another book on catalogues? That's a good question, and I hope my answer will satisfy you.

More and more Americans are using mail order to do more and more of their shopping, and I expect that a lot of people will find this book useful in discovering mail-order sources they didn't know about. There are many wonderful mail-order houses that are familiar to everyone—like Sears, for example—but there are also thousands of much smaller firms that have marvelous products for sale. In this book I will tell you about Sears and other large companies, of course, but I will also tell you about some of those thousands of small operations that just might have the perfect product for you.

An estimated 6.7 billion catalogues were mailed to Americans in 1983, and an even larger number is expected to be sent out in the coming years. One of the homes to receive some of these catalogues will no doubt be yours.

There are numerous reasons for this great rise in mail-order sales. One of the most important is the increasing number of two-income families. With both husband and wife at work five days a week, there is less time for traditional shopping trips to convenient outlets. In these cases, the mail-order catalogue is often not only a convenience, but even a necessity.

Another reason is selection. Many catalogues offer a greater variety of a particular kind of merchandise than even the largest stores, let alone the smaller ones. This is certainly the case in some of the areas I emphasized in this book. By mail you can buy unusual foods that otherwise could be bought only by visiting, for example, some backwater in the Appalachians, good books published by such unheralded sources as university presses, and seeds for plants that you might not know even exist. In addition, there are many more cataloguers than there are retailers in your area, so the likelihood of your finding what you want is greater when you shop by mail.

Furthermore, being members of an extremely mobile society, we cannot always control where we are going to wind up. A family transferred to a sparsely populated section of the upper Middle West can take with it tastes acquired in New York, Chicago, or Los Angeles and be able to satisfy many of their cravings through the mails.

Another factor in the rise of mail order has been the availability of toll-free telephone numbers. During the energy crunches of the 1970's, the cataloguers tried to advertise the patriotism of shopping by mail or phone instead of car. There is no such energy crisis as I write this, but who knows what the future may bring? It may become again patriotic to shop from mail-order catalogues.

Finally, many mail-order companies advertise that they have lower prices than conventional outlets, despite postage, printing, and other costs.

The Consumers Union conducted a survey of its members on mail order and reported the results in the October 1983 issue of *Consumer Reports*. Only 14 percent of the people who responded said that the main reason they bought through direct mail was low prices. Thirty-two percent said the reason was that the merchandise was not available to them elsewhere, and almost as many, 31 percent, cited convenience. Nineteen percent said they were attracted by the high quality of the goods. On the other hand, 60 percent said that a major disadvantage was that they could not see the merchandise before putting in the order.

In many matters of taste, I am an admirer of my colleague Warren Weaver Jr., a veteran correspondent in the Washington Bureau of *The New York Times*. Just before a recent national election, Warren popped some letters in the mail and announced to those of us nearest him that he had taken care of another year's Christmas shopping. War-

ren is obviously much more organized than the rest of us. I don't start thinking about Christmas shopping until mid-December; here it was the beginning of November and Warren was just about finished.

Over the years, Warren had gradually learned to discipline himself and to plan ahead. "The Christmas catalogues these days start arriving around the end of August and stop around the end of October," Warren told me. "I save them, I read them, and when I find something I like, I turn down the corner of the page." He is on so many mailing lists that he will receive 15 to 20 catalogues a day during peak periods, and he at least skims every one of them. One thing he has found is that many mail-order companies will be offering identical things that are popular at a particular time. In those cases, it is easy enough for the mail-order shopper to look for the company with the lowest price.

I asked Warren if he had ever had a bad experience in ordering by mail. "Financially, no," he answered. "Sometimes you get something that isn't right. Once I ordered a laurel wreath—you pick off the leaves and use them for bay leaf in cooking as you need it—but it was rotten. We sent it back and got a substitute."

Since both Warren and his wife work, they have the purchases sent to his office, which is always open, instead of home. "Sometimes that creates a problem—especially if the package is too big, because then it has to be dragged home."

Warren is kind of my guru in this field. It was he who put me on to a record supplier in Pennsylvania that was able to come up with some records of Ella Fitzgerald that I wanted for my daughter Michele. Who would have thought that I would find an answer to a problem like that in the middle of Pennsylvania? But I found records there that I couldn't find in the best record stores in Washington. That was one of my inspirations for this book.

I have selected for listing in this book mail-order companies that sell products that appeal to me and my family, that I suspect would be interesting to others with specialized interests, or that sell products that would satisfy popular tastes and hobbies. In many ways, this could be viewed as more than a compendium of catalogues, but rather a statement of American tastes and interests at this point in our history. I sent questionnaires to thousands of mail-order companies and thousands of them filled them out and returned them to me along with samples of their catalogues; some of the places that sell food even sent samples of their merchandise.

Buying by Mail Order

Catalogue Frequency.   The number of catalogues that a company issues each year is important because something in the fall number may not be available in the spring if a company publishes four catalogues a year. However, if it is a once-a-year catalogue, there should be no problem in ordering later. A company that really wants your business will go out of its way to provide objects from previous catalogues. In some cases, catalogues are not published on a regular basis, but instead are issued in the same form for many years, with a price list updated from time to time for inclusion.

Catalogue Cost.   Although many companies put price tags on their catalogues, most of them will send a catalogue without fee if you simply ask for it. For some reason, this is particularly prevalent among gardening firms. For reasons best known to marketing geniuses, many of these catalogues carry cover prices although they actually are free. One company officer said his catalogue was free but carried a price tag because it was placed on the counter of his retail operation as a free give-away, and the price tag discouraged people from taking more than one. Some of the superbly printed garden catalogues, however, really will cost you some money. Most catalogues are free because the customer is the important character in the plot. The company advertises the availability of its catalogue, sends out the catalogue, and hopes for a sale. If you ask for a catalogue, you are presumed to be part way down the path toward a sale. If you get on a mailing list, in fact, you may find it a permanent circumstance. And if the company rents out its list to another company, yet another catalogue will wing its way toward you.

Discount Operations.   I asked companies whether they had discount prices. I have made note of those that responded in the affirmative, but that is their own description. You still have to do your homework and use your common sense. (I have marked operations that claim to be discounters with an asterisk, for quick reference.) There are three basic kinds of discounters—wholesalers that sell large quantities at a discount, merchants that usually sell at list price but occasionally have sales, and true discounters that sell merchandise retail and at below list price.

Manner of Payment. Although some companies responded to my questionnaire by saying that they would accept cash as payment, I would urge that no one make mail-order purchases with cash. Almost all companies responded that they accepted checks or money orders. However, some companies will not ship a purchase until the check clears the bank, which can take a week or so. This is not necessary with money orders. My preferred method of payment is with credit cards. This gives you the same record as a check, and it also gives you the muscle of the credit card company in case there is a problem. In addition, the company can send out the purchase the same day it receives the order, rather than waiting for a check to clear. For any purchases of a high-price item, I think it's a good idea always to ask whether you can get a discount for paying by check or money order instead of by credit card.

Manner of Shipment. Many companies prefer United Parcel Service over the Postal Services for reasons of cost and supposed reliability. I have neither compared nor tested these services, but the Postal Service goes everywhere and United parcel does not or cannot. For example, United Parcel cannot deliver to a Post Office box. If you do not have an address served by United Parcel, you must make sure that the seller will use the Postal Service; failing that, have the package delivered by United Parcel to the home of a friend served by that agency.

Returns Policy. I have tried to include as much consumer information as possible. However, in those cases where I had to omit some consumer information—otherwise, this

book would have been so big and the price so high that no one would have bought it—or the firm did not provide it, the reader is advised to determine the refund policy.

Postage Cost. One thing to look for is whether the company includes the postage in its price. Not many do, but those that do actually are offering a lower price than what is apparent because there are no additional shipping fees.

Telephone Service. Some companies do not accept phone orders. Where no phone number is listed, the company has no phone either for orders or for complaints or problems. There has been a great rise in the number of companies with toll-free 800 numbers. Since they change from time to time, it is good to keep in mind that there is an information number that may be called to see if the company you are interested in has a toll-free number. The information numbers is (800) 555-1212. You can also call this number to find out if you have to dial 1 at the beginning of a particular 800 number from your area.

Gift Services. Many of the firms listed here offer gift service. These are indicated throughout by a dagger (†) preceding the entry.

The Law

Because virtually all catalogue sales cross state lines and because the mails are usually involved, there is a clear federal role in protecting consumers against fraud. Here are the rules that the Federal Trade Commission enforces:

- A mail-order company must send ordered goods within the time period specified in its advertisements or within 30 days if no shipping date is specified.
- If the company cannot meet this deadline, it must send notification (before the deadline) and permit the consumer either to receive a prompt refund or to agree to a delay. The notice must include the new shipping date, instructions on how to cancel the order, and a postge-paid means of reply.
- If the consumer agrees to a new shipping date and the company is again unable to meet it, the company must send a second notice. Unless the consumer signs and returns this postage-paid notice, the company must automatically cancel the order.
- If the consumer chooses a refund, the company must refund the money within seven business days after receiving the consumer's request for orders paid in cash, or credit the account within one billing cycle for orders paid by credit card.

These rules do not apply to photofinishing services, magazine subscriptions after the first issue, C.O.D. orders, and seeds and plants. There is another curious exception that you ought to be aware of, and it is so odd that it probably would never have occurred to you: These rules do not protect the buyer if the order was made by telephone. Until that is changed, FTC officials recommend that people concerned about their rights send their payments by mail instead of using their credit cards with telephone orders. On the other hand, sometimes it might be an advantage to use a credit card. An American Express officer once told me that the credit card company will always put pressure on a mail-order firm to satisfy complaints. Otherwise, he said, American Express could choose to make the refund itself to the consumer and bill the mail-order firm for the cost. If the mail-order firm refuses to pay, it runs the risk of losing the valuable ability of offering people the opportunity to make purchases with American Express cards.

If you feel you have gotten a raw deal from a mail-order company, you can also complain to your credit card company (if such means of payment was used), to the Federal Trade Commission, or to the Direct Marketing Association, the organization that most reputable mail-order companies belong to. The Direct Marketing Association can attempt to straighten things out; the FTC cannot, but rather collects complaints to determine if there is a pattern that might suggest government action against the company involved. The FTC has many local offices, so check your telephone directory under U.S. Government. If there is no office in your area, the headquarters is at Sixth Street and Pennsylvania Ave., N.W., Washington, D.C. 20580. An FTC leaflet on direct mail may be obtained by writing to the Washington address or telephoning (202) 523-3598. With all the millions of mail-order purchases, the FTC gets perhaps 9,000 complaints a year.

The FTC offered the following suggestions on making mail-order purchases:

- Note the shipping date specified in the ad and order early to allow plenty of time for delivery.

- Examine the company's return policy. If the ad does not tell you what it is, inquire before you order.
- When in doubt, check the firm's reputation with the local Better Business Bureau or state or local consumer protection agency.
- Keep copies of the company's name and address, the date of the order, the advertisement or catalogue from which you ordered, the order form, and the canceled check or charge-account records.

- Once the order arrives, keep all papers, such as invoices and packing slips. If the product is damaged, is the wrong size, or is otherwise unsatisfactory and there are no enclosed instructions on what to do about it, write to the company, explain the problem, and ask how to return the purchase. If the goods appear to have been damaged in shipment, call the Postal Service or the delivery agency.

❖1 The Big Selection

Here are places that have goods that might not be found down the street. Gimbels may not tell Macy's (or is it the other way 'round?), but both of them will tell you. Here are the country's largest merchandisers, including the very largest, Sears, and sources of some of the most unusual things available anywhere in the world.

And when it comes to thoughts of worldwide sources, what can be better than Harrods, the landmark store in the West End of London?

Department Stores and Mail-Order Giants

ABRAHAM & STRAUS, *P.O. Box 731, Brooklyn, N.Y. 11202. Tel. (718) 625-6000. Free 24- to 32-page catalogue issued frequently.*

Clothing, furniture, housewares, linens, audio and video equipment, perfume and cosmetics. Payment by check, money order, or A & S charge.

B. ALTMAN & CO., *361 Fifth Avenue, New York, N.Y. 10016. Tel. (212) 689-7000, (800) 228-5444 (except in Nebraska) or (800) 642-8777 (in Nebraska). Free 100-page-plus catalogue issued frequently.*

One of New York's nicest stores for furniture, gifts, clothing. Payment by check, money order, American Express, Visa, Mastercard, Diners Club, or Altman's charge. Shipment by truck in local area and Postal Service outside it.

BERKELEY HOUSE ENTERPRISES, *815 New York Avenue, Martinsburg, W.Va. 25401. Tel. (304) 267-2673. Free 24-page catalogue issued 4 times a years.*

A large assortment of clothing, housewares, tools, computer hardware and software, and gardening equipment. Payment by check, money order, Visa, or Mastercard. Shipment by Postal Service or United Parcel. Purchases may be returned within 10 days for refund.

BLOOMINGDALE'S BY MAIL, *115 Brand Rd., Salem, Va. 24156. Tel. (800) 368-3438. Free 100-page catalogue issued frequently.*

This store considers itself to be America's trend setter, and not too many would disagree. People visiting New York for the first time ought to stop in at Bloomie's flagship store at 59th Street and Lexington Avenue. Clothing, luggage, indoor and outdoor furniture, housewares, audio and video equipment, fine china, silver, and crystal.

MARSHALL FIELD'S, *111 North State St., Chicago, Ill. 60690. Tel. (312) 781-1000. Catalogue costs $2.*

GIMBELS, *Broadway and 33rd Street, New York, N.Y. 10001. Tel. (212) 736-5100. Frequent catalogues of varying size.*

Clothing and accessories, furniture and furnishings, stamps and coins. Payment by check, money order, or Gimbel's charge.

GOKEY'S, *84 South Wabasha, St. Paul, Minn. 55107. Tel (612) 224-4300. Free catalogue.*

*GREAT WESTERN, *P.O. Box 1126, Lewiston, Idaho 83501. Tel. (208) 746-3605, (800) 635-5802 (except in Idaho), or (800) 632-2043 (in Idaho). Free 432-page catalogue issued annually.*

This huge catalogue has discount prices on many, many items and is aimed primarily at people in the Western states. Payment by check, money order, Visa, or Mastercard. Shipment by Postal Service or United Parcel. Purchases may be returned within 10 days for refund.

HANOVER HOUSE INDUSTRIES, *Hanover, Pa. 17331. Tel. (717) 637-1600, (800) 621-5800 (except in Illinois), or (800) 972-5858 (in Illinois). Enormous assortment of catalogues.*

This looks like the General Motors of mail order. It has 20 catalogue divisions, including *Hanover House, Cosmopedics, Lakeland Nurseries Sales, Adam York, New Hampton General Store, Hampton Farms, Night 'N Day Intimates, First Editions, Pennsylvania Station, Old Village Shop, Chelsea Collection,* and *Imprints.* In a recent year the company issued 230 million catalogues. Payment by check, American Express, Visa, Mastercard, Diners Club, or

* Indicates firms that discount, offer a discount for bulk purchases, or have special sale catalogues or catalogue items.

Carte Blanche. Delivery by Postal Service or United Parcel. Purchases may be returned within 14 days for refund.

HARRODS, *Brompton Road, Knightsbridge, London SW1X 7XL, England. Tel. (01) 730-1234. Semiannual 150-page catalogue costs $5.50 when mailed to the United States (it costs 1.50 pounds sterling in Britain).*

One of the most famous (and expensive) department stores in the world for food, furnishings, clothes, and gifts. Payment by check, money order, American Express, Visa, Mastercard, Diners Club, or Harrods charge. Shipment by Postal Service, United Parcel, or air or sea freight. Purchases may be returned within 30 days for refund.

HECHT'S, *P.O. Box 50130, F Street Station, Washington, D.C. 20004. Tel. (202) 626-8000 in Washington or (301) 685-4444 in Baltimore. Free catalogues of varying sizes issued several times a year.*

This Washington-based chain has a good reputation and good merchandise.

JELMOLI-VERSAND, *8112 Otelfingen, Switzerland. Tel. (01) 849-11-11. Free 700-page catalogue issued twice a year.*

This is a very large catalogue written in German and with the prices given in Swiss francs. It seems to have everything.

MILES KIMBALL OF OSHKOSH, *41 W. Eighth Ave., Oshkosh, Wis. 54901. Tel. (414) 231-3800. Free 64-196-page catalogue issued 5 times a year.*

This is a very varied catalogue of housewares, toys, gifts, and personal items from a very large mail-order firm. Payment by check

or money order. Purchases may be returned for refund or replacement.

L. L. BEAN. *See listing under* Casual and Sports Clothing, Western Wear, Printed T-Shirts, and Team Jackets.

LORD & TAYLOR, *424 Fifth Avenue, New York, N.Y. 10018. Tel. (212) 391-3344. Free 40- to 100-page catalogues.*

Fine furniture, clothing, gifts.

MACY'S, *Broadway and 34th Street, New York, N.Y. 10001. Tel. (212) 971-6000. Catalogues of varying size issued frequently; 3 catalogues $3 a year in the United States and $10 outside the country.*

Mail-order offerings from the world's largest store. You can find almost anything here from clothing and cosmetics to furniture, housewares, and audio and video equipment.

NEIMAN-MARCUS, *1618 Main St., Dallas, Tex. 75201. Tel. (808) 634-6267. The 32-to-118 page catalogues are priced at $5 to $7.*

This company has become widely known beyond its Texas base through the merchandising skills and promotional instincts of its longtime boss, Stanley Marcus. Its merchandise, including clothing, kitchenware, and gifts, is of the highest quality.

J. C. PENNEY, *P. O. Box 2056, Milwaukee, Wis. Tel. (800) 222-6161. Free catalogues of varying size.*

Catalogues for, among other things, men's clothing, women's and half-size clothing, professional apparel for women and men, as well as home furnishings, cookware, some appliances and sporting goods. The Christmas catalogue also has toys. This is the country's second largest cataloguer.

SEARS, ROEBUCK & CO., *Sears Tower, Chicago, Ill. 60684. Tel. (312) 875-2500. There are 2 general catalogues a year of about 1,300 pages, sent free to customers who have placed at least 2 catalogue orders of at least $30 within 6 months. It is also available in stores for $4, redeemable on any purchase of $20 or more.*

This is the world's leading cataloguer. One of the reasons may be the company's attention to details: Instead of filling out and returning my questionnaire for this book, the company detailed an employee to answer all of my questions in a very complete letter. Another reason is the quality of the merchandise. I have never been disappointed with a Sears purchase. Besides the main catalogue, Sears is now offering the following specialty catalogues, which it calls Specialogs (ugh!): *Women's and Half Sizes; Big and Tall Men; Mother-to-Be and Baby; Western; Uniforms; Home Health Care; Home Improvement; Kitchen and Bath; Kenmore Appliances; Carpeting; Farm, Ranch and Garden; Power and Hand Tools; Mobile Homes; Office Supplies; Sears Calling; Especially for Cooks; Stitch 'n Latch Crafts; Cameras and Photo Supplies; Toys; Recreational Vehicles and Camping; and Boating.* Payment by check or Sears credit card. Delivery by Postal Service or motor carrier, or merchandise can be picked up at catalogue centers. Merchandise

may be returned for refund, without time limit.

SPIEGEL, *1515 W. 22nd St., Oak Brook, Ill. Tel. (800) 345-4500. Catalogue as large as 528 pages costs $3, refundable against purchase.*

This is said to be the fastest-rising cataloguer in the United States. After some years in the doldrums, it is now the third largest cataloguer in the country and is attracting increasing numbers of customers with more expensive merchandise, including fine clothing, than that offered by most large cataloguers. The huge, beautifully put together catalogue is indicative of the company's attention to quality.

WOODWARD & LOTHROP, *Washington, D.C. 20013. Tel. (202) 783-7600 in the Washington area, or (301) 256-8030 in the Baltimore area. Free catalogues.*

One of the best department stores in the Washington area.

See also *Specialty Department Stores.*

Country and General Stores

COUNTRYSIDE GENERAL STORE, *Route 1, Box 7, Waterloo, Wis. 53594. Tel. (414) 478-2115 or (414) 478-2139. Free 36-page catalogue issued 3 times a year.*

All kinds of equipment for cooking food, including a cherry pitter, a corn cutter, a walnut huller, an inertial nutcracker—even a food dehydrator. There are also books on cooking, Aladdin and other oil lamps, scythes and other farm implements, and books and equipment for gardening, raising poultry, rabbits, goats, cows, and sheep, and cheese-making. Payment by check, money order, Visa, Mastercard, or C.O.D. Shipment by Postal Service or United Parcel. Refunds for goods returned within 30 days.

HARVARD COOPERATIVE SOCIETY (*The Coop*), *1400 Massachusetts Ave., Cambridge, Mass. 02238. Tel. (617) 492-1000, (800) 343-5570 (except in Massachusetts), or (800) 792-5170 (in Massachusetts). Free annual 36-page catalogue.*

The society follows the principles established when it was formed in 1882 to provide members of the Harvard-M.I.T. community with merchandise at competitive prices and to distribute the earnings among the members. Goods available include books, records, men's and women's clothing, sports equipment and clothing, prints, posters, and many other things.

JENIFER HOUSE, *New Marlboro Stage, Great Barrington, Mass. 01230. Tel. (413) 528-1500. Twice-a-year 104-page catalogue costs 50 cents.*

The furniture includes chairs, rockers, and loveseats. Among the other products are rugs, china, lamps, pewter, cookware, clocks, bedding, children's furniture and toys, hardware, and a large line of women's dresses, skirts, blouses, and sleepwear. Payment by check, money order, American Express, Visa, or Mastercard. Shipment by Postal Service or United Parcel. Refunds or credit for goods returned within 7 days of receipt.

OLD FORGE HARDWARE, *Old Forge, N.Y. 13420. Tel. (315) 369-6100 or (315) 357-3524.*

A-frames, baskets, bedding, books, campfittings, fireplace accessories, gourmet supplies, housewares, paints, sporting goods, sweaters, stoneware, woodenware. If you are vacationing in the southern Adirondacks, this is a great place to spend a rainy day.

ORVIS, *10 River Rd., Manchester, Vt. 05254 Tel. (802) 362-1300. Free 56- or 96-page catalogues issued 7 times a year.*

Besides being one of the oldest mail-order companies in the United States, Orvis says it is also the oldest fishing rod manufacturer in existence. The orientation, of course, is toward the outdoors, and there are fishing tackle, hunting clothes, guns, traditional country clothing, and gifts.

THE VERMONT COUNTRY STORE, *Route 100, Weston, Vt. 05161. Tel. (802) 824-3184. The 96-page catalogue issued 3 times a year costs 25 cents.*

This catalogue is subtitled "Voice of the Mountains." It offers bedding, men's and women's clothing, and some food items such as popcorn and griddle-cake mix.

Sales and Surplus Goods

GRAND FINALE, *P.O. Box 340, Farmers Branch, Tex. 75234. Tel. (214) 934-9777. Free 32-page catalogue.*

Here is a real miscellaneous catalogue. The premise is that Grand Finale buys manufacturers' closeouts and thereby offers good merchandise at low prices.

JERRYCO, *601 Linden Place, Evanston, Ill. 60202. Tel. (312) 475-8440. Quarterly 48-page catalogue costs 50 cents.*

This company sells, at discount prices, industrial and military surplus that will appeal to teachers, tinkerers, lab experimenters, manufacturers, model makers, collectors of the bizarre, atronomers, artists, do-it-yourselfers, small retailers, flea marketeers, the curious, or anyone seeking hard-to-find items. Some examples: U.S. Navy practice bombs (empty), Swiss music box movements (without the power source to rotate the drum that makes the music), magnets, rabbit fur, acupuncture dolls, tools, switches, motors, and scientific equipment.

See also *Army and Navy Goods.*

❖2 Food and Drink

Food may be the area covered by this book with the most surprises and delights for readers. There are many mail-order food companies, some of which advertise and some of which do not. You will find both here. You will also find, if you obtain enough of the catalogues noted here, that there are several compulsions abroad in the land. In New England, there is a compulsion that leads otherwise normal firms to break out in offers of maple syrup. New England must be afloat in the stuff. On the other hand, in California, otherwise normal firms seem driven to offer nuts.

You will pay more for mail-order food than you would pay for what is stocked at your local A & P, but these catalogues give you the opportunity to buy things not normally available in your neighborhood or shopping center store. Many companies sent me samples of their offerings—although I did not request them—and just about everything that was sent to me was a cut above anything I could buy locally.

There has been a rise in the number of mail-order food companies in recent years.

Perhaps this is one way of compensating for our loss of neighborhood shops like those that still exist in Europe. The supermarket, which has forced out of business most neighborhood butchers, greengrocers, bakeries, cheese stores, fish markets, poultry stores and, in some areas, even wine shops, can carry only what is a sure popular seller. Perhaps the mail-order company will some day become a replacement of our neighborhood specialty food shop.

Some of the best specialty food stores in the country are in New York City, and many of them have mail-order operations, including some that have been started just recently. Some of the better known ones listed here include Balducci's, Caviarteria, Cheese of All Nations, Dean & DeLuca, Schapira Coffee Co., and Paprikas Weiss. There clearly is not too much cheese-making or paprika grinding going on in New York City, but the quest for the best in all kinds of food has been so strong there for so long that the merchants have had a tradition of stocking just about anything. There are plenty of non-New York mail-order companies that are closer to the source of the foods they sell. Some of those that have been around for a long while or are enjoying recent popularity include the Omaha Steaks, Blue Channel Corp., Grandma Brown's Beans, Gazin-Robinson (want some kosher Creole food?), Gethsemani Farms, Legal Seafoods, Latta's, Mrs. Field's Cookies, Pinnacle Orchards, and Ray's Chilli.

There are foods offered by monks and nuns, by companies in business a century, and by others operating for just a year. Some are foods with no salt, some with no artificial ingredients; some are plain old junk foods that just taste good. There are lots of suprises,

such as the very large number of small companies offering specialty items like cheeses and smoked meats, and there are the expected, such as firms selling expensive steaks and fresh fruits. Americans can order up the cornucopia, by mail.

Note that wine and liquor cannot be sent across state lines.

Gourmet, Ethnic, and Special Foods

†ALASKA FOOD & GIFT CACHE, *819 W. Fourth Ave., Anchorage, Alaska 99501. Tel. (907) 279-3912. Four-page catalogue costs 50 cents and is issued twice a year.*

Canned salmon, halibut, smoked salmon, and reindeer sausage.

AMERICAN SPOON FOODS, *411 E. Lake St., Petoskey, Mich. 49770. Tel. (616) 347-9030. Free 12-page catalogue issued 3 times a year.*

Preserves, honeys, and jellies from Michigan's north woods area, plus local maple syrup, dried morel mushrooms, black walnuts, hickory nuts, butternuts, wild rice, smoked buffalo, and pork sausages. Check, money order, Visa, and Mastercard accepted. Shipment is by Postal Service and United Parcel. Money-back guarantee.

†APPLE VALLEY STORE, *P.O. Box 608, Darby, Mont. 59829. Tel. (406) 821-3281. Free annual 48-page catalogue.*

The offerings include gift packages of Montana beef, syrups and preserves, local cheeses and sausages, soup mixes, and spices.

In addition to the food, the company offers the work of Montana artists and craftspeople. Payment by check, money order, Visa, or Mastercard. Shipment by Postal Service or United Parcel. Purchases may be returned within 30 days for refund or credit.

BAKEWELL CREAM, BYRON H. SMITH & CO., *54 Perry Rd., Bangor, Me. 04401. Tel. (207) 942-5531 or (800) 432-1621 (except in Maine). Brochure.*

The one product offered here is a highly regarded powdered leavening agent that may be substituted in most recipes for baking powder or cream of tartar. It contains no sodium pyrophosphate or starch additives. Payment by check or money order. Shipment by Postal Service or United Parcel. If unsatisfied with results after 2 or 3 efforts, return unused portion promptly for refund.

BALDUCCI'S, *424 Avenue of the Americas, New York, N.Y. 10011. Tel. (212) 673-2600. Annual 16-page catalogue costs $2.*

This is one of New York's great stores and is located on a street which most New Yorkers, including the people at Balducci's, call Sixth Avenue. It has only recently begun issuing catalogues. There's plenty of caviar, mushrooms, pâté, smoked salmon, trout and eel, cheeses, and truffles (including the special white truffles from Italy). A very nice catalogue that will get better as the Balducci family decides which foods to emphasize in its mail-order business. The first catalogue cover had a painting by Joan Landis of 22 members of the family. Check, money order, or American Express for payment. United Parcel for delivery. Returns may be made within 2 weeks.

BETTER FOODS FOUNDATION, *P.O. Box 9, Greencastle, Pa. 17225. Tel. (717) 597-3105 or (800) 233-7032 (except in Pennsylvania). The 8-page catalogue, issued 3 times a year, costs $1.*

This company specializes in natural foods, cookies, cereals, and snacks.

BICKFORD FLAVORS, *282 S. Main St., Akron, Ohio 44308. Tel. (216) 762-4666. Free annual 8-page catalogue.*

Payment by check, money order, Visa, or Mastercard. Shipment by Postal Service or United Parcel. No refunds except in case of shipping error.

†CABLE CAR MARKETS, *20143 Suisun Dr., P.O. Box 454, Cupertino, Calif. 95015. Tel. (408) 298-9789. Free annual 28-page catalogue.*

San Franciso sourdough bread, jams made from varietal wine grapes, Sonoma Jack cheese. Gift packages. Payment by check, money order, American Express, Visa, or Mastercard. Delivery by Postal Service or United Parcel. Cash refund if dissatisfied.

---

† Indicates firms that offer gift packages.

CALEF'S COUNTRY STORE, *Box 57, Barrington, N.H. 03825. Tel. (603) 664-2231. Free brochure issued twice a year.*

The business is over 100 years old and the current owners are the fifth generation to operate this country store. The Calef family has customers in all 50 states, what they sell is "a taste of New England" in the form of its own kind of cheddar and cans of maple syrup. Payment by check or money order. Delivery by United Parcel. Refunds are in cash or merchandise.

CALIFORNIA SUNSHINE FINE FOODS, *144 King St., San Francisco, Calif. 94107. Tel. (415) 543-3007. Brochure price list.*

This company describes itself as a specialty gourmet wholesaler/distributor to the white-tablecloth restaurant trade that also sells mail order. Among its offerings are caviar, foie gras, and fresh seafood.

LA CASA ROSA, *P.O. Box 380, San Juan Bautista, Calif. 95045. Tel. (408) 623-4563. Christmas catalogue costs 25 cents.*

Sells chutneys, preserves and jellies, and salad dressings.

†CASADOS FARMS, *P.O. Box 1269, San Juan Pueblo, N.M. 87566. No tel. Brochure costs $1.*

Natural foods from New Mexico—chiles, corn, flour, spices, and nuts, with some, including ristas (chiles tied on a string), put up as unusual and nice gifts. Payment by check, money order, Visa, or Mastercard. Shipment by United Parcel. Refunds for returned purchases.

†CAVIARTERIA, *29 E. 60th St., New York, N.Y. 10022. Tel. (212) 759-7410 or (800) 221-1020 (except in New York, Alaska, and Hawaii). Free annual 16-page catalogue.*

While a store that sells caviar, smoked salmon, pâté, and foie gras is somewhat reluctant to describe itself as a discount shop, Caviarteria does say that its prices are perhaps 40 percent lower than those in New York gourmet food shops. Check, money order, American Express, Visa, and Mastercard for payment. Postal Service, United Parcel, and Federal Express are used for delivery. They will pay postage on unsatisfactory goods that are sent right back and will issue a refund in money or credit toward another purchase.

COMMUNITY CAFE, *P.O. Box 3778, Baton Rouge, La. 70821. Tel. (800) 535-9901. Monthly brochure.*

The main product here is coffee, but they also offer a wide assortment of tea and things to nibble on while drinking their coffee or tea—candies, cookies, cakes, and nuts. There is also a line of fine kitchenware. Payment by check, American Express, Visa, or Mastercard.

CREOLE DELICACIES CO., *533 Saint Ann St., New Orleans, La. 70116. Tel. (504) 525-9508. Annual brochure price list costs 50 cents.*

†DAKIN FARM, *Rt. 7, Ferrisburg, Vt. 05456. Tel. (802) 887-2936. Free 16-page catalogue issued twice a year.*

Maple syrup, ham, bacon, cheddar cheese, jam, marmalade, jelly, and relish, much of it done up in gift packages. Payment by check, money order, Visa, or Mastercard. Delivery by United Parcel. Dakin "takes care of any complaints immediately."

DEAN & DELUCA, *121 Prince St., New York, N.Y. 10012. Tel. (212) 431-1691 or (800) 221-7714 (except in New York State). Free 16-page catalogue issued 2 or 3 times a year.*

This is another of New York's great food stores, its first mail-order catalogue was issued in 1985. Among the specialties it offers are pasta, including garlic-parsley linguine and fettuccine. Check, money order, American Express, Visa, and Mastercard accepted. Shipment by Postal Service, United Parcel, or Federal Express. Food items are not returnable; nonfood items may be returned within 30 days for replacement or credit.

†EASTMAN'S MARKET, *P.O. Box 637, Manchester Center, Vt. 05255. Tel. (802) 362-1203. Free brochure price list issued twice a year.*

Smoked ham, lox, cheddar cheese, brie, and maple syrup. Nice gift possibilities. Payment by check, money order, American Express, Visa, or Mastercard. Delivery by Postal Service, United Parcel, or Purolator Courier. Cash refunds if not satisfied.

EGERTONS, *Lyme St., Axminster, Devon, England EX13 5DB. Tel. (0297) 32742, cable Postagift Axminster. The catalogue is free by surface mail but $2 by air.*

A place like this makes me aware of how difficult regulations can make life in the United States. In Britain, as in much of the rest of the world, you can send a gift bottle of wine to a friend; you cannot in the United States except within a state or with some kind of arrangement among cooperating merchants. Egerton's is a place that could take care of much of your gift giving if you have friends in Britain. It is a bit pricey. There are biscuits (we call them cookies), gingerbread, pies, cakes, preserves, fish, ham, pheasants, partridge, quail, cheeses, and lots of wine and whiskey to wash it down. American Express, Visa, Mastercard, and Diner's Club are all accepted, and it is much easier to order with them than with checks, which can get complicated.

ELLIS FOODS CORP. *See listing below under Stokes Canning Co.*

†FAMIGLIA PETRUCCI, *P.O. Box 7035, Santa Rosa, Calif. 95407. Tel. (707) 544-8825. Free 4-page catalogue issued twice a year.*

The Petrucci family offers lots and lots of olives—Spanish-style, Italian-style, hot, pitted, stuffed, smoked, in oil, wine, vermouth. Many gift suggestions. Payment by check, money order, Visa, or Mastercard. Shipment by United Parcel. Refunds in cash.

†FIGI'S, *Dairy Lane, Marshfield, Wis. 54405. Tel. (715) 384-6101 to place an order or (715) 387-6311 to make an inquiry. Free 80-page catalogues.*

The emphasis in the food catalogue is on gift giving, especially of cheese, sausages, nuts, and smoked meats. There is a separate Figi's catalogue on cookware. Payment by check, money order, American Express, Visa, or Mastercard. If not completely satisfied, customer may return any item for exchange or refund.

†**FRESNO TRADING CO.,** *P.O. Box 7600, Fresno, Calif. 93747. Tel. (209) 251-5700, (800) 344-7317 (except in California), or (800) 742-1611 (in California only). Free 12- to 20-page catalogue issued once or twice a year.*

Pistachios, "sinful chocolates," and almonds.

FRIGO FOOD PRODUCTS CO., *P.O. Box 446, Torrington, Ct. 06790. Tel. (203) 482-8127. Brochure price list issued twice a year.*

Italian foods, especially cheeses, and featuring asiago, "the champagne of Italian cheeses." Not everyone in my family shared my enjoyment of the piece they sent, so it may be an acquired taste. Payment by money order, Visa, or Mastercard. Shipment by United Parcel. There is no time limit on returns, and Frigo will provide cash refunds.

GAZIN-ROBINSON, *P.O. Box 19221, New Orleans, La. 70179. Tel. (504) 482-0302. Quarterly 30-page catalogue costs 50 cents.*

Good food, New Orleans style, with emphasis on Creole, Cajun, and French cooking. The catalogue has a cookbook section which includes books on not only such expected dishes as Creole gumbo but also such surprises as kosher Creole cooking and Southern cooking with a microwave oven. Payment by check, money order, Visa, or Mastercard. Shipment by United Parcel; Postal Service parcel post is used for delivery to Alaska, Hawaii, Canada, and APO and FPO addresses.

†**GREEN MOUNTAIN SUGARHOUSE,** *R.F.D. 1, Ludlow, Vt. 05149. Tel. (802) 228-7151. Free 16-page catalogue issued every fall.*

Four kinds of maple syrup and a short explanation of why this delicious food costs so much: It takes 40 gallons of boiled down sap to make 1 gallon of syrup, at great cost in fuel and labor. Other items include cheeses, bacon, maple candy, and mincemeat pie. Payment by check, money order, American Express, Visa, or Mastercard. Delivery by United Parcel. Unsatisfactory goods may be returned for refund within 30 days.

HALE PLACE—1752, *P.O. Box 217, Goshen, Conn. 06756. Tel. (203) 491-3466. Free quarterly 4- to 6-page catalogue.*

Imported gourmet foods include truffles, foie gras, olive and walnut oils, and pumate (sun-dried tomatoes in olive oil). Payment by check or money order. Delivery by Postal Service or United Parcel.

HARRINGTON'S, *618 Main St., Richmond, Vt. 05477 Tel. (802) 434-4444. Free 32-page catalogue issued 6 times a year.*

Primarily smoked ham and other pork products, but also smoked turkey, pheasant, beef, and salmon, plus some maple syrup and cheddar cheese. Payment by check, money order, American Express, Visa, Mastercard. Delivery by Postal Service and United Parcel. They claim to resolve any problems in short order.

†**HICKIN'S MOUNTAIN MOWING FARM,** *R.F.D. 1, Black Mountain Rd., Brattleboro, Vt. 05301. Tel. (802) 254-2146. Free 12-page catalogue, but you have to provide a self-addressed stamped envelope.*

Fruit jams, jellies, preserves, butters, and maple products, including a maple fruitcake, plus cheeses and smoked meats. Payment by check or money order. Shipment by United Parcel.

†HICKORY FARMS, *P.O. Box 75, Maumee, Ohio 43537. Tel. (419) 893-6446. Free 24-page catalogue.*

*J. & K. SALES CO., *10808 Garland Dr., Culver City, Calif. 90230. Tel. (213) 836-3334. Brochure price list issued 3 or 4 times a year.*

"Affordable gourmet foods." The company uses a snail as its symbol on its stationery, and escargots are among the gourmet fare offered at discount, along with caviar and saffron. J. & K. asks $45 for an ounce of saffron that they say is comparable to saffron selling for $90 an ounce. Payment by check or money order. Delivery by Postal Service or United Parcel. Money back or credit toward another purchase if the goods are returned right away.

KINGSMILL FOODS CO., LTD., *1399 Kennedy Rd., Unit 17, Scarborough, Ont., Canada MIP 2L6. Tel. (416) 755-1124. Brochure price list issued 6 times a year.*

Over 60 products for people on low-protein, gluten-free, metabolic disorder- and allergy-related diets. Payment by check, money order, or Visa. Shipment by Postal Service or Purolator. Refund or credit for returned goods.

†*LATTA'S, *P.O. Box 1377, Newport, Ore. 97365. Tel. (503) 265-3238 or after hours (503) 265-7675. Free 24-page catalogue issued 3 times a year.*

* Indicates firms that discount, offer a discount for bulk purchases, or have special sale catalogues or catalogue items.

Latta's sent me a tin of smoked salmon decorated with sea shells and a tiny star fish—a nice way to receive a package when you live far away from the sea. Latta's main offerings are more to be eaten than gazed at, though the salmon tin's wrapper turned out to be an actual rubbing from a blueback salmon. Other foods from the sea in Latta's catalogue include Dungeness crab, shrimp, tuna, and sturgeon. There are also dried fruit, nuts, honey, tea, coffee, preserves and jellies, herbs and spices. There are two fliers a year that offer 25 to 50 percent off regular prices. Payment by check, money order, American Express, Visa, or Mastercard. Shipping by United Parcel. Everything is 100 percent guaranteed.

†MAISON GLASS, *52 E. 58th St., New York, N.Y. 10022. Tel. (212) 755-3316. Annual 116-page catalogue costs $5.*

"This is the finest and most comprehensive catalogue of gourmet foods and distinctive delicacies published in the world," the company says. It certainly is impressive, from the caviar at the front (American and Russian) to pâtés, ducks, geese, pheasants, quail, wild turkeys, cheeses, mushrooms, steaks and chops, fruits, honey, and even teas and candies. It is very pricey, as one might expect. Payment by check, money order, American Express, Visa, Mastercard, Diners Club, Carte Blanche, or Maison Glass charge account. Shipment by Postal Service, United Parcel, Express Mail, or Federal Express. There is a 10-day limit on the return of nonperishables, and credits are given for returns.

13

†MATTHEWS 1812 HOUSE, *15 Whitcomb Hill Rd., Cornwall Bridge, Conn. 06754 Tel. (203) 672-6449. Free annual 12-page catalogue.*

This firm sells mostly gourmet cakes. The Matthews' newest offering is a lemon rum cake. Check, money order, American Express, Visa, Mastercard. Deliveries usually by United Parcel but sometimes by the Postal Service. Money back guarantee.

†THE MAURY ISLAND FARMING CO., *Route 3, Box 238, Vashon, Wash. 98070. Tel. (206) 463-9659. Free annual catalogue.*

Jams, jellies, and other foods from islands in Puget Sound, with many of the foods put in gift packages. Payment by check, money order, Visa, or Mastercard. Shipment usually by United Parcel, but Postal Service used if necessary. Refunds for unsatisfactory purchases.

LA MISE EN PLACE, *82A S. Bayles Ave., Port Washington, N.Y. 11050. Tel. (516) 883-8700. Price list.*

Vinegars, preserves, sauces, cakes, cookies—all pricey and all terrific looking. One example: almond torte with raspberry puree and whipped cream for $17.95 plus $5 for shipping. Payment by check, money order, American Express, Visa or Mastercard. Shipment by United Parcel. Money-back guarantee within 10 days.

*MISTER BULKY'S FOODS, *116 Seaview Dr., Secaucus, N.J. 07094. Tel. (201) 867-2821. Price list.*

Mister Bulky claims savings of 10 to 70 percent. Some examples of Mister Bulky prices versus brand-name food prices: mixed nuts without peanuts, $3.51 (instead of $5.72); yellow popping corn, 39 cents (instead of $1.44); and chocolate drink, 98 cents (instead of $1.69). The firm sells some eight hundred different food products. Payment by check, money order, Visa, or Mastercard. Shipment by United Parcel. Cash or credit for returns made within 7 days of delivery.

NESTLE COMPANY, *100 Bloomingdale Rd., White Plains, N.Y. 10605. Tel. (914) 697-2403. Free 24-page catalogue issued 3 times a years.*

†NORTHWEST CACHE/GRANITE FALLS PICKLERY, *9306 N.E. 40th St., Bellevue, Wash. 98004. Tel. (206) 455-4719. Brochure price list.*

There are several enticing things here, including smoked salmon, preserves, teas, apples, and pickles, many of them put up in gift boxes. Payment by check, Visa, or Mastercard. Shipment by United Parcel. Purchases may be returned for refund, credit, or exchange.

PAPRIKAS WEISS IMPORTER, *1546 Second Ave., New York, N.Y. 10028. Tel. (212) 288-6117. Quarterly 32-page catalogue costs $1.*

An institution in New York's Yorkville section, on the city's Upper East Side, for the past fifty years, this firm specializes in Hungarian foods but carries other delectables as well. The proprietor, Edward Weiss, is happy to autograph his book, *The Paprikas Weiss Hungarian Cookbook* if you'd like to buy it. The Hungarian specialties include sausage, bacon and, of course, paprika—hot, half-sweet, and sweet. Payment by check, money order, Visa, or Mastercard. Shipment by Postal Service or United Parcel. "You must be thoroughly satisfied or just return the merchandise in good

condition within 15 days of receipt for full refund, no questions asked."

†PAXTON & WHITFIELD LTD., *93 Jermyn St., London,
SW1Y 6JE, England. Tel. (01) 930-0250. Free 12-
page catalogue.*

English food can be excellent, despite
the snobbish criticism that you hear about it
in this country. Here is a fine provisioner that
offers just a few cheeses and teas for shipment
abroad but lots of good things within Britain.
They put up gift packages, something to keep
in mind if you have friends in the U.K. Prices
for shipment to the United States and Canada are listed separately, but your check or
money order must be in pounds sterling.
Shipment by Postal Service. Refunds in cash,
credit, or replacement.

PIGGIE PARK ENTERPRISES, *P.O. Box 6847, West
Columbia, S.C. 29171. No tel. Brochure price list.*

This is Maurice Bessinger's "World's
Best Hickory Barbeque," featuring ham barbeque, Carolina hash, and barbeque sauce.
Payment by check or money order. Shipment
by United Parcel.

PRESENT HAPPINESS CO., *P.O. Box 9129, Santa Fe,
N.M. 87504. Tel. (505) 988-2468. Free annual price
list.*

This company sells cakes. Payment by
check, money order, Visa or Mastercard. Delivery by United Parcel but, on request, also
by Postal Service. Cash refund within 10 days
if unsatisfied.

RAY'S CHILI, *Ray's Brand Products, P.O. Box 1000,
Springfield, Ill. 62705. Tel. (217) 523-2777. Price list.*

I share Mimi Sheraton's opinion that
this is the best canned chili in the United
States. Payment by check or money order.
Shipment by United Parcel. If not satisfied,
Ray's will give you your money back or a
credit.

*S. E. RYKOFF & CO., *P.O. Box 21467, Market St.
Station, Los Angeles, Calif. 90021. Tel. (213) 624-
6094 or (800) 421-9873 (except in Alaska and Hawaii). Free 48-page catalogue issued 4 times a year.*

This company is a wholesale food distributor that sells to restaurants, and they encourage case-lot purchases for which they
offer discount prices. They carry "25,000
items for our wholesale distribution, so if
there is a product the consumer has seen in a
restaurant but has been unable to purchase,
we may be able to send it." There are pâtés,
quail eggs, artichoke hearts and truffles, plus
several no-salt and low-sodium foods; also
some kitchenwares. Payment by check,
money order, American Express, Visa, or
Mastercard. Delivery by Postal Service or
United Parcel. Refunds made in cash or
credit, with full satisfaction guaranteed if notified within 15 days.

†SEY-CO PRODUCTS CO., *7651 Densmore Ave., Van Nuys, Calif. 91406. Tel. (818) 785-0421, (800) 423-2942 (except in California), (800) 423-0218 (in California, except in 818 area code). Semiannual 32-page catalogue costs $1.*

Sey-co says that its best-selling items are American caviar, king crab meat, French pâté de foie gras with truffles, tuna fish, and pistachio nuts. Check, money order, American Express, Visa, Mastercard, and Diners Club accepted for payment. Shipment by Postal Service, United Parcel, or truck. Goods may be returned within 30 days for refund or credit against next purchase.

†SIR THOMAS LIPTON COLLECTION, *Mail-Order Division, P.O. Box 215, 105 Oak St., Norwood, N.J. 07648. Tel. (800) 526-0359, ext. 64 (except in New Jersey) or (800) 932-0878, ext. 64 (in New Jersey). Free 32-page catalogue.*

Teas and things to eat while sipping them, such as amaretto cake, fruitcake, and Scottish shortbread.

SNACK WORLD, *418 Moss St., Reading, Pa. 19604. Tel. (215) 376-5478. Brochure price list.*

Gift food items from Pennsylvania Dutch country, including pretzels, shoofly pie, and cheese. Payment by check or money order. Shipment by Postal Service or United Parcel.

STOKES CANNING CO./ELLIS FOODS CORP., *Mail Order Department, P.O. Box 4506, Denver, Colo. 80204. Tel. (303) 629-1333. Price list.*

These two companies offer chile, tamales, Stokes-brand green chili sauce with pork (the most popular item), and similar products. Payment by check or money order. Shipment by United Parcel, but Postal Service sometimes used. Refunds for purchases returned.

†SUGARBUSH FARM, *R.F.D. B, Woodstock, Vt. 05091. Tel. (802) 457-1757. Free 4-page catalogue issued 3 times a year.*

Their products include cheese (no coloring, preservatives or additives) and maple syrup and maple candy (also with nothing added). The aged cheddar I received was the best I've had in years. Payment by check, money order, American Express, Visa, Mastercard, Diners Club. Shipment mainly by United Parcel (the Postal Service is used in shipments to postal boxes). Everything is unconditionally guaranteed.

*SULTAN'S DELIGHT, *Box 253, Staten Island, N.Y. 10314. Tel. (718) 720-1557. Free 16-page catalogue issued twice a year.*

Middle Eastern foods, such as stuffed grape leaves, chick pea flour, Turkish figs, olives, chutney. Prices are 50 percent below supermarket prices; for example super colossal pistachios sell for $6.50 a pound, compared with $7.95 to $19.95 elsewhere. Belly dancer and musical items also available. Payment by check, money order, Visa, or Mastercard. Delivery by United Parcel in 48 states, by Postal Service elsewhere. Refund or credit against another purchase for unsatisfactory goods returned within 30 days.

SUMMERLAND BULK FOOD EMPORIUM, *P.O. Box 838, Summerland, B.C., Canada V0H 1Z0.*

The original product here was "fruit leathers," fruit that has been pounded into thin sheets and then dried, made of apples, apricots, raspberries, peaches, and pears. Other fruits and foods are also available. Payment by check or money order. Shipment by Postal Service. No returns.

SUNNYLAND FARMS, *P.O. Box 549, Albany, Ga. 31703. Tel. (912) 883-3085. Free annual 48-page catalogue.*

This company sells pecans.

†THE SWISS COLONY, *1112 Seventh Ave., Monroe, Wis. 53566. Tel. (608) 246-2000. Free 152-page catalogue.*

Cheeses, hams, sausages and things, all done up in nice packages for gift giving, with an emphasis on Christmas. Check, money order, Choose 'n' Charge, American Express, Visa, Mastercard, Diners Club, or Carte Blanche. The catalogue says that every item is warranted to be exactly as advertised and that requests for adjustment should be made within 10 days if the merchandise is unsatisfactory in any way.

†TODARO BROS. MAIL ORDER, *557 Second Ave., New York, N.Y. 10016. Tel. (212) 679-7766. Annual 16- to 24-page catalogue costs $1.*

Some luxury items (a recent catalogue featured black truffles on the cover at $35 an ounce and white truffles at $40 an ounce); also more reasonably priced items, such as mushrooms, vinegar, all Italian specialties, and montasio cheese made from unpasteurized milk. (Most cheese imported into the United States is made from pasteurized milk, which is good public-health policy, but bad gastronomy.)

†TRENCHERMAN'S LTD., *Lambourn Woodlands, Nr. Newbury, Berkshire, RG16 7TP, England. Tel. Lambourn (0488) 71426 or 71753. Free annual 16-page catalogue.*

Excellent gifts of food and wine to send to your friends in England, Scotland, and Wales, especially at Christmastime. Payment by check or postal money order. Delivery by Postal Service. In event of dissatisfaction, purchases will be exchanged.

TRUZZOLINO FOOD PRODUCTS CO., *104 N. Parkmont Industrial Park, Butte, Mont. 59701. Tel. (406) 494-3132. Brochure price list.*

Here are some appetizing foods—beef or turkey tamales, salsa, chili, smoked trout, beef enchilades, refried beans, and beef tamales in chili sauce. I have fond memories of the now-departed Alamo chili house on West 43d St. in Manhattan, where the taste of the tamales, enchiladas, and chili lingered with you for hours (if not days). Payment by check, money order, Visa, or Mastercard. Shipment usually by United Parcel, but Postal Service available. Refund or credit for purchases returned within 2 weeks.

†WILLIAM'S SMOKE HOUSE, *1001 Main St., Bennington, Vt. 05201. Tel. (802) 442-2326. Brochure price list.*

Smoked hams (with no water, "liquid smoke," or smoked flavorings added), sausages, dried beef, pork, scrapple, trout, cheeses, jams, jellies, preserves, honey and, of course, maple syrup. Payment by check, money order, Visa, or Mastercard. Delivery by United Parcel.

WOK TALK, *15 Barston Rd., Great Neck, N.Y. 11021. Tel. (516) 829-3540. Free 12-page newsletter issued 6 times a year.*

This is primarily a newsletter for cooks interested in Chinese food, but it also offers 50 products for sale in each issue. The number they sent me, for example, included Chinese recipes on computer disks, cookbooks in more conventional formats, kitchen equipment (including, of course, woks), and some packages of basic foods used in Chinese recipes. While the last mentioned might not have great appeal to those of us lucky enough to be living in areas where such ingredients are easily available, this could be important to someone living in a smaller town without access to the things that go into one of the world's greatest cuisines. Payment by check, money order, Visa, or Mastercard. Delivery by Postal Service or United Parcel. Refunds in cash or credit of returns within 30 days.

ZAB'S BACKYARD HOTS, *1504 Scottsdale Rd., Rochester N.Y. 14623. Tel. (716) 436-4890. Brochure price list.*

Hotdogs (natural-seasoned and all-natural) plus a notable hot sauce called "America's best hot sauce" by a gastronome who tried to rate such things. Payment by money order, American Express, Visa, or Mastercard. Shipment by Postal Service, United Parcel, or air freight. No returns.

Meat, Fish, and Seafood

†AMANA MEAT SHOP AND SMOKEHOUSE, *Amana, Iowa 52203. Tel. (319) 622-3113. Brochure price list.*

Smoked meats from a place that put up its smokehouse in 1858. I have a weakness for the things offered here—hams, bacon, sausages. The company provides a gift service. Payment by check. Shipment by United Parcel. No returns.

†BARKER'S FINE SEAFOODS, *P.O. Box 577, 83 Elm St., Camden, Me. 04843. Tel. (207) 236-4841 or (800) 227-1113 (except in Maine, Alaska, and Hawaii) Several 8- to-12-page catalogues issued each year at $1 each.*

This is a very attractive catalogue with a lot of things that people along the coast, especially in the Northeast, tend to take for granted. I would imagine that the vast middle of the country would see things here that are not ordinarily available to them. Lobsters, clams, oysters, mussels, fresh salmon, smoked salmon and sturgeon, caviar, and more. Very pricey, but seafood is also expensive when you can get it at your corner market, and these items make impressive gifts. Payment by check, money order, American Express, Visa, or Mastercard. Delivery by United Parcel or Federal Express.

†BLUE CHANNEL CORP., *P.O. Box 128, Port Royal, S.C. 29935. Tel. (803) 524-3153. Free annual 40-page catalogue, and an annual calendar that costs $1.*

The specialties here are she-crab soup, oyster stew, and clam chowder, and there is also a selection of crabmeat. The handsome catalogue has many fine recipes I'd like to try. There are bargains to be had from time to time, such as a recent offer in which an order of 9 cans of soup brought 3 cans of New England clam chowder at no extra cost. Payment by check, money order, American

Express, Visa, or Mastercard. Shipment by Postal Service, United Parcel, or, if you really have a hankering, Federal Express. No time limit on returns, and refunds in exchanges or cash.

ENZED TRADERS, *P.O. Box 7108, Ann Arbor, Mich. 48107. Tel. (313) 663-6987. Free annual brochure.*

Venison and other specialty meats. Payment by check or money order. Delivery by Postal Service and United Parcel. Guaranteed wholesome on delivery or Enzed will replace the order.

†GASPAR'S SAUSAGE CO., *P.O. Box 436, North Dartmouth, Mass. 02747. Tel. (617) 998-2012 or (800) 343-8086 (except in Massachusetts). Brochure price list.*

GENE'S RESTAURANT, *Interstate 65 and Highway 99, Columbia, Tenn. 38401. Tel. (615) 381-1700. Free brochure price list.*

Hams, sausages, and bacon. Payment by check, money order, American Express, Visa, or Mastercard. Delivery by Postal Service. Returns may be made within 30 days for cash refund.

†*GWALTNEY OF SMITHFIELD, *P.O. Box 489, Smithfield, Va. 23430. Tel. (804) 357-3131. Free annual catalogue.*

These are very good hams and are well known through most of the country. A recent price list offers a whole ham for $39.95, but the price falls to $29.95 per ham for business customers who buy up to 25 hams, and the price falls by 5 cents a pound more if the order exceeds 25. Payment by check, money order, American Express, Visa, and Mastercard. Delivery by Postal sevice and United

Parcel. The hams are guaranteed and should be returned for replacement within a reasonable time if unsatisfactory.

HARRINGTON'S. *Smoked meats. See listing under Gourmet, Ethnic, and Special Foods, above.*

†HEGG & HEGG SMOKED SALMON, *801 Marine Dr., Port Angeles, Wash. 98362. Tel. (206) 457-3344. Brochure and price list issued annually.*

HIGH VALLEY FARM. *14 Alsace Way, Colorado Springs, Colo. 80906. Tel. (303) 634-2944. Free annual 8-page catalogue.*

Gourmet smoked foods—turkey, chicken, ham, beef, cornish game hen, pheasant—that are suggested for gifts. Payment by check or money order. Delivery by United Parcel. No returns.

ROY L. HOFFMAN & SONS, *Route 6, Box 5, Hagerstown, Md. 21740. Tel. (301) 739-2332. Brochure price list.*

This place has a highly regarded line of smoked meats—ham, bacon, and turkey. Payment by check, money order, Visa, or Mastercard. Shipment by United Parcel. Purchases may be returned within 30 days for refund or credit.

JOHNSONVILLE SAUSAGE CO., *P.O. Box 119, Sheboygan Falls, Wis. 53085. Tel. (414) 467-2641 or (800) 558-4455. Free annual 4-page catalogue.*

*V. W. JOINER & CO., *P.O. Box 387, Smithfield, Va. 23430. Tel. (804) 357-2161. Brochure price list.*

Aged Smithfield hams from Virginia, with a 10 percent discount available on orders of 25 hams or more. Payment by check, money order, American Express, Visa, Mastercard, Diners Club, and Carte Blanche. Shipment by Postal Service or United Parcel. Refunds available in cash or in credit toward another purchase.

†*LAWRENCE'S SMOKE HOUSE, *Route 30, R.R. 1, Box 28, Newfane, Vt. 05345. Tel. (802) 365-7751. Free 8- to 12-page annual catalogue.*

Corncob-smoked products, including ham, boneless ham, bacon and Canadian-style bacon, poultry, fish, specialty meats, and cheeses. There are also nonsmoked foods and, this being Vermont, maple syrup is available. Gift packages are put together and there are discounts of up to 30 percent for quantity buyers. Payment by check, money order, Visa, or Mastercard. Shipment by United Parcel. Refund, credit, or replacement for unsatisfactory goods if company is notified within 3 days and approval given.

†LEGAL SEAFOODS, *33 Everett St., Allston, Mass. 02134. Tel. (617) 783-8084 or (800) 343-5804 (except in Massachusetts). Free 8-page catalogue issued twice a year.*

"If it isn't fresh, it isn't Legal" is the motto of this noted seafood purveyor. However, it is expensive, as seafood usually is. Lobsters, clams, shrimp, mussels, scallops, and oysters, plus caviar and salmon and various other kinds of fish. These make impressive gifts. Payment by check, money order, American Express, Visa, Mastercard, or Diners Club. Most deliveries by United Parcel; no deliveries to postal boxes. Lobsters are guaranteed to arrive alive, and seafood is guaranteed to be fresh. Credit given if dissatisfied.

†MEADOW FARMS COUNTRY SMOKEHOUSE, *P.O. Box 1387, Bishop, Calif. 93514 Tel. (619) 873-5311. Brochure price list.*

The samples sent me weighed 18 pounds, including a note which said, "I'm not trying to influence your editorial opinion, but it will." Roi Ballard is one smart butcher. The meats were excellent, and I especially like the lean, thick bacon that did not disappear in the frying pan. Meats smoked over mahogany fires, including hams, bacon, turkey, various sausages, and jerky, with many of the items available as gifts. Payment by check, money order, Visa, or Mastercard. Shipment by Postal Service, United Parcel, or Greyhound. Refund, credit, or exchange for purchases returned within a "reasonable" time.

MONTANA RANCH PRODUCTS, *Gilt Edge Rd., Lewistown, Mont. 59457. Tel. (406) 538-9805. Brochure price list.*

Several canned beef products, including taco filling, hash, and plain beef (without salt!), which the company says are particularly well suited for R.V. owners, yacht owners, and sportsmen because of their long shelf life. Payment by check, money order, Visa, or Mastercard. Shipment by United Parcel. Purchases may be returned for refund within 2 weeks.

NAUVOO CHEESE CO. *Smoked meats. See listing under* Cheese, *below.*

†NEW SKETE FARMS, *Monks of New Skete, Cambridge, N.Y. 12816. Tel. (518) 677-3928. The 8-page catalogue costs $1.*

Smoked poultry, including turkey and chicken breasts and whole ducks and chicken, plus bacon, ham, sausage, cheddar cheese, and flavored cheese spreads. Gift boxes are available. Payment by check or money order. Shipment by United Parcel. Refund or credit for "reasonable complaints, spoilage, etc."

NORTH ATLANTIC SMOKEHOUSE, *245 E. 19th St., 3D, New York, N.Y. 10003. Tel. (212) 777-1179. No catalogue.*

Smoked salmon, smoked eel, and mackerel. Ask for prices. Payment by check, Visa, or Mastercard. Shipment by United Parcel. They promise to replace any fish found unsatisfactory.

†NUESKE HILLCREST FARM MEATS, *Route 2, Wittenberg, Wis. 54499. Tel. (715) 253-2226. Free annual 12-page catalogue.*

All the smoked meats are smoked over an open applewood fire in an old-fashioned way that the company has used for over 50 years. The products include ham, bacon, sausages, smoked turkey and chicken, dried beef, and smoked pork loin, much of it available in gift packages. Payment by check, money order, Visa, or Mastercard. Shipment by United Parcel.

OMAHA STEAKS, *4400 S. 96th St., P.O. Box 3300, Omaha, Neb. 68103. Tel. (402) 391-3660 or (800) 228-9055 (except in Nebraska). Free annual 24-page catalogue.*

My wife, Iris, once bought me some of these steaks for a gift. They were very good and very pricey. They make impressive gifts for special occasions or for trying to impress a potential customer. Payment by check, money order, American Express, Visa, Mastercard, Diners Club, Carte Blanche, or Omaha Steaks charge account. Satisfaction guaranteed; if not satisfied, you get your money back or another order.

OSCAR'S HICKORY HOUSE, *205 Main St., Warrensburg, N.Y. 12885. Tel. (518) 623-3431. Brochure price list.*

Smoked meats, including ham, boneless ham, bacon, pork, sausage, pepperoni, and beef, plus cheddar cheese. Shipment by United Parcel. Refunds for returned purchases.

THE SAUSAGE MAKER, *177 Military Rd., Buffalo, N.Y. 14207. Tel. (716) 876-5521. Free annual 88-page catalogue.*

†SEND-A-SALAMI, *P.O. Box 3185, Silver Spring, Md. 20901. Tel. (301) 251-1022. Free brochure price list.*

Here are 2½-pound kosher salamis done up in costumes for holidays (Valentine's Day, St. Patrick's Day, Mother's Day, Fourth of July, and the traditional time for eating salami, Thanksgiving, of course) and to note certain occupations (dentist, doctor, logger). Also included are instructions on eating salami. A nice level of whimsy. Payment by check, money order, Visa, or Mastercard. Shipment by United Parcel. The return policy is described as "generous," with refunds in cash or credit.

*SMITHFIELD HAM AND PRODUCTS CO., *P.O. Box 487, Smithfield, Va. 23430. Tel. (804) 357-2121. Annual brochure price list.*

†TENDER JUICY MEAT CO., *8806 L St., Omaha, Neb. 68127. Tel. (402) 331-5111, (800) 228-8812 (except in Nebraska) or (800) 652-0001 (in Nebraska). Brochures and price list.*

Expensive cuts of prime beef from Limousin cattle, a breed developed in France and not found widely in the United States. These make impressive gifts. Payment by check, money order, American Express, Visa, or Mastercard. Shipment by United Parcel. Full refund if not satisfied.

USINGER'S FAMOUS SAUSAGE, *1030 N. Third St., Milwaukee, Wis. 53203. Tel. (414) 276-9100. Brochures and an order form instead of a catalogue.*

Gourmet hot dogs? Usinger's says it smokes a frank for more than 3 days, compared to the 1-hour smoking the more plebian of this most plebian food gets. I hope the pigs appreciate the honor. This firm has been in business since 1880. The prices are higher than what you would pay at your local supermarket, but reports say they are worth the extra money.

VIRGINIA VEAL FARMS, *Standardsville, Va. 22973. Tel. (804) 985-3481 or (800) 446-1749. Brochure and price list.*

WIMMER'S MEAT PRODUCTS, *126 W. Grant St., West Point, Neb. 68788. Tel. (402) 372-2437, (800) 228-6600 (except in Nebraska), or (800) 642-9900 (in Nebraska). Free annual 24-page catalogue.*

Ham, Canadian bacon, cheeses, and gift packages of sausages, cheeses, bolognas, and wursts. Payment by check, money order, American Express, Visa, Mastercard, and Diners Club. Shipment by United Parcel. Full satisfaction or refund, credit, or replacement.

WINDSOR FARMS. *Lamb. See listing under* Needle-crafts, *of all places. What? you may ask. This company primarily sells lamb's wool to people in the needlecrafts.*

†WOODSHED BUTCHER, *Lees Mill Rd., Moultonboro, N.H. 03254. Tel. (603) 476-8434 or (800) 633-3888 (except in New Hampshire). Brochure price list.*

Lobster clambake from a place named Woodshed Butcher? They do offer it, in addition to aged beef and lamb chops. Check, money order, American Express, Visa, Mastercard, Diners Club, and Carte Blanche are all accepted for payment. Delivery by Postal Service. Cash refunds offered in the event of unsatisfactory goods.

Cheese

†CHEESE JUNCTION, *1 W. Ridgewood Ave., Ridgewood, N.J. 07450. Tel. (201) 445-9211. Free 20-page catalogue.*

†CHEESE OF ALL NATIONS, *153 Chambers St., New York, N.Y. 10007. Tel. (212) 964-0024. Annual 64-page catalogue costs $1.*

This is a very nice catalogue, both for the wide selection of cheeses it offers and for its chatty notes about cheese: "If mold appears, simply scrape if off. . . . To avoid breakage in cutting, use a thin-bladed knife or wire cutter." There are almost 400 cheeses from France and more than a hundred from Italy; hundreds more from elsewhere in the world. There are also kosher cheeses, even imported kosher cheeses. American Express, Visa, and Mastercard for purchases. United Parcel for delivery. Replacements made if unsatisfactory products are returned within 10 days.

†COQUILLE VALLEY DAIRY CO-OP AND BANDON CHEDDAR CHEESE, *P.O. Box 515, 680 E. Second St., Bandon, Ore. 97411. Tel. (503) 347-2461. Annual brochure.*

Mostly cheddar offerings, but also some sausages and fish, put up in gift boxes. No credit cards, but checks and money orders are accepted. Most shipments are by United Parcel.

†CROWLEY CHEESE, *Healdville, Vt. 95758. Tel. (802) 259-2340. Annual brochure price list.*

Cheese made in what is called Vermont's oldest cheese factory, plus maple syrup. Check, money order, Visa, and Mastercard accepted. Shipment by United Parcel. Unsatisfactory products will be replaced if returned within 15 days.

†GETHSEMANI FARMS, *Trappist, Ky. 40051. Tel. (502) 549-3117. Free annual brochure price list.*

Trappist cheese and fruitcake, some of it in gift packages, made in this monastery in Kentucky. Payment by check or money order. Most of the business consists of Christmas gift packages. Shipment by United Parcel, except for Postal Service parcel post for post office box holders. Refunds in cash or credit if dissatisfied.

HELUVA GOOD CHEESE, *6152 Barclay Rd., P.O. Box C, Sodus, N.Y. 14551. Tel. (315) 483-6971. Free annual 16-page catalogue.*

IDEAL CHEESE SHOP, *1205 Second Ave., New York, N.Y. 10021. Tel. (212) 688-7579. Price list.*

The list includes 55 items from France, and one of them is a personal favorite not widely available—brie made from unpasteurized milk. Ten other countries are represented, with new offerings including American versions of brie, bleu, and chevre. Payment by check, money order, American Express, Visa, or Mastercard. Shipment by United Parcel.

†KOLB LENA CHEESE CO., *301 W. Railroad St., Lena, Ill. 61048. Tel. (815) 369-4577. Brochure price list issued twice a year.*

Lots of domestic versions of European cheeses, including a brie that the Kolb folks are particularly proud of. Gift packages available. Payment by check or money order. Delivery by United Parcel. As for return policy, "we always stand behind our cheeses and satisfy the customer."

MAYTAG DAIRY FARMS, *Box 806, RR 1, Newton, Iowa 50208. Tel. (515) 792-1133, (800) 247-2458 (except in Iowa), or (800) 258-2437 (in Iowa). Free 20-page catalogue issued twice a year.*

The specialty is a blue cheese that has been made here since 1941; the cheddars and other cheeses are also made here. Payment by check, money order, Visa, or Mastercard. Delivery by Postal Service, United Parcel, or, at extra cost to customer, express or courier service.

†*NAUVOO CHEESE CO., *P.O. Box 188, Nauvoo, Ill. 62354. Tel. (217) 453-2213. Free annual 16-page catalogue.*

The specialty here is a blue cheese, but there are other cheeses as well, and some smoked meats. Discounts available on bulk purchases: 5 percent off for 8 to 14 boxes, 10 percent off for 15 or more. Payment by check, money order, Visa, or Mastercard. Most deliveries by United Parcel but some by Postal Service. Unsatisfactory goods should be returned within 30 days for money back.

NEW SKETE FARMS. *See listing under* Meat, Fish, and Seafood, *above.*

†PLYMOUTH CHEESE CORP., *P.O. Box 1, Plymouth, Vt. 05056. Tel. (802) 672-3650. Annual price list.*

This company was founded in 1890 by 5 Plymouth farmers, one of whom was Col. John C. Coolidge, the father of Calvin Coolidge. It closed in 1934, during the Great Depression, and then was reopened in 1960 by John Coolidge, son of the president. The offerings are Plymouth cheese, available in mild or medium sharp, plus maple syrup. Payment by check or money order. Delivery mostly by United Parcel but some by Postal Service. Refunds in cash if not satisfied.

†SARAH'S MART, *P.O. Box 462, Faribault, Minn. 55021. Tel. (507) 334-6143. Brochure price list issued annually.*

The specialty here is Treasure Cave blue cheese. Payment by check or money order. Delivery by United Parcel. Cheese replaced if dissatisfied.

SONOMA CHEESE FACTORY, *Galaxy Products, 2 Spain St., Sonoma, Calif. 95476. Tel. (707) 938-5232. Free 8-page catalogue issued twice a year.*

†*STEVE'S CHEESE, *Route 2, Denmark, Wis. 54208. Tel. (414) 863-2397. Brochure price list.*

Lots of kinds of cheese, some done up in gift boxes. Prices are consistently cheaper than other mail-order firms. Payment by check, money order, or Steve's charge account. Delivery by United Parcel except for Postal Service parcel post on foreign orders. They have never received returns, but will give money back or apply a credit if dissatisfied.

†THE SWISS CHEESE SHOP, *Highway 69 North, P.O. Box 429, Monroe, Wis. 53566. Tel. (608) 325-3493. Free annual 8-page catalogue.*

†WIMMER'S MEAT PRODUCTS. *See listing under* Meat, Fish, and Seafood, *above.*

†WISCONSIN CHEESEMAN, *P.O. Box 1, Madison, Wis. Tel. (608) 837-4100. Free 96-page catalogue.*

†W. S. U. CREAMERY, *Troy Hall 101, Pullman, Wash. 99164. Tel. (509) 335-4014. Brochure price list.*

The initials stand for Washington State University, and the product for sale is cheese made in the college's Department of Food Science and Human Nutrition. The offerings are cheddar, Cougar, Gold, Viking, and hot pepper. A gift service is available. Payment by check or money order. Shipment by United Parcel. Refunds for returned purchases.

Fruit and Nuts

†ACE PECAN CO., *County Fair, Box 65, Ninth & Harris, Cordele, Ga. 31015. Tel. (800) 323-9754. Free 18-page catalogue.*

Cashews, pistachios, pecans, almonds, walnuts, and, of course, peanuts—this being a Georgia firm. Check, money order, American Express, Visa, Mastercard, Diners Club for payment. Postal Service and United Parcel for delivery. Money-back guarantee.

†LEE ANDERSON'S COVALDA DATE CO., *P.O. Box 908, 51-392 Highway 86, Coachella, Calif. 92236. Tel. (619) 398-3441. Free brochure price list issued twice a year.*

Dates, many of them done up in gift packages. Payment by check or money order. Delivery by Postal Service or United Parcel. Refunds for defective goods if requested within 30 days.

BENECH FARMS OF ALMADEN, *2296 Senter Rd., P.O. Box 6387, San Jose, Calif. 95150. Tel. (408) 298-9789. Free 20-page catalogue issued 6 times a year.*

Dried fruits—apricots, figs, nectarines, raisins, apple rings, peaches, prunes, pears, dates, bing cherries—that made me hungry as I read the catalogue. Gift packages put up. Payment by check, money order, American Express, Visa, or Mastercard. Delivery by Postal Service or United Parcel. Complete satisfaction guaranteed, with cash refunds.

BUTTERFIELD FARMS. *Nuts. See listing under* Baked Goods, Sweets, and Snacks, *below.*

DYMPLE'S DELIGHT, *Route 4, Box 53, Mitchell, Ind. 47446. Tel. (812) 849-3487. Annual price list sent free if you send self-addressed stamped envelope.*

Canned persimmons, plus persimmon seeds and recipes. Payment by check or money order. Shipment by United Parcel. No returns.

*FRAN'S PECANS, *P.O. Box 188, Harlem, Ga. 30814. Tel. (404) 556-9172. Free 4-page price list.*

Extra fancy, extra large, halves, pieces, jumbos, seedlings, mammoths, roasted, and salted. Discounts for quantity purchases and for prepayment; they also do a lot of business as a fund-raising vehicle for groups. Payment by check, money order, Visa, or Mastercard. Shipment by United Parcel. Unsatisfactory shipments must be returned within 5 days for refund, replacement, or credit against another order.

†GOURMET NUT CENTER, *1430 Railroad Ave., Orland, Calif. 95963. Tel. (916) 865-5511. Free annual 8-page catalogue.*

†HALE INDIAN RIVER GROVES, *Indian River Plaza, Wabasso, Fla. 32970. Tel. (305) 589-4334, (800) 327-6060 (except in Florida), or (800) 432-6040 (in Florida). Free annual 24-page catalogue.*

Oranges, grapefruit, mangoes—but mostly oranges. There are many gift possibilities to choose from, especially for Christmastime, when Northerners could use a dose of Florida cheer.

†HAWAIIAN PLANTATIONS, *1311 Kalakaua Ave., Honolulu, Hawaii 96826. Tel. (808) 955-8888 or (800) 367-2177. Free semiannual 24-page catalogue.*

HOUSE OF ALMONDS, *P.O. Box 11145, Bakersfield, Calif. 93389. Tel. (800) 235-4070 (except in California) or (800) 235-4070 (in California). Free annual 24-page catalogue.*

†HYATT FRUIT CO., *Lockbox 4239, Fort Lauderdale, Fla. 33338. Tel. (305) 566-7868 or (800) 327-5810 (except in Florida). Free annual 16-page catalogue.*

Oranges, grapefruit, candies, and jellies.

JAFFE BROS., *P.O. Box 636, Valley Center., Calif. 92082. Tel. (619) 749-1133. Free annual brochure price list.*

Large selection of organically grown and untreated natural foods, including dried apples, apricots, figs, peaches and pears, prunes and raisins, dehydrated mushrooms, dates, almonds, cashews. Payment by check, money order, Visa, or Mastercard. Delivery by Postal Service, United Parcel, or air freight.

†THE KIWI RANCH, *192 Highway 99, Gridley, Calif. 95948. Tel. (916) 695-1448. Brochure price list.*

Boxes of kiwis by themselves or with preserves or chutney, and recipes; a bowl that is supposed to promote the even ripening of all fruit, and handmade dolls that children are asked to believe grow on kiwi trees. Many gift items included. Payment by check, money order, Visa, or Mastercard. Shipment by Postal Service, United Parcel, or common carrier. Refunds for unsatisfactory purchases.

*KOINONIA PARTNERS, *Route 2, Americus, Ga. 31709. Tel. (912) 924-0391. Free annual 16-page catalogue.*

Pecans in halves, in pieces, and in the shell, stuffed into dates, hickory-smoked, spiced, and put in chocolate bars. There are also fruitcakes and other things. The company offers discounts on quantity purchases. Payment by check or money order. Shipment by Postal Service, United Parcel, or truck. Purchases may be returned within 15 days for refund or replacement.

LIBERTY ORCHARDS, *117 Mission Ave., Cashmere, Wash. 98815. Tel. (509) 782-2191. Free semiannual 8-page catalogue issued every year.*

A confection made from the produce of the Pacific Northwest—apples, apricots, walnuts—that contains no artificial flavors, colors, or preservatives is sold under the company's brand, "Aplets & Cotlets." Check, money order, Visa, or Mastercard for payment. Postal Service or United Parcel for delivery.

†MAUNA LOA MACADAMIA NUT CORP., *Star Route 3, Hilo, Hawaii 96720. Tel. (808) 966-9301. Free 16-page catalogue.*

Payment by check, money order, American Express, Visa, or Mastercard. Shipment by Postal Service and United Parcel. Replacement or refund if customer is dissatisfied.

†MISSION ORCHARDS, *P.O. Box 6947, San Jose, Calif. 95150. Tel. (408) 297-5056. Free 28-page catalogue.*

†MISSOURI DANDY PANTRY, *212 Hammons Dr. East, Stockton, Mo. 65785. Tel. (417) 276-5121 (ask for "The Pantry"). Free 16-page catalogue issued twice a year.*

The specialty here is black walnuts, which the company does not want you to confuse with other walnuts, since the black walnut is very different. Payment by check, money order, Visa, or Mastercard. Shipment is by United Parcel, except when the address is a box number, in which case Postal Service is used. If not satisfied, money refunded or walnuts replaced within a reasonable length of time.

*NUTS ON CLARK, *3830 N. Clark St., Chicago, Ill. 60613. Tel. (312) 871-8777. Free quarterly 12-page catalogue.*

Reduced prices on nuts and fruits. Colossal pistachios (these nuts seem to be sized the same enthusiastic way as canned olives) for $4.25 to $5.50 a pound, compared to what Nuts on Clark says is a normal price elsewhere of $9.95; jumbo cashews for $4.65 to $5.50 a pound, $8.95 elsewhere; Australian apricots for $5.25 a pound, $12.50 elsewhere. Check, money order, American Express, Visa, and Mastercard o.k. for payment, but a minimum of $20 is needed for credit card purchases. Cash refunds made within 3 days in event of error.

PECAN PRODUCERS INTERNATIONAL, *P.O. Box 1301, Corsicana, Tex. 75110. Tel. (214) 872-1337. Brochure and price list.*

†PINNACLE ORCHARDS, *P.O. Box 1068, Medford, Ore. 97501. Tel. (503) 772-6271 or (800) 547-0227 (except in Oregon). Free annual 32-page catalogue.*

The catalogue is illustrated with photos of great-looking golden and red Delicious apples and Comice pears from the Pacific Northwest. These, as an orchardist friend of

mine in New York used to say, are for lookin' as well as eatin'. Payment by check, money order, American Express, Visa, or Mastercard. Delivery by United Parcel. Refunds in cash or credit against another purchase if not satisfied.

PRIESTER PECAN CO., *P.O. Drawer B, Fort Deposit, Ala. 36032. Tel. (205) 227-4301 or (800) 633-5725. Free annual 20-page catalogue.*

J. H. SHERARD, *P.O. Box 75, Sherard, Miss. 38669. Tel. (601) 627-5165 or (800) 647-5518 (except in Mississippi). Price list.*

Lots of pecans, shelled or unshelled. Payment by check, money order, Visa, or Mastercard. Shipment by Postal Service or United Parcel. Refund or replacement for purchases returned within 30 days.

†SHIELDS DATE GARDENS, *80-225 Highway 111, Indio, Calif. 92201. Tel. (619) 347-0996. Brochure price list.*

†SQUIRE'S CHOICE, *35 S. Main St., Yardley, Pa. 19067. Tel. (215) 493-8668 or (800) 523-6163 (except in Pennsylvania). Brochure price list.*

Lots of nuts—cashews, macadamias, pecans, almonds, and pistachios, all but the pistachios available without salt if desired. Payment by check, American Express, Visa, or Mastercard. Shipment by United Parcel; first-class mail is used to Hawaii, Alaska, and foreign addresses.

†STERNBERG PECAN CO., *Box 193, Jackson, Miss. 39205. Tel. (601) 366-6310. Free annual 6-page catalogue.*

This family-run company sells only 1 unroasted, uncandied, unsalted, unsugared, unspiced, uncooked product—fancy mammoth shelled pecan halves. Suggested for gifts, especially to friends outside the United States, since pecans are grown only in this country. Payment by check or money order. Shipment by Postal Service or United Parcel.

†SUN COUNTRY, *20143 Suisun Dr., P.O. Box 454, Cupertino, Calif. 95015. Tel. (408) 996-2928. Free 28-page catalogue issued twice a year.*

Fancy fruits, including pears, kiwis, apples, cherries, grapefruit, tangelos, grapes, and oranges, arranged for gift giving. Payment by check, money order, American Express, Visa, or Mastercard. Delivery by Postal Service or United Parcel. Cash refunds any tme if dissatisfied.

†H. M. THAMES PECAN CO., *P.O. Box 2206, Mobile, Ala. 36652. Tel. (205) 433-1689 or (800) 633-1306. Free annual 20-page catalogue.*

TIMBER CREST FARMS, *4791 Dry Creek Rd., Healdsburg, Calif. 95448. Tel. (707) 433-8251. Free 24-page catalogue.*

Unsulphured dried fruits and nuts, with several good-looking gift packages put together. Payment by check, money order, Visa, or Mastercard. Shipment by Postal Service or United Parcel. Purchases may be returned within 2 weeks for refund or credit.

†*VIRGINIA DINER, *P.O. Box 310, Wakefield, Va. 23888. Tel. (804) 899-3106. Brochure and order form.*

The offering here is gourmet peanuts, if that does not seem to be too much of a contradiction in terms. Those of us trying to limit our consumption of salt will appreciate their offering 5 salt-free items. If only more companies would do that! Peanuts from "The Peanut Capital of the World" in bags and buckets, in or out of their shells; they could make novel gifts for businesses, and Virginia Diner offers quantity discounts, so that might be worth an inquiry. They also offer T-shirts that proclaim the wearer to be the World's No. 1 Nut ($5). Check, money order, Visa, and Mastercard, plus billing after credit is established. Postal Service, United Parcel, and truck. Full credit for goods returned within 3 months.

WINE AND THE PEOPLE. *Grapes and grape juice. See listing under* Wine- and Beer-Making Supplies.

Grains and Vegetables, Natural and Freeze-Dried Foods

BROWNVILLE MILLS, *Brownville, Neb. 68321. Tel. (402) 825-4131. Free annual 6- to 8-page catalogue.*

A large line of "natural" foods, including stone ground flours, meals, grains, seeds, cereals, and nuts, plus vitamins. Payment by check or money order. Shipment by Postal Service, United Parcel, or truck freight. Purchases may be returned for refund or credit within 10 days of delivery.

*BRUMWELL FLOUR MILL, *Box 126, South Amana, Iowa 52334. Tel. (319) 622-3455. Brochure price list.*

This company turns out small quantities of 21 milled grains, including unbleached flour, whole wheat flour, and soy flour. No chemicals, no preservatives. There is a discount for quantity purchases. Payment by check or money order. Shipment by Postal Service or United Parcel. Refund or replacement of unsatisfactory purchases.

CASADOS FARMS. *Natural foods from New Mexico. See listing under* Gourmet, Ethnic, and Special Foods, *above.*

CHIEFTAIN WILD RICE CO., *Rt. 9, Hayward, Wis. 54843. Tel. (715) 462-3280. Brochure issued 3 times a year.*

This is luxury stuff, so use it sparingly, maybe with a roast duck, or extend it with some brown rice. A recent catalogue offered the wild rice for $15.95 a pound. Payment by check only. Delivery by United Parcel.

CHS POTATO FARMS *(Carl Hessler & Son), 7665 Eleven Mile Rd., Rockford, Mich. 49341. Tel. (616) 874-6511. No catalogue or price list.*

Yes, really, potatoes offered by mail. CHS says it is the only source of a very special kind of a potato called Golden Gourmet, similar to those grown in Europe and unlike what Americans are used to. I'd suggest trying them baked, with caviar from Caviarteria (see *Gourmet, Ethnic, and Special Foods,* above) and sour cream. Payment by check, money order, Visa, or Mastercard. Shipment by United Parcel. Money back or order reshipped if not satisfied.

CONNER FARMS, *P.O. Box 1566, Dalton, Ga. 30720. Tel. (404) 226-5674. Free catalogue.*

Some people consider Vidalia onions the ambrosia of the gods. Here is a notable supplier of such. Payment by check, money order, Visa, or Mastercard. Shipment by Postal Service or United Parcel. Credit for goods damaged in shipment.

†DELEGEANE GARLIC FARMS, *1518 Yountville Cross Rd., Napa Valley, Calif. 94558. Tel. (707) 944-8019. Free brochure price list.*

If you really love garlic, this is for you. We received a gift of elephant garlic for Christmas once from friends several hundred miles away; I guess that was far enough. It was very good and the cloves lasted all winter. The Delegeanes like garlic so much that they've made up some large cloves as Chirstmas tree ornaments. Payment by check, money order, Visa, or Mastercard. Delivery by United Parcel, but Postal Service available at extra cost. Refund or exchange if not satisfied, so long as shipment is returned within 10 days.

DRI-LITE FOODS, *1540 Charles Dr., Redding, Calif. 96003. Tel. (916) 241-9280. Free annual 4-page catalogue.*

The specialty here is the feeding of the backpacker, one of whose biggest considerations is weight, so the catalogue gives both the price and weight of each item. There are meats, vegetarian meals, fruits, and snacks. Check or money order for payment. United Parcel for delivery.

EREWHON, *236 Washington St., Brookline, Mass. 02146. Tel. (617) 738-4516, (800) 222-8028 (except in Massachusetts, Hawaii, and Alaska), or (800) 222-8029 (in all of United States). Free annual 16-page catalogue.*

Nuts, grains, beans, seeds, flours, granola, dried fruit in bulk quantities. The emphasis is on what has come to be known as natural foods, with the catalogue designating those foods that have been organically grown. Unusual incidental: A list of the company's products with a kosher designation is available. Payment by check, money order, C.O.D., Visa, or Mastercard. Shipment by Postal Service or United Parcel. Credit given for unsatisfactory shipments returned within 2 weeks.

GRANDMA BROWN'S BEANS, *P.O. Box 230, Mexico, N.Y. 13114. Tel. (315) 963-7221. Price list, plus free 24-page recipe book.*

Chiefly baked beans from a recipe developed, the story goes, during the Depression by Lulu Brown, who was able to support herself by selling the beans that had made her so popular at church suppers. There's nothing like good baked beans; one of my fondest memories is the delicious beans Horn & Hardardt used to put in those little pots. Payment by check or money order. Delivery by United Parcel.

HARTENTHALER'S NATURAL FOODS & HERBS. *See Herbs and Spices, below.*

*INTER-STATE FOOD RESERVES, *1295 Bayshore Blvd., Dunedin, Fla. 33528. Tel. (813) 733-5608 or (800) 447-8673 (except in Florida). Free catalogue.*

This is freeze-dried food to keep you alive in case of emergency. Payment by check, money order, wire transfer, Visa, or Mastercard. Shipment by Postal Service, United Parcel, or national carriers.

JAFFE BROS. *Organically grown foods. See listing under Fruit and Nuts, above.*

KENNEBEC BEAN CO., *Main St., North Vassalboro, Me. 04962. Tel. (207) 873-3473. Price list.*

KENYON CORN MEAL CO., *P.O. Box 221, West Kingston, R.I. 02892. Tel. (401) 783-4054. Brochure price list.*

"We stone grind our grains. Nothing is added or taken out, other than sifting to remove the shells." The specialty, of course, is grains (corn meal, whole wheat flour, rye meal, etc.); there are also mixes, clam cakes, syrups, preserves, and jelly. Payment by check, money order, Visa, or Mastercard. Shipment by Postal Service or United Parcel. Refund or replacement for returned purchases.

LUNDBERG BROWN RICE, *P.O. Box 369, Richvale, Calif. 95974. Tel. (916) 882-4551. Price list.*

Use a check or money order to buy brown and other rice by the 25-pound bag; no credit cards. Delivery by United Parcel.

MAINE EDIBLE SEAWEED, *Box 15, Steuben, Me. 04680. Tel. (207) 546-2875. Brochure price list.*

Six North Atlantic "sea vegetables"—kelp, dulse, alaria, digitata kelp, Irish moss, and nori—by the pound or in smaller packages. Payment by check or C.O.D. Shipment by United Parcel.

†NORTHERN LAKES WILD RICE CO., *P.O. Box 28, Cass Lake, Minn. 56633. Tel. (218) 335-6369. Brochure.*

This company sells hand-harvested native wild rice, which it says is greatly superior to the domesticated "wild" rice normally found in stores. This is very expensive, and it would make an impressive gift. Payment by check or money order. Shipment by Postal Service or United Parcel. Purchases may be returned for refund at any time.

PROVISIONS UNLIMITED, *P.O. Box 456, Oakland, Me. 04963. Tel. (207) 465-3212. Free 32-page catalogue.*

Such foods as grains, beans, seeds, nuts, dehydrated foods, and freeze-dried meats, fruits, vegetables, and dairy products, plus water purifiers, radiation detectors, windmills, tools. Payment by check, money order, Visa, or Mastercard. Shipment by United Parcel unless Postal Service is requested. Purchases may be returned, in new condition, for refund or credit within 30 days.

*RAINY DAY RESERVE, *1653 Kensington Rd., N.W., Calgary, Alba., Canada T2N 3R2. Tel. (403) 283-2211. Annual catalogue costs $2.*

This company offers discount prices on storable dehydrated and freeze-dried foods. An example: One year's supply of food for one person (fruits, vegetables, and protein) costs $900. Since the food lasts for so long a time, it is suggested that the material is a good thing to have around just for convenience's sake. Payment by check or money order. Shipment by Postal Service. Purchases may be returned for replacement.

S. & H. ORGANIC ACRES, *P.O. Box 27, Montgomery Creek, Calif. 96065. Tel. (916) 337-6305. Brochure price list.*

Elephant garlic, which we first received as a gift, is really good stuff. Flavorful and very mild, the heads are so big that they last a long time. This company will sell you garlic for eating now or smaller plants for growing in your own garden. Other garlics, shallots and onions are also available. Payment by check, money order, Visa, or Mastercard. Shipment is usually by United Parcel, but Postal Service is used when necessary. Purchases may be returned for refund.

*STARFLOWER NATURAL FOODS & BOTANICALS, *885 McKinley, Eugene, Ore. 97402. Tel. (503) 686-2151 or (800) 452-2643. Quarterly 96-page catalogue is free for the first 2 issues but costs $1.50 after that.*

This place is geared for buying clubs, co-ops, and the like, and the minimum order is $200. It sells a wide variety of what have come to be called "natural" foods, including meats without chemicals, hormones, steroids, or antibiotics, plus cereals, cheeses, beans, rice, herbs, etc. The company offers many discounts, such as lower prices on low-fat yogurt and long-grain brown rice. Payment by check only. Delivery by United Parcel and truck. Unsatisfactory goods must be reported within 48 hours if perishable or within 5 days if nonperishable for refunds less a 10 percent restocking fee.

SURVIVAL CENTER, *Box 707, Ravenna, Ohio 44266. Tel. (216) 678-4000 or (800) 321-2900. Brochure issued 3 or 4 times a year costs $2.*

Here are freeze-dried foods, dehydrated foods, grains, and dried fruit, plus water purifiers, heaters and lamps, windmills to generate electricity, and bomb shelters. A note on security from the company: "Some folks use love and others use guns. Just make sure you know the power and consequences each carries."

TUTHILLTOWN GRIST MILL, *Box 18, Albany Post Rd., Gardiner, N.Y. 12525. Tel. (914) 255-5695. Brochure price list.*

This mill is on the National Register of Historic Places, having been build in 1788. It offers stone ground flours, meals, and cereal products. Payment by check or money order. Shipment by United Parcel. Purchases may be returned, immediately upon receipt, for credit.

†WAR EAGLE MILL, *R.R. 5, Box 411, Rogers, Ark. 72756. Tel. (501) 789-5343. Free annual 16-page catalogue.*

This is a working water-powered grist mill that sells wholegrain flours, meals, and mixes from grains ground at the mill. Other products include jams, jellies, and honey, much of it suggested as gift items. Payment by check, money order, Visa, or Mastercard. Shipment by Postal Service of United Parcel. Refunds for returned purchases.

Baked Goods, Sweets, and Snacks

ASTOR CHOCOLATE CORP., *48-25 Metropolitan Ave., Glendale, N.Y. 11386. Tel. (718) 386-7400. Free annual 8-page catalogue.*

BALDWIN HILL BAKERY, *Baldwin Hill Rd., Phillipston, Mass. 01331. Tel. (617) 249-4691. Brochure.*

Two kinds of sourdough bread—whole wheat and traditional European—are offered. Payment by check or money order. Shipment by United Parcel. No returns accepted.

BISSINGER'S, *205 W. Fourth St., Cincinnati, Ohio 45202. Tel. (513) 241-8182. Semiannual 16- and 8-page catalogues cost 50 cents each.*

Candies, mostly chocolates, with specialties for Easter. Payment by check, money order, Visa, or Mastercard. Shipment by United Parcel. Refunds for returns of damaged or spoiled candies.

†BUTTERFIELD FARMS, *330 Washington St., Marina Del Rey, Calif. 90291. Tel. (213) 822-0700. Free 8-page catalogue.*

Fruitcake, Bavarian mints, chocolate chip cookies, pistachios, almonds. Payment by check, money order, American Express, Visa, Mastercard, Diners Club, or Carte Blanche.

†BYRD COOKIE CO., *2233 Norwood Ave., Savannah, Ga. 31406. Tel. (912) 355-1716. Brochure price list.*

†CAFE BEAUJOLAIS BAKERY, *P.O. Box 730, Mendocino, Calif. 95460. Tel. (707) 964-0292. Free annual catalogue.*

There is a holiday fruitcake and an interesting confection called a Panforte di Mendocino, which comes in almond, hazelnut, walnut, and macadamia flavors and is supposed to have been modeled in Italy after a concoction created during the Crusades "for its long-lasting nutritious and energy-giving qualities." One may accept that with a grain of nutmeg, considering the folklore handed down over the centuries about the Crusades, but that would not rule out its being delicious. Someone with a memory of Italian desserts would have a yearning for this one. Suggested for gifts. Payment by check, money order, American Express, Visa, or Mastercard. Shipment by United Parcel. Credit for unsatisfactory shipments, but only if confirmed by telephone.

†C'EST CROISSANT, *P.O. Box 1987, Allentown, Pa. 18105. Tel. (215) 821-5511. Brochure price list.*

Croissants—butter, almond, raspberry, and chocolate—for yourself or in gift packages. Payment by check, money order, American Express, Visa, or Mastercard. Shipment by United Parcel. Guaranteed to be "absolutely fresh" or money refunded.

THE CHOCOLATE CATALOGUE, *3983 Gratiot St., St. Louis, Mo. 63110. Tel. (314) 534-2402 or (800) 325-8881 (except in Alaska and Hawaii). Free 16-page catalogue issued 4 times a year.*

CHOCOLATE PHOTOS, *200 W. 57th St., New York, N.Y. 10019. Tel. (212) 979-4340. Brochure and price-list.*

Your face in chocolate—or your company's symbol, or your team's mascot. The chocolates (not really photographs but copies of them made from molds) come in various sizes and assortments, somewhat pricey but certainly novel. Payment by check, money order, American Express, Visa, or Mastercard.

†*COLLIN STREET BAKERY, *401 W. Seventh St., Corsicana, Tex. 75110. Tel. (214) 872-3951 or, in the fruitcake season only (October, November, December), (800) 453-1214 (except in Alaska and Hawaii). Brochure issued twice a year.*

The specialty here is fruitcake. Discounts are offered for people making large orders—something that a business might take into consideration when selecting gifts to send to customers. A fruitcake also makes a nice gift for a relative serving overseas in the military or foreign service. After the Christmas holidays, Collin Street swings into pecan pies and rum cakes. Payment by check, money order, American Express, Visa, Mastercard, or Diners Club. Delivery by Postal Service or United Parcel. There is an unconditional money-back guarantee.

COOKIE OF THE MONTH, *63 Ivy Rd., Wilmington, Del. 19806. Tel. (302) 656-5993. Free brochure and price list.*

For as many months as you like, you can have cookies sent to a favorite person (even yourself) every month, although it could get a bit expensive. The brochure I got listed a price of $8.50 per month—for 1½ lbs. of very good cookies—plus $2.50 shipping. Payment by check, money order, Visa, or Mastercard.

†DI CAMILLO BAKING CO., *811 Linwood Ave., Niagara Falls, N.Y. 14305. Tel. (416) 282-2341. Brochures and order form.*

This family-owned business sent me samples, which were very good indeed. Some of their products are sold by the Wine Enthusiast (see listing under *Wine- and Beer-Making Supplies*)and by some of the leading gourmet food stores in the country. They are inexpensive, but they certainly taste good, and the canister that the focaccia (Italian flat bread) came in is so attractive that we are using it to store pasta on a countertop. Other products include cookies and cakes, none of which are for people watching their calories. Payment by check, money order, American Express, Visa, or Mastercard. Shipment by United Parcel. Credit given for returns made within 10 days.

†EILENBERGER'S BUTTER NUT BAKING CO., *P.O. Box 710, Palestine, Tex. 75801. Tel. (214) 729-2176. Brochure price list.*

Apricot cake, pecan cake, and fruitcake. Gift service available. Payment by check, money order, American Express, Visa, or Mastercard. Shipment by Postal Service or United Parcel. Refund or credit for returned goods.

FISHER'S POPCORN, *200 South Boardwalk, Ocean City, Md. 21842. Tel. (301) 289-5638. Price list.*

FRALINGER'S, *1325 Boardwalk, Atlantic City, N.J. 08401. Tel. (609) 345-2177. Free annual catalogue.*

When I see this name, I'm taken back quite a few years to summertimes in Atlantic City—the Boardwalk, the beach, the piers, including Heinz Pier (where they gave out free plastic pickles to pin onto your shirt). Much of what I remember about Atlantic City is gone, but Fralinger's remains. I used to walk on the Boardwalk, trying to decide whether to spend my quarter on salt-water taffy at Fralinger's or James'. Fralinger's boasts "only the finest candies and confections the Atlantic City Boardwalk has had to offer since 1885." Take that, James'! Payment by check, money order, Visa, or Mastercard. Shipment by Postal Service or United Parcel. Purchases may be returned for refund after telephoning for authorization.

GETHSEMANI FARMS. *Fruitcake. See listing under Cheese, above.*

†GRAND FINALE CONFECTIONS, *200 Hillcrest Rd., Berkeley, Calif. 94705. Tel. (415) 655-8414. Brochure price list.*

This place bills itself as California's smallest licensed candy factory, a distinction that won't last long if it continues to turn out tasty caramels like those they sent me. There are also sauces recommended for dripping over ice cream or cake or dipping your finger into. Some of the sweets would make excellent gifts. Payment by check, American Express, Visa, Mastercard, Diners Club, or Carte Blanche. Delivery by United Parcel. Money back if dissatisfied.

†ROBERT D. GRIMM MARKETING, *246 E. 46th St., New York, N.Y. 10017. Tel. (212) 206-8520. Brochure price list.*

Giant chocolate chip cookies, as big as pizzas, and birthday cakes, available for shipment all over the country. These would make very nice surprise gifts. There are also nonfood gift items, including boxes of balloons. Payment by check, money order, American Express, Visa, or Mastercard. Shipment by United Parcel.

†HARBOR SWEETS, *P.O. Box 150, Marblehead Mass. 01945. Tel. (617) 745-7648. Free quarterly 12- to 16-page catalogue.*

The proprietor, Benneville N. Strohecker, sent me a package of his candy with a note saying that his goal was to make the best candy in the world. My family seems to have concluded that Mr. Strohecker was well on his way toward his goal, as they left me only one piece. The candies make very nice gifts; one of them is a copy in chocolate of Romeo and Juliet kissing (from the bas-relief sculpture series at the Folger Shakespeare Library in Washington) for Valentines Day. Payment by check, money order, Visa, or Mastercard. Delivery by United Parcel, by Postal Service if necessary, or by air freight, for very eager Romeos. Refund, credit, or replacement if not satisfied.

†HONEY BEE GARDENS, *1863 Lane 11½, Lovell, Wyo. 82431. Tel. (307) 548-2543. Brochure price list.*

Candies made with only one sweetener, honey. Their Q-Bee Pecan Pearl (a honey pecan praline) is the "queen of all candies." Bring your sweet tooth. Payment by check or money order. Shipment by Postal Service or United Parcel. Purchases may be returned for credit within 10 days.

IMMACULATE HEART HERMITAGE, *Camaldolese Monks, Big Sur, Calif. 93920. Tel. (408) 667-2456. Price list.*

Here are fruitcakes and date nut cakes with a large following. Payment by check or money order.

KERNEL POPPINS, *319 Avenue of the Americas, New York, N.Y. 10014. Tel. (212) 989-6588. Price list.*

Everything you've ever wanted in popcorn, and then some. Popcorn with caramel, cheese, butter, or combinations thereof, and you can order it with or without salt. Payment by check, money order, American Express, Visa, or Mastercard. Delivery by United Parcel. Replacements are sent if packages arrive damaged or opened.

KOINONIA PARTNERS. *Chocolate bars and fruitcake. See listing under* Fruit and Nuts, *above.*

†LAMMES CANDIES, *P.O. Box 1885, Austin, Tex. 78767. Tel. (512) 472-3114. Free annual 12-page catalogue.*

This company has been around since 1885, and its leading product is a pecan praline that my daughter Ellen found quite remarkable and probably worth the extra miles she had to run to use up the considerable number of calories absorbed. There is a gift service with which to spoil your friends and business acquaintances. Payment by check, money order, Visa, or Mastercard. Shipment by Postal Service, United Parcel, or truck freight. The candies are guaranteed to be fresh.

MADAME CHOCOLATE, *1940-C Lehigh Ave., Glenview, Ill. 60025. Tel. (312) 729-3330. Free 16-page catalogue issued 4 times a year.*

This company sells more kinds of chocolate than I thought existed, as well as cookware items to prepare chocolate dishes. It claims to be the only place in the country where noncommercial purchasers can buy "the same kinds of chocolate used in the finest candy stores, bakeries, and restaurants." Payment by check, money order, Visa, or Mastercard. Shipment by Postal Service or United Parcel. Refunds or credit for damaged goods.

MAID OF SCANDINAVIA. *Candies and cake toppings. See listing under* Cookware and Dinnerware.

MAIL ORDER MUFFINS, *910 Orange St., Wilmington, Del. 19801. Tel. (302) 656-6500 or (800) 441-7527, ext. 804. Annual catalogue folder.*

"We don't need salt, so we don't use it." Muffins come in 17 varieties. Payment by check, money order, Visa, or Mastercard. Delivery by United Parcel. They ask that nothing be returned; they will send another batch or give a refund if the muffins aren't fresh.

MARGE'S COUNTRY KITCHEN, *Route 1, Box 164A, Duncan, Okla. 73533. Tel. (405) 255-0753. No catalogue.*

Marge Murray makes only one item, pound cake, and it is, by all accounts, sensational. Who would have thought you could develop a national following with pound cake? Payment by check or money order. Shipment by Postal Service or United Parcel. Ms. Murray has never had a cake returned.

MARSHALL'S MACKINAC TRAIL, *308 E. Central Ave., Mackinaw City, Mich. 49701. Tel. (616) 436-5379. Free catalogue.*

The 3 kinds of fudge I got to taste test—chocolate pecan, peanut butter, and chocolate chip—were very good. Shipment by Postal Service or United Parcel.

†MARY OF PUDDIN HILL, *P.O. Box 241, Greenville, Tex. 75401. Tel. (214) 455-2651. Free 14- to 30-page catalogue issued twice a year.*

Nice chocolates, many fixed up for gift giving. Payment by check, money order, American Express, Visa, or Mastercard. Delivery by Postal Service or, outside Texas, United Parcel. Refunds in cash or credit—everything is fully guaranteed—if claim made within a reasonable amount of time.

MINERVA STREET CHOCOLATE, *1052 Olivia, Ann Arbor, Mich. 48104. Tel. (313) 665-8661. Brochure price list.*

Chocolate truffles that look appropriately sinful. Payment by check or money order. Shipment by United Parcel. Replacement of unsatisfactory purchases.

†MORAVIAN SUGAR CRISP CO., *Route 2, Clemmons, N.C. 27012. Tel. (919) 764-1402. Brochure price list.*

"The best homemade cookies in the world," including their traditional sugar crisp, ginger crisps, and chocolate crisps. These are suggested for gifts at Christmas and other jolly times. Payment by check. Delivery by Postal Service or United Parcel. No returns except in case of mistake by the cookie company.

†MRS. FIELDS COOKIES, *P.O. Box 680370, Park City, Utah 84068. Tel. (801) 649-2404 or (800) 344-CHIP (except in Utah). Brochure price list issued annually.*

Lots of chocolaty cookies made without preservatives, including Chocolate Frost-Bites—cookies topped with chocolate mousse, dipped in chocolate and frozen. Mrs. Fields suggests that the freezing contracts the chocolate, thus decreasing the number of calories. If I could only believe that, I'd go on a chocolate ice cream diet! Mrs. Fields seems to have just the right combination of good taste and whimsy. "It is estimated that 6,020,000 square miles or about 10.4 percent of the earth's land is permanently glaciated," she writes. "Wouldn't it be wonderful if it were all chocolate?" Payment by check, money order, Visa, or Mastercard. Delivery by United Parcel. Refunds in cash or credit if not satisfied.

MRS. SNYDER'S CHOCOLATE CHIPPERY *is run by the same Cathy Snyder who sends out Mail Order Muffins, see listing above.*

NANCY'S CANDIES, *Rt. 1, Box 490, Pine Mountain, Ga. 31822. Tel. (404) 663-4583. Brochure price list sent out 3 times a year.*

Here is another food company boasting that it doesn't use preservatives. This limits Nancy's shipments to October through March. Nancy makes chocolate pecan crunch and pecan toffee and, judging by the speed with which the samples disappeared after being sent to my home, they have a certain attraction for a person with a sweet tooth. Payment by check, money order, American Express, Visa, or Mastercard. Shipment by

United Parcel. There is an unconditional money-back guarantee.

OLE SALTY'S OF ROCKFORD, *1447 Charles St., Rockford, Ill. 61108. Tel. (815) 229-3590. Price list.*

Accounts suggest that these are the best potato chips in the country. No preservatives are used and, best of all for people like me who are trying to limit their use of salt, the chips come regularly salted, lightly salted, and unsalted. Payment by check or money order. Shipment by United Parcel. Refunds for returned purchases.

ORRELL'S MARYLAND BEATEN BISQUITS, *P.O. Box 7 Wye Mill, Md. 21679. Tel. (301) 822-2065. No catalogue.*

PINAHS COMPANY, *3914 W. Center St., Milwaukee, Wis. 53210. Tel. (414) 873-7310. No catalogue.*

Despite the lack of a catalogue, word is spreading wide and fast about Pinahs Rye Chips, which come in garlic, plain, onion, and hickory. You could write to the company for a quote on how much it would cost to ship a case to you, the price ranging from $14.50 to $17 at this writing, depending on how far you are from Milwaukee. Payment by check or money order. Shipment by United Parcel. No returns except in case of defective product.

†THE POPCORN FACTORY, *P.O. Box 453, Lake Bluff, Ill. 60044. Tel. (312) 362-9600 or (800) 228-5000. Free quarterly 16- to-24-page catalogue.*

†PRIMMER'S COUNTRY STORE, *310 South K Ave., Vinton, Iowa 52349. Tel. (319) 472-5088. Brochure price list.*

Snack foods for eating or giving as gifts. There are packs of popping corn, with and without oil, plus other munchies. Payment by check, money order, Visa, or Mastercard. Shipment by United Parcel. Purchases may be returned within 7 days for refund.

R. & R. HOMESTEAD KITCHEN, *803 Morning Glory Lane, De Pere, Wis. 54115. Tel. (414) 336-7574 or 336-8244. No catalogue.*

R. & R. offers hot fudge topping, German Christmas stollen, fruit cake, and glazed walnuts. *Diversion* magazine said its hot fudge topping was the best in the country and a must for chocolate freaks. Payment by check or money order. Shipment by United Parcel. No returns.

†ARNOLD REUBEN JR.'S CHEESE CAKES, *15 Hillpark Ave., Great Neck, N.Y. 11021. Tel. (516) 466-3685. Free brochures.*

The name makes clear the specialty, and the cheesecakes are widely regarded as excellent. Cheesecake is expensive; Arnold Reuben Jr.'s cheesecakes, not surprisingly, are very expensive. A terrific gift for a homesick ex-New Yorker. Payment by check, money order, American Express, Visa, or Mastercard. Shipment by Postal Service or United Parcel. No returns since the "product is frangible"; if there are any probems, they'll send another cake.

†SANTA FE COOKIE CO., *110 W. San Francisco St., Santa Fe, N.M. 87501. Tel. (505) 983-7707 or (800)*

243-0353 (except in New Mexico). Free brochure issued twice a year.

Six kinds of cookies, including traditional Santa Fe shortbread with piñon. The gift packages are somewhat expensive, but they sure look good. Payment by check, money order, Visa, or Mastercard. Shipment by United Parcel. The cookies are guaranteed to be fresh; credit given for unsatisfactory deliveries.

SCHIMPFF'S, *347 Spring St., Jeffersonville, Ind. 47130. Tel. (812) 283-8975. Brochure price list issued 4 to 6 times a year.*

This company, founded in 1858 by Gus A. Schimpff, the great-grandfather of the company's current candymaker, Sonny Schimpff, says it is the oldest single-family owned retail candy manufacturer in the United States. You can select the composition of your own box of candy, choosing from, for example, 26 milk chocolates and 17 dark vanilla chocolates. Sonny's "only desire in life is to be known as the world's best candymaker," and he goes to great lengths to further this desire. Payment by check, money order, Visa, or Mastercard. Shipment by Postal Service or United Parcel. Credit for purchases returned within 10 days of receipt.

†KAY SILVER'S NUTCORN, *9459 Charleville Blvd., Beverly Hills, Calif. 90212. Tel. (213) 274-3220. Brochure price list.*

Gift packages of nutcorn—caramel-coated pecans, almonds, and popcorn—and other tempting nut combinations. Payment by check, money order, Visa, or Mastercard. Shipment by United Parcel.

TEUSCHER CHOCOLATES OF SWITZERLAND, *620 Fifth Ave., New York, N.Y. 10020. Tel. (212) 246-4416. Brochure price list issued annually.*

Mimi Sheraton found these to be "rich bittersweet or mellow chocolates that many connoisseurs consider to be the world's finest." The chocolates contain no preservatives, additives, or artificial food coloring and fresh shipments are flown from Zurich to New York every week. As one might expect, they are very pricey. Money order, American Express, Visa, and Mastercard accepted. Delivery by United Parcel. Credit given for unsatisfactory shipments.

†**TOUT SWEET,** *P.O. Box 5343, Portland, Ore. 97228. Tel. (503) 646-7999. Free brochure price list.*

Expensive candies, properly sinful—classic truffles, framboise, Grand Marnier, noisette. Gifts any recipient will pay attention to. Payment by check, Visa, or Mastercard. Shipment by Postal Service or United Parcel. Unconditionally guaranteed; return any unused portion, and you'll receive a check immediately.

†**TRAPPISTINE CREAMERY CARAMELS,** *R.R. 3, Dubuque, Iowa 52001. Tel. (319) 556-6330. Brochure.*

These caramels, which provide the main source of income for an abbey of Cistercian nuns, come in vanilla, chocolate, licorice, and honey. A gift service is available, and Christmas boxes are offered. Payment by check or money order. Shipment by United Parcel unless Postal Service is requested. Purchases may be returned for refund or exchange within 10 days.

TRAPPISTINE QUALITY CANDY, *300 Arnold St., Wrentham, Mass. 02093. Tel. (617) 528-1282. Brochure price list.*

Candy made by the nuns of Mt. St. Mary's Abbey, including fudge, maple fudge with walnuts, caramels, plus fruit preserves from the monks of St. Joseph's Abbey in Spencer, Mass., and fruitcake from the monks of Gethsemani Farms in Kentucky. Payment by check or money order. Shipment by Postal Service or United Parcel. Purchases may be returned for replacement.

VELVET CREME POPCORN CO., *4710 Belinder, Shawnee Mission, Kans. 66205. Tel. (913) 236-7742. Brochure price list.*

Popcorn with a wide following, put up in containers with dividers that allow the simultaneous purchase of popcorn with various flavorings, one of which is unsalted. Payment by check or money order. Shipment by Postal Service or United Parcel or, on large orders, truck. Refunds for purchases returned within a "reasonable" time.

WOLFERMAN'S, *2820 W. 53rd St., Fairway, Kans. 66205. Tel. (913) 432-6131 or (800) 255-0169 (except in Kansas). Semiannual 8- to 12-page catalogue costs $1.*

Famous muffins from a company started in 1888. *Esquire* calls Wolferman's English muffins the best in the United States. You can sign up for the Muffin of the Month Club. Payment by check, money order, Wolferman charge, American Express, Visa, or Mastercard. Delivery by United Parcel, except by Postal Service to Hawaii and Alaska. Cash refund or credit for unsatisfactory goods.

Coffee, Tea, Condiments, and Preserves

BAINBRIDGE'S FESTIVE FOODS, *P.O. Box 150805, Nashville, Tenn. 37215. Tel. (615) 383-5157. Brochure price list.*

Cuisine magazine praised this company's black walnut jelly, spiced sweet pickles, and apple pie jelly. There are a dozen other products. Payment by money order, Visa, or Mastercard. Shipment by United Parcel. No returns without prior written approval.

BELLA COFFEA, *1602 Grant Ave., Suite 209, Novato, Calif. 94947. Tel. (415) 897-3928. Free price list to people who send in a self-addressed stamped envelope.*

Eighteen coffees that range from Colombian to French vanilla. Payment by check, money order, American Express, Visa, or Mastercard. Delivery by United Parcel. Damaged goods may be returned within 5 days for credit against future purchases.

†BLANCHARD & BLANCHARD LTD., *Upper Pasture Rd., Norwich, Vt. 05055. Tel. (802) 649-1327. Free 8-page catalogue.*

Seven kinds of mustard, 6 salad dressings, and 6 dessert sauces are among the products available, plus several gift assortments. Payment by check or money order. Shipment by United Parcel. Purchases may be returned for credit within 1 week, but only if the product was spoiled.

BOSTON FARMS, *R.D. 1, Stillwater, Pa. 17878. Tel. (717) 864-3632. Free 16-page catalogue.*

"Boston jellies and preserves cannot and do not rub elbows on supermarket shelves with commercial products, machine-produced from seed to store;" the company offers strawberry, huckleberry, peach, blueberry, and tomato-with-lemon preserves, plus concord grape, apple-cinnamon, and quince jellies. Payment by check or money order. Shipment by United Parcel. If unsatisfied, send back purchases within 30 days and get a credit toward another purchase.

CHERRY HILL COOPERATIVE CANNERY, *MR 1, Barre-Montpelier Rd., Barre, Vt. 05641 Tel. (802) 479-2558. Brochure.*

Maple cream, applesauce (unsweetened or sweetened with honey), creamed honey, cider jelly, and maple syrup. Payment by check, money order, or C.O.D. Shipment by United Parcel or common carrier.

CHERRY HUT PRODUCTS, *Beulah, Mich. 49617. Tel. (616) 882-4431. Brochure price list.*

A large line of preserves, jams, jellies, and sauces made from many fruits, especially cherries, available as gifts. Payment by check or money order. Shipment by United Parcel.

CHICAMA VINEYARDS, *Stoney Hill Rd., West Tisbury, Mass. 02575. Tel. (617) 693-0309. Price list.*

Vintage vinegars. There have been nice things written about these vinegars from Martha's Vineyard, which include unflavored red and white wine vinegars, and herb- and fruit-flavored vinegars. Payment by check, money order, Visa, Mastercard, or C.O.D. Shipment by United Parcel. No returns.

CLANCY'S FANCY, *410 W. Washington, Ann Arbor, Mich. 48103. Tel. (313) 663-4338. Brochure.*

This company has only one product—Clancy's Fancy Irish Hot Sauce. Anything with 5 cloves of garlic in one little bottle has got to be good, and this also has honey, ginger root, hot peppers and vinegar. The Irish provenance is somewhat shaky, having derived from Colleen Clancy's recollection of sauces concocted at an Irish school by classmates from Trinidad, Mexico, Spain, and points south. Payment by check or money order. Shipment by Postal Service or United Parcel. No returns.

*CLARK HILL SUGARY, *Canaan, N.H. 03741. Tel. (603) 523-7752. Brochure issued annually.*

Pure maple syrup is not cheap, and Clark Hill's is no exception, with a recent price list offering a pint for $6, a quart for $10, and a half gallon for $17. A discount of 20 percent is offered, however, on orders of 100 or more. Payment by check, money order, Visa, or Mastercard. Delivery by United Parcel unless Postal Service is requested. Full refund in cash if not satisfied.

COMMUNITY CAFE. *Coffee and Tea. See listing under* Gourmet, Ethnic, and Special Foods, *above.*

GRANITE FALLS PICKELRY. *See listing for Northwest Cache/Granite Falls Pickelry under* Gourmet, Ethnic, and Special Foods.

KOZLOWSKI FARMS, *5566 Gravenstein Highway, Forestville, Calif. 95436. Tel. (707) 887-2104. Brochure price list.*

Old-fashioned jams, sugarless jams, California wine jellies (the latest being cabernet sauvignon), berry vinegars, and mustard. Payment by check, money order, Visa, or Mastercard. Shipment by United Parcel. Purchases may be returned for refund within 2 weeks.

LUZIANNE BLUE PLATE FOODS, *640 Magazine St., New Orleans, La. 70130. Tel. (504) 524-6131 or (800) 692-7895 (except in Louisiana). Free brochure.*

Coffee blends, tea, and salad dressing. Payment by check, Visa, or Mastercard. Delivery by United Parcel. Unconditional guarantee, with refunds in cash or credit.

PALMER'S MAPLE SYRUP, *Waitsfield, Vt. 05673. Tel. (802) 496-3696. Brochure.*

This business is a "small family affair," run by Everett Palmer, and his wife, Kathryn. Though it is small, it has a fine reputation among maple syrup aficionados. Payment by check. Shipment by United Parcel.

†PEPPER PATCH, *1250 Old Hillsboro Rd., Franklin, Tenn. 37064. Tel. (615) 790-1012. Annual catalogue costs $1.*

Marmalades, jellies, sauces made from fruits, peppers, and other vegtables but never with any arrtificial coloring, flavoring, or chemical preservatives. The newest offerings are sweet potato butter, green tomato marmalade, and prune marmalade. Payment by check, money order, Visa, or Mastercard. Delivery by United Parcel. They promise to replace any damaged merchandise promptly.

L. E. ROSELLI'S FOOD SPECIALTIES, *R.D. 1, Box 342, Medford, N.J. 08055. Tel. (609) 654-4816. No catalogue.*

This small family business has a large following for its spaghetti sauces, which contain no sugar or preservatives. The varieties are marinara, meat, mushroom, pizza, meatless, and no-salt. Isn't it interesting that so many places are offering foods without salt added? They ship by United Parcel and include the bill. Payment by return check.

SCHAPIRA COFFEE CO., *117 W. 10th St., New York, N.Y. 10011. Tel. (212) 675-3733. Price list.*

The next time someone asks you what's so great about New York City, you could answer, "Schapira's, for one thing." Not too many cities have such a gem. A recent price list offered 20 kinds of coffee, 12 kinds of loose tea and 14 kinds of tea bags, plus various pots and machines for brewing. We bought an espresso machine, aptly named the Vesuviana many years ago at Schapira's, and it continues to spout coffee when called upon. Payment by Visa or Mastercard.

TALK O' TEXAS BRANDS, *435 S. Oakes, San Angelo, Tex. 76903. Tel. (915) 655-6077 or (915) 658-6408. Price list.*

Red bell pepper relish, hot crisp okra pickles, and mild crisp okra pickles. Payment by check.

†TRINITY ABBEY HONEY, *Huntsville, Utah 84317. Tel. (801) 745-3784. Brochure price list.*

This is a Trappist monastery that has developed a creamed honey spread in natural and other flavors, including cinnamon,

lemon, date pecan, toasted almond, black walnut, and maple. A gift service is available if you want to give a very unusual present. Payment by check. Shipment by United Parcel. Purchases may be returned for refund within 5 days.

†WILDS OF IDAHO, *1308 W. Boone, Spokane, Wash. 99201. Tel. (509) 326-0197. Brochure.*

Gourmet huckleberry products—jam, topping, syrup, and huckleberry-chocolate—some of them put together in gift assortments. Payment by check, money order, Visa, or Mastercard. Shipment by United Parcel. Purchases may be returned within 10 days for refund.

WOOD'S CIDER JELLY, *R.F.D. 2, Box 266, Springfield, Vt. 05156. Tel. (802) 263-5547. Brochure price list.*

The 2 foods available here—cider jelly and maple syrup—got high marks in, of all places, *Money* magazine. Payment by check or money order. Shipment by United Parcel. Purchases may be returned within 15 days for refund or credit.

Herbs and Spices

ATTAR HERBS & SPICES, *Playground Rd., New Ipswich, N.H. 03071. Tel. (603) 878-1780. Annual 8-page catalogue costs 25 cents.*

THE COLORADO SPICE & TEA MERCHANT, *2217 E. 21st Ave., Denver, Colo. 80205. Brochure price list.*

The emphasis here is on spices, more than 50 of them, and there are also teas, nuts and dried fruits. Cookbooks are offered at discounts, including some by Julia Child, James Beard, and Craig Claiborne. Payment by check or money order. Shipment by Postal Service or United Parcel. Purchases may be returned within 10 days for refund.

CULPEPER LTD., *Hadstock Rd., Linton, Cambridge, England, CB1 6NJ. Tel. Cambridge 891196. Free 8-page price list.*

A fine selection of herbs for cooking, or, if you are so inclined for medicinal purposes. The prices for herbs and seeds are reasonable, but with substantial shipping charges. Americans interested in raising their own herbs might be interested in buying some seeds for plants not normally found in this country. Payment, in sterling, by check, money order, American Express, Visa, and Diners Club. Delivery by Postal Service. Credit given for faulty goods.

FAITH MOUNTAIN HERBS, *Box 199, Main St., Sperryville, Va. 22740. Tel. (703) 987-8824. Semiannual 16-page catalogue costs $2.*

Herbs and spices, as well as handicrafts from Appalachia. See also entry under *Crafts to Buy.* Payment by check, money order, American Express, Visa, or Mastercard. Delivery by United Parcel. Unsatisfactory goods may be returned within 20 days for refund.

GRAND MONDE DES HERBES (Wide World of Herbs), *11 St. Catherine St. East, Montreal, Que., Canada H2X 1K3. Tel. (514) 842-1838. Catalogue costs $2.*

HARTENTHALER'S NATURAL FOODS & HERBES, *1854 Delmar Dr., Folcroft, Pa. 19032. Tel. (215) 583-1644.*

Annual 30 page catalogue costs $1, deductible against first order.

Lots of herbs and spices for cooking and health care, with "very reasonable" prices on bulk orders. Payment by check, money order or Visa. Shipment by Postal Service or United Parcel. Unsatisfactory items should not be returned but cash refund or credit is promised if customer is not happy.

LES HERBES FRANÇAISES ET EPICERIE TRADING INC., *P.O. Box 253, Gedney Station, White Plains, N.Y. 10605. Tel. (914) 681-0548. Brochure.*

Here are whole bay leaves and bay leaves wrapped around fennel, sage, thyme, or taragon in a classic bouquet garni. Payment by check or money order. Shipment by Postal Service, United Parcel, or truck. No returns.

†JOSEPHINE, *P.O. Box 249, 38 E. Sycamore St., Columbis, Ohio 43216. Tel. (614) 228-0494. Catalogue costs $1.*

Herbs for tea, vitamin sources, health care, and especially seasoning, with some for meat, some for seafood, and some for poultry and game. A gourmet basket from here would make a nice gift. Payment by check, money order, Visa, or Mastercard. Delivery by Postal Service or United Parcel. Refunds in cash.

MEADOWBROOK HERBS & THINGS, *Whispering Pines Rd., Wyoming, R.I. 02898. Tel. (401) 539-7212. The 30-page catalogue costs $1.*

*MR. SPICEMAN, *615 Palmer Rd., Yonkers, N.Y. 10701. Tel. (914) 961-7776. The 24-page catalogue issued 3 times a year costs $1, but you can then deduct twice the cost of the catalogue from your first order.*

This very nice catalogue includes a list of spices and, for those of us concerned about sodium and high blood pressure, notes 150 items without salt. Lots of teas and herbal teas proffered along with breezy advice, such as: "Use spice often. Practice makes perfect." The prices are said to be way below what is charged in supermarkets: cinnamon, 62 percent lower; paprika, 62 percent lower; and ground garlic, 53 percent lower. Payment by check, money order, Visa, or Mastercard. Shipment by Postal Service or United Parcel. Refunds in cash or credit for goods returned within 10 days.

PAPRIKAS WEISS IMPORTER. *See listing under* Gourmet, Ethnic, and Special Foods, *above.*

PENN HERB CO., *603 N. Second St., Dept. 28, Philadelphia, Pa. 19123. Tel. (215) 925-3336 or (800) 523-9971 (except in Pennsylvania). Annual 80-page catalogue costs $1, but that is refundable with order and includes free samples.*

These herbs are aimed at health and well-being, but the company is careful to say that herbs do not substitute for a doctor's care. There are lots of herbal teas that are recommended for both health and flavor, and the catalogue provides this advice on making your own vanilla extract: "Cut vanilla bean into several large pieces and add to a pint of brandy; close cap and allow to sit for several weeks, shaking the bottle every day." Payment by check, money order, C.O.D., Visa, or Mastercard. Delivery by Postal Service or United Parcel. Credit or cash refunds.

RAM ISLAND FARM HERBS, *Ram Island Farm, Cape Elizabeth, Me. 04107. Tel. (207) 799-0011. Annual 16-page catalogue costs $1.*

RILEY'S SEASONING AND SPICES, *R.R. 2, Box 17, Griggsville, Ill. 62340. Tel. (217) 833-2207. Brochure price list.*

Wayne Riley developed his all-purpose seasoning to flavor the whole hogs that he cooked up for groups and private parties. It has become very popular. He has also developed a salt-free version. Payment by check or money order. Shipment by United Parcel. No returns.

STARFLOWER NATURAL FOODS & BOTANICALS. *See listing under* Grains and Vegetables, Natural and Freeze-Dried Foods, *above.*

TAYLOR'S HERB GARDEN, *1535 Lone Oak Rd., Vista, Calif. 92083. Tel. (619) 727-3485. Annual 32-page catalogue costs $1.*

Lists lots of herbs that will provide a fresh taste in your kitchen while bringing beauty to the garden. Payment by check, money order, or C.O.D. ($2 service charge on C.O.D.). Complete satisfaction or money back or replacements sent.

UNITED SOCIETY OF SHAKERS, *Sabbathday Lake, Poland Spring, Me. 04274. Tel. (207) 926-4597.*

Herbal teas, culinary herbs, Shaker potpourri, and rose water. Some books are also available. Payment by check or money order. Shipment by United Parcel. Purchases may be returned for refund or credit within 4 weeks.

WALTER'S, *WSM Co., Box 52, Chappaqua, N.Y. 10514. Tel. (914) 238-3665. No catalogue.*

Walter Mills makes one product, a dry mixture of herbs spices and salt to which you add vinegar, water, and/or other liquids to make dressings for salads, chicken, fish, or whatever other dishes your sense of adventure and taste encourage you to enhance.

See also *Seeds and Plants* and *Vitamins, Herbs, and Health Guides*.

Wine and Liquor

EGERTONS. *Wine and liquor for friends in Britain. See* Gourmet, Ethnic, and Special Foods, *above.*

†**NATIONWIDE GIFT LIQUOR SERVICE,** *800 Speed Order Systems and Express-a-Gift, P.O. Box 32070, Phoenix, Ariz. 85016. Tel. (602) 957-4923, (800) 528-6148 (except in Arizona), or (800) 243-4787 (in Arizona). Brochure.*

This company is trying to accomplish something difficult—working out a system of liquor dealers who will deliver gifts of wine and liquor. Because of the hodge-podge of state liquor laws, wine and liquor cannot be sent everywhere. Payment by check, money order, American Express, Visa, Mastercard, Diners Club, or Carte Blanche. Purchases may be returned for refund or credit.

TRENCHERMAN'S LTD. *Wine and spirits to send to friends in the British Isles. See listing under* Gourmet, Ethnic, and Special Foods, *above.*

❖3 Food Companions

I cannot remember any subject coming along with such force and staying power as the recent interest in cooking, serving and, of course, eating good food. A look at a current television schedule will provide ample evidence of this; among the listings are to be found a cooking program featuring Julia Child, specials on Cajun, Chinese, and "frugal" gourmet cooking, a series on cooking in New Orleans' best restaurants, and another on the same in New York.

Pots and pans are no longer hidden in cabinets. Copper pots are hung on the wall (I can see seven of them on our kitchen wall) to become a focal point of the room, and those big aluminum pots are meant to do the same. Just to show you that people are serious about this, one of the mail-order companies sells kits of supplies needed to put new tin linings on the insides of copper pots. It wasn't too long ago that most Americans didn't know that copper pots were lined with tin; now they're learning to rejuvenate them at home.

Two groups of comestibles that can make food better tasting and more fun to eat—herbs and spices and also wine and beer—have been used for these purposes since long before anyone started wondering about them. In both cases, the user can also be the provider, growing the herbs and spices, vinting the wine, brewing the beer. Those interested in growing herbs and spices or even raising wine grapes should consult the For the Garden chapter.

Finally, what better accompaniment to a glass of beer or wine than some cheese— perhaps even a special cheese made with herbs and spices? Here are some supplies for making your own wine, beer, and cheese.

Cookware and Dinnerware

*AMERICAN ARCHIVES LTD., *Division of American Slicing Machine Co., 5535 N. Long Ave., Chicago, Ill. 60630. Tel. (312) 774-2020, (800) 621-5809 (except in Illinois) or (800) 972-5858 (in Illinois). Free 24-page catalogue issued twice a year.*

Silverware and tableware at discount prices, like a 56-piece set of Interlude by International offered at $375, said to have a list price of $650. Payment by check, money order, American Express, Visa, Mastercard, Diners Club, or Carte Blanche. Shipment by United Parcel. Purchases may be returned for refund or credit within 30 days.

†AMERICA'S WINELAND CRAFTS, *Box J, Rolling Hills Estates, Calif. 90274. Tel. (213) 539-5005 or (800) 824-7888, Operater 999. Semiannual 36-page catalogue costs $2. Free 36-page* Wine Ambiance Catalogue.

Gourmet accessories. The *Wine Ambiance Catalogue* offers glasses, coolers, and other accoutrements for enjoying wine, much of it a bit too pricey for those who enjoy plain old wine by the jugful. There are many gift ideas and many books here. Payment by check, money order, American Express, Visa, Mastercard, or Diners Club. Shipment by Postal Service or United Parcel. Purchaes may be returned for refund within 30 days.

ANYTHING LEFT HANDED. *Kitchen gadgets for lefties. See listing under* Novelty Items and Gag Gadgets.

AUX CUISINES, *43 Saddle Ranch Lane, Hillsdale, N.J. 07642. Tel. (201) 664-8775. No cataogue.*

This company offers kits for retinning the insides of copper pots. Do it yourself and save a lot of money. Rather than a catalogue, they will send you copies of newspaper articles about the ease of retinning. Payment by check or money order. Delivery by Postal Service or United Parcel. Refunds for goods returned within 30 days. Be fairly certain that you want to make the effort, before you order, as the owner does not approve of window-shoppers.

BERRY-HILL LTD. *Specialty kitchen equipment, such as grindstones. See listing under* Garden Tools, Equipment, and Furniture.

M. & S. BLOOM, *920 Andersen Dr., San Rafael, Calif. 94901. Tel. (415) 453-1640, (800) 227-3900 (except in California), or (800) 632-2122 (in California). Free 24-page catalogue issued 3 times a year.*

Kitchen gadgets, equipment, and cookbooks. The shipment cost is included in the price, not extra. Payment by check, money order, American Express, Visa, or Mastercard. Shipment by Postal Service or Federal Express. Merchandise may be returned for refund or credit within 60 days.

BOSTON PROPER MAIL ORDER. *Kitchen gadgets and food-serving accessories. See listing under* Women's Clothing.

*BRADLEY'S, *P.O. Box 1300, Columbus, Ga. 31993. Tel. (404) 324-5617 or (800) 241-8981. (Except in Georgia). Free 24-page catalogue issued 4 times a year.*

Barbecue grills and equipment for cooking with charcoal or gas. Those who order by telephone can take advantage of daily specials that include discounts of 15 to 50 pecent on featured items. Payment by check, money order, Visa, or Mastercard. Shipment by United Parcel. Refunds for goods returned within 30 days.

BROOKSTONE, *1053 Vose Farm Rd., Peterborough, N.H. 03458 Tel. (603) 924-7181 or 924-9511. Free 48-page Homewares catalogue issued 3 times a year.*

Lots of equipment for cooking, much of it suitable for gift giving. Many of the things are gadgets you would never have thought of like a cheese grater that snaps onto its own bowl, thereby keeping the cheese from flying all over the counter. Brookstone makes other catalogues, including one listed under *Tools and Equipment*. Payment by check, money order, American Express, Visa, or Mastercard. Shipment by United Parcel. Goods may be returned for refunds.

CENTURY FAMILY PRODUCTS, *3628 Crenshaw Blvd., Los Angeles, Calif. 90016. Tel. (213) 731-0900, (800) 421-4662 (for credit card orders, except in California), or (800) 252-4631 (for credit card orders in California). Free 52-page catalogue issued quarterly.*

Recipe collectors, kitchen implement organizers (this looks like a good idea that would get rid of the clutter in some drawers in our kitchen), kitchenware, plus planners to keep track of appointments, personal inventory registers, photo albums and frames, and magazine binders.

CHATHAM FIELDS, *Pewter, glass, and silver. See listing under* Crafts to Buy.

THE CHEF'S CATALOGUE *3915 Commercial Ave., Northbrook, Ill. 60062. Tel. (312) 480-9400. The 32-page catalogue issued 5 times a year costs $1.*

Lots of kitchen equipment, including copperware, knives, machines, and books, plus recipes printed as filler material. Payment by check, money order, American Express, Visa, Mastercard, Diners Club, or Carte Blanche. Shipment by Postal Service or United Parcel. Refunds for goods returned within 30 days.

THE CHINA CLOSET, *6807 Wisconsin Ave., Chevy Chase, Md. 20815. Tel. (301) 656-0203. Free 16-page catalogue.*

China, glassware, pots, pans, knives, and other kitchen equipment. Payment by check, money order, American Express, Visa, Mastercard, or Choice. Refund or exchange for goods returned within 30 days of receipt.

COLLECTION VENISE SIMPLON ORIENT-EXPRESS. *China and silver. See listing under* Railroadiana.

†COMMUNITY KITCHENS. *This is the parent company of Community Cafe listed under* Gourmet, Ethnic, and Special Foods.

The colorful, 54-page catalogue offers many items for cooking and serving food and lots of gift suggestions.

CROSS IMPORTS, *P.O. Box 128, Newton Highlands, Mass. 02161. Tel. (617) 965-1187. Annual 48-page catalogue costs $1.*

Machines (an electric device to make pasta) and all manner of pots, pans, and other things for the kitchen. Though the company doesn't consider itself a discount firm, all of its prices are below list. Payment by check, money order, American Express, Visa, or Mastercard. Shipment by Postal Service or United Parcel. Refunds if not satisfied.

DELFT BLUE LTD., *3735 St. Paul St., Ellicott City, Md. 21043. Tel. (301) 465-4220. The 8-page catalogue costs $1.*

This is a company started by a family from the area in Holland where delft earthenware pottery originated. It makes cups, plates, soup tureens, and wall tiles. Payment by check, Visa, or Mastercard. Shipment by Postal Service or United Parcel. Purchases may be returned for refund within 30 days.

†EPICURE/BATTERIE DE CUISINE, *65 E. Southwater, Chicago, Ill. 60601. Tel. (312) 977-3740; for orders call (800) 228-5000 (except in Nebraska), or (800) 642-8777 (in Nebraska). Free 32-page catalogue issued frequently.*

*THE GAILIN COLLECTION, *P.O. Box 53921, Fayetteville, N.C. 28305. Tel. (919) 864-7372. No catalogue.*

This company acts as a buying service; you tell them what you want, and they get it for you. What they can get includes Aynsley, Coalport, Crown Staffordshire, Minton, Royal Crown Derby, Royal Worchester, Spode, and Wedgwood china from England,

as well as Edinburgh, Stuart, and Waterford crystal, and French and German products. "The lowest prices in the United States." Payment by check, money order, Visa, or Mastercard. Shipment by United Parcel, air or sea freight. There are no returns accepted except in case of error by the company, so be sure of what you want.

GRIFFITH POTTERY HOUSE. *See listing under* Railroadiana.

†HOFFRITZ FOR CUTLERY, *515 W. 24th Street, New York, N.Y. 10011. Tel. (212) 924-7300 or (800) 972-1000 for orders only. The 40-page catalogue issued 3 times a year costs $1.*

This is one of New York City's best known specialty stores, and it has been in business for 50 years. I have listed it here because I think of it first as a source for kitchen knives, but it also has lots of other kitchen equipment, as well as gifts and things that have absolutely nothing to do with slicing bread (a razor for trimming a mustache, for example, and small electronic equipment). Payment by check, money order, American Express, Visa, Mastercard, Diners Club, Carte Blanche, or Choice. Delivery by Postal Service or United Parcel. Goods may be returned within 30 days for refund or credit.

HOMESPUN CRAFTS. *Pewter tableware. See listing under* Bedding, Linens, and Towels.

*INTERNATIONAL HOUSEWARES, *P.O. Box 1826, Pittsfield, Mass. 01202. Tel. (413) 499-2370. Free 16-page catalogue.*

Mostly coffeepots and other pots from Chemex, plus accessories suitable for both Chemex and other glass cookware, much of which would make fine gifts.

JACQUELYNN'S CHINA MATCHING SERVICE, *4770 N. Oakland Ave., Milwuakee, Wis. 53211. Tel. (414) 962-7213. No catalogue.*

This company buys and sells discontinued patterns of Lenox, Oxford, and Temperware. Customers send self-addressed stamped envelopes with the name, the number, or a photo of the pattern they are seeking. The service then finds what is needed from its stock or keeps the request on file until something comes in. Payment by check or money order. Shipment by United Parcel. Purchases may be returned for refund within 5 days of receipt.

†*KITCHEN BAZAAR, *4455 Connecticut Ave., N.W., Washington, D.C. 20008. Tel. (202) 363-4625. The 32- to-48 page catalogue is issued 5 times a year, and costs $1.*

Kitchenware and serving pieces at discount prices, with this example: 25 percent off for Royal Worcester Evesham. The company stocks 10,000 items and suggests that tourists in the nation's capital also make a visit to its store. It is on the same street as the main entrance to the National Zoo, so you could visit the pandas on the same trip. Payment by check, money order, American Express, Visa, or Mastercard. Shipment by Postal Service or United Parcel. Returns accepted on all merchandise for refund or credit.

LEHMAN HARDWARE AND APPLIANCES. *See listing under* Tools and Equipment for Craftspeople, Tinkerers, and Do-It-Yourselfers.

MADAME CHOCOLATE. *Molds and other equipment for making chocolate candy and deserts. See listings under* Baked Goods, Sweets, and Snacks.

MAID OF SCANDINAVIA, *3244 Raleigh Ave., Minneapolis, Minn. 55416. Tel. (612) 927-7996 or (800) 328-6722 (except in Minnesota, Alaska and Hawaii.) Annual 240-page catalogue costs $1.*

All manner of baking equipment, including pans, molds (Bugs Bunny, Mickey Mouse, the Cookie Monster), tubes, flutes, springforms, cookie cutters—all in a catalogue the size of a small city's telephone directory. Payment by check, money order, Visa, or Mastercard. Shipment by Postal Service or United Parcel. Refunds or credit for goods returned within 30 days of purchase, less a 10 percent charge; food, used, and personalized goods not returnable.

MUSEUM OF FINE ARTS, *Boston. Tea and coffee services. See listing under* Museum, Botanic Garden, and Public Radio Gift Catalogues.

DEN PERMANENTE, *8 Vesterbrogade, DK-1620, Copenhagen V, Denmark. Tel. 01-12 44 88. Annual 64-page catalogue costs $1.*

This place has permanent displays of Danish arts and crafts and furnishings for the kitchen and dining room, including such products as Dansk glass. Payment by check, money order, American Express, Visa, Mastercard, or Diners Club. Shipment by Postal Service. Purchases may be returned for credit.

QUIMPER FAIENCE INC., *141 Water St., Stonington, Conn. 06378. Tel. (203) 535-1712. The 16-page catalogue issued every 2 years costs $2.*

This is the American importer of the Quimper pottery, which has been made in the French province of Brittany since 1690. The tableware in this catalogue emphasizes traditional simplicity in design and coloring. It is, as you would guess, very pricey. Payment by check or money order. Shipment by United Parcel (except by Postal Service outside U.S.) Purchases may be returned at any time for refund or exchange.

REPLACEMENTS LTD., *1510 Holbrook St., Greensboro, N.C. 27403. Tel. (919) 275-7224. No catalogue.*

This company says it has the world's largest inventory of discontinued china and crystal patterns. A person's needs are kept in a computer until the request is met. Payment by check, money order, American Express, Visa, Mastercard, or C.O.D. Shipment by United Parcel. Purchases may be returned within 10 days for refund.

SCHAPIRA COFFEE CO. *See listing under* Coffee, Tea, Condiments, and Preserves.

STURBRIDGE YANKEE WORKSHOP. *China, glassware, flatware. See listing under* Furniture and Furnishings.

*THE UNDERGROUND. *See listing under* Lamps and Lighting Fixtures.

VITA MIX CORPORATION, *8615 Usher Rd., Olmsted Falls, Ohio 44138. Tel. (216) 235-4840. Annual free 6-page catalogue.*

This company makes the Vita Mix machine which grinds grain, kneads dough, squeezes juice, and makes yogurt, purees, baby food, and peanut butter, among other things.

*WESTON BOWL MILL, *Main St., Route 100, Weston, Vt. 05161. Tel. (802) 824-6219. Semiannual catalogue costs 50 cents.*

This company makes 200 wooden household and kitchen items and sells them at 25 to 40 percent below normal prices. Payment by check, money order, Visa, or Mastercard. Shipment by Postal Service or United Parcel. Refund or credit for goods returned undamaged within 30 days.

†WILLIAMS-SONOMA, *P.O. Box 7456, San Francisco, Calif. 94120. Tel. (415) 652-9007 (for orders) or (414) 652-1555 (for customer service). The 64-page catalogue issued 6 times a year costs $1.*

This catalogue contains a large selection of nice-looking and useful pieces of cookware, many suitable for gifts. Payment by check, money order, American Express, Visa, Mastercard, Diners Club, or Carte Blanche. Shipment by United Parcel usually, but Postal Service parcel post is available on request. Anything may be returned for refund or credit.

†*THE WINE ENTHUSIAST, *P.O. Box 63, Chappaqua, N.Y. 10514. Tel. (914) 238-9799, (800) 228-2028, ext. 412 (except in Nebraska) or (800) 642-8300, ext. 412 (in Nebraska). The 36-page cataogue issued 3 times a year costs $1.*

That catalogue fee is deductible toward your first purchase, which because of our bluenose laws cannot be of wine but rather of what goes with wine—glasses, decanters, china, wine racks, even a bar ($349 plus $39 shipping), wine-making equipment and some good things to nibble on while sipping. Payment by check, money order, American Express, Visa, or Mastercard. Shipping by Postal Service or United Parcel. Returns within 10 days, cash refunds if desired, with the company paying the return postage.

†WORLD'S FARE, *P.O. Box 5678, Smithtown, N.Y. 11788. Tel. (516) 231-0353, (800) 621-5199 (except in Illinois), or (800) 972-5855 (in Illinois). The 28-page catalogue issued 3 times a year costs $1.*

This catalogue offers a "gourmet and gift collection." There are lots of copper and stainless steel pots and other kitchenware, marble pieces, terra cotta bakeware, pasta machines, espresso pots (why do most people, even restaurant owners writing their menus, spell that "expresso," which sounds like a fast train?), and ceramics. Payment by check, money order, American Express, Visa, or Mastercard. Shipment by Postal Service or United Parcel. Purchases may be returned within 30 days of receipt for refund or credit.

†THE WOODEN SPOON, *Route 6, P.O. Box 852, Mahopac, N.Y. 10541. Tel. (914) 628-3747 or (800) 431-2207 (except in New York). The 64-page catalogue issued 3 times a year costs $1.*

Tools and gadgets for the kitchen, many of which would make nice gifts; a Danish-made heart-shaped waffle iron caught my attention in that regard. Payment by check, money order, American Express, Visa, or Mastercard. Shipment by United Parcel. Refunds for goods returned within 30 days.

YIELD HOUSE. *Stainless steel flatware. See listing under* Furniture and Furnishings.

See also **Gourmet, Ethnic, and Special Foods, Audio and Video Equipment** for gadgets and appliances, *and* **Fine and Unusual Gifts.**

Wine- and Beer-Making Supplies

BARREL BUILDERS, *1085 Lodi Lane, St. Helena, Calif. 94574. Tel. (707) 963-7914. Free newsletter 6 times a year.*

This is a manufacturer of wine barrels that also offers a line of hot tubs, for which there is also a brochure available. Payment by check or money order. Delivery by Postal Service or United Parcel.

BLUE BROS., *701 Seventh Ave., New York, N.Y. 10036. Tel. (212) 757-6300. The 20-page catalogue costs $1.*

CAPE COD BREWER'S SUPPLY CO., *126 Middle Rd. Box 1139, South Chatham, Mass. 02659. Tel. (617) 432-5417. Free annual 24-page catalogue.*

THE COMPLEAT WINEMAKER, *1219 Main St., Saint Helena, Calif. 94574. Tel. (707) 963-9681. Free annual 10-page catalogue.*

Wide variety of winery supplies for both the home wine-maker and large winery operations. Payment by check, money order, Visa, or Mastercard; credit terms available after credit check. Shipment by Postal Service or United Parcel. Credit issued for returned goods, but no electrical parts can be returned.

GREAT FERMENTATIONS, *87 Larkspur, San Rafael, Calif. 94901. Tel. (415) 459-2520. Free annual 16-page catalogue, plus free newsletter to customers.*

"You'll learn more about wine by making your own than you'll ever get out of a book." Wine-making and beer-making equipment, plus ingredients for the beer, but no grapes are shipped. Payment by check, money order, Visa, or Mastercard. Shipment by Postal Service or United Parcel. Cash refunds if goods are defective or missent.

HAMMACHER SCHLEMMER. *See listing under* Audio and Video Equipment, Computers, Electronics, Appliances, and Gadgets.

*E. C. KRAUS, *P.O. Box 7850, Independence, Mo. 64053. Tel. (816) 254-7448. Free 16-page catalogue issued 4 times a year.*

Books and equipment for making wine and beer, plus the ingredients for the beer, including several varieties of yeast, malt, grain, and hops. Prices 25 to 50 percent below those charged in retail wine shops. Payment by check, money order, Visa, or Mastercard. Delivery by Postal Service or United Parcel. Cash refunds (less shipping cost) for returned merchandise.

LA MAISON EDERY, *477 Madison Ave., New York, N.Y. 10022. Tel. (212) 371-2595 or (800) 221-1042 (except in New York). Brochure.*

This company makes containers for home storage of bottles of wine. They are finished in walnut or French provincial oak, one for 200 bottles and one for 65.

NICHOLS GARDEN NURSERY. *Winemaking equipment. See listing under* Seeds and Plants.

NORDIC SAUNA. *Wine cellars. See listing under* Hot Tubs and Saunas.

PRESQUE ISLE WINE CELLARS, *9440 Buffalo Rd., North East, Pa. 16428. Tel. (814) 725-1314. Free catalogue.*

This is an exceptionally well-written catalogue that also serves as an introduction to the joys—and the hazards—of making wine at home. "On that soul-satisfying day when you discover that you can consistently make good wines to enhance the flavor of food and to enjoy with friends" the catalogue notes, "it will be the product of good judgment, good grapes, patience and careful observation. There are no shortcuts, no magical additives. It is an art." That goes for much of life. Presque Isle sells grapes, juice, books, chemicals, and equipment with which you may start on your way toward establishment of a Chateau Lafite (or, better, Mouton) Rothschild in the U.S. Payment by check, money order, Visa, or Mastercard. Delivery by Postal Service, United Parcel, or truck freight, but special arrangements must be made to ship grapes and juice. Cash refund within 30 days if unsatisfied.

SEMPLEX OF U.S.A., *P.O. Box 12276, Minneapolis, Minn. 55412. Tel. (612) 552-0500. Free 24-page catalogue.*

"Any adult may make wine and beer for personal family use. No registration is necessary." Lots of equipment, ingredients, and books on making wine and beer. Payment by check, money order, C.O.D., Visa, Mastercard, Diners Club, Carte Blanche, and Shopper's Charge. Refund in cash or credit toward another purchase.

WILLOW VALLEY CO. *T-shirts for wine-makers and wine drinkers. See listing under* Casual and Sports Clothing.

*WINE AND THE PEOPLE, *907 University Ave, Berkeley, Calif. 94710. Tel. (415) 549-1266. The 30- to 40-page catalogue is issued about once a year (plus newsletter updates) and costs $1.50.*

Fresh grapes are sold in the Berkeley area only. Elsewhere, fresh or frozen grape juice is shipped. The offerings consist of high quality varietal grapes—chardonnay, gewurztraminer, sauvignon blanc, and riesling for white wine; barbera, cabernet franc, cabernet sauvignon, malbec, merlot, pinot noir, and zinfandel for red. There are also the ingredients for home beer-making, plus the equipment to make wine and beer. Good discounts, especially on large orders. The Bavarian gold malt is listed at $1.69 a pound for up to 10 pounds, $1.52 a pound for 10 to 40 pounds, and $1.37 a pound for more than 40 pounds. Customers from the Northeast (east of Ohio and north of Virginia) should write to the eastern distributors, Steve and Lynn Kampers, 9917 E. Moccasion Trail, Wexford, Pa. 15090. Canadians should ask for names and addresses of distributors in their country. Payment by check, money order, Visa or Mastercard. Delivery by United Parcel or freight shipping. Generally credit is given toward another purchase for such problems as faulty equipment, but cash refunds are also made.

Cheese-Making Supplies

ERIE CHEESEMAKING SUPPLY CO., *7700 W. Bargain Rd., Erie, Pa. 16509. Tel. (814) 838-2841. Free 24-page catalogue.*

This informative catalogue proclaims the ease of making cheese. The equipment is not expensive.

NEW ENGLAND CHEESEMAKING SUPPLY CO., *P.O. Box 85, Ashfield, Mass. 01330. Tel. (413) 628-3808. Free 28-page catalogue.*

This catalogue, illustrated with color photos, is more elaborate than Erie Cheesemaking's, and offers more complex (and more expensive) equipment. There are also herbs and spices to flavor the cheese and several books on the subject. Payment by check, money order, Visa, and Mastercard. Shipment by United Parcel, but Postal Service available at extra charge.

Cookbooks

BOOKS FOR COOKS CATALOG, *7188 Cradlerock Way, Columbia, Md. 21045. Tel. (301) 547-9066. Annual 24-page catalogue costs $1.*

This company has 2,500 books in stock, only some of them included in the catalogue, so you should ask for anything not listed. There is a full page on wine books.

THE COLORADO SPICE AND TEA MERCHANT. *See listing under* Herbs and Spices.

THE COOKBOOK GALLERY, *1012 Locust St., Kansas City, Mo. 64106. Tel. (816) 842-3188 or (800) 821-5745 (except in Missouri). Free 8-page catalogue issued 6 times a year.*

This is a book club that sells cookbooks to members at a discount.

*JESSICA'S BISCUIT, *Box 301, Newtonville, Mass. 02160. Tel. (617) 963-0530, (800) 225-4264 (except in Massachusetts), or (800) 332-4027 (in Massachusetts). Three 64-page catalogues each year, cost $1, plus 5 newsletters.*

A catalogue of cookbooks that does not seem to miss much: Betty Crocker, Julia Child, James Beard, and Craig Claiborne. It includes original edition of the latter's *New York Times Cookbook,* which is hard to find because it is so good. A few years ago I saw one copy of it in the window of a Times Square bookshop whose main trade was in pornography but kept some other books on the unlikely chance that a judge might need to be convinced that it was a legit book store. The proprietor sold it to me with some reluctance. Jessica's Biscuit sells cookbooks only and, from time to time, offers some at a discount.

BARBARA WEINDLING, *69 Ball Pond Rd., Danbury, Conn. 06810. Tel. (203) 746-2514. Semiannual 10-page catalogue costs $1.*

Nonflashy list of hundreds of cookbooks.

See also *Gourmet, Ethnic, and Special Foods.*

❖ 4 Clothing and Accessories

Clothing makes up one of the largest segments of the mail-order business, and one of the oldest as well. Catalogue sales of clothing and accessories is so competitive that some of the companies with higher priced lines of products seem to let their catalogue designers go all out. Good-looking catalogues in this section include those issued by Banana Republic, L. L. Bean, Camp Beverly Hills, Lands' End, Saint Laurie Ltd., Patagonia Mail Order, and Esprit de Corp. As a general rule, I would suggest that you might expect to pay higher prices for the good things in these well made catalogues.

Did you ever notice that men look very self-conscious while modeling clothes and women do not? I wonder why that is. Another thing that I wonder about (although this is not as compelling) is why so many American companies, especially clothiers, have tacked "Ltd." after their names. It might make some sense as a harmless affectation if the product is very English, but it often is used when the goods are real Americana.

Life used to be simpler. A place like

Brooks Brothers sold men's clothing, and a place like Talbot's sold women's. Now most places that used to specialize in women's clothing include something for men, and vice versa.

There are many other articles of clothing and accessories in The Great Outdoors and Gifts chapters. This is one area where the price of the catalogue really doesn't mean much. Once you get on a mailing list, it's probably a lifetime relationship between you and the company, with the catalogue fee seldom charged.

A sociological note, if I may be allowed one: The world depicted in the photographs in most of these catalogues is one dominated by middle-class white people who seem to have a perpetual age of twenty-two or so. This is not to say that others need not apply, but rather to suggest that a gentle hint might be in order from customers who want to suggest that America is much more diverse than what most catalogues show. A compliment is due those companies that are not limited in their choice of models. (End of sermonette.)

Specialty Department Stores

BERGDORF GOODMAN, *754 Fifth Avenue, New York, N.Y. 10019. Tel. (212) 753-7300. The 72-page catalogue issued several times a year costs $5 a year.*

Main catalogue lists fine women's and children's clothes and accessories. A men's-only catalogue is also available, listing fine men's furnishings and spotswear.

†**BULLOCKS WILSHIRE,** *3050 Wilshire Blvd., Los Angeles, Calif. 90010. Tel. (213) 382-6161 or (800) 228-2028 (except in Nebraska). Free 44-page catalogue.*

Handsome clothing and accessories, mainly for women, plus some gift items. Payment by check, money order, American Express, Visa, Mastercard, or Bullocks Wilshire account. Purchases may be returned for refund, credit, or exchange but personalized items are not returnable.

†**GARFINCKEL'S,** *1401 F St., N.W., Washington, D.C. 20004. Tel. (301) 459-9633, or (800) 345-8501 (except in Pennsylvania), or (800) 662-5180 (in Pennsylvania). Catalogue issued 5 to 7 times each year costs $3.*

High fashion women's clothing from a company that calls itself Washington's premier specialty store. Other catalogues feature gifts and clothing for men and children. Payment by check, money order, American Express, Visa, Mastercard, Diners Club, Choice, or Garfinckel's credit card. Delivery by United Parcel. Purchases may be returned for refund or credit within 30 days.

I. MAGIN, *185 Berry St., San Francisco, Calif. 94107. Tel. (800) 227-4828 (all states). The 60-page catalogue issued 7 times a year costs $2.50 for a year's subscription.*

SAKOWITZ, *1111 Main Street, Houston, Tex. 77521. Tel. (713) 759-1111. The 76-page catalogue costs $2, but the Christmas issue costs $3.*

Clothing, shoes, accessories, and gifts.

†SAKS FIFTH AVENUE, *449 W. 14th St., New York, N.Y. 10014. Telephone (212) 940-5333 or (800) 221-3505 (except in New York State) Free catalogues.*

Saks is one of the benefits of living in New York. It is one of the finest stores in the world, and it has men's, women's and children's clothing as well as handsome accessories. If you can't get to a Saks Fifth Avenue store, you can at least get a Saks catalogue. The store is well equipped to send out gift purchases. Payment by check, money order, American Express, Visa, Mastercard, Diners Club, or S.F.A. account. Purchases may be returned for refund, credit, or replacement.

Men's and Women's Clothing

ASCOT CHANG CO. LTD., *2/F, Block D, 41 Man Yue St., Hung Hom, Kowloon, Hong Kong. Tel. 3-644384. Free brochure and sample swatches.*

This company supplies custom-made shirts for men and women. Payment by check or money order. Shipment by United Parcel. Purchases may be returned for refund or credit within 1 month of receipt.

BAKER STREET SHIRTMAKERS, *281 Centennial Ave., Piscatway, N.J. 08854. Tel. (201) 885-5000, (800) 528-6050 (except in Arizona), or (800) 352-0458 (in Arizona). Semiannual 32-page catalogue costs $1.*

This company is mainly known for its men's shirts, as the name suggests, but the catalogue, called *The Baker Street Collection*, includes men's and women's slacks, tailored clothing, and outerwear. Payment by check, money order, American Express, Visa, or

Mastercard. Shipment by United Parcel. Purchases may be returned for refund or credit.

BANANA REPUBLIC, *410 Townsend St., San Francisco, Calif. 94130. Tel. (415) 777-0250 or (800) 527-5200. The 32-page catalogue costs $1.*

This is a clever, well-designed catalogue of travel and safari clothing, much of which, I'm sure, is worn elsewhere than on safari. There are shirts, trousers, vests, socks, sweaters, jackets, hats, skirts, and dresses. Payment by check, money order, American Express, Visa, Mastercard, or Carte Blanche. Delivery by Postal Service or United Parcel. Purchases may be returned within 30 days for refund or credit.

JOS. A. BANK CLOTHIERS, *123 Market Place, Baltimore, Md. 21202. Tel. (301) 837-1700. Free 90-page catalogue issued 6 times a year.*

This company makes a very nice line of clothes for men and women—men's suits, blazers, sport coats, and slacks, plus women's suits, dresses, shirts, and skirts. Payment by check, money order, American Express, Visa, or Mastercard. Shipment by Postal Service or United Parcel. Purchases may be returned for refund or credit.

BROOKS BROTHERS, *346 Madison Ave., New York, N.Y. 10017. Tel. (212) 682-8800, (800) 247-1000 (except in New Jersey), or (800) 272-1035 (in New Jersey). Free 16- to 48-page catalogue issued 8 times a year.*

A recent catalogue featured a women in a handsome wool skirt and jacket, so I'm finally convinced that Brooks Brothers is no longer the place for only buttoned-down male executives. For women, there are suits, dresses, skirts, slacks, and sweaters; for men, slacks, jackets, suits, ties, and, of course, oxford shirts with button-down collars. Payment by check, money order, American Express, Visa, Mastercard, Diners Club, or Brooks Brothers charge. Shipment by Postal Service or United Parcel. Purchases may be returned for refund.

CAROL BROWN, *Putney, Vt. 05346 Tel. (802) 387-5875. Brochure.*

Here are Irish and Welsh tweeds, capes, and coats for men and women. A handwritten note from the owner (a woman in her 90's), said her tweed capes are most suited to mail-order sales; this, it seems, is a personal place. Payment by check, money order, Visa, or Mastercard. Shipment by United Parcel. Purchases may be returned for refund.

BURBERRY'S, *9 E. 57th St., New York, N.Y. 10022. Tel. (212) 371-5010. Free catalogue.*

These are the best known raincoats in the world.

CABLE CAR CLOTHIERS/ROBERT KIRK LTD., *150 Post St., San Francisco, Calif. 94108. Tel. (415) 397-7733. Free 64-page catalogue.*

They sell mostly men's suits, jackets, slacks, shirts, and accessories, but some women's fashions as well.

CAMBRIDGE WOOLS LTD. *Aran sweaters. See listing under* Needlecrafts.

THE COTTON COMPANY, *P.O. Box 631, 1800 S. Watkins St., Chattanooga, Tenn. 37401. Tel. (615)* 622-7340 or (800) 421-4548. Quarterly 24- to 36-page catalogue costs $2.

All-cotton shirts, pants, blouses, skirts, shorts, dresses, sweaters, women's lingerie, and men's underwear. There is also a line of bed sheets. Payment by check, money order, American Express, Visa, or Mastercard. Shipment by United Parcel. There is an "absolute, unconditional return policy, no strings attached."

THE CUSTOM SHOP, SHIRTMAKERS, *715 Fifth Ave., New York, N.Y. 10019. Tel. (800) 221-9982 (except in New York State) or (800) 522-5229 (in New York). Brochure.*

DEERSKIN TRADING POST, *119 Foster St., Peabody, Mass. 01960. Tel. (617) 532-2260. Free 56-page catalogue issued 4 times a year.*

Leather products, including suede jackets, vests, and coats, sheepskin coats and jackets, plus clothing made of lamb's wool and camel hair, and cowhide flight jackets. There are some expensive furs, such as mink, and there are shoes. Payment by check, money order, American Express, Visa, or Mastercard. Shipment by Postal Service or United Parcel. Purchases may be returned within 14 days for refund.

*DREAMY DOWN FASHIONS, *Suite 185, 287 W. Butterfield Rd., Emhurst, Ill. 60126. Tel. (312) 941-3840. Free 20-page catalogue.*

Offers merchandise at 40 to 60 percent off retail prices.

ESPECIALLY MAINE, *Kennebunkport, Me. 04046. Tel. (207) 985-3749. The 16- to 38-page catalogue is issued 3 times a year costs $1.*

Women's clothing includes jumpers, pants, sweaters, and skirts; men's wear includes sweaters, ties, and socks. The clothing featured is indigenous to Maine. Payment by check, money order, Visa, or Mastercard. Shipment by United Parcel unless Postal Service is requested. Purchases may be returned for refund or credit.

THE FREED CO., *P.O. Box 394, Albuquerque, N.M. 87103. Tel. (505) 247-9311. Brochures.*

Men's leather coats, lap robes, and silk scarves are among the clothing items available here. Other offerings include rugs, Mexican sarapes, and strands of semi-precious stones. In addition, the company offers new white cotton flour bags—a scarce item today. Shipment by Postal Service. Purchases may be returned within 3 days of credit.

FRENCH CREEK SHEEP & WOOL CO., *R.D. 1, Elverson, Pa. 19520. Tel. (215) 286-5700. The 32- to 48-page catalogue issued 3 times a year costs $2.*

Payment by check, money order, American Express, Visa, or Mastercard. Shipment by Postal Service or United Parcel. Purchases may be returned within 2 weeks for refund or credit.

*GOHN BROS., *Box 111, Middlebury, Ind. 46540. Tel. (219) 825-2400. Free 8-page catalogue issued 8 times a year.*

Here is a no-frills catalogue that lists, without glossy illustrations, scores of items at what the company says are discount prices.

The company specializes in "Amish and plain clothing." The business is geared "primarily to serve the Amish people, and those wishing to return to the simple way of life." There are hats, caps, shoes, socks, gloves, underwear, hosiery, work clothes, and made-to-order Amish suits. There are also fabrics, if you want to make it yourself, at prices 30 to 40 percent below competitors'.

*HABAND CO., *265 N. Ninth St., Paterson, N.J. 07530. Tel. (201) 942-2600. Many free catalogues and brochures.*

Discount prices for just about every article of clothing from a company whose prez, Duke Habernickel, as he calls himself, interjects exclamation points and a no-holds-barred style. About discounts, Duke said, "Shirts! Three-layer coats $29.95!! Excellent values on women's clothing! We sell 100,000 pairs of pants per week! Discounts! ALL MADE IN U.S.A.! ALL SIZES! OVER 3 MILLION CUSTOMERS!" I learned recently that Duke was unsuccessful in his efforts to buy Tiffany's. Too bad! He would have shaken up Fifth Avenue. Payment by check, money order, Visa, or Mastercard. Shipment by Postal Service or United Parcel. Refunds for purchases "within 30 days if you don't want to wear it."

HOG WILD!, *Faneuil Hall Market, 280 Friend St., Boston, Mass. 02114. Tel. (617) 523-PIGS. The 20-page catalogue issued 6 times a year costs $1.*

Clothing from the Pork Avenue Collection. Get it? It gets worse. ("What's the pig idea?" and clothes designed by Calvin Swine.) Many articles of clothing and accessories with the pig motif. There is also some ham and bacon available. If your needs are urgent you can call the hog line.

*HUNTINGTON CLOTHIERS AND SHIRTMAKERS, *1285 Alum Creek Dr., Columbus, Ohio 43209. Tel. (614) 252-4422 or (800) 848-6203 (except in Ohio) Free catalogue issued 8 times a year.*

Discount prices available on most items because the company manufactures most of the clothing in its catalogue. For example an oxford cotton button-down shirt that sells elsewhere for $29 is $17.50 at Huntington. Payment by check, money order, American Express, Visa, Mastercard, Diners Club, or Carte Blanche. Shipment by United Parcel or, on request only, by Postal Service. Purchases may be returned for refund or credit.

INFINITE CONCEPTS, *West Looe, Cornwall, PL3 2EN, England. Tel. Looe (05036) 4170. Free brochure and fabric swatches.*

This company makes Harris tweed jackets for men and women. You send them your measurements, your choice of fabric, and your payment, and they send you back your jacket. Payment by check, American Express, Visa, Access/Mastercard, Diners Club, or Eurocard. Shipment by Postal Service.

*KENNEDY OF ARDARA, *Ardara, County Donegal, Ireland. Tel. Ardara 6. Annual 6- to 10-page catalogue costs $2.*

While this company does not describe itself as discount, I would, since the prices it charges for mail-order purchases are the same that it charges to American department stores that carry its handmade knitwear—

B. Altman, Bloomingdale's, Marshall Field's, Neiman-Marcus, and I. Magnin. There are men's and women's sweaters, skirts, and other items from a company that uses 900 cottage knitters. Payment by money order, American Express, Visa, Mastercard, or Diners Club. Shipment by Postal Service. Purchases may be returned within 7 days for refund or credit.

KINLOCH ANDERSON, *John Knox House, 45 High St., Edinburgh, EH1 1SR, Scotland. Tel. (031) 556-6961. Brochure price list.*

Here are Scottish Highland day and evening dress articles for men, including kilts, plus skirts, blouses, and "kilted skirts" for women. Payment by check, money order, American Express, Visa, Mastercard, or Carte Blanche. Shipment by Postal Service. Purchases may be returned, as soon as possible, for refund or credit.

VICTOR LAURENCE (MERCHANTS) LTD., *Laurence Corner, 62 Hampstead Rd., London, NW1 2NU, England. Tel. (01) 388-6811. The 40- to 60-page catalogue costs $2.*

This place has a nice combination of useful and funky surplus clothing. The catalogue is intended to "not only interest but also entertain you." There are raincoats, military greatcoats, camouflage jackets, sweaters, boots, gloves, shirts, firefighter helmets, those funny potlike French military caps like the one De Gaulle wore, police jackets, and many theatrical costumes. Payment by check, money order, American Express, Visa, Mastercard, or Diners Club. Shipment by Postal Service. No returns.

NORMAN J. LAWRENCE LTD., *Lawrence of London, 417 Fifth Ave., New York, N.Y. 10016. Tel. (212) 889-3119. Brochure.*

"We've been doing one thing right since 1947—raincoats." There are raincoats in silk, raincoats with fur lining, raincoats in cotton and in Ultrasuede. Payment by check, money order, Visa, Mastercard, Diners Club, or Carte Blanche. Shipment by United Parcel. Purchases may be returned at any time for refund.

LONG JOHN SHIRTS, *3580 Willow Lane, Thousand Oaks, Calif. 91361. Tel. (805) 496-0380 or (800) 821-3327. Free 14-page catalogue.*

"Simple and straight-forward" classic pullover shirts for outdoor work and recreation. Payment by check, money order, Visa, Mastercard, or C.O.D.

*D. MACGILLIVRAY & CO., *Balivanich, Benbecula, Western Isles, PA 88 5LA, Scotland. Tel. Benbecula 2265. Catalogue costs $3 (for mailing fees).*

Discount prices on fabrics and Harris tweeds. There are suits, tartans, coats, jackets, sweaters and other knitwear, plus rugs made of wool and of sheepskin. Payment by check money order, American Express, Visa, Mastercard, or Access. Shipment by Postal Service. Purchases may be returned for refund or credit.

LEW MAGRAM, *250 W. 54th St., New York, N.Y. 10019. Tel. (212) 586-4828 or for orders only, (800) 228-5000. Semiannual 80-page catalogue costs $2.*

There are some nice looking things for men and women here—skirts and blouses for casual or office wear, suits, sweaters, and ac-cessories. Payment by check, money order, American Express, Visa, Mastercard, Diners Club, or Carte Blanche. Shipment by Postal Service or United Parcel. Purchases may be returned within 30 days for refund or credit.

MARK, FORE & STRIKE, *P.O. Box 640, Delray Beach, Fla. 33444. Tel. (305) 276-0366 or (800) 327-3627. Free 24-page catalogue.*

Most of the clothing here is for women, and most is what I would call preppy—good-looking skirts, blouses and sweaters, plus dresses, Ultrasuede suits, and slacks. Two pages are devoted to men's clothing. Payment by check, American Express, Visa, Mastercard, Diners Club, or M.F.&S. account. Purchases may be returned within 3 weeks of receipt for refund or replacement.

DAVID MORGAN, *Box 70190, Seattle, Wash. 98107. Tel. (206) 282-3300 or (206) 782-7028. Semiannual 96-page catalogue costs 25 cents.*

This company sells a wide variety of imported clothes, including Akubra hats from Australia, Welsh and Alpine caps and hats, and Welsh smocks, shirts and vests, and English and Irish sweaters. Others products available here include jewelry based on Welsh and Scottish designs, and books and maps on Britain, with an emphasis on Wales, one of the nicest places in the world.

THE PERUVIAN CONNECTION LTD., *West Canaan Farm, Tongonoxie, Kans. 66086. Tel. (913) 845-2450. Quarterly 36-page catalogue costs $2.*

Handsome clothing, especially articles of alpaca, for men and women. There are hand-made sweaters, blouses, vests, ponchos, and skirts, plus blankets. Payment by check, money order, American Express, Visa, or Mastercard. Shipment by United Parcel.

CARROLL REED, *Mill St., Conway, N.H. 03818. Tel. (603) 447-2511. The 28-to 68-page catalogue is issued 10 times a year and costs $1.*

This shop has a nice line of casual and sports clothes, a large selection of women's shoes, plus some suits and dresses for the office. Most items are for women, but there are some for men.

*W. S. ROBERTSON (OUTFITTERS) LTD., *Bank St., Galashiels, TD1 1EP, Scotland. Tel. 0896-2152. Brochure price list issued twice a year costs $5.*

Discounts on knitwear. For example, a Pringle sweater that costs $200 in a Manhattan store could be bought from Robertson for $107, including air mail and duty. The sweaters come in cashmere, Shetland wool, lamb's wool, and cotton. Payment by check or money order. Shipment by Postal Service. Purchases may be returned for refund.

*SAINT LAURIE LTD., *897 Broadway, New York, N.Y. 10003. Tel. (212) 473-0100 or (800) 221-8660 (except in New York State). Free 32-page catalogue issued twice a year.*

This place has discount prices, with savings of 30 to 50 percent on hand-tailored garments. Women's sizes range from 2 petite to 18 tall and come in 9 styles of suits, while men's range from 36 short to 48 extra long in 6 styles. The catalogues are handsomely illustrated with both photos and line drawings. Payment by check, money order, American Express, Visa, Mastercard, Diners Club, or

Carte Blanche. Shipment by Postal Service or United Parcel. Purchases may be returned—if not worn or altered and the tickets are not removed—for refund or credit within 2 weeks.

SATIN SALES, CO., *7 S. Fifth St., Minneapolis, Minn. 55402. Tel. (612) 333-5045 or (800) 328-0965 (except in Minnesota). Semiannual 16-page catalogue costs $1.*

Spandex jeans, satin pants, satin kimonos, black denim jeans, motorcycle jackets, and other clothing items favored by rock singers and some of their followers.

*SICKAFUS SHEEPSKINS, *Route 78, Exit 7, Strausstown, Pa. 19559. Tel. (215) 488-1782. Annual 16-page catalogue costs 50 cents.*

Discount prices on sheepskin coats and other sheepskin products. The prices are reported to be at least 25 percent lower than normal, with some savings ranging as high as $100 or $200. Payment by check, money order, American Express, Visa, or Mastercard. Shipment by Postal Service or United Parcel. Purchases may be returned within 14 days for refunds.

SKINNY'S DOWN UNDER. *Sheepskin jackets. See listing under* Automotive Needs.

THE TALBOTS, *175 Beal St., Hingham, Mass. 02043. Tel. (617) 749-7600. The 56-page catalogue issued 8 times a year costs $2.*

Here is the Valhalla of preppydom. This company has a well earned reputation for high-quality clothing, especially smart clothing for women, such as suits, dresses, blouses, jackets, and sweaters. There are some items for men, but Talbots has made its reputation on women's clothes. Payment by American Express, Visa, Mastercard, or Diners Club. Shipment by United Parcel. There is an "unlimited returns guarantee."

WALKER, *Box 99306, San Francisco, Calif. 94109. Tel. (415) 863-2839. Free catalogue and fabric swatches.*

Skirts, dresses, shirts, and neckties, plus totes and handbags. Payment by check, money order, Visa, or Mastercard.

THE WHITE PINE CO. LTD., *P.O. Box 3512, Madison, Wis. 53704. Tel. (608) 241-2225. Free 16- to 24-page catalogue issued 4 times a year.*

This company says it has the largest selection of knitted silkwear available by mail in the country. The silk is used for long underwear, sleeping bag liners, turtleneck sweaters, nightshirts, polo shirts, men's briefs and women's silk lace undergarments. Payment by check, money order, American Express, Visa, or Mastercard. Shipment by United Parcel unless Postal Service is requested. Purchases, if in "as-new" condition, may be returned for refund or credit within 30 days.

See also *Crafts to Buy* and *Supplies and Services for the Physically and Visually Handi-* *capped.* For costumes see *Dance and Theater Supplies and Costumes.*

Casual and Sports Clothing, Western Wear, Printed T-Shirts, and Team Jackets

A & A FIBERGLASS. *Driving caps and jackets. See listing under* Automotive Needs.

L. L. BEAN, *9960 Spruce St., Freeport, Me. 04033. Tel. (207) 865-3111. Free 64- to 136-page catalogue issued 4 times a year.*

This company has received an awful lot of attention in recent years, perhaps because of a good publicity effort, but also because the products enjoy a fine reputation. Here are outdoor clothes and casual clothes for those not necessarily going camping. There is also a large line of outdoor shoes, sports equipment, and bicycle gear. List prices include postage and handling, something to be aware of when comparison shopping. Payment by check, money order, American Express, Visa, or Mastercard. Shipment by Postal Service or United Parcel. Purchases may be returned, at any time, for refund, credit, or replacement.

CAMP BEVERLY HILLS, *9615 Brighton Way, Beverly Hills, Calif. 90210. Tel. (213) 202-0069, (800) 323-1717 (except in Illinois), or (800) 942-8881 (in Illinois). The 24-page catalogue costs $2.*

Casual and sports clothing, à la California in both conception and cut.

CAMPMOR. *See listing under* Camping Equipment.

COUNTRYWEAR, *P.O. Box 1466, Nevada City, Calif. 95959. Tel. (916) 265-8222. Free 24- to 56-page catalogue issued twice a year.*

Here are skirts, pants, sweaters, jumpsuits, jackets, ponchos, and dresses for women, men's slacks, shorts, and shirts.

J. CREW OUTFITTERS, *18 Lincoln Pl., Garfield, N.J. 07026. Tel. (201) 471-7084 or (800) 562-0258 (except in New Jersey, Alaska, and Hawaii). Free 40-page catalogue issued twice a year.*

Here are nice casual sports clothes, including sweaters in cotton and wool, rugby pants and running shorts, jeans, trousers, skirts, and oxford blouses and shirts. Payment by check, money order, American Express, Visa, or Mastercard. Shipment by Postal Service or United Parcel. Purchases may be returned, at any time, for refund, credit, or exchange.

DALLAS ALICE, *4956 Boiling Brook Parkway, Rockville, Md. 20852. Tel. (301) 468-6996. Semiannual 12- to 24-page catalogue costs $1.*

This company has what an officer described as the country's most complete line of T-shirts and sweatshirts, the company's own as well as merchandise from other manufacturers.

†DUNHAM'S OF MAINE, *P.O. Box 707, Waterville, Me. Tel. (800) 341-0471 (except in Maine), or (207) 873-6165 (in Maine). Free 24-page catalogue.*

Men's and women's clothing, including shirts, ties, shoes, jackets, suits, dresses, skirts, blouses, and sweaters in a good-looking casual style. Payment by check, American Express, Visa, Mastercard, Diners Club, Carte Blanche, or Dunham's charge. Shipment by United Parcel unless Postal Service is requested. Purchases may be returned, "promptly," for refund, credit, or exchange.

DUNNS. *See listing under* Camping Equipment.

*EISNER BROS., *76 Orchard St., New York, N.Y. 10002. Tel. (212) 475-6868 or (212) 431-8800. Free 28-page catalogue issued 3 times a year.*

Discounts of 20 to 50 percent on T-shirts, baseball and painter's caps, sweatshirts and sweatpants, and sports clothing—shirts for golf, soccer, tennis, baseball, and football. Payment by certified check or money order. Shipment by United Parcel. Purchases may be returned within 10 days, and only if damaged, for refund or credit.

*M. FRIEDMAN SPECIALTY CO., *P.O. Box 5777, Baltimore, Md. 21208. Tel. (301) 922-9450. The 8- to 16-page catalogue issued 4 to 6 times a year costs $1.*

Discount prices on jackets for rock groups and baseball and football teams, baseball batting practice jerseys, and other equipment. A New York Yankees jacket that ordinarily costs $78 to $88 is priced at $55. Payment by check, money order, Visa, or Mastercard. Shipment by Postal Service or United Parcel. Purchases may be returned within 7 days for refund.

*THE FINALS, *21 Minisink Ave., Port Jervis, N.Y. 12771. Tel. (212) 431-1414, (800) 431-9111 (except in New York), or (800) 452-0452 (in New York).*

Discount prices for running togs: $100 warmup suits for $50, $200 Gore-Tex running suits for $130. Swimwear also available. Payment by check, money order, American Express, Visa, or Mastercard. Shipment by Postal Service or United Parcel. Refund or credit for goods returned within 30 days, 90 days for fabric or workmanship defects. No returns for custom-printed items.

FUN-WEAR BRANDS, *141 E. Elkhorn Ave., Box 2800, Estes Park, Colo. 80517. Tel. (303) 586-3361. Annual 32-page catalogue is free.*

Everything for the cowboy and cowgirl—boots, Levi's, fringed shirts, OshKosh bib overalls, hats, children's clothing.

*GRIZZLY SPORTS SUPPLY, *P.O. Box 4265, Burlingame, Calif. 94011. Tel. (415) 692-2819. Free 8-page catalogue issued 2 or 3 times a year.*

Discounts for quantity or team orders in the purchase of sports clothing. For example, rugby shirts that cost $40 to $45 in the store cost $30 to $36 here or even $23 to $29 for large orders. Soccer boots that cost $40 to $75 are priced at $32 to $68 here. Much of the stuff is imported from Britain and New Zealand.

INTERNATIONAL MALE, *2800 Midway Dr., San Diego, Calif. 92110. Tel. (619) 226-8751 or, for sales only, (800) 854-2795 (except in California). The 42- to 56-page catalogue issued 5 or 6 times a year costs $2.*

Despite the name, some of these things are for women. The products are geared to-

ward an active, outdoor, sports life, and the clothing is handsome. Some shoes are available.

JAMES RIVER TRADERS, *James River Landing, Hampton, Va. 23631. Tel. (804) 827-6000. Free 48-page catalogue.*

Good-looking casual clothing, including sweaters, shirts, jeans, blazers, and shoes. Payment by check, money order, American Express, Visa, Mastercard, or Diners Club. Shipment by United Parcel. Purchases may be returned for refund or exchange.

LANDS' END, *Lands' End Lane, Dodgeville, Wis. 53595. Tel. (608) 935-9341 or (800) 356-4444 (except in Hawaii and Alaska). Free 100-page catalogue issued 4 times a year.*

This is a fine catalogue of goods from a superior seller of casual and sportswear. There are shirts, shoes, bright rugby shirts, sweaters, slacks, culottes, shorts, foul weather gear, and many other things, including a line of luggage. Payment by check, money order, American Express, Visa, or Mastercard. Shipment by Postal Service or United Parcel. Purchases may be returned for refund or credit.

MID-WESTERN SPORT TOGS, *150 W. Franklin St., Berlin, Wis. 54923. Tel. (414) 361-2555. Free annual 36-page catalogue.*

This company, founded in 1869 as the Berlin Whip Co., offers a very unusual service. Deer hunters send the skin from their kills to the company, which tans it for them and returns it to them as deerskin or fashions it into deerskin clothing. "It gives him an opportunity to 'wear his trophy,' not just look at the mounted antlers." If you don't happen to have a deerskin around the house, the company also sells deerskin products including jackets, coats, shirts, and vests, shoes, and gloves and mittens. Payment by check or money order. Shipment by Postal Service or United Parcel. Purchases may be returned within 10 days for refund or credit.

*JIM MORRIS ENVIRONMENTAL T-SHIRTS, *P.O. Box 2308, Boulder, Colo. 80306. Tel. (303) 444-6430. Free catalogue of 24 to 32 pages is issued 1 to 3 times a year.*

Discounts for quantity purchases of T-shirts, which proclaim various environmental causes like, the protection of dolphins, whales, wolves, eagles, and wetlands. The traditional designs are nice, and there are some anthropomorphic drawings that avoid becoming silly or too cute. Payment by check, money order, Visa, or Mastercard. Shipment by Postal Service or United Parcel.

OPUS-T, *5446 Highway 290 West, Suite 301, Austin, Tex. 78735. Tel. (512) 892-4870. Brochure price list.*

Here are T-shirts for fans of the Bloom County newspaper comic strip, featuring drawings of the anti-hero penguin. At least I think it's a penguin.

PATAGONIA MAIL ORDER, *Division of the Great Pacific Iron Works, P.O. Box 150, Ventura, Calif. 93002. Tel. (805) 648-3386. Free 60-page catalogue issued twice a year.*

Here are clothes to keep you dry and warm in the worst of weather while you are doing such things as climbing mountains, paddling a raft across a river, sleeping in a tent atop a mountain, fishing in a stream, crewing a sailboat, or just plain walking. Payment by check, money order, American Express, Visa, or Mastercard. Shipment by Postal Service or United Parcel. Satisfaction is guaranteed.

PALM BEACH SPORTS, *345 Wilson Ave., Norwalk, Conn. 06854. Tel. (203) 838-3601. Free annual 16-page catalogue.*

Discounts for quantity purchases of this company's line of sports and casual wear. The company, club, or organization name or logo can be embroidered onto these clothes, making them good vehicles for premium, incentive, and identity programs. Payment by check, money order, Visa, or Mastercard. Shipment by United Parcel. Purchases may be returned, only if defective, within 10 days for replacement.

PALO ALTO BICYCLES. *See listing under* Bicycles and Motorcycles.

PRO TEAM CORNER, *P.O. Box 2322, Loves Park, Ill. 61131. Tel. (815) 877-4002. Free 24-page catalogue issued twice a year.*

Football jerseys with N.F.L. colors, T-shirts with team logos, football and baseball posters, baseball jerseys with Major League logos, plus lots of items immortalizing teams of various universities, some of which are also notable as educational institutions. There are a lot of good gift ideas here for the sports nut. Payment by check, money order, American Express, Visa, or Mastercard. Shipment by Postal Service or United Parcel. Refund or credit for merchandise returned at any time as long as it is not used or damaged.

*ROBIN CONCEPTS, *8033 Sunset Blvd., Suite 909, Hollywood, Calif. 90046. Tel. (213) 669-0606. The 7-page catalogue costs $1.*

Here is another T-shirt maker, with wholesale prices for quantity purchases. A recent catalogue had such designs as a spider, a skull, a dragon, and British, American, and Canadian flags. Payment by check or money order. Shipment by Postal Service. Purchases may be returned, if not worn, for refund or credit.

SABA'S WESTERN WEAR, *7254 E. Main St., Scottsdale, Ariz. 85251. Tel. (602) 947-8351, (602) 949-7404, (800) 528-6600 (except in Arizona), or (800) 352-0458 (in Arizona). Annual 32-page catalogue costs $1.*

Cowboy and cowgirl stuff, including jeans, blazers, jackets, skirts, shirts, vests, and the like in fabrics and animal skins. To really make you look like a Westerner, there are boots and Stetson hats. Payment by check, money order, American Express, Visa, or Mastercard. Shipment by Postal Service or United Parcel. Purchases may be returned within 30 days for refund.

*SHEPLERS INC., *P.O. Box 7702, Wichita, Kans. 67277. Tel. (316) 946-3780 or (800) 835-4004. Free 16- to 96-page catalogue issued 6 times a year.*

Western clothing, such as sandals, shirts, blouses, and jeans, some at discount prices, like a dress shirt for $13 and dress slacks for $17. Payment by check, American Express, Visa, or Mastercard. Shipment by Postal Service or United Parcel.

NORM THOMPSON, *P.O. Box 3999, Portland, Ore. 97208. Tel. (503) 644-2666 or (800) 772-7226 (ex-* *cept in Alaska and Hawaii). Free 24- to 100-page catalogue issued several times a year.*

Men's and women's shoes, sandals, pants, shirts, jackets, hats, leather goods for outdoor activity especially, but also clothing and shoes for business wear, bedding, underwear, and dresses and skirts. There is also a section and an occasional catalogue on foods that include salmon specialties, one of which has no salt added.

WILLOW VALLEY CO., *P.O. Box 9257, Madison, Wis. 53715. Tel. (608) 255-1397. Semiannual 4-page catalogue costs 50 cents.*

Any of 5 wine sayings printed on T-shirts in any of 5 languages (English, French, German, Italian or Spanish). The sayings, English version, are "In wine there is truth," "Old friends and old wine are best," "Good wine needs no crier," "When wine is in, wit is out," and "Wine makes glad the heart of man." Payment by check or money order. Shipment by Postal Service or United Parcel. Cash refund if returned within 30 days.

See also *Sporting Goods* and *Army and Navy Goods* and *Horse Supplies and Riding Equipment.*

Work Clothes and Uniforms

BENCONE UNIFORMS, *121 Carver Ave., Westwood, N.J. 07675. Tel. (201) 666-4210 or (800) 631-4602. Free 32-page catalogue issued 3 times a year.*

Professional uniforms and accessories, some offered at discounts. Many of these items are for people in the health professions, including slacks, shirts, and skirts, in traditional white as well as modern pastels; laboratory and operating room clothing; maternity clothes; plus hosiery and shoes. Most items are for women, but there are some for men as well. Payment by check, money order, American Express, Visa, Mastercard, Diners Club, or Carte Blanche.

*EASTERN WEAR-GUARD, *33 Everett St., Boston, Mass. 02134. Tel. (800) 343-4406 (except in Massachusetts) or (800) 362-4305 (in Massachusetts). Free 48-page catalogue.*

The company sells uniforms, work clothes, shoes, and accessories. Personalizing is available—your company name on the back of a shirt and the employee's name on the front. Payment by check, money order, American Express, Visa, or Mastercard.

JAMES G. FAST CO., *Box 7000, Conway, Ark. 72032. Tel. (501) 327-6049 or (800) 643-8378. Free 36-page catalogue issued 6 times a year.*

Professional apparel for women, especially some nice-looking nurse's uniforms. There are also shoes, maternity clothes, lab jackets, doctor's smocks, and underwear. Payment by check, money order, Visa, or Mastercard. Shipment by Postal Service or United Parcel. Purchases may be returned within 30 days for refunds.

*RALPH MARTIN INC., *115 E. Fifth St., Rochester, Ind. 46975. Tel. (800) 223-5501 (except in Indiana) or (800) 223-0088 (in Indiana). Free 24- to 32-page catalogue issued 3 or 4 times a year.*

Discount prices of 10 to 30 percent on work garments for men and women—poplin and twill shirts, pants, coats, coveralls, jumpsuits, gloves, and vests.

SARA GLOVE CO., *P.O. Box 4069, Waterbury, Conn. 06704. Tel. (203) 574-4090 or (800) 243-3570 (except in Connecticut). Semiannual 32-page catalogue costs $1.*

Here are articles of clothing and equipment for safety on the job, including gloves, aprons, shoes, hard hats, plus jeans, jackets, and rainwear.

Women's Clothing

ADRIAN AVERY FOR BROWNSTONE STUDIO. *See listing below under Brownstone Studio.*

ALLIANCE EDITIONS, *P.O. Box 207, North Adams, Mass. 01247. Tel. (413) 664-6318. Semiannual 16-page catalogue costs $1.*

Silk screen printing on women's sportswear including T-shirts, turtlenecks, and dresses.

AVON FASHIONS, *Avon Lane, Newport News, Va. 23630. Free 96-page catalogue.*

Many classic and modern designs in dresses, skirts, blouses, shoes, slacks, lingerie, swimwear, and sportswear. Payment by check, money order, American Express, Visa, or Mastercard. United Parcel first choice for delivery, but other methods used as well. Purchases may be returned for refund or exchange.

BEAUTIFUL & CO., *800 Third Ave., New York, N.Y. 10022. Tel. (212) 758-8877, (800) 523-9882 (except in Arizona), or (800) 523-0695 (in Arizona) Free 32-page catalogue issued 4 to 6 times a year.*

Business, casual, and evening fashions. The company also offers the bonus of "size a la carte," which lets you pick one size for tops and another for bottoms in suits and 2-piece dresses. Payment by check, money order, American Express, Visa, or Mastercard. Shipment by Postal Service or United Parcel. Refunds for returned purchases.

BEDFORD FAIR, *157 Kisco Ave., Mt. Kisco, N.Y. 10549. Tel. (914) 666-6400. Free 48-page catalogue.*

Many suits, dresses, blouses, slacks, and sportswear. Payment by check, money order, American Express, Visa, or Mastercard. Refund for purchases returned within 15 days.

HENRI BENDEL, *10 W. 57th St., New York, N.Y. 10019. Tel. (212) 706-2222. The 64-page catalogue issued 3 times a year costs $3.*

This is one of New York's finest high-fashion stores, with prices to match. The clothes look great. Payment by check, money order, American Express, Visa, Mastercard, or Bendel charge. Shipment by United Parcel. Refunds for purchases returned within 2 weeks (or by January 15 in the case of the Christmas catalogue).

†BOSTON PROPER MAIL ORDER, *1 Boston Plaza, P.O. Box 2027, Nashua, N.H. 03061. Tel (603) 882-9496 or (800) 243-4300 (except in New Hampshire, Alaska, and Hawaii). Quarterly 36-page catalogue costs $2 a year.*

Products aimed at the working woman. These are good-looking clothes for office and casual wear, as well as many products for the home, including kitchen gadgets and food-serving items, many of which would make nice gifts. Payment by check, money order, American Express, Visa, or Mastercard. Shipment by Postal Service or United Parcel. Purchases may be returned within 30 days for refund or credit.

BROWNSTONE STUDIO, *1 E. 43rd St., New York, N.Y. 10017. Tel. (212) 883-1090, (800) 221-2468 (except in New York), or (800) 442-8422 (in New York). There are 3 distinct catalogues.*

Adrian Avery for Brownstone Studio: Higher priced clothing, especially knits, with designer accessories.

Jean Grayson's Brownstone Studio: Wardrobes with coordinated accessories in sizes 4 to 20; free quarterly 36-page catalogues.

Intime for Brownstone Studio: The appeal here is for somewhat younger women, with an emphasis on robes, gowns, and leisure wear; free 32-page catalogue issued 3 times a year.

Payment by check, money order, American Express, Visa, Mastercard, or Diners Club. Delivery by United Parcel unless customer requests otherwise. Refunds for goods returned within 30 days.

CAREER GUILD, *6412 Vapor Lane, Niles, Ill. 60648. Tel. (312) 492-1400, (800) 538-5380 (except in Illinois), or (800) 972-9999 (in Illinois). Free 32-page catalogue issued 4 times a year.*

A buying club for coordinated fashions designed for working women. Members receive a 25 percent discount after a 1-time $5 membership fee. Nonmembers may purchase at the full rate. Payment by check, money order, American Express, Visa, or Mastercard. Shipment by Postal Service or United Parcel. Purchases may be returned within 15 days for refund.

ELIZABETH K., *Elizabeth K. Plaza, Pleasantville, N.J. 08232. Tel. (800) 222-0044 (except in New Jersey) or (800) 222-0043 (in New Jersey). Free 36-page catalogue.*

ESPRIT DE CORP, *950 Tennessee St., San Francisco, Calif. 94107. Tel. (415) 648-6900, (800) 4-ESPRIT (except in Hawaii and Alaska), or (800) 237-7748 (for customer service). Issues 3 catalogues that cost $2 each.*

Esprit: Women's fashions; 40-page catalogue.
Esprit Sport: Women's sportswear; 40-page catalogue.
Esprit Kids; Children's fashions; 24-page catalogue.
Payment by check, money order, American Express, Visa, Mastercard, or Diners Club. Delivery by Postal Service, United Parcel, or Federal Express. Purchases may be returned within 14 days for refund or credit.

FACETS, *P.O. Box 81425, Atlanta, Ga. 30366. Tel. (404) 449-6186 or (800) 228-5000. Free 36-page catalogue.*

Some handsome, high-fashion clothing for women. A recent catalogue, for example, featured a Mollie Parnis suit. Payment by check, money order, American Express, Visa, Mastercard, or Diners Club. Shipment by Postal Service or United Parcel. Unused merchandise may be returned for refund or exchange.

F.B.S., *659 Main St., New Rochelle, N.Y. 10801. Tel. (914) 632-5777. The 48- to 80-page catalogue issued 4 to 6 times a year costs $2 for a 1-year subscription.*

Good-looking casual clothing, swimwear, and shoes. Payment by check, money order, American Express, Visa, or Mastercard. Delivery by Postal Service or United Parcel. Purchases may be returned within two weeks for refund.

FIRST EDITIONS, *340 Poplar St., Hanover Pa. 17331. Tel. (717) 637-1600, (800) 621-5839 (except in Illinois), or (800) 972-5858 (in Illinois). Free 48-page catalogue.*

†**HIGHLAND HOUSE,** *130 N. Broad St., Lancaster, Ohio 43130. Tel. (614) 653-7716, (800) 848-5098 (except in Ohio), or (800) 848-5099 (in Ohio). Annual 46-page catalogue costs $1.*

Blazers, blouses, shawls, jackets, skirts, vests, and suits, with emphasis on woolen knits. There are also several items for children, such as Peter Rabbit books and tea sets, and gifts. Payment by check, money order, American Express, Visa, or Mastercard. Shipment by Postal Service or United Parcel. Refund or credit for returned purchases.

HONEYBEE, *2745 Philmont Ave., Huntingdon Valley, Pa. 19006. Tel. (215) 947-6517. Quarterly 64-page catalogue costs $2.*

Casual clothing, swimwear, evening clothes, and business suits.

THE INGRAM COLLECTION, *214 W. 39th St., New York, N.Y., 10018. Tel. (800) 223-5679 (except in New York) or (800) 522-3939 (in New York). Free 32-page catalogue.*

Casual, dressy, and business attire. Payment by check, money order, American Express, Visa, Mastercard, or Diners Club. Purchases may be returned within 30 days for refund.

INTIMATE BOUTIQUE. *Swimwear. See listing under* Hosiery, Lingerie, Underwear, and Lounge Wear, *below.*

J. JILL LTD., *Stockbridge Rd., Great Barrington, Mass. 01230. Tel. (413) 528-1500. Free 40-page catalogue issued 3 times a year.*

"Country clothes" designed and made out of natural fibers, including cotton, wool, and silk. Payment by check, money order, American Express, Visa, or Mastercard. Delivery by Postal Service or United Parcel. Refund or credit for purchases returned within 7 days of receipt.

A. B. LAMBDIN, *2050-E Carroll Ave., Chamblee, Ga. 30341. Tel. (404) 451-1057 or (800) 554-9231 (except in Georgia). Quarterly 32- or 48-page catalogue costs $1 per year.*

M.G.A., *771 E. Ninth St., Los Angeles, Calif. 90021. Tel. (213) 488-1277 or (800) 262-4MGA (except in Alaska and Hawaii). The 20- to 30-page catalogue issued 3 times a year costs $2.*

A handsome catalogue that depicts nice looking clothes. Payment by check, money order, American Express, Visa, or Mastercard. Shipment by United Parcel. Purchases

may be returned within 14 days for refund or credit.

PREMIER EDITIONS, *Unique Merchandise Mart, Building 12, Hanover, Pa. 17333. Tel. (717) 637-1600, (800) 621-5800 (except in Illinois), or (800) 972-5858 (in Illinois). Free 48-page catalogue.*

A wide range of women's fashions, dressy and sporty.

ROYAL SILK, *Royal Silk Plaza, 45 E. Madison Ave., Clifton, N.J. 07011. Tel. (800) 22-ROYAL (except in New Jersey) or (201) 340-2400 (in New Jersey). The 36- to 40-page catalogue issued 7 times a year costs $1.*

Although not a "discount" operation, Royal charges 40 to 60 percent below retail because it designs, manufactures, and markets its own silk blouses, T-shirts, scarves, belts, skirts, and dresses, some of them silk-cotton blends. Payment by check, money order, American Express, Visa, Mastercard, Diners Club, or Carte Blanche. Shipment by Postal Service or United Parcel. Refund or credit for purchases returned within 10 days.

LA SHACK, *19 the Plaza, Locust Valley, N.Y. 11560. Tel. (516) 671-1091 or (800) 645-3524 (except in New York). Free 32-page catalogue.*

Handsome fashions for work, play, and otherwise.

SHAKER WORKSHOPS. *Vests. See listing under* Furniture and Furnishings.

SHELLY'S TALL FASHIONS, *747 Towne Ave., Los Angeles, Calif. 90021. Tel. (213) 627-TALL. Free 24-page catalogue issued twice a year.*

Good-looking clothes for women 5 feet 7 inches or taller. Payment by check, money order, Visa, Mastercard, or Shelly's charge. Shipment by Postal Service or United Parcel. Refund or credit for returned purchases.

SHOPPING INTERNATIONAL, *Palo Verde at 33rd, P.O. Box 27600, Tucson, Ariz. 85726. Tel. (602) 747-5000. Free 48-page catalogue.*

Clothing from Morocco, Pakistan, India, Italy, China, Taiwan, Mexico, Guatemala, Greece, and elsewhere not to mention the United States. Payment by check, money order, Visa, Mastercard, or Diners Club. Purchases may be returned within 15 days for refund or exchange, but altered, personalized, or soiled items are not returnable.

16 PLUS, *3250 S. 76th St., Philadelphia, Pa. 19153. Tel. (215) 492-9619. Free 16- to 48-page catalogue.*

This company provides fashions for large women that are not tents. The clothing is available by mail as well as in stores. Payment by check, money order, American Express, Visa, or Mastercard. Delivery by Postal Service or United Parcel. Purchases may be returned for refund.

SOFWEAR. *See listing under* Shoes and Other Footwear, *below.*

SPORTPAGES, *2007 Royal Lane, Suite 100, Dallas, Tex. 75229. Tel. (214) 247-3101, (800) 527-3166 (except in Texas), (800) 442-3823 (in Texas, except Dallas), or 484-8900 (in Dallas only). Free 32-page catalogue.*

Casual clothes, swimwear, and lingerie. Payment by check, money order, American Express, Visa, Mastercard, Diners Club, or Carte Blanche. Shipment by Postal Service

or United Parcel Service. Purchases may be returned within 30 days for refund, but personalized items, swimwear, lingerie, and sale items are not returnable.

NANCY STONE AND ANTHONY RICHARDS. *Dresses, coats, and lingerie. See listing for Stork-kit under* Mothers and Mothers-to-Be.

*SUNUP/SUNDOWN, *979 N.E. 45th St., Ft. Lauderdale, Fla. 33334. Tel. (305) 771-6190. Free brochure issued 5 or 6 times a year.*

Mostly swimwear, at discounts. Payment by check, money order, Visa, Mastercard, Diners Club, or C.O.D. Shipment by Postal Service. Purchases may be returned within 10 days for refund.

*THAI SILKS, *252 State St., Los Altos, Calif. 94022. Tel. (415) 948-8611. Annual brochure price list costs 35 cents.*

Prices 30 to 50 percent lower than retail for silk hankies, scarves, blouses, dresses, and fabrics.

THE TOG SHOP, *Lester Square, Americus, Ga. 31710. Tel. (912) 924-8800. Free 128-page catalogue issued 4 times a year.*

Traditional clothing, mostly sportswear including dresses and shoes. Payment by check, money order, American Express, Visa, Mastercard, or Diners Club. Shipment by Postal Service or United Parcel. Refund or exchange for returned purchases.

THE VERY THING, *P.O. Box 7427, Charlottesville, Va. 22906. Tel. (703) 456-8177 or (800) 336-4051 (except in Virginia). Free 32-page catalogue.*

Nice looking casual fashions. Payment by check, money order, American Express, Visa, or Mastercard. Purchases may be returned for refund within 30 days, but monogrammed items may not be returned unless defective.

WATER WITCH, *P.O. Box 329-C, Maine St., Castine, Me. 04421. Tel. (207) 326-4884. Free 12-page catalogue.*

Handsome dresses and other clothing made of all-cotton Dutch wax batiks and Java prints imported from the Netherlands and of wool-cotton Viyellas from Britain. Payment by check, money order, American Express, Visa, or Mastercard. Delivery by United Parcel is preferred, but Postal Service will be used on request. Merchandise may be returned for refund or credit within 2 weeks if in good condition.

MARTHA WEST, *179 E. Post Rd., White Plains, N.Y. 10601. Tel. (914) 949-4271 or (914) 949-4240. Free 16- to 24-page catalogue issued 3 times a year.*

Classic clothing in sizes 6 to 42 and 10½ to 26½. Payment by check, Visa, Mastercard, or Martha West charge. Shipment by United Parcel. Refund or credit for purchases returned within 10 days.

See also *For Mothers and Mothers-to-Be.*

Men's Clothing

BACHRACH, *2354 Hubbard Ave., Decatur, Ill. 62526. Tel. (217) 875-1020, (800) 637-5840 (except in Illinois), or (800) 252-1582 (in Illinois). Free 48- to 64-page catalogue issued 4 times a year.*

Good-looking clothing that leans toward the casual or sporty, although the jackets and slacks certainly would do in today's office. The offering also include blazers, shirts, and sweaters. Payment by check, money order, Visa, Mastercard, or Bachrach charge. Shipment by Postal Service or United Parcel. Purchases may be returned at any time for refund or credit.

BURTON LTD., *14 E. 41st St., New York, N.Y. 10017. Tel. (212) 685-3760.*

This company specializes in neckties with animal motifs. One shows a cat another a teddy bear. Payment by check, money order, Americn Express, Visa, or Mastercard. Shipment normally by United Parcel, but Postal Service will be used on request. Refund or credit for merchandise returned within 10 days.

CHIPP INC., *14 E. 44th St., New York, N.Y. 10017. Tel. (212) 687-0850. Free catalogue issued twice a year plus special mailings.*

Preppy clothing, including Shetland jackets, gabardine trousers, oxford button-down shirts, and rep ties. "Traditional with a sense of humor," it features items like a necktie said to be from the Darien Rifles, which fled Khartoum when the gin ran out.

†THE COCKPIT/AVIREX LTD. *Clothing, much of it leather, and accessories for the well-dressed pilot. See listing under* Aviation.

EASTON STUDIOS, *207 Wilson Rd., Easton, Conn. 06612. Tel. (203) 268-2385. Semiannual 4- to 6-page catalogue costs $1, refundable with purchase.*

Ascots, dickeys, and mufflers from Scotland. Payment by check, money order, Visa, or Mastercard. Shipment usually by United Parcel but Postal Service used if necessary. Refund or credit for goods returned within 30 days.

JOHN FIELDS BOW TIES, *Kenwood, Calif. 95452. Tel. (707) 833-6668. Free 8-page catalogue issued 3 times a year.*

"I sense a Renaissance in bow ties;" the owner regards those who wear them as an elite minority. Payment by check. Delivery by Postal Service.

*FRAME NECKWEAR CO. LTD., *P.O. Box 422, Birmingham, Mich. 48012. Tel. (519) 886-5410. Free annual 20-page catalogue.*

Neckties with embroidered motifs that include national flags, sports, and professions. Discounts given for quantity purchases. Payment by check, money order, Visa, or Mastercard. Delivery by Postal Service or United Parcel. Returns accepted any time for refund or credit.

*HIGHLANDER COMPANY, *1072 N. Jacoby Rd., Copley, Ohio 44321. Tel. (216) 666-6748 Free 24- to 32-page catalogue issued 3 or 4 times a year.*

Discounted oxford button-down shirts and orlon acrylic sweaters. Payment by check, money order, American Express, Visa, Mastercard, or Diners Club. Shipment by Postal Service, United Parcel, or Emery. Refund or credit for returned merchandise.

HUGH MACPHERSON (SCOTLAND) LTD., *17 W. Maitland St., Edinburgh, EH12 5EA, Scotland. Tel (031) 225-4008. Price list.*

Highland dress for day and evening wear, with many clans' tartans in stock. Books and tape cassettes on Scotland also available. Payment by check, money order, American Express, Visa, Mastercard, or Diners Club. Delivery by Postal Service. Returns allowed for credit only if goods are faulty or the wrong size.

JOEL MCCAY INC., *620 N. Lake Ave., Pasadena, Calif. 91101. Tel. (818) 793-1027. Free annual 12-page catalogue.*

Chiefly men's jumpsuits, but also some robes and safari suits.

PAUL STUART, *Madison Avenue at 45th St., New York, N.Y. 10017. Tel. (212) 682-0320. Semiannual 32-page catalogue costs $2.*

This is one of America's leading stores for men's and boy's clothing.

S. REDMAYNE LTD., *The Old Mill, Warwick Bridge, Carlisle, CA4 8RR, England. Tel. 0228-61661. Free 8- to 16-page catalogue.*

This firm specializes in "bespoke" (custom) tailoring, but also operates a mail-order business offering outerwear, both raincoats and overcoats. For suits, the company offers a copying service; you select the fabric and style and then send a suit of yours, and Redmayne will make a suit based on the size and shape of the one you sent. Both are then mailed to you. Also offered are leather briefcases and outdoor wooden furniture, a curious combination. Payment by check or money order. Shipment by Postal Service. "Satisfaction guaranteed."

THE SQUIRE SHOP, *4548 Main St., Buffalo, N.Y. 14226. Tel. (716) 839-4242. Free 10-page catalogue issued twice a year.*

Clothing and accessories with the buffalo symbol on them, even formal wear.

TIE-ONE-ON, *P.O. Box 40225, Philadelphia, Pa. 19106. Tel. (215) 625-2855. Brochure price lists.*

Novelty ties, one for the WASP, the other for people in the computer business.

Furs

BOREAL SPECIALTIES, *Box 219, Star Route 3, Dairyland, Wis. 54830. Tel. (715) 244-3343.*

Beaver artifacts, including totems, necklaces, and furs.

*CORNELIUS FURS (HOLDING) PTY. LTD., *G.P.O. Box 3775, Sydney, New South Wales, 2201, Australia. No telephone. Free 14-page catalogue.*

Discounts on furs during sales. Payment by American Express, Visa, Mastercard, Diners Club, Carte Blanche, or telegraphic transfer. Delivery by surface or air parcel post. "Garments are unusually not returned."

*HY FISHMAN FURS, *305 Seventh Ave., New York, N.Y. 10001. Tel. (212) 244-4844. Free catalogue.*

Discount prices on furs. For example: $2,300 for a mink coat that ordinarily sells for $5,500; $2,995 for a $7,000 fox coat. Payment by check, money order, Visa, Mastercard, Diners Club, or Carte Blanche. Shipment by United Parcel. Purchases from stock may be returned within 10 days for refund; no returns on goods made to order.

Hosiery, Lingerie, Underwear, and Lounge Wear

ANDREW BARRY ASSOCIATES, *565 Potter Rd., Framingham, Mass. 01701. Tel. (617) 877-3131. Brochure.*

Knee-high's, stockings, panty hose, and foot shells. Besides women's hosiery for everyday wear, there is a full line in white for those whose professions require it.

*LOUIS CHOCK INC., *74 Orchard St., New York, N.Y. 10002. Tel. (212) 473-1929. Semiannual 64-page catalogue costs $1.*

Discounts of 25 percent off prices of men's, women's, and children's hosiery. Payment by check or money order. Shipment by United Parcel. Purchases may be returned within 30 days for refund.

†CUDDLEDOWN, *106 Main St., Yarmouth, Me. 04096. Tel. (207) 846-9781. Annual 36-page catalogue costs $1.*

Things to wear to bed, like camisoles and snuggies for women, plus 100 percent silk and 100 percent cotton long underwear, pajamas, and nightgowns. Another main product line consists of bedding—down comforters, pillows, sheets, and pillowcases. Payment by check, money order, American Express, Visa, or Mastercard. Shipment by United Parcel, but Postal Service on request. Purchases may be returned for refund or credit.

*D. & A. MERCHANDISE CO., *22 Orchard St., New York, N.Y. 10002. Tel. (212) 925-4766. Free 16-page catalogue issued twice a year.*

Discounts of 25 percent off normal retail price are reported by the owner of this shop, who calls himself the Underwear King. For women the offerings include Hanes hosiery, Olga, Bali, and Warner's bras, and Danskin leotards; for men Jockey, BVD, and Munsingwear T-shirts and shorts. Payment by check, money order, Visa, Mastercard, or C.O.D. Shipment by United Parcel. Purchases may be returned within 30 days for refund.

JAMES G. FAST. *Underwear. See listing under* Work Clothes and Uniforms, *above.*

INTIMATE BOUTIQUE, *P.O. Box F, Wheeling, Ill. 60090. Tel. (312) 537-8560 or (800) 323-6153. The 16-page catalogue issued 3 times a year costs $1.*

Lingerie and swimwear. Payment by check, money order, American Express, Visa, or Mastercard. Shipment by Postal Service or United Parcel. Purchases may be returned for refund within 3 weeks.

INTIME FOR BROWNSTONE STUDIO. *See listing for Brownstone Studio under* Women's Clothing, *above.*

INTIMIQUE, *Winterbrook Way, Meredith, N.H. 03253. Tel. (603) 279-7081 or (800) 258-4738. Free 48-page catalogue issued annually.*

Lingerie and women's nightwear. Payment by check, money order, American Express, Visa, Mastercard, Diners Club, or Carte Blanche. Shipment by Postal Service or United Parcel. Merchandise may be returned for refund or credit.

NATIONAL WHOLESALE CO., *400 National Blvd., Lexington, N.C. 27292. Tel. (704) 249-0211. Free 64-page catalogue issued 7 times a year.*

Hosiery, panty hose, lingerie, long winter underwear, and socks. Payment by check, money order, American Express, Visa, or Mastercard. Delivery by Postal Service or United Parcel. Refund for returned merchandise.

NIGHT 'N DAY INTIMATES, *Unique Merchandise Mart, Building 22, Hanover, Pa. 17333. Tel. (717) 637-1600, (800) 621-5800 (except in Illinois), or (800) 972-5858 (in Illinois). Free 32-page catalogue.*

Sexy lingerie.

SCINTILLA SATIN SHOP, *4802 N. Broadway, Chicago, Ill. 60640. Tel. (312) 728-2590. Free 12-page catalogue.*

Clothes of satin for the boudoir, including nighties, slips, panties, loungers, robes, and pajamas. There are also blankets, spreads, and bed covers. Payment by check, money order, American Express, Visa, Mastercard, or Diners Club. Shipment by United Parcel or, if requested, Postal Service. Purchases, except personalized or special-cut items, may be returned for refund or exchange within 30 days.

SPORTPAGES. *Lingerie. See* Women's Clothing, *above.*

T.L.C. WEAR, *6253 W. 74th St., Box 2001, Bedford Park, Ill. 60499. Tel. (312) 496-4900, (800) TLC-WEAR (except in Illinois, Alaska, and Hawaii), or (800) TLC-5255 (in Illinois). Free 24-page catalogue issued twice a year.*

This is a company that specializes in "sensual, soft, romantic lingerie and loungewear" for (blush, blush) honeymooners and those who wish to prolong the notion of a honeymoon. The clothing does seem to fit the bill. Payment by check, money order, Visa, or Mastercard. Shipment by United Parcel. Purchases may be returned within 15 days for refund or credit.

UNDERGEAR. *This is a division of International Male, listed above under* Casual and Sports Clothing, *specializing in men's underwear, including some articles cut especially for women.*

VICTORIA'S SECRET, *P.O. Box 16589, Columbus, Ohio 43216. Tel. (614) 276-3131, (800) 821-0001 (except in Ohio), or (800) 321-4881 (in Ohio). Catalogue runs 30 to 48 pages, costs $3, and is issued 4 times a year.*

Women's designer lingerie. Payment by check, money order, American Express, Visa, or Mastercard. Shipment by Postal Service, United Parcel, or Federal Express. Refund or credit for purchases returned within 30 days.

See also *Bedding, Linens and Towels.*

Shoes and Other Footwear

THE ARCTIC TRADING CO., *Box 910, Churchill, Manitoba, Canada R0B 0E0. Tel. (204) 675-8804. Annual 72-page catalogue costs $10.*

Mukluks, which are boots made of mooseskin, insulated by animal fur and decorated with beads, plus sheepskin and leather slippers also decorated with beads. Payment by check, money order, American Express, Visa, or Mastercard. Shipment by Postal Service. Credit for merchandise returned within 15 days.

AUSTIN-HALL BOOT COMPANY, *491 N. Resler, Suite B, P.O. Box 12368, El Paso, Tex. 79912. Tel. (915) 581-2124. Annual 30-page catalogue costs $1.*

Western boots from a company that promises to do its best to accommodate special needs, such as a larger calf, an extra narrow foot, or an extra large size. Payment by check, money order, Visa, or Mastercard. Delivery by Postal Service or United Parcel. Boots without lettering or brands may be returned within 10 days for refund or exchange.

AVON FASHIONS. *See listing under* Women's Clothing, *above*.

BIARRITZ, *P.O. Box 590, Auburn, Me. 04210. Tel. (207) 782-2200. Free 16-page catalogue published twice a year.*

Casual shoes and espadrilles, mostly for women, but there are Japanese slipper-type espadrilles for both men and women. Payment by check, money order, American Express, Visa, or Mastercard. Shipment by Postal Service or United Parcel. Refund or credit for shoes returned within 2 weeks.

MILTON BODNER SHOES, *38 Lexington Ave., Passaic, N.J. 07055. Tel. (201) 777-8623. Free 20-page catalogue issued twice a year.*

Many dress and casual women's shoes. Shoes may be returned within 10 days for refund or credit.

BOSTONIAN, C. & J. CLARK LTD., *111 N. Forney Ave., Hanover, Pa. 17331. Tel. (717) 632-7575 or (800) 345-8500, Ext. 120. Free 32-page catalogue issued twice a year.*

Dress and professional men's shoes from Bostonian and casual footwear from Clark's. Refund or replacement for shoes returned within 10 days.

CHURCH'S ENGLISH SHOES, *428 Madison Ave., New York, N.Y. 10017. Tel. (212) 755-4313. Brochure price list.*

English, French, and Italian styles.

F. B. S. *See listing under* Women's Clothing, *above*.

THE HANOVER SHOE, *111 N. Forney Ave., Hanover, Pa. 17331. Tel. (717) 632-7575 or (800) 345-8500, Ext. 33. Free 40-page catalogue issued twice a year.*

Traditional men's shoes from the same company that makes Bostonian shoes, (listed above). Though not a "discount" company, it does offer $5 off with each order and advertises "factory direct savings." Unworn shoes may be returned within 10 days for refund or replacement.

HILL BROTHERS, *99 Ninth St., Lynchburg, Va. 24504. Tel. (804) 528-1000 (for information), (800) 446-0999 (for orders, except in Virginia). Free quarterly 48-page catalogue.*

Dress and casual shoes and slippers for women. Payment by check, money order, American Express, Visa, Mastercard, Diners Club, Carte Blanche, or C.O.D. Shipment by Postal Service or United Parcel. Their good return policy allows you to wear shoes for up to 14 days and return them for refund or exchange if not satisfied by then.

MAXWELL SHOE COMPANY, *310 Legion Ave., Annapolis, Md. 21401. Tel. (301) 267-9690. Free 12-page catalogue issued 3 times a year.*

Women's casual and dress shoes. Unworn shoes may be returned within 30 days for refund or exchange.

MOONEY & GILBERT, *314 Fifth Ave., New York, N.Y. 10001. Tel. (212) 564-3055. Free 12-page catalogue issued twice a year.*

A very large selection of women's casual, sports, and dress shoes, including many in extra-narrow widths, Unworn shoes may be returned within 10 days for refund.

NIERMAN'S TALL GIRL SHOES, *17 N. State St., Suite 1202, Chicago, Ill. 60602. Tel. (312) 346-9797, (800) 323-6556 (except in Illinois), or (800) 942-6345 (in Illinois). Free 16-page catalogue issued twice a year.*

This company was started in 1923 and sells only hard-to-find shoes for tall women (in narrow, medium, and wide widths), both casual and dress styles. Refund or credit for unworn shoes returned within 2 weeks.

OTTEN & SON, *Postbus (P.O. Box) 55655, 1007 ND, Amsterdam, Netherlands. Tel. (20) 729724. Brochure price list.*

Real wooden clogs with leather uppers for men, women, and children in white, black, and blue. I won't try to list specific prices because of currency fluctuations, but they are not expensive—around $20 plus postage—and could make very nice gifts for friends, whether of Dutch extraction or not. Payment by check, money order, American Express, Visa, or Mastercard. Shipment by Postal Service. Forget about refunds on something like this.

*QUODDY CRAFTED FOOTWEAR, *1515 Washington St., Braintree, Mass. 02184. Tel. (617) 843-2226. Free 6-page catalogue issued 4 times a year.*

Sports and casual shoes at discount. Boat shoes that retail for $55 are offered here

at $36.95; men's penny loafers that retail for $68 offered here at $44.95. Refund or credit for returned shoes.

RICHLEE SHOE CO., *5 Norfolk Ave., South Easton, Mass. 02375. Tel. (617) 238-4355 or (800) 343-3810 (except in Massachusetts). Free 32-page catalogue.*

These are men's shoes with the elevator feature designed to make men appear taller. They come in many dress and casual styles. The box carries the Richlee name and does not indicate that the shoes are elevators. Unworn shoes may be returned within 60 days for refund or exchange.

SHAKTI SHOES AND SANDALS, *309 Spring St., Herndon, Va. 22070. Tel. (703) 437-0404 or (800) 336-3394 (except in Washington, D.C., metropolitan area). Brochure price list.*

Men's and women's casual shoes. Refunds for shoes returned within 21 days.

THE SHOE FACTORY, *P.O. Box 09370, Bexley, Ohio 43209. Tel. (614) 443-2251. Brochure price lists.*

Casual women's shoes.

SHOE-OVER, *18 Wallace Dr., Spring Valley, N.Y. 10977. Catalogue costs $2.*

SKINNY'S DOWN UNDER. *Sheepskin slippers from New Zealand and Australia. See listing under Automotive Needs.*

SOFWEAR, *1811 San Jacinto, Houston, Tex. 77002. Tel. (713) 650-0916. Free 40-page catalogue.*

Hundreds of kinds of women's shoes, plus such apparel as sweaters, blouses, dresses, and slacks, but the emphasis is on footwear. Purchases may be returned for refunds within 15 days of receipt.

TODD'S, *5 S. Wabash Ave., Chicago, Ill. 60603. Tel. (312) 372-1335. Free annual 24-page catalogue.*

Men's and women's western, Frye, work, and walking boots, moccasins, and other casual shoes. Returns may be made within 30 days for refund or credit.

THE TOG SHOP. *See listing under* Women's Clothing, *above.*

T. WAYNE PRODUCKTIONS, *687 Church St., Mountain View, Calif. 94041. Tel. (415) 968-4311. Brochure.*

Sweet-looking slippers in the shape of ducks, rabbits, and carrots. I assume these are intended for children, but who knows? Payment by check, money order, Visa, or Mastercard. Shipment by United Parcel. No set return policy; only 2 pairs were returned in the past 4 years.

WEST COAST SHOE COMPANY, *P.O. Box 607, Scappoose, Ore. 97056. Tel. (503) 543-7114. The 4-page catalogue costs $1.*

Logger, lineman, and work boots, some home slippers. Payment by check or money order. Delivery by Postal Service or United Parcel. No returns on special orders; returns must be made within 10 days of receipt for factory defect.

See also *Men's and Women's Clothing, Work Clothes and Uniforms,* and *Casual and Sports Clothing,* above, *and Bicycles and Motorcycles, Sporting Goods, Camping Equipment, Army and Navy Goods,* and *Horse Supplies and Riding Equipment.*

Gloves and Scarves

*AMEDEO PERRONE, GLOVEMAKER, *92 Piazza di Spagna, 00187 Rome, Italy. Tel. (06) 6783101. Price list.*

Gloves of suede, antelope, deer, kid, and silk; also embroidered gloves. From time to time they have discount specials, such as the recent offering of kid leather golf gloves for $10. Payment by check, American Express, Visa, Mastercard, Diners Club, or Carte Blanche. Shipment by Postal Service. Purchases may be returned immediately upon receipt for exchange.

J. G. SLOAN LTD., *1309 E. Broward Blvd., Fort Lauderdale, Fla. 33301. Tel. (305) 463-4363.*

This company imports cashmere scarves from Alex Baggs of Ayr, Scotland, in navy, camel, scarlet, or gray, or, at extra cost, white. Payment by check, money order, or American Express. Satisfaction is guaranteed. No catalogue seems to be available, but company will reply to queries.

Luggage, Handbags, Briefcases, Canes and Umbrellas, Travel Clocks.

*ACE LEATHER PRODUCTS, *2211 Avenue U, Brooklyn, N.Y. 11229. Tel. (718) 645-3534 or (800) DIAL-ACE (except in New York State). Free annual 32-page catalogue.*

Luggage is the specialty, but there are other gift suggestions, including a telescope, briefcases, and travel alarm clocks. The merchandise is said to be offered at a discount. Payment by check, Visa or Mastercard. Shipment by United Parcel. Purchases may be returned within 14 days for credit or exchange.

DOONEY & BOURKE, *P.O. Box 841, South Norwalk, Conn. 06856. Tel. (203) 853-7515 or (800) 243-5598 (except in Connecticut). Free annual 8-page catalogue.*

This company sells leather handbags.

FIBERBILT CASES, *601 W. 26th St., New York, N.Y. 10001. Tel. (212) 675-5820 or (800) 847-4176 (except in New York State). Free annual 16-page catalogue.*

Here are briefcases for salesmen and executives, protective cases for carrying computers, and assorted other protective cases. Payment by check, money order, American Express, Visa, or Mastercard. Shipment by United Parcel or common carrier. Purchases may be returned for refund or credit within 30 days with receipt and authorization.

LANE'S LUGGAGE, *1146 Connecticut Ave., N.W., Washington, D.C. 20036. Tel. (202) 452-1146. Free 32-page catalogue.*

A large line of pricey things. Payment by check, money order, American Express, Visa, Mastercard, Diners Club, or Choice.

LEATHER LUGGAGE INC., *210 Pharr Rd. NE, Atlanta, Ga. 30305. Tel. (404) 233-7956 or (800) 874-7871. Brochure price list.*

This company is a direct importer of cowhide from Colombia. Its luggage is said to be priced 25 percent below normal retail. Payment by check, money order, American Express, Visa, or Mastercard. Shipment by United Parcel. Purchases may be returned within 30 days for refund or credit.

LEWIS LEATHERS, *120 Great Portland St., London, W1A 2DL, England. Tel. (01)-636-4314. Free annual 52-page catalogue.*

Payment by check, money order, Visa, or Mastercard. Shipment by Postal Service or air freight. Purchases may be returned within 7 days for refund or credit.

PORT CANVAS. *Duffles, handbags, beachcomber totes. See listing under* Sporting Goods.

THE PERERA COLLECTION, *Guardian Cane Co., Caller Box 310, Kansas City, Mo. 64141. Tel. (816) 221-3581 or (800) 821-5157. Free 40-page catalogue.*

Walking canes, some with brass heads molded into bird shapes, some with African animals carved on them, a combination cane-flashlight and, of course, the trusty sword cane, plus a cane gun and an electric-shock prod.

S. REDMAYNE LTD. *Briefcases. See listing under* Men's Clothing, *above.*

SWAINE ADENEY BRIGG & SONS LTD., *185 Picadilly, London, W1V OHA, England. Tel. (01) 734-4277. Free annual catalogue.*

The offerings here are extremely handsome and priced to match. One main product is fine luggage, and there also are canes, umbrellas, men's briefcases and women's handbags, plus a full line of saddlery and clothing for horsemen and horsewomen. Payment by check, money order, American Express, Visa, Mastercard or Diners Club. Shipment by Postal Service or Emery Air Freight. No returns.

WALKER, *Box 99306, San Francisco, Calif. 94109. Tel. (415) 863-2839. Brochure price list is free in black-and-white, $1 in color.*

Good-looking casual handbags, accessory bags, school bags, and belts.

Belts, Buckles, and Buttons, Uniform Insignia

THE BELT BUCKLE BUSINESS, *P.O. Box 4170, Jackson, Miss. 39216. Tel. (601) 353-9190. The 24-page catalogue costs $1, refundable with order.*

Here is real Americana—United States flags, World War II fighter planes, animals, etc. Payment by check, money order, Visa, or Mastercard. Shipment by Postal Service or United Parcel. Purchases may be returned within a year for refund or credit.

FASHION TOUCHES, *P.O. Box 804, Bridgeport, Conn. 06601. Tel. (203) 333-7738. Brochure price list.*

This company custom covers belts, buckles, and buttons, from the customer's own fabric or from Fashion Touches' stock.

B. ROBBINS LTD., *P.O. Box 2294, New York, N.Y. 10185. Tel. (212) 496-8347. Annual 6-page catalogue costs $1.*

Here are ornamental blazer buttons and jacket crests for the very preppy. Many of the items are British designs.

MILITARIA, *14691 Alder Lane, Tustin, Calif. 92680. Tel. (714) 730-1640. Free annual 12-to 16-page catalogue.*

Yachting and uniform insignia, gold bullion blazer badges, and woven neckties using a symbol or pattern provided by the buyer.

THE BEN SILVER CORP., *149 King St., Charleston, S.C. 29401. Tel. (803) 577-4556. Free catalogues.*

Blazer buttons marking colleges and universities, plus those of professions and pastimes.

WALKER. *Belts. See* Luggage, Handbags, Briefcases, Canes and Umbrellas, Travel Clocks, *above.*

Jewelry, Watches, Diamonds, and Gems

ANTIQUE IMPORTS UNLIMITED. *Antique jewelry. See listing under* Antiques.

GIOVANNI APA, *Via E. de Nicola, 2, P.O. Box 190, 80059 Torre Del Greco, Italy. Tel. (081) 8811125. Free 28-page catalogue.*

Cameos made by craftsmen in a firm established in 1848.

BUCHERER LTD., *CH-6000, Lucerne, Switzerland. Free annual 68-page catalogue.*

This company calls itself the largest watch and jewelry retailer in Switzerland and also has a branch in New York City (41 E. 42nd St., New York, N.Y. 10017, tel. (212) 697-9636). Payment by check, money order, American Express, Visa, Mastercard, Diners Club, or Carte Blanche. Shipment by Postal Service. Purchases may be returned for credit.

CARTIER, *653 Fifth Ave., New York, N.Y. 10022. Tel. (212) 753-0111. Annual 48-page catalogue costs $5 but is free to private clients.*

Expensive jewelry, watches, diamonds, and gems.

*RENNIE ELLEN DIAMONDS, *15 W. 47th St., New York, N.Y. 10036. Tel. (212) 869-5525. The 12-page catalogue costs $2.*

The proprietor says she sells to the public at wholesale prices. There are diamonds, settings, and rings. Payment by money order, bank tellers check, or personal check, but allow 10 to 15 days for clearance of the latter. Shipment by Postal Service. Purchases may be returned for refund within 5 days.

*EMPIRE DIAMOND CORP., *350 Fifth Ave., New York, N.Y. 10118. Tel. (212) 564-4777. Free annual 92-page catalogue.*

Discount prices promised; the purchases are guaranteed to be at least 25 percent below retail or the buyer's money will be refunded and the cost of the appraisal will be paid. Bank reference is needed for 10-day inspection. Shipment by registered mail. Purchases may be returned for refund within 60 days.

*GOLD 'N' STONES, *Box 636, Sterling, Alaska 99672. Tel. (907) 262-9713 or (907) 262-5050. Annual 8-page catalogue costs $1.*

This company makes jewelry out of Alaskan jade from the Kobuck area of the Arctic, plus some Canadian jade from British Columbia. Retail customers will be given a 30 percent discount on purchases over $25. Payment by check or money order. Shipment by Postal Service. "Five-year guarantee on jade jewelry"; they will replace or repair unsatisfactory pieces for $2 handling fee.

ITRACO WATCH CO. LTD., *P.O. Box 289, CH-8027, Zurich, Switzerland. Tel. (01) 720.04.97; telex 54 112 ITRA CH. The 32-page catalogue costs $3.*

A large line of Swiss watches. Payment by bank check or bank or postal money order. Shipment by Postal Service. No returns, but the company has repair centers in New York and Los Angeles.

KENYA DIVISION OF DAY & FRICK INC., *1760 N. Howard St., Philadelphia, Pa. 19122. Tel. (215) 739-4080. Free annual 16-page catalogue.*

This company describes itself as the oldest and leading simulated diamond firm in the mail order field. Purchases may be returned for refund within 10 days.

MARCUS & CO., *9460 Wilshire Blvd., Beverly Hills, Calif. 90212. Tel. (213) 271-6244. Catalogue costs $4.*

One of America's largest discount jewelers. Much of their merchandise is "purchased at or below wholesale from distressed jewelers, private parties, estate trustees, and 'out-of-pawn' from [their] Beverly Hills and San Francisco loan offices." Payment by check, Visa, or Mastercard. Shipment by Postal Service. "Items are 100 percent guaranteed to be as represented or your money will be immediately refunded."

THE NECKLACE SHOP, *P.O. Box 620366, Woodside, Calif. 94062. No telephone. Price list.*

Because there is a considerable variation in the values of this type of merchandise, the owner is reluctant to characterize her shop as "discount." However, other places are said to ask up to 4 times as much as does this shop for similar pieces. The gemstone necklaces "are not Tiffany quality, or the prices would not be what they are, but they are good quality, genuine, and many of them—depending upon the integrity of the suppliers—are excellent."

THE SHARPER IMAGE. *Gems, jewelry, and watches. See listing under* Audio and Video Equipment.

†TAIWAN VARIETY & NOVELTY SUPPLIES, *2 Alley 11, Lane 174, Section 2, Pa-Teh Rd., Taipei, Taiwan. Tel. (02) 771-6801 or (02) 771-8541. Packet of brochures costs $5 by airmail.*

Rings, pendants, earrings, necklaces, tie clips, cufflinks, and other objects in 14k gold, silver, and brass, with such stones as coral, opal, Taiwan and Australian jade, tiger eye, agate, and garnet. Payment by bank check or money order. Shipment by Postal Service.

*VANITY FAIR DIAMONDS, *55 E. Washington St., Chicago, Ill. 60602 Tel. (312) 977-0318 or (800) 235-3000. Free annual 32-page catalogue.*

Discount prices on jewlry, diamonds, and watches. One cited by the company: $847 for a 1.00 carat diamond that is said to list for $1,515.

See also *Antiques* and *Museum, Botanic Garden, and Public Radio Gift Catalogues* and *Fine and Unusual Gifts.*

Wigs

*PAULA YOUNG, *Box 483, Brockton, Mass. 02403. Tel. (617) 584-7360 or (800) 343-9695 (except in Massachusetts). Free 22-page catalogue issued twice a year.*

Discount prices on designer wigs. Payment by check, money order, Visa, or Mastercard. Shipment by United Parcel. Purchases may be returned for refund or exchange.

See also *Dance and Theater Supplies and Costumes.*

Hats

See individual listings for *Specialty Department Stores, Men's and Women's Clothing, Casual and Sports Clothing* in this section; *Army and Navy Goods* in *The Great Outdoors;* and *Dance and Theater Supplies and Costumes* in *The Performing Arts.*

❖5 Parents and Children

Some very nice looking maternity clothing is now widely available, and a good thing, too, since so many women work and choose to stay on the job much farther along in pregnancy than had been the case in the past.

Children have always been a special target of the mail-order companies, and the selection of things for children is extremely wide. Many things listed here are probably available only by mail. The classic Jamesville coaster wagons, available from the Wisconsin Wagon Co., have a special appeal to me.

NOTE TO GRANDPARENTS: Most of the things here would make nice gifts.

For Mothers and Mothers-to-Be, and for Fathers, Too

BABY LOVE, *P.O. Box 127, Laguna Beach, Calif. 92652. Tel. (714) 494-6748. Free 4-page catalogue issued twice a year.*

Fashions for nursing mothers. "Mom deserves some special attention at this very special time in her life." The company also has many books on childcare.

JAMES G. FAST. *Maternity wear. See listing under* Work Clothes and Uniforms.

MOTHERS WORK, *P.O. Box 40121, Philadelphia, Pa. 19106. Tel. (215) 625-9259. Annual 32-page catalogue costs $3.*

Clothing for the pregnant business executive; swatch card included with the catalogue.

MOTHERCARE LTD. *See listing under* For Children, *below.*

ORANGE CAT GOES TO MARKET. *Books on birth and parenting, a word that fills a need despite my normal aversion to neologisms. See listing under* General Booksellers.

*REBORN MATERNITY, *1449 Third Ave., New York, N.Y. 10028 Tel. (212) 737-8817. Semiannual 64-page catalogue costs $2.*

Discount prices on better maternity clothing. For example, Belle France dresses that are $118 to $130 elsewhere are $92 to $98 here. Payment by check, American Express, Visa, or Mastercard. Shipment by United Parcel. Purchases may be returned within 2 weeks for refund, but sales of dressier silks and evening wear are final.

STORK-KIT, *6864 Engle Rd., Cleveland, Ohio 44130. Tel. (216) 826-1900. Several free annual 24-page catalogues.*

Catalogues include *Mothers Place* for maternity clothes, and *Nancy Stone and Anthony Richards* for dresses, coats, and lingerie.

See also *For Children,* **below, for kits that parents can buy to make things for their children.**

For Children

†HANNA ANDERSSON, *5565 S.W. Hewett Blvd., Portland, Ore. 97221. Tel. (503) 292-8664. Free 16-page catalogue.*

Nice looking clothes and sturdy toys and furniture. Gift services are available. Payment by check, money order, Visa, or Mastercard. Purchases may be returned for refund or exchange, but clothes that have been worn or laundered are not returnable.

ANTIQUE DOLL REPRODUCTIONS, *Route 1, Box 103, Milo, Mo. 64767. Tel. (417) 826-4785. The 10-page catalogue costs $2.*

These are lovingly handmade china or bisque reproductions, some of 100-year-old originals. Payment by check or money order. Shipment by Postal Service. Purchases may be returned for refunds within 10 days.

BAILEY'S. *Toys. See listing under* Camping Equipment.

BEAR-IN-MIND, *20 Beharrell St., Concord, Mass. 01742. Tel. (617) 369-5987. Semiannual 48-page catalogue costs $1.*

Everything about bears—stuffed bears, Paddington Bears, bear books, bear T-shirts. Payment by check, money order, American Express, Visa, or Mastercard. Delivery by Postal Service or United Parcel. Refund or credit for purchases returned within 30 days.

THE BEAR NECESSITIES, *P.O. Box C-10, Belmont, Mass. 02178. Tel. (617) 647-9365 or (800) 543-3450. Free 24-page catalogue.*

More on bears, including Paddington, of course, and lots of puns (the designer Bierre Cardin, music to your bears, wunderbear, bear mitzvahs—for Jewish bears. Payment by check, money order, American Express, Visa, or Mastercard. Delivery by Postal Service or United Parcel.

B. J. BABY, *River Road, Worthington, Mass. 01098. Tel. (413) 238-7757 or (413) 238-5919. Brochures.*

A bedroom light in the shape of a goose head, a child's sink that hooks onto a bathtub, and other products of a clever imagination.

BELLEROPHON BOOKS, *36 Anacapa St., Santa Barbara, Calif. 93101. Tel. (805) 965-7034. Free 8-page catalogue to those who provide self-addressed stamped envelope.*

Art books, posters, coloring books, cutouts, and calendars especially for children. There are books on dogs, airplanes, and cowboys, and also on music (Beethoven, Bach, Mozart); ballet (*Nutcracker* and *Sleeping Beauty*) and literature (Chaucer and Shakespeare). What a nifty way to learn!

BOOKS OF WONDER. *New and old children's books. See listing under* Rare and Finely Printed Books, Juvenalia.

CAPRILANDS HERB FARM. *Dolls. See listing under* Seeds and Plants.

*CHERRY TREE TOYS, *P.O. Box 369, Belmont, Ohio 43718. Tel. (614) 484-1746. The 20-page catalogue costs $1.*

Discount prices available for a large line of pre-cut kits of wooden toys that need only to be sanded and glued together. Sounds like something even I could handle.

CHILD LIFE PLAY SPECIALTIES, *55 Whitney St., Holliston, Mass. 01746. Tel. (617) 429-4639. Free annual 24-page catalogue.*

Wooden swing sets, jungle gyms, and other wooden backyard play equipment. Payment by check, money order, Visa, or Mastercard. Shipment by Postal Service, United Parcel, or motor freight. Unused purchases may be returned within 60 days for refund.

CHILD SAFETY INSTITUTE, *P.O. Box 1019, Port Washington, N.Y. 11050. Tel. (201) 935-3434. Brochure price list.*

Safety equipment to prevent injuries to children, such as cabinet and medicine cabinet locks, shields and caps for electrical outlets. Payment by check, money order, American Express, Visa, or Mastercard. Shipment by United Parcel. Refunds for purchases returned within 30 days.

CHILDREN'S BOOK & MUSIC CENTER, *P.O. Box 1130, Santa Monica, Calif. 90406. Tel. (213) 829-0215 or (800) 443-1856 (except in California). Annual catalogue costs $1 but is sent free to teachers, schools, and libraries if requested on official letterhead.*

Books, records, and tapes for young children, from infancy to about kindergarten. Words and music to grow on.

CHILDWISE PRODUCTS, *P.O. Box 282, Westwood, N.J. 07675. Tel. (201) 573-8668. Free annual 14-page catalogue.*

Toys, diaper-changing pads and bags, baby seats.

THE CLAPPER COMPANY. *Toys and tools for the garden. See listing under* Garden Tools, Equipment, and Furniture.

COMMUNITY PLAYTHINGS, *Rifton, N.Y. 12471. Tel. (914) 658-3141. Annual 60-page catalogue costs 50 cents.*

Children's furniture, such as cribs and playpens, plus such play equipment as slides, gyms, swings, and seesaws. The products are made by a religious group called the Hutterian Society of Brothers. There are also books of religious, inspirational, or instructional nature. Payment by check or money order. Shipment by Postal Service, United Parcel, or truck. Returns are not accepted.

CONSTRUCTIVE PLAYTHINGS, *2008 W. 103rd Terr., Leawood, Kans. 66206. Tel. (913) 642-8244 or (800) 255-6124 (except in Kansas.) Free annual 32-page home catalogue; annual 200-page school catalogue costs $2.*

The company has a well-earned reputation for excellent toys, educational products, books, and music, including some with which I remember our daughters grew up. Payment by check, money order, Visa, or Mastercard. Shipment by Postal Service, United Parcel, or truck. Purchases may be returned within 30 days for refund, but authorization must be obtained first.

COTTONTAILS, *1325 43rd St., Los Alamos, N.M. 87544. Tel. (505) 662-4558. Annual 6-page catalogue costs $1.*

Good-looking clothing for children.

CR'S CRAFTS. *Stuffed toys to buy or make. See listing under* Needlecrafts.

DOVER PUBLICATIONS. *Books, paper dolls, and toy books. See listing under* Art and Illustrated Books.

*DOLL HOUSE FACTORY OUTLET, *325 Division St., Boonton, N.J. 07005. Tel. (201) 335-5501. Annual 32-page catalogue costs $2.*

Discount prices for dolls and toys, with some prices 75 percent lower than those charged in stores.

DUNNS. *Outdoor Clothing. See listing under* Camping Equipment.

THE ENCHANTED DOLL HOUSE, *Route 7, Manchester Center, Vt. 05255. Tel. (802) 362-3030. Annual 88-page catalogue costs $1.*

Traditional dolls and some not so traditional, like Marilyn Monroe and Mark Twain, plus dollhouses. It looks as though a lot of thought has gone into these products.

ESPRIT DE CORP. *Children's Clothing. See listing under* Women's Clothing.

RICHARD HANTEN FOR CHILDREN, *6137 N. Scottsdale Rd., Scottsdale, Ariz. 85253. Tel. (602) 991-8222. The 8- to 36-page catalogue issued 3 or 4 times a year costs $1 per catalogue.*

Good-looking clothes for children. Payment by check, money order, American Express, Visa, or Mastercard. Delivery by Postal Service or United Parcel. Purchases may be returned within 2 weeks for refund or credit.

GOOD HEARTED BEARS, *3 Pearl St., Mystic, Conn. 06355. Tel. (203) 536-2468. Annual brochure costs $1.*

More bears, more bear puns (Humphrey Beargart), and Aloysius from *Brideshead Revisted.* Payment by check, money order, Visa, or Mastercard. Shipment by Postal Service or United Parcel. Purchases may be returned within 14 days in resaleable condition for refund or credit.

HIGHLAND HOUSE. *Children's clothing. See listing under* Women's Clothing.

H.U.D.D.L.E., *3416 Wesley Ave., Culver City, Calif. 90230. Tel. (213) 836-8001. Catalogue costs $2.*

Beds, including a baby bed that converts to a twin-size day bed, and other furniture for growing children, including tables, toy boxes, desks. Payment by check, money order, Visa, or Mastercard. Shipment by United Parcel or freight companies. Except for defective furniture, there are no returns since everything is manufactured to specifications.

HUTCHINSON BOOKS, *Chestnut St., Lewiston, Me. 04240. Tel. (207) 783-6329 or (800) 341-0403 (except in Maine, Alaska, and Hawaii). Free 24-page catalogue issued twice a year.*

This company publishes books for children under the Ladybird imprint. One particularly good idea is a set of books in French that are translations of some of Ladybird's most popular books for the very young. *Telling the Time* becomes *Apprenons l'heure* when published under the La Coccinelle symbol. Payment by check, money order, Visa, or Mastercard. Delivery by United Parcel. Refund or replacement if not satisfied.

ELIZABETH JAMES, *P.O. Box 357, Beverly, Mass. 01915. Tel. (617) 927-6171. Brochure issued 3 times a year costs 75 cents.*

Vests and hodded bath towels for infants.

JUDI'S DOLLS, *P.O. Box 607, Port Orchard, Wash. 98366. Tel. (206) 876-3954. Annual 16-page catalogue costs $1.50.*

Imaginative dolls. I especially liked that dolls of children of various races were available. Payment by check or money order. Shipment by Postal Service or United Parcel. Purchases may be returned for refund or credit within 30 days if in original, undamaged condition.

JUST FOR KIDS!, *Winterbrook Way, Meredith, N.H. 03253. Tel. (603) 279-7081. Free 64- to 100-page catalogue issued twice a year.*

Toys, including stuffed animals, a log cabin playhouse, and swing sets, plus children's books, records, and clothes—it looks like a lot of fun.

KID COTTONS, *197 Main St., Northfield, Mass. 01360. Tel. (413) 498-4423. Free 32-page catalogue.*

Children's clothing. The catalogue is nicely illustrated with fine line drawings.

THE KIWI RANCH. *Dolls. See listing under* Fruit and Nuts.

LEARNING THINGS, *68A Broadway, P.O. Box 436, Arlington, Mass. 02174. Tel. (617) 646-0093. Free annual 28-page catalogue.*

This is a catalogue of materials for science, mathematics, and technology education. Among the products available are microscopes, binoculars, and telescopes, cameras, math and chemistry aids, and classroom supplies. Payment by check or money order. Shipment by United Parcel. Purchases may be returned within 30 days for refund.

LIBERTYVILLE SADDLE SHOP. *Riding clothes. See listing under* Horse Supplies and Riding Equipment.

MOTHERCARE, *P.O. Box 145, Watford, Herts., WD2 5SH, England. Tel. (0923) 31616. Free 164-page catalogue issued twice a year.*

A thick catalogue of nice English clothing, toys, prams, books, and things for children, plus a large line of maternity fashions. Payment by check, international money order, Mastercard, or Eurocard. Shipment by surface mail or air mail. Purchases may be returned within 2 weeks of receipt for refund.

MUSEUM OF MODERN ART. *Toys. See listing under* Museums, Botanic Garden, and Public Radio Gift Catalogues.

NEDOBECK GRAPHICS, *P.O. Box 20737, Milwaukee, Wis. 53220. Tel. (414) 327-0761. Free 12-page catalogue issued annually.*

Nedobeck, the author-artist of a series of children's books, cards, and graphics, will incorporate the child's name, hometown, etc., into the work. Payment by check or money order. Delivery by United Parcel. Refunds on returns within 30 days if not satisfied.

THE OFFICIAL STICKER CATALOGUE, *P.O. Box 17, Long Beach, Calif. 90801. Tel. (213) 603-8890. Free 16-page catalogue issued twice a year.*

When my daughter Ellen was quite small, she covered her bedroom door with stickers that she picked up here and there. It was truly a one-of-a-kind. Payment by check, money order, American Express, Visa, or Mastercard. Delivery by Postal Service or United Parcel. Refund or credit for goods returned within 14 days.

OPPORTUNITIES FOR LEARNING, *8950 Lurline Ave., Chatsworth, Calif. 91311. Tel. (818) 341-2535. Free subject catalogues issued twice a year.*

This company issues several education-oriented catalogues. Some of the subjects covered are special students, microcomputer software, math, reading and language, and social studies.

ORANGE CAT GOES TO MARKET. *Children's books. See listing under* General Booksellers.

RAMS HEAD. *Stuffed animals. See listing under* Automotive Needs.

RESOURCES FOR THE GIFTED, *P.O. Box 15050, Phoenix, Ariz. 85060. Tel. (602) 840-9770. Free annual 24- to 32-page catalogue.*

Materials for use at home and in the school to help in the education of gifted children, who frequently are not adequately challenged in normal settings.

SAN FRANCISCO MUSIC BOX CO. *See listing under* Music Boxes.

DALE SEYMOUR PUBLICATIONS, *P.O. Box 10888, Palo Alto, Calif. 94303. Tel. (415) 324-2800 or (800) 872-1100. Free 68-page catalogue.*

Instructional material on mathematics, computers, language, and science. Payment by check, Visa, or Mastercard. Shipment by United Parcel. Purchases may be returned within 30 days for refund.

SOMETHING TO CROW ABOUT, *P.O. Box 51056, Palo Alto, Calif. 94303. Tel. (800) 227-3900 (except in California) or (800) 632-2122 (in California). Free 16-page catalogue.*

Nice children's clothing, including bib overalls, flannel shirts, and raincoats. Payment by check, money order, Visa, or Mastercard. Purchases, except for personalized items, may be returned for refund.

SUZO, *Box 10, Chester, Vt. 05143. Tel. (802) 875-3980. Semiannual 30-page catalogue costs $1.25.*

Animal suits so children can dress up like penguins, rabbits, pandas, and other creatures.

SWALLOWHILL, *Box 34, Midland, Ont., Canada L4R 4K6. Tel. (705) 526-6713. Catalogue costs $1, refundable with first order.*

Doll kits for the do-it-yourselfer, with an emphasis on porcelain dolls. Payment by check or money order. Shipment by Postal Service. Purchases may be returned for refund or credit within a "reasonable time."

THREE BEARS BABY IMPORTS, *10 Wells St., Westerly, R.I. 02891 Tel. (401) 596-7725. Semiannual 24-page catalogue costs $1, refundable with order.*

Much of the clothing is from West Germany, but some is from other countries, and it is very cute. There are also toys and stuffed animals.

TOYS TO GROW ON, *P.O. Box 17, Long Beach, Calif. 90801. Tel. (213) 603-8890. Free 32- to 36-page catalogue issed twice a year.*

Clever, colorful, and educational toys. Payment by check, money order, American Express, Visa, or Mastercard. Shipment by Postal Service or United Parcel. Purchases may be returned within 30 days for refund or credit.

T. WAYNE PRODUCKTIONS. *Slippers. See listing under* Shoes and Other Footwear.

THE WORLD OF PERIPOLE. *See listing under* Musical Instruments.

U.S. CAVALRY STORE. *See listing under* Army and Navy Goods.

WISCONSIN WAGON CO., *10 S. Locust St., Janesville, Wis. 53545. Tel. (608) 754-0026. Brochure price list.*

Classic Janesville coaster wagons and other toys, plus a nice traditional wooden cradle. Payment by check, money order, Visa, or Mastercard. Shipment by United Parcel or truck freight. Purchases may be returned for refund without time limit.

THE WOODEN NEEDLE, *Box 908, Kamloops, B.C., Canada V2C 5M8. Tel. (604) 554-1624. Annual catalogue costs $1, refundable with first order.*

Wooden toys. Payment by check, money order, or Visa. Shipment by Postal Service. Merchandise in good condition may be returned at any time for refund.

THE WOODEN SWING CO., *45 New York Ave., Framingham, Mass. 01701. Tel. (617) 620-1909. Free annual 12-page catalogue.*

Sturdy wooden swing sets, one with a tent on top and a basketball backboard on the side. Payment by check, money order, Visa, or Mastercard. Shipment by United Parcel or truck freight. Refund or credit for purchases returned within 30 days.

WOODPLAY INC., *P.O. Box 27911, Raleigh, N.C. 27611 Tel. (919) 832-2970. Free annual 10-page catalogue.*

Another line of wooden swings, seesaws, treehouses, and the like that seem solidly built. Payment by check, money order, Visa, or Mastercard. Shipment by United Parcel or common carrier. Refunds or credit for purchases returned within 30 days.

YARDS OF FUN, *P.O. Box 119, North Manchester, Ind. 46962. Tel. (219) 982-6067 or (800) 348-5400 (except in Indiana). Free 10-page catalogue.*

Swing sets, slides, and seesaws. Payment by check, money order, Visa, or Mastercard. Shipment by United Parcel or common carrier. Refund, credit, or exchange for returned purchases.

See also *Specialty Department Stores* and *Casual and Sports Clothing, Sporting Goods, Games and Toys,* and *Crafts to Buy.*

❖6 For the Home

The Victorian revival in the United States is picking up momentum, perhaps as a delayed reaction to the stark modernity of post-World War II design, and there is an emphasis on heavy, dark woods and on intricate brass fittings and accessories. The sweeping changes in taste are evident in the catalogues listed in this chapter.

In compiling the furniture list, I realized something that I'd known but hadn't given much thought to: North Carolina is the great center for furniture in the United States. However, what is made here is primarily factory productionware—good, solid furniture, but not the kind made by hand one piece at a time. The latter continues to be crafted largely in New England, as the reader will see from the addresses in the following list. By necessity, the handmade furniture is much more expensive. Who knows how long we will continue to have two such industries in our country? We need them both, I think.

Some of the companies will send you, at lower cost, furniture in unfinished or semifinished condition. You put the pieces together and then sand and paint them. That's a good cost-saving idea for people with the tools and skill already in place; it may not be such an idea for people like me, since up until recently my experience has been limited to hammering nails into walls for pictures to be hung on.

This is a broadly based chapter, embracing some things, such as wood stoves, in which interest comes and goes. In the case of stoves, this is a function of the price and scarcity of oil and gas, and wood stoves have the advantage of being attractive (or at least interesting); it's hard to find a good-looking solar panel. And remember that old saying about firewood: It heats you twice, once when you cut it and once when you burn it.

Some of the hardware suppliers listed here do most of their business with retail dealers but will also sell directly to the public. However, there frequently is a fee for returns (called a "restocking" charge) that can run quite high, so the buyer is cautioned to be fairly certain of the purchase. Whenever a great deal of hand work is involved in the making of an object (as in the case of some of the hardware) or if an object is completely handmade (as with some of the furniture and lamps), the price can be very high.

Catalogues that I found particularly good or interesting include Cohasset Colonials, the Country Bed Shop, Thos. Moser Cabinetmakers, the Seraph, Shaker Workshops, Sion-Fuk Enterprises, Charles Webb, Cannondale's, the Company Store, Isabel Brass Furniture, Lisa Victoria Brass Beds, Nowell's, St. Louis Antique Lighting Co., Strike One (Islington), Bryant Stove Works, Anglo-American Brass Co., Ball & Ball, Remodeler's Supply Co., and the Renovator's Supply.

Furniture and Furnishings

*AMERICAN FURNITURE SYSTEMS, *805 Kings Highway, Brooklyn, N.Y. 11223. Tel. (718) 258-3500 or (800) 221-6969. Free 64-page catalogue.*

Most of the things here are for the office and school, but many are suitable for the home. The company says its prices represent savings of up to 45 percent. There are chairs, tables, bookcases, desks, computer furniture, files, safes, lecterns, shelving, lockers. Payment by check, American Express, or Visa. Money-back guarantee.

ANDEAN PRODUCTS. *See listing under* Crafts to Buy.

*ANNEX FURNITURE GALLERIES, *P.O. Box 958, High Point, N.C. 27261. Tel. (919) 882-8195 or (800) 334-7391 (except in North Carolina). Free catalogue.*

Discounts of 40 to 50 percent off retail are offered by the company, which is an authorized dealer for many brand-name companies. Payment by check, Visa, Mastercard, or C.O.D. Delivery by truck service, and returns must be made at time of delivery.

ARISE FUTON MATTRESS CO., *37 Wooster St., New York, N.Y. 10013. Tel. (212) 925-0310. Catalogue costs $2.*

Japanese-style mattresses and wood frames. Payment by check, money order, American Express, Visa, or Mastercard. Shipment by United Parcel or common carrier.

*BALES FURNITURE MANUFACTURING, *Space Beds, 1300 17th St., San Francisco, Calif. 94107. Tel. (415) 552-8616. Free 28-page catalogue.*

Beds, wall beds, chests, hutches, cabinets, dressers, and bookcases at discount prices. Payment by check, money order, American Express, Visa, Mastercard, Diners Club, or Carte Blanche. Shipment by common carrier. No returns are accepted. Any damage must be reported at the time of delivery to the freight company.

*BARNES & BLACKWELDER, *1804 Pembroke Rd., Greensboro, N.C. 27408. Tel. (919) 373-8504 or (800) 334-0234 (except in North Carolina). Free brochure.*

Furniture for the home at discount prices. An example given was a $3,220 rice-carved queen-sized bed by Henkel-Harris available for $1,820. Payment by check. Shipment by United Parcel or truck. No returns if the right item is delivered.

THE BARTLEY COLLECTION LTD., *747 Oakwood Ave., Lake Forest, Ill. 60045. Tel. (312) 634-9510 or (800) 227-8539. Catalogue costs $1.*

Tables, benches, silver chests, bureaus, highboys, beds, and desks, finished or in kits at lower price for finishing at home. Payment by check, money order, Visa, or Mastercard. Shipment by United Parcel. Merchandise may be returned, if in original condition, within 30 days for refund.

BEDLAM BRASS, *19-21 Fair Lawn Ave., Fair Lawn, N.J. 07410. Tel. (201) 796-7200. Catalogue costs $1.*

Brass beds. Payment by check, money order, Visa, Mastercard, Diners Club, or C.O.D. Credit for returns.

*THE BEDPOST, *795 Bethel Rd., Columbus, Ohio 43214. Tel. (614) 559-0088. Semiannual 8-page catalogue costs $1.95.*

Waterbeds, hot tubs, etc., at discount prices.

THE BOMBAY COMPANY, *P.O. Box 79186, Fort Worth, Tex. 76179. Tel. (800) 535-6876 (except in Texas) or (817) 232-5650 (in Texas). Free 16- to 32-page catalogue issued 4 times a year.*

Tables, chests, and accessories of traditional style. Payment by check, money order, American Express, Visa, Mastercard, or Diners Club. Delivery by United Parcel. Purchases may be returned for refund or credit within 60 days.

*CANNONDALE'S, *Route 113 South, P.O. Drawer 1107, Berlin, Md. 21811. Tel. (301) 641-4477 or (800) 552-1776 (except in Maryland). Free 12-page catalogue issued 6 times each year.*

This company claims to be the world's largest direct marketer of solid brass and white iron beds and to offer the beds at discount prices.

COHASSET COLONIALS, *95 Ship St., Cohasset Harbor, Mass. 02025. Tel. (617) 383-0110. The 16- to 32-page catalogue issued 4 times a year costs $1.*

Fine reproductions of classic early American furniture, provided in easy-to-put-together kits. There are also lamps and other furnishings.

LAURA COPENHAVER INDUSTRIES, *Rosemont, Marion, Va. 24354. Tel. (703) 783-4663. The 24-page catalogue costs $1.*

Traditional mountain crafts and styles ("in the hope that these historic arts will survive our generation"), including canopies for four-poster beds, quilts, valances, coverlets, curtains, rugs, and furniture (the canopy beds themselves, handmade).

CORNUCOPIA INC., *P.O. Box 30, Westcott Rd., Harvard, Mass. 01451 Tel. (617) 456-3201. Annual 16-page catalogue costs $2.*

Reproductions of classic early American chairs, tables, hutches, and other pieces.

THE COUNTRY BED SHOP, *Charles E. Thibeau, Cabinetmaker-designer, Box 222, Groton, Mass. 01450. Tel. (617) 448-6336. The 32-page catalogue issued every 3 or 4 years, costs $4.*

This is a handsome catalogue of the shop's offerings—handmade reproductions of American furniture of the 17th and 18th centuries. Among the pieces available are post and other beds, cradles, cribs, chairs, tables, chests, and cupboards. The prices are high, reflecting, the company says, the cost of the labor and materials to produce the objects.

THE COUNTRY LOFT, *South Shore Park, Hingham, Mass. 02043. Tel. (617) 749-7766 or (800) 225-5408. Approximately 48-page catalogue costs $5 (but people I know get it free).*

Early American and Shaker reproduction furniture and accessories are offered. There are also lamps, rugs, and fabrics. Payment by check, money order, American Express, Visa, Mastercard, Diners Club, and Carte Blanche. United Parcel used for delivery whenever possible, with freight carrier for furniture. Any item may be returned for refund or replacement.

*COUNTRY WORKSHOP, *95 Rome St., Newark, N.J. 07105. Tel. (201) 589-3407, (800) 526-8001 (except in New Jersey, Alaska, and Hawaii), or (800) 259-0936 (in New Jersey). Annual 12-page catalogue costs $1, and there are free notices and newsletters.*

This company says its prices are half or less what one would pay for comparable furniture from a dealer or department store. The pieces include unfinished bookcases, cabinets, chests, tables, desks, beds, and butcher block tops.

EMPEROR CLOCK COMPANY. *See listing under* Clocks, *below.*

ERKINS. *Garden furniture. See listing under* Sculpture.

E. J. EVANS. *Webbing and cushion fabrics for Danish chairs and sofas. See listing under* Basket-Making, Caning, *and* Furniture Webbing.

FOREIGN TRADERS, *The Old Mexico Shop, P.O. Box 1967, Santa Fe, N.M. 87501. Tel. (505) 983-6441. Free gift catalogue; decorator's catalogue issued every 2 or 3 years costs $2.*

Spanish Colonial furniture and accessories, tables and chairs, decorative tiles, lamps, chandeliers, and sculpture.

FURNITURE OF SHAKER SIMPLICITY, *Lawrence M. Lengel, 22 N. Main St., Mercersburg, Pa. 17236. Tel. (717) 328-5777. Annual 6-page catalogue costs $1.*

Handcrafted chairs, tables, and clocks. Payment by check or money order. Delivery by Postal Service or common carrier. The company will refund price, repair, or replace item for any reason within a "reasonable" time.

*FURNITURE TRADITIONS, *Box 5067, Hickory, N.C. 28601. Tel. (704) 324-0611. The 40-page catalogue costs $3.*

A discount company with a very wide range of furniture, including many reproductions. Their most popular piece is their Hi-Lo table, which sells for $375, but would cost about $450 in a retail store. The line includes chests, dining room, bedroom, and living room furniture, and there are some leather pieces. Payment by check or money order. Delivery by common carrier. Furniture may be returned only if damaged.

FUTON-TO-SLEEP-ON, *33 W. Eighth Ave., Vancouver, B.C., Canada V5Y 1M9. Tel. (604) 877-1271. Free semiannual 20-page catalogue.*

Besides futons, there are bed frames, couches, tatami mats, sheets, quilts, and pillows. Payment by money order, Visa, or Mastercard. Shipment by Postal Service. Unsatisfactory purchases may be returned within 30 days for refund.

GARDENER'S EDEN. *Outdoor furniture. See listing under* Garden Tools, Equipment, and Furniture.

GUMPS. *See listing under* Fine and Unusual Gifts.

HAMMACHER SCHLEMMER. *Outdoor Furniture. See listing under* Audio and Video Equipment.

HISTORIC CHARLESTON REPRODUCTIONS. *See listing under* Museum, Botanic Garden, and Public Radio Gift Catalogues.

ISABEL BRASS FURNITURE, *120 E. 32d St., New York, N.Y. 10016. Tel. (212) 689-3307 or (800) 221-8523 (except in New York). Annual 24-page catalogue costs $4.*

A catalogue of good-looking brass beds, very pricey. Payment by check, money order, American Express, Visa, or Mastercard. Shipment by motor carrier. Merchandise can be returned immediately for refund if customer is not satisfied with quality and workmanship.

JENNIFER HOUSE. *Furniture, bedding, lamps, children's furniture. See listing under* Country and General Stores.

*JONES BROTHERS FURNITURE, *P.O. Box 991, Smithfield, N.C. 27577. Tel. (919) 934-4162. No catalogue.*

Instead of issuing a catalogue this company asks customers to tell them what they are interested in; they will then send back individual brochures from various manufacturers and offer the furniture in them at discounts of 35 to 40 percent off regular retail prices.

JAMES LEA, CABINETMAKER, *9 West St., Rockport, Me. 04856. Tel. (207) 236-3632. Annual 20-page catalogue costs $3.*

Handmade reproductions of 18th-century American furniture. Among the pieces are a Queen Anne bonnet top highboy, a Chippendale looking glass, and a bow back Windsor chair. The prices for these fine objects are high. Payment by check or money order. Delivery by common carrier. Pieces may be returned for credit within 30 days.

LEATHERCRAFTERS, *303 E. 51st St., New York, N.Y. 10022. Tel. (212) 759-1955. The 32-page catalogue costs $1.*

Leather-covered chairs. Payment by check, money order, Visa, or Mastercard. Shipment by United Parcel, truck, air, or boat. No returns.

†**THE LENNOX SHOP,** *Route 179, Box 64, Lambertville, N.J. 08530. Tel. (609) 397-1880. Annual 42-page catalogue costs $1.*

Reproductions of early American pine furniture—bookcases, tables, benches, cupboards. There are also lamps and sconces, and a line of giftware, including pewter reproductions.

LISA VICTORIA BRASS BEDS, *17106 S. Crater Rd., Petersburg, Va. 23805. Tel. (804) 862-1491. The 20-page catalogue costs $4.*

Great looking brass beds, custom-made to designs exclusive with this company. Payment by check, money order, Visa, or Mastercard. Shipment by freight. Refunds for returned goods.

*MAGNOLIA HALL, *726 Andover, Atlanta, Ga. 30327. Tel. (404) 351-1910. The 80-page catalogue issued twice a year costs $2.*

Discount prices on Victorian, Louis XIV, and early American reproduction tables, mirrors, desks, lamps, sofas, chairs, and clocks.

MONDRIAN CUSTOM CABINETRY, *1021 Second Ave., New York, N.Y. 10022. Tel. (212) 355-7373. Catalogue costs $3.*

Here are wall units, Parsons tables, wardrobes, chests, cabinets, bookcases, beds, desks, and files, all offered in both sharp edge ("T-Square") and in rounded edge ("Deco") styles. They are good-looking pieces.

THOS. MOSER CABINETMAKERS, *Cobbs Bridge Rd., New Gloucester, Me. 04260. Tel. (207) 926-4446. Annual 44-page catalogue costs $3.*

Handsome pieces of handmade furniture, with special attention given to early American reproductions. Some clocks also included. Payment by check, money order, Visa, or Mastercard. Shipment by common carrier.

MOULTRIE MANUFACTURING CO., *P.O. Box 1179, Moultrie, Ga. 31776. Tel. (912) 985-1312 or (800) 841-8674 (except in Georgia). Semiannual 30-page catalogue costs $1.*

Wrought iron outdoor furniture, gates, and fences for an elegant country house or for those smallers houses the owners would like to think of as elegant.

*MURROW FURNITURE GALLERIES, *P.O. Box 4337, Wilmington, N.C. 28406. Tel. (919) 799-4010 or (800) 334-1614 (except in North Carolina). The 80-page catalogue costs $5.*

Discounts of 30 to 50 percent on every line of furniture.

MUSEUM OF MODERN ART. *See listing under* Museum, Botanic Garden, and Public Radio Gift Catalogues.

ORLEANS CARPENTERS, *Box 107-C, Rock Harbor Rd., Orleans, Mass. 02653. Tel. (617) 255-2646. Annual 16-page catalogue costs 50 cents.*

Colonial and Shaker reproductions. The owner says it is the only shop in the country making museum-quality Shaker boxes in quantity. Payment by check, money order, Visa, or Mastercard. Delivery by United Parcel. Merchandise may be returned within 30 days for refund.

OUTER BANKS PINE PRODUCTS, *Box 120 Lester, Pa. 19113. Tel. (215) 534-1234. Annual catalogue costs 50 cents.*

This company makes corner cabinets from pine designed to be given their final finish by the purchaser, plus a line of clocks, finished and unfinished.

*PRIBA FURNITURE SALES, *P.O. Box 13295, Greensboro, N.C. 27405. Tel. (919) 855-9034 or (800) 334-2498 (except in North Carolina). Brochure.*

The company sends customers mailers issued by furniture manufacturers. It offers discounts of up to 40 percent off retail prices on living room, dining room, bedroom, and other furniture, plus clocks, lamps, fabrics, carpets, wallpaper, shades and blinds, mattresses and springs, and other bedding.

PUTNAM ROLLING LADDER CO. *Patio furniture. See listing under* Tools and Equipment for Craftspeople, Tinkerers, and Do-It-Yourselfers.

*JAMES ROY INC., *15 E. 32d St., New York, N.Y. 10016. Tel. (212) 679-2565. Brochure price list.*

This company sells things at a third off the retail price. For example, the Sealy Mod-

ule, Style 5124, Grade E, which lists for $1,500, sells here for $1,000. Payment by check, money order, Visa, or Mastercard. Shipment by Postal Service, United Parcel, commercial carrier, or Roy truck. Refunds for returns made within 7 days.

S. & C. HUBER, ACCOUTREMENTS, *82 Plants Dam Rd., East Lyme, Conn. 06333. Tel. (203) 739-0772. Annual 36-page catalogue costs $1.50.*

This company produces copies of 18th- and early 19th-century goods and carries a line of antique furniture as well. There are also stenciling supplies for those who want to try their hand at that old art. Payment by check or money order. Shipment by Postal Service.

THE SERAPH, *P.O. Box 500, Sturbridge, Mass. 01566. Tel. (617) 347-2241. The 12-page catalogue costs $3.*

Reproduction handmade furniture of designs from the 18th and early 19th centuries. There are chairs, sofas, tables, and cupboards, plus chandeliers, lamps, and sconces.

SHAKER WORKSHOPS, *P.O. Box 1028, Concord, Mass. Tel. (617) 646-8985. The 40-page catalogue issued 3 times a year, costs 50 cents.*

Here are reproductions of classic Shaker furniture, either in finished form or in kits for completion at home. There are chairs, tables, beds, shelves, and rockers, plus books, chandeliers and sconces, prints, women's vests, and rugs.

*SHAW FURNITURE GALLERIES, *P.O. Box 576, Randleman, N.C. 27317. Tel. (919) 498-2628 or*

(800) 334-6799 (except in North Carolina). Assorted brochures.

This company sells the furniture of 300 manufacturers and says it offers discounts of up to 47 percent. Payment by check, money order, Visa, or Mastercard. Shipment by Postal Service, United Parcel, common carrier, or home delivery service. Goods should not be returned without permission of the company.

SIMMS & THAYER CABINETMAKERS, *P.O. Box 35, North Marshfield, Mass. 02059. Tel. (617) 585-8606. Annual 24-page catalogue costs $3.*

This is a specialist in handcrafted reproductions of early American furniture. There are tables, hutches, cupboards, chairs, and chests.

SION-FUK ENTERPRISES, *George & Sons Co., 60 Tahsen Third Rd., Kaohsiung, Taiwan. Tel. (07) 751-5648 or (07) 201-2772. The 20-page catalogue costs $5.*

There are many handsome pieces in this catalogue, including rattan, hand-carved, inlaid, and teak tables, chairs, sofas, screens, desks, and rockers, mostly in Chinese and Japanese style. The Western pieces include grandfather clocks from West Germany and brass beds.

STONE LEDGE CO. *See listing under* Wood Stoves, *below.*

†**STURBRIDGE YANKEE WORKSHOPS,** *Blueberry Rd., Westbrook, Me. 04092 Tel. (207) 774-9045 or (800) 343-1144 (except in Maine). The 48- to 72-page catalogue issued 6 times a year costs $1.*

Traditional American reproductions, including such furniture as rolltop desks, chairs, sofas, tables, and beds, plus clocks, lamps, sconces, hardware, rugs, curtains, art reproductions, china, glassware and flatware, and lots of gifts. Payment by check, money order, American Express, Visa, Mastercard, or Diners Club. Shipment by Postal Service, United Parcel, or common carrier. Refund or credit for purchases returned within 10 days.

VERMONT TUBBS, *P.O. Box 148, Forestdale, Vt. 05745. Tel. (802) 247-3414. Brochure price list.*

Part of the business here is the manufacture of snowshoes, but another part is the making of furniture based on snowshoe construction—rawhide stretched over wooden frames. There are chairs, rockers, and tables. The company also makes a line of contemporary bentwood furniture.

WALPOLE WOODWORKERS, *767 East St., Walpole, Mass. 02081. Tel. (617) 668-2800 or (800) 343-6948 (except in Massachusetts and Hawaii). The 28-page catalogue costs $1.*

The specialty here is handmade indoor and outdoor furniture of cedar, used for its qualities of drying easily, resisting twisting and warping, and resisting decay. There are tables, chairs, benches, stools, carts.

CHARLES WEBB, *Designer/Woodworker, 7 Thorndike St., Cambridge, Mass. Tel. (617) 491-2390. The 30-page catalogue costs $2.*

Handcrafted beds, sofa beds, benches, tables, chests, desks, chairs, mirrors, shelf systems, and bookcases. Payment by check or money order. Shipment by United Parcel, common carrier, or furniture mover. Refunds for goods returned in a "reasonable" number of days.

ROBERT WHITLEY STUDIO, *Box 69, Solebury, Pa. 18963. Tel. (215) 297-8452. The 16-page catalogue costs $4.*

There is one product in this catalogue, a handmade rocking chair that has been much honored. Payment by check or money order. Delivery by Postal Service. Rockers must be returned within 3 days for refund.

*YIELD HOUSE, *North Conway, N.H. 03860. Tel. (800) 258-4720 (except in New Hampshire) or (800) 552-0320 (in New Hampshire). Free 76-page catalogue.*

This company provides discounts of up to 45 percent on furniture, accessories, and gifts. There is a nice anachronism: a home computer stand in an antique finish. There are many pieces for the bath, bedroom, dining room, kitchen, and sewing room, plus lamps, hardware, and cookware. Payment by check, money order, American Express, Visa, or Mastercard. Shipment by Postal Service, United Parcel, or common carrier, and the shipping cost is included in the price of many items. There is an excellent return policy: Anything may be returned for refund or credit within 90 days.

*RICHARD B. ZARBIN & ASSOCIATES, *225 W. Hubbard St., Chicago, Ill. 60610. Tel. (312) 527-1570. No catalogue.*

This is a discount dealer in furniture, bedding, carpets, and accessories. The prices are 40 percent below retail.

See also *For Children, Antiques,* and *Fine and Unusual Gifts.*

Clocks and Clock-Making Kits

ARTISANS COOPERATIVE. *See listing under* Crafts to Buy.

CRAFT PRODUCTS CO. *See listing under* General Craft Supplies.

*EMPEROR CLOCK COMPANY, *Emperor Industrial Park, Fairhope, Ala. 36532. Tel. (205) 928-2316. Free catalogue for clocks; catalogue for other furniture costs $1; free brochures sent 6 to 8 times a year.*

The company says it has discount prices and is the world's largest manufacturer of grandfather clocks, both finished and in kits that need to be assembled and finished. Besides the clocks, which are made in Germany, the company offers a Queen Anne secretary, dining room table and chairs, desks, and other furniture.

KEITH HARDING. *Clocks and clock parts. See listing under* Music Boxes.

HURST ASSOCIATES LTD., *151 Nashdene Rd., Unit 14, Scarborough, Ont., Canada M1V 2T3. Tel. (416) 293-4497. Free annual 44-page catalogue.*

Clocks and parts, plus kits for people who want to do the final assembly themselves. Payment by check, money order, Visa, or Mastercard. Delivery by Postal Service, United Parcel, or Canpar. Refunds for goods returned within 21 days.

MASON & SULLIVAN, *586 Higgins Crowell Rd., West Yarmouth, Mass. 02673. Tel. (617) 775-4643. Quarterly 48-page catalogue costs $1.*

This company provides kits for making clocks according to skill level from the clumsy, like me, to the very skilled. Besides the inner workings and the wooden bodies, clock-making tools are also available. The finished products in the catalogue are handsome. Payment by check, money order, American Express, Visa, Mastercard, Diners Club, or Carte Blanche. Shipment by Postal Service or United Parcel. Purchases may be returned for refund or credit within 30 days after first calling customer service at (617) 778-1056.

S. T. PRESTON & SON. *See listing under* Boating and Fishing Supplies.

EUGENE & ELLEN RENO. *Antique Clocks. See listing under* Antiques.

STRIKE ONE (ISLINGTON) LTD. *Antique Clocks. See listing under* Antiques.

VIKING CLOCK COMPANY, *P.O. Box 490, Foley, Ala. 36536. Tel. (205) 943-5081. Free 16-page catalogue plus 4 flyers each year.*

Clocks made in the factory or provided in kits for final assembly at home. Many models available, including grandfather.

See also *Furniture and Furnishings,* above, and *Fine and Unusual Gifts.*

Bedding, Linens, and Towels

AGATHA'S COZY CORNER, *Woodbury Plaza, Portsmouth, N.H. 03801. Tel. (603) 436-0102 or (800) 258-0857 (except in New Hampshire). Free 36-page catalogue issued twice a year.*

Linens, flannel sheets, down comforters, and towels. Payment by check, money order, American Express, Visa, or Mastercard. Shipment by Postal Service or United Parcel. Purchases may be returned within 30 days for refund.

ARTISANS COOPERATIVE. *See listing under* Crafts to Buy.

EDDIE BAUER. *See listing under* Sporting Goods.

BETTER SLEEP, *New Providence, N.J. 07974 and 57 Industrial Rd., Berkeley Heights, N.J. 07922. Tel. (201) 464-2200. Free 16-page catalogue issued twice a year.*

Pillows, "slants" to raise portions of mattress, cushions for people with arthritis, rheumatism, or fractures. Payment by check, money order, Visa, or Mastercard. Shipment by Postal Service or United Parcel. Refund or credit for merchandise returned within 20 days of receipt.

LAURA COPENHAVER INDUSTRIES. *Quilts, valances, bed canopies, see listing under* Furniture and Furnishings, *above.*

THE COMPANY STORE, *1205 S. Seventh St., La Crosse, Wis. 54601. Tel. (608) 785-1400, (800) 356-9367 (except in Wisconsin), or (608) 788-9910 in Wisconsin. (Call collect). Free 20- to 30-page catalogue issued 4 to 6 times a year.*

All down products, at least 50 percent off the list price, they say, that "one pays if one buys our merchandise from the retailers we supply—Nieman-Marcus, Bloomies, Marshall Field's, Saks, Lord & Taylor." Besides down comforters and pillows, there are Bill Blass coats and Gloria Vanderbilt robes.

THE COTTON COMPANY. *See listing under* Men's and Women's Clothing.

CUDDLEDOWN. *See listing under* Hosiery, Lingerie, Underwear, and Lounge Wear.

DOWN HOME COMFORTS, *Box 281, West Brattleboro, Vt. 05301. No Telephone. The 8-page catalogue costs $1.*

Department of Yankee Independence: Most places in this book that don't have phones are in New England. This is a small company dealing with made-to-order new and remade comforters, pillows, and featherbeds. Payment by check or money order. Shipment by Postal Service or United Parcel. In answer to my inquiry about return policy, the owner said, "Will revise order to fit. Bedding laws prevent return of used merchandise."

FEATHERED FRIENDS, *155 Western Ave. W., Seattle, Wash. 98119. Tel. (206) 282-5673 or (800) 426-2724 (except in Washington State, Alaska, and Hawaii). Annual 16-page catalogue costs $1.*

Down comforters and sleeping bags.

DAS FEDERBETT, *961 Gapter Rd., Boulder, Colo. 80303. Tel. (303) 494-2343. Free brochures.*

A featherbed, it is explained to us New Worlders, is an unquilted shell filled with down. It encloses the sleeper and keeps him or her (or both?) warm and is something widely used in Europe and Asia. Payment by check or money order. Shipment by United Parcel. No returns.

FUTON-TO-SLEEP-ON. *Quilts, sheets, pillows. See listing under* Furniture and Furnishings, *above.*

GARNET HILL, *Box 262, Franconia, N.H. 03580. Tel. (603) 823-5545. Semiannual 28- to 52-page catalogue costs $1 for a 2-year subscription that includes flannel swatches with the first catalogue.*

This company started the Flannel Sheet Revolution. Its very nice catalogue shows natural-fiber sheets, comforters, pillows, blankets, sleepwear, and underwear. The firm's good neighbors served as models, and they look a little nervous in their underwear, but who wouldn't? Payment by check, money order, American Express, Visa, Mastercard, or Diners Club. Shipment by Postal Service or United Parcel. Goods may be returned unused within 30 days for refund or credit.

HALLIE GREER. *Pillows and bed linens, as well as napkins and coasters for the dining table. See listing under* Wall Coverings and Curtains, *below.*

HOMESPUN CRAFTS, *Box 1776, Blacksburg, S.C. 29702 Tel. (704) 937-7611. Semiannual 24-page catalogue costs $1.25.*

This company has lots of things for Colonial homes. The emphasis is on bedspreads, blankets, sheets, ruffles, and sleepwear. Other products include curtains, rugs, pewter flatware, and towels.

ROBINSON'S WALLCOVERINGS. *See listing under* Wall Coverings and Curtains, *below.*

RUSSELLS QUILT CO., *4032 Tweedy Blvd., South Gate, Calif. 90280. Tel. (213) 569-1512. Brochure price list costs $1.*

Down and feather quilts, comforters, and pillows.

*J. SCHACHTER CORP., *115 Allen St., New York, N.Y. 10002. Tel. (212) 533-1150. Annual 16-page catalogue costs $1.*

This company has discounts of 20 to 40 percent below retail on sheets, comforters (including down), towels, mattress pads, and blankets.

SCINTILLA SATIN SHOP. *See listing under* Hosiery, Lingerie, Underwear, and Lounge Wear.

THE SHOPPERS' PARADISE. *See listing under* Fine and Unusual Gifts.

ST. PATRICK'S DOWN, *St. Patrick's Mills, Douglas, Cork, Ireland. Tel. 021-931111. Quarterly 24-page catalogue costs $1.*

This shop sells a featherbed for warmth, a patchwork quilt, and other bedding. A recent catalogue offered a free Irish wool sweater with each purchase of a comforter or other major item. Payment by check, money order, American Express, Visa, Mastercard, or Diners Club. Purchases may be returned within 14 days for credit.

†THE STEVENS CATALOGUE, *7 Commercial Dr., Greenville, S.C. 29607. Tel. (803) 233-6770 or (800) 845-8793. Free 32-page catalogue issued 4 times a year.*

Sheets, pillow cases, women's sleepwear, comforters, draperies, and towels from one of America's best known manufacturers. A gift service is available. Payment by check, money order, American Express, Visa, or Mastercard. Delivery by United Parcel. Goods may be returned for refund or credit within 2 weeks of delivery, but monogrammed, used, or laundered items are not returnable.

NORM THOMPSON. *See listing under* Casual and Sports Clothing.

TOUCH OF CLASS CATALOGUE, *Huntingburg, Ind. 47542. Tel. (812) 683-3707 or (800) 457-7456 (except in Indiana, Alaska, and Hawaii). Free 40-page catalogue.*

Bed linens, down pillows and comforters, women's nightgowns. Payment by check, money order, American Express, Visa, Mastercard, Diners Club, or Carte Blanche. Shipment by United Parcel whenever possible; Postal Service is used otherwise. Returns accepted for refund.

*WARM THINGS, *180 Paul Drive, San Raphael, Calif. 94903. Tel. (415) 472-2154. Free annual 8-page catalogue.*

Down quilts, pillows, covers, and robes. Warehouse sales, inventory clearance, and white sales offer discounts of 20 to 65 percent. Payment by check, money order, Visa, or Mastercard. Shipment by Postal Service or United Parcel. Refund or credit for returns within 15 days.

See also *Army and Navy Goods.*

Lamps and Lighting Fixtures

ALADDIN SERVICE & PRODUCTS, *Box 100960, Nashville, Tenn. 37210. Tel. (615) 748-3693, (800) 251-4535 (except in Tennessee). In Tennessee (615) 748-3000. A 4-page brochure price list.*

Electric lamps, many made of brass, and ceramic lampshades. Genuine oil lamps and kerosene heaters also available. Payment by check, money order, Visa, or Mastercard. Shipment by Postal Service or United Parcel. Refunds or credit for merchandise returned within 30 days or warranty period.

AUTHENTIC DESIGNS, *The Mill Road, West Rupert, Vt. 05776. Tel. (802) 394-7713. The 64-page catalogue costs $3.*

Handcrafted re-creations and adaptations of early American lighting fixtures. They are handsome items. Payment by check, money order, Visa, or Mastercard.

Shipment by Postal Service, United Parcel, or truck. Refunds for items returned within 6 months.

THE BRASS LANTERN, *353 Franklin St., Duxbury, Mass. 02332. Tel. (617) 837-2591. The 12-page catalogue costs 25 cents.*

The shop provides superior handcrafted brass lamps at reasonable prices.

BRUBAKER METALCRAFTS, *P.O. Box 353, Eaton, Ohio 45320. Tel. (513) 456-5834. Free brochure price list.*

Offered here are handmade reproductions of Colonial candle holders and lanterns.

CHASE COLLECTION. *See listing under* Fine and Unusual Gifts.

THE COPPER HOUSE, *R.F.D. 1, Route 4, Epsom, N.H. 03234 Tel. (603) 736-9798. Catalogue costs $1.*

Many copper lamps and also a large line of weather vanes.

DUTCH PRODUCTS & SUPPLY CO. *See listing under* Wall Coverings and Curtains, *below.*

HERITAGE LANTERNS, *70A Main St., Yarmouth, Me. 04096. Tel. (207) 846-3911. The 48-page catalogue costs $2.*

Copper, brass, and pewter lamps, lights, lanterns, globes, and sconces for electric lights or candles. Payment by check, money order, Visa, or Mastercard. Shipment by United Parcel. Refund or credit for returned goods, except for custom-made pieces.

HISTORIC CHARLESTON REPRODUCTIONS. *See listing under* Museum, Botanic Garden, and Public Radio Gift Catalogues.

HURLEY PATENTEE LIGHTING, *R.D. 7, Box 98a, Kingston, N.Y. 12401. Tel. (914) 331-5414. The 16-page catalogue costs $2.*

Handmade reproductions of Colonial sconces, lamps, and chandeliers, some for use with candles and others with electric light bulbs.

IRVIN'S CRAFT SHOP, *R.D. 1, Box 45, Mt. Pleasant Mills, Pa. 17853. Tel. (717) 539-8200. The 28-page catalogue costs $1.*

Handcrafted reproductions of lamps, lanterns, and candle holders in tin, copper, and brass, most also available with electrical wiring.

CHARLES KEATH LIMITED. *See listing under* Fine and Unusual Gifts.

KING'S CHANDELIER CO., *P.O. Box 667, Eden, N.C. 27288. Tel. (919) 623-6188. Annual 96-page catalogue costs $2.*

This company has been in business for 50 years; it says its prices are comparable to (and often lower than) wholesale prices for chandeliers of comparable quality elsewhere.

GEORGE KOVACS LIGHTING, *24 W. 40th St., New York, N.Y. 10018. Tel. (212) 944-9606. Annual 12-page catalogue costs 50 cents.*

Contemporary lighting fixtures. Payment by check, money order, American Express, Visa, or Mastercard. Shipment by United Parcel or freight carrier. Refunds on returned mail orders.

LEHMAN HARDWARE & APPLIANCES. *See listing under* Tools and Equipment for Craftspeople, Tinkerers, and Do-It-Yourselfers.

NOWELL'S, *Box 164, Sausalito, Calif. 94966. Tel. (415) 332-4933. The 52-page catalogue costs $3.50.*

This is a handsome catalogue of Victorian lighting fixtures, with many nice brass items. Payment by check, money order, Visa, or Mastercard. Shipment by Postal Service or United Parcel. Returns accepted for refund within 5 days.

S. T. PRESTON & SON. *See listing under* Boating and Fishing Supplies.

ST. LOUIS ANTIQUE LIGHTING CO., *25 N. Sarah, St. Louis, Mo. 63108. Tel. (314) 535-2770. Catalogue costs $3.*

This company has a large line of attractive reproductions of Victorian ceiling lights, lamps, and sconces. Payment by check, money order, Visa, or Mastercard. Shipment by United Parcel. Refund or credit for lamps returned within 30 days, less 20 percent restocking fee.

*THE UNDERGROUND, *311-1/2 S. 11th St., Tacoma, Wash. 98402. Tel. (206) 383-2041. Semiannual catalogue of 12 to 14 pages costs $1.50.*

Discount prices on Aladdin lamps and other items, including cookware and water purifiers.

VERMONT INDUSTRIES, *The Blacksmith Shop, Box 301, Route 103, Cuttingville, Vt. 05738. Tel. (802) 492-3451. Semiannual 10-page catalogue costs $1.*

Lamps and candle holders are among the principal handmade products made at this re-creation of a late 19th-century hand-forging shop. Other items include fireplace equipment and iron and wood benches.

WASHINGTON COPPER WORKS, *Washington, Conn. 06793. Tel. (203) 868-7527. Annual 44-page catalogue costs $2.*

Handmade lamps, lanterns, and sconces, to be used with candles, kerosene, or electricity. Payment by check, Visa, or Mastercard. Shipment by United Parcel. Refunds for returned goods.

LT. MOSES WILLARD, *Tinker/Whittler, 7805 Railroad Ave., Cincinnati, Ohio 45243. Tel. (513) 561-3942. Catalogue costs $2.*

This is a manufacturer of Colonial and folk art reproduction lighting. It previously was known as Colonial Tin Craft. Payment by check, money order, Visa, or Mastercard. Shipment by United Parcel or common carrier. Goods may be returned within 5 days for refund.

See also *Furniture and Furnishings,* **above,** *Hardware for the Home,* **below, and** *Country and General Stores.*

Wall Coverings and Curtains

DELFT BLUE LTD. *Wall tiles. See listing under* Cookware and Dinnerware.

DUTCH PRODUCTS & SUPPLY CO., *P.O. Box 296, Yardley, Pa. 19067. Tel. (215) 493-4873. The 4-page catalogue costs $1.*

Royal Delft tiles for walls, fireplace facings, and accent spots in the kitchen, bathroom, or playroom. This company also offers Colonial chandeliers in brass or brass with Delft-Polychrome or Limoges parts, and there are also some of pewter. The company is mainly wholesale and prefers to do business through retail stores, but it does make literature available and will sell to people who do not live near a store carrying its products.

HALLIE GREER, *P.O. Box 165, Cushing Corners Rd., Freedom, N.H. 03836. Tel. (603) 539-6007. Semiannual 10-page catalogue costs $2.*

Curtains, drapes, and wall coverings in country fabrics. One print has medallions of farm animals flanked by floral borders, another uses heather to cover the full fabric. The fabrics are also made up into napkins and coasters for the dining table, pillows and bed linens, and sundresses and jackets.

LOVELIA ENTERPRISES, *356 E. 41st St., New York, N.Y. 10017. Tel. (212) 490-0930. The 20-page catalogue costs $4.*

Fine tapestries from Belgium, France, and Italy. These can be used not only for wall hangings but also put in frames, to upholster furniture, and cover pillows. The company says it is the largest importer of tapestries in the country.

*MUTUAL WALLPAPER & PAINT CO., *812 W. Main St., Louisville, Ky. 40202. Tel. (502) 583-0525. Catalogues, issued every 2 years, cost 35 cents for regular wallpaper and $1 for vinyl and for flock.*

These are utilitarian catalogues with pages made of wallpaper samples and the descriptions printed on the undecorated sides. Prices are 50 percent below retail.

KAREN NELSON, *P.O. Box 425, 80 Franklin St., New York, N.Y. 10013. Tel. (212) 925-5582. Catalogue costs $5.*

Miss Nelson makes tapestries that are priced from $3,000 to $10,000, so after seeing the reproductions in the catalogue and before writing out a check you might want to look at the real thing. Payment by check.

*ROBINSON'S WALLCOVERINGS, *225 W. Spring St., Titusville, Pa. 16354. Tel. (814) 827-1893. Annual 58-page catalogue costs $1.*

Another discount wallpaper company that uses its wallpaper for the pages of its catalogue. Besides a large selection of wallpaper, the company offers such bedroom furnishings as curtains, bedspreads, and quilts.

See also *Furniture and Furnishings,* and *Bedding, Linens, and Towels,* above.

Floor Coverings

THE FREED CO. *See listings under* Men's and Women's Clothing.

HERITAGE RUGS, *P.O. Box 404, Lahaska, Pa. 18931. Tel. (215) 794-7229. Brochure price list.*

These are hand-woven rag rugs custommade to meet particular needs. "Just send us the colors you would like to have woven into your rug by paint colors, wallpaper samples or fabric swatches and we will create the rug especially for your room," the brochure says. Payment by check, money order, Visa, or Mastercard. Shipment by United Parcel or motor freight. No returns on custom-made articles.

HOMESPUN CRAFTS. *See listing under* Bedding, Linens, and Towels, *above.*

CHARLES W. JACOBSEN, *Oriental Rugs, 401 S. Salina St., Syracuse, N.Y. 13202. Tel. (315) 422-7832. A 16-page catalogue.*

This company imports and sells Oriental rugs. The customer makes a tentative selection and the rugs are shipped by motor freight or United Parcel. After 7 days, if the customer wants to keep a rug, he or she sends a check or money order; if not, the rugs are shipped back to the company at its expense. The company also sells books about Oriental rugs.

D. MACGILLIVRAY & CO. *See listing under* Men's and Women's Clothing.

MOTOR SHEEP. *Sheepskin rugs. See lisiting under* Automotive Needs.

THE SHOPPER'S PARADISE. *See listing under* Fine and Unusual Gifts.

THOS. K. WOODARD, *American Antiques & Quilts, 835 Madison Ave., New York, N.Y. 10021. Tel (212) 988-2906. Annual 16-page catalogue costs $5.*

Rugs, stair runners, and mats in classic early American designs. Payment by check, money order, American Express, Visa, or Mastercard. Shipment by United Parcel. Rugs may be returned within 2 days of receipt for refund.

See also *Furniture and Furnishings,* **above, and** *Crafts to Buy.*

Closet Accessories and Storage Trunks

ANTIQUE TRUNK CO., *3706 W. 169 St., Cleveland, Ohio 44111. Tel (216) 941-8618. The 12-page catalogue costs 50 cents.*

This company says it is the country's largest supplier of antique trunk repair parts. Shipment by Postal Service or United Parcel. Purchases may be returned within 60 days for refund.

CHARLOTTE FORD TRUNKS, *Box 536, Spearman, Tex. 79081. Tel. (806) 659-3027. The 40-page catalogue costs $1.*

"Heirloom Treasures From Antique Trunks" is the motto of this company. Pay-

ment by check or money order. Shipment by Postal Service or United Parcel. Purchases may be returned for refund.

CLOSET SHOP AT HOME, *7833 Spring Ave., Elkins Park, Pa. 19117. Tel. (215) 825-5821. Annual 16-page catalogue costs $1.*

Is your closet a mess? This company makes closet organizers to get things under control. Payment by check, money order, Visa, or Mastercard. Shipment by Postal Service or United Parcel. Purchases may be returned for credit.

Hardware for the Home

ANGLO-AMERICAN BRASS CO., *P.O. Box 9792, San Jose, Calif. 95157. Tel. (408) 246-0203, (408) 246-3232, or (800) 222-7277 (except in California). Annual 20-page catalogue cots $1.50.*

Fine brass reproductions of handles, hinges, locks, keys, keyholes, and hooks available direct from this manufacturer. Lots of Victorian influence here.

BALL & BALL, *463 W. Lincoln Highway, Exton, Pa. 19341. Tel. (215) 363-7330. The 108-page main catalogue costs $5; quarterly supplemental catalogues are free.*

This manufacturer of reproduction Victorian hardware (also available are reproduction 18th-century lighting fixtures and even earlier house hardware and accessories), is more than 50 years old, and has a huge selection of pulls, escutcheons, knobs, hinges, finials, and clock fittings. Among its reproductions are a half dozen chandeliers from the meeting room of Independence Hall in Philadelphia, which it copied from the single surviving original of the set. There are also many other chandeliers and lighting fixtures, for candles or light bulbs, made by Ball & Ball.

*BLAINE HARDWARE INTERNATIONAL, *1919 Blaine Dr., Route 4, Hagerstown, Md. 21740. Tel. (301) 797-6500, Ext. 707, or (800) 638-3042 (except in Maryland). Annual 48-page catalogue cots $2.50.*

Replacement hardware for homes, institutions, and commercial places, including parts for patio doors, windows, screens, handles, rollers. There is a page of grab bars for the handicapped. Quantity discounts are available.

THE BROADWAY COLLECTION, *250 N. Troost, Olathe, Kans. 66061. Tel. (913) 782-6244 or (800) 255-6365. The 100-page catalogue costs $5.*

The mail order division of this company sells to people who do not live near Broadway's dealers. The catalogue is encyclopedic, including European and American styles in bathroom sink and tub fittings, switch plates, knockers, hooks, hinges, pulls, escutcheons, door knobs.

ELGIN ENGRAVING CO., *940 Edwards Ave., Dundee, Ill. 60118. Tel. (312) 428-1992. Free Annual 18-page catalogue.*

Engraved metal objects, including brass doorplates, door knockers, dog tags, even your name engraved on the head of a pin.

DAVID H. FLETCHER, *Blue Mist Morgan Farm, 68 Liberty St., Haverhill, Mass. 01830. Tel. (617) 374-8783. Annual 20-page catalogue costs $3.*

Handcrafted copper weather vanes and lanterns from a 100-year-old concern that has 75 models from which to choose, and if that isn't enough, they'll do custom work.

HORTON BRASSES, *Nooks Hill Rd., P.O. Box 120, Cromwell, Conn. 06416. Tel. (203) 635-4400. The 36-page catalogue costs $2.*

This company makes 450 kinds of reproduction pieces from the 1680's to the 1920's. There are pulls, escutcheons, knobs, hinges, clock parts, even reproductions of nails, plus how-to and history books on furniture and houses. Payment by check or money order. Shipment by Postal Service or United Parcel. Goods may be returned within 30 days for refund, less 15 percent restocking charge.

KAYNE & SON CUSTOM FORGED HARDWARE, *Route 4, Box 275A, Candler, N.C. 28715. Tel. (704) 667-8868. The 16-page catalogue on Colonial hardware costs $2; 24-page catalogue on hand-forged hardware also costs $2; both of them cost $3.50.*

The Colonial line is made of cast bronze and brass (hinges pulls, handles, knockers, etc.) and the hand-forged pieces include steel pulls, latches, hinges, fireplace tools, and kitchen equipment. Payment by check, money order, or C.O.D. Shipment by Postal Service or United Parcel. Refund or credit for returned merchandise.

*PAXTON HARDWARE LTD., *7818 Bradshaw Rd., Upper Falls, Md. 21156. Tel. (301) 592-8505. Annual 62-page catalogue cots $2.50.*

Discounts are offered for quantity purchases of such things as doorknobs (Victorian, antique, ceramic, and brass), pulls, escutcheons, casters, hooks, hinges, locks, and latches, plus many parts for lamps and chandeliers, and many glass lamp shades.

REMODELER'S SUPPLY CO., *P.O. Box 92, Highway 18, Garrison, Minn. 56450. Tel. (612) 692-4498. Brochure price lists.*

Good-looking brass and chrome-plated plumbing fixtures for kitchens and bathrooms; hot tubs and whirlpool baths; toilets and bidets. There are also accessories for stoves and fireplaces, plus lamps and lighting fixtures.

THE RENOVATOR'S SUPPLY, *Old Mill, Millers Falls, Mass. 01349. Tel. (413) 659-2211. The 56-page catalogue issued 4 to 6 times a year costs $1.*

Many pieces for restoring an old house, including hardware (pulls, escutcheons, hinges, latches, and doorknobs), lamps and lighting fixtures, candlesticks, plumbing fixtures, weathervanes, and fireplace fixtures. Payment by check, money order, Visa, or Mastercard. Shipment by Postal Service or United Parcel. Refunds for purchases returned within 30 days.

S. CHRIS RHEINSCHILD, *2220 Carlton Way, Santa Barbara, Calif. 93109. Tel. (805) 962-8598. The 10-page catalogue costs $1.35.*

How many catalogues have a toilet on the front page? This one does! It probably violates every marketing rule in the textbooks but is very effective, since the toilet is one of those old-fashioned types that you see from time to time in England, but almost never in the U.S., with the water tank about 6 feet above the floor and ready to roar into a torrent at the pull of a chain. Mr. Rheinschild makes reproductions of Victorian toilets, bathroom and kitchen sinks, and bathtubs. This is one supplier I'll keep in mind when we move into our Victorian house in Washington.

SQUAW ALLEY, *401 S. Main St., Naperville, Ill. 60540. Tel. (312) 357-0200. The 76-page catalogue costs $3.*

Brass reproduction pulls, knobs, escutcheons, hinges, locks, some wood, some porcelain. This catalogue is very descriptive and nicely organized. There is a separate section on lighting, with copies of antique fittings and glass shades. The company also carries antiques.

SUNRISE SPECIALTY & SALVAGE CO., *2210 San Pablo Ave., Berkeley, Calif. 94702. Tel. (415) 845-4751. The 16-page catalogue costs $2.*

This place has lots of old-fashioned fittings and fixtures for the bathroom. There are faucets, drains, spouts, shower heads, tubs, showers, water closets, and towel bars. The materials are brass, china, and wood. The catalogue is well illustrated and the products are obviously handsome.

YIELD HOUSE. *See listing under* Furniture and Furnishings, *above.*

Wood Stoves, Solar Devices, Insulating Materials, Heaters, Windmills, and Armageddon Supplies

ALADDIN SERVICES & PRODUCTS. *Kerosene heaters. See listing under* Lamps and Lighting Fixtures, *above.*

ANCHOR TOOLS & WOODSTOVES, *2761 N.W. Savier, Portland, Ore. 97210. Tel. (503) 224-7868 or (503) 223-3452. No catalogue.*

This compnay is a custom finding service. It seeks out archaic, rare, or out-of-production materials, especially hand-operated woodworking tools. Write and let them know what you are looking for. Payment by check, money order, Visa, or Mastercard. Shipment by Postal Service, United Parcel, or air or motor freight. No returns are accepted.

BRYANT STOVE WORKS, *P.O. Box 2048, Thorndike, Me. 04986. Tel. (207) 568-3665. The 24-page catalogue costs $2, and there is a free brochure.*

They certainly should know a lot about keeping warm in Maine. These pieces look great. They are low-tech—they don't make music, solve problems, or answer riddles; they just keep you warm.

THE CONSERVATION STORE, *1889 Avenue Rd., Toronto, Ont., Canada M5M 3Z9, Tel. (416) 789-4159. Semiannual catalogue costs $1.*

All kinds of ways to keep the cold out, including window quilts.

CORNERSTONES. *Information on insulation and solar equipment. See listing under* Building and Architectural Supplies, *below.*

THE DRAWING-ROOM GRAPHIC SERVICES LTD., *Box 86627, North Vancouver, B.C., Canada V7L 4L2. No Telephone. Free annual 20-page catalogue.*

Books on "how to live comfortably in concert with the natural cycles of the earth," covering such things as solar heating and insulation. Payment by check, money order, American Express, Visa, or Mastercard. Shipment by Postal Service. Refund or credit for returned books.

ENERGY ALTERNATIVES LTD., *P.O. Box 671, Amherst, N.S., B4H 4B4, Canada. Annual 40-page catalogue costs $1.*

Here are wood stoves that keep homes warm and good-looking, plus lots of energy-saving accessories. Payment by check, money order, Visa, or Mastercard. Delivery by Postal Service.

ENERSHADE LTD., *40 Norwich St. East, Guelph, Ont. Canada N1H 2G6. Tel. (519) 821-8998. Free 4-page brochure sent to people who provide a stamped self-addressed envelope.*

Insulating shades and curtains to keep your heat from escaping through your windows; these are finished in attractive colors and designs. Payment by check or money order. Delivery by Postal Service. Goods may be returned within 30 days for credit.

HEARTHSTONE, *R.D. 1, Morrisville, Vt. 05661. Tel. (802) 888-4586. The 16-page catalogue costs $1.*

Informative, colorful catalogue of soapstone stoves.

113

LEHMAN HARDWARE & APPLIANCES. *See listing under* Tools and Equipment for Craftspeople, Tinkerers, and Do-It-Yourselfers.

LEMEE'S FIREPLACE EQUIPMENT, *815 Bedford St., Bridgewater, Mass. 02324. Tel. (617) 697-2672. Biennial 36-page catalogue costs $1.*

Payment by check or money order. Shipment by United Parcel. Credit given for returns made "within a few weeks."

O'BROCK WINDMILL DISTRIBUTORS, *9435 12th St., North Benton, Ohio 44449. Tel. (216) 584-4681. Semiannual 40-page catalogue costs $2, refundable with order.*

Harness the Wind is the name of this catalogue, which offers windmills, towers, pumps, etc. Here's a good idea: For a $25 refundable deposit, you can borrow a video tape that shows windmills being erected. Payment by check or money order. Shipment by Postal Service, United Parcel, or motor freight. Purchases may be returned for refund within 30 days.

PATENTED PRODUCTS. *Electric bed warmers. See listing under,* Audio and Video Equipment.

PROVISIONS UNLIMITED. *Windmills. See listing under* Grains and Vegetables, Natural and Freeze-Dried Foods.

R. D. ASSOCIATES, *P.O. Box 99, New Rochelle, N.Y. 10804. Tel. (914) 636-8699. Annual 44-page catalogue costs $1, refundable with order.*

The catalogue, called *Energy Savers,* is filled with devices to do just that. There are devices to get more heat out of radiators, to keep hot water hot, to get more hours out of light bulbs.

REMODELER'S SUPPLY CO., *See listing under* Hardware for the Home, *above.*

SOLAR COMPONENTS CORP., *P.O. Box 237, Manchester, N.H. 03105. Tel. (603) 668-8186 or (800) 258-3072 (for credit card orders). Free 88-page catalogue issued twice a year.*

This company sells greenhouses, sunspaces, solar rooms, glazing systems, and the like.

STONE LEDGE, *170 Washington St., Marblehead, Mass. 01945. Tel. (617) 631-8417. Brochure price list costs $1.*

This company is the U.S. importer of wood-burning and coal-burning stoves and furniture manufactured by Godin of France. The stoves are as decorative as they are warming. Americans may not be familiar with the artistic designs of those handsome European stoves with the ironwork first embossed and then painted in enamel. Most of the stoves are sold through dealers, but Stone Ledge will sell directly to consumers who do not live near those dealers. The Godin furniture, including such pieces as lawn benches and pedestal tables, also relies on cast iron.

THE SURVIVAL CENTER. *Windmills, bomb shelters, heaters. See listing under* Grains and Vegetables, Natural and Freeze-Dried Foods.

THERMAX CORP., *1 Mill St., Burlington, Vt., 05401. Tel. (802) 658-1098. (In Canada, 39 Main St., Vankleek Hill, Ont. K0B 1R0. Tel. (613) 678-3322. Brochure price list.*

Windmills to generate electricity. Payment by check, money order, American Express, Visa, or Mastercard. Shipment by Postal Service or United Parcel. Purchases may be returned for refund or credit within 15 days.

VERMONT STOVE COMPANY, *Route 7, Box 368, Shelburne, Vt. 05482. Tel. (802) 862-7081 or (800) 343-2577 (except in Vermont). Frequent 24-page catalogues cost $1 or nothing.*

Available here are fireplace inserts that are designed to cut down on the amount of wood burned while increasing the heat provided. Payment by check, money order, American Express, Visa, or Mastercard. Stoves are shipped by common carrier, parts by United Parcel. Refund or credit for material returned within 30 days.

†THE WARMING TREND, *Box 1184, Manchester Center, Vt. 05255. Tel. (802) 362-4111. Semiannual 32-page catalogue costs $1.*

Accessories for woodstoves and fireplaces, plus devices for improving their efficiency. Also, insulating materials and related products for the home.

WINDOWBLANKET CO. *107 Broadway, P.O. Box 540, Lenoir City, Tenn. 37771. Tel. (615) 986-2115. Free brochure.*

This company makes a replacement for drapes that is supposed to keep the cold out in the winter, the heat out in the summer, and the noise out year round.

Hot Tubs and Saunas

BARREL BUILDERS. *See listing under* Wine- and Beer-Making Supplies. *That sounds weird but it isn't, since Barrel Builders makes wine barrels, and it's an easy leap from there to hot tubs.*

*THE BEDPOST. *See listing under* Furniture and Furnishings, *above.*

NORDIC SAUNA, *941 E. San Carlos Ave., San Carlos, Calif. 94070. Tel. (415) 592-1818. Free catalogue.*

This company manufactures its own saunas and wine cellars and sells directly to the public, thus avoiding "middle-man" markups. Payment by check. Shipment by United Parcel or, on larger items common carrier. Refunds for returns within guarantee period, usually a year.

REMODELER'S SUPPLY CO. *See lisitng under* Hardware for the Home, *above.*

SPRING MOUNTAIN ENERGY SYSTEMS, *2617 San Pablo Ave., Berkeley, Calif. 94702. Tel. (415) 841-3000. Brochure price list.*

Hot tubs and heaters to warm the water. Payment by check or money order. Delivery by Postal Service or truck freight. Refunds given on defective equipment returned within 15 days.

Building and Architectural Supplies

THE BLAIRHAMPTON ALTERNATIVE, *Box 748, Haliburton, Ont., Canada K0M 1S0. Catalogue costs $5.*

This is for people who want to build their own log cabins. The suppliers are ecologically concerned people who pledge to plant trees to replace all those used in their buildings and those of their customers. Payment by check or money order. Shipment by Postal Service. Purchases may be returned for refund if they are unused.

CORNERSTONES, *54 Cumberland St., Brunswick, Me. 04011. Tel. (207) 729-6701. Annual 36-page catalogue costs $2.*

The product here is information: courses in building houses, insulating existing houses, and installing solar equipment. There is a large selection of house-building books.

CROWTHER OF SYON LODGE. *Architectural antiques. See listing under* Antiques.

DILWORTH MANUFACTURING CO., *P.O. Box 158, Honey Brook, Pa. 19344. Tel. (717) 354-8956. Brochure price list.*

Heavy-duty Plexiglas covers that fit over basement window wells. Payment by check, money order, Visa, or Mastercard. Shipment by United Parcel or freight. Purchases may be returned for refund within 30 days.

HOME PLANNERS INC., *23761 Research Dr., Farmington Hills, Mich. 48024. Tel. (313) 477-1850. Several catalogues ranging in price from $2.75 to $8.95.*

If you are serious about building your own house, this company has many plans available. One catalogue offers 165 affordable house plans, another 400 plans in early American, Tudor, and other designs, and one is an encyclopedia of 450 house plans.

MYLEN INDUSTRIES, *650 Washington St., Peekskill, N.Y 10566. Tel. (914) 739-8486, (212) 585-6767, or (800) 431-2155 (except in New York State.) Annual catalogue costs 50 cents.*

This company supplies architectural and spiral stairways. Payment by check or money order. Shipment by common carrier.

❖7 Collectibles and Decorations

All kinds of things, some of them very ordinary—such as old maps, lead soldiers, posters, and even old milk pails—can find new life as antiques. A surprisingly wide selection of art and antiques is available by mail, including statues, paintings, prints, posters and antique pottery.

Film posters were hardly recognized as an art form when Hollywood started printing movie posters to draw customers into the-aters. Now thay are in great demand, with originals fetching high prices, especially for such cult movies as *Casablanca* or such big hits as *Gone With the Wind*. Reproductions can be purchased at reasonable prices.

The focus in this chapter is mainly on things people buy for display, although many of the items—such as antique clocks and jewelry—can be used as well.

Antiques

*ANTIQUE IMPORTS UNLIMITED, *P.O. Box 2978, Covington, La. 70434. Tel. (504) 892-0014. Catalogue costs $1.*

A wholesaler that says its prices are 40 to 60 percent below retail, this company specializes in antique and collectible jewelry and also carries many antique maps. It formerly operated in Ireland and England under the name of Gand Ltd. Payment by check, money order, Visa, or Mastercard. Shipment by Postal Service. Full refund, less postage and packing charge, for purchases returned within 10 days of receipt and in the same condition.

N. BLOOM & SON (ANTIQUES) LTD., *40 Conduit St., London, W1, England. Tel. (01) 629-5060. Annual 8-page catalogue costs $3.*

More than 200 items are shown in the catalogue, including Victorian, Edwardian, Art Deco, and Imperial Russian pieces of jewelry. Payment by check, American Express, Visa, Mastercard, Diners Club, or bank-to-bank transfer. Shipment by air mail. Any unsatisfactory item may be returned promptly in same condition for refund.

*BURNHAM-CAMPBELL GALLERIES LTD., *200 Front St., Greenport, N.Y. 11944. Tel. (516) 477-2121. Free annual 20-page catalogue.*

Antiques and old furniture. Reproductions are offered at discount prices; for example, an English brass lamp that lists for $120 is offered here for $72. Payment by check, money order, American Express, Visa, or Mastercard. Shipment by United Parcel. Purchases may be returned within 30 days for refund.

CROWTHER OF SYON LODGE, *Syon Lodge, London Road, Isleworth, Middlesex, TW7 5BH, England. Tel. (01) 560-7978. Free annual catalogues.*

One catalogue offers period paneled rooms from old English houses, and another has architectural antiques, such as a wrought iron gate from a manor built in 1740.

CHARLES EDE LTD., *37 Brook St., London, W1Y 1AJ, England. Tel. (01) 493-4944. Annual subscription to about 9 subject catalogues costs 5 English pounds sterling; there is no charge for a single catalogue.*

The catalogues in a recent year were *Attic Pottery, Corinthian and East Greek Pottery, Cypriot Pottery, Egyptian Sculpture, Etruscan Pottery, Greek Pottery from South Italy, Persian Bronzes, Roman Glass, Terra Cotta Scuplture,* and *Writing and Lettering in Antiquity.* Payment by check or money order. Shipment by Postal Service or air freight. No returns accepted, but objects are guaranteed to be as catalogued.

ELIZABETH EDGE STUDIOS. *Reproductions of antique toys. See listing under* Fine and Unusual Gifts.

FOREIGN TRADERS. *See listing under* Furniture and Furnishings.

*A. GOTO, *1-23-9 Hiashi, Shibuya-ku, Tokyo, Japan. Price list costs $1.*

Since the stock is subject to change on a weekly basis, there is no catalogue; instead, the company sends out price lists with current offerings. The antiques are said to be from about 1850 to 1900 and include wood block prints, carvings, silver, scrimshaw, cloisonné, snuff and opium boxes, beads, and bottles. The prices are said to be ¼ or ½ of what one would expect to pay in a retail store. Payment by money order. Shipment by Postal Service. No returns accepted.

KENDAL PLAYING CARD SALES. *See listing under* Games and Toys.

EUGENE & ELLEN RENO, *Box 191, Lawrence, Mass. 01842. Tel. (603) 898-7426. Quarterly 4-page price list costs $3 per year.*

A wide range of antiques, including china, glass, toys, dolls, miniatures, jewelry, clothing, and clocks. Payment by check or money order. Shipment by Postal Service or United Parcel. Purchases may be returned for refund within 10 days.

RONIN GALLERY, *605 Madison Ave., New York, N.Y. 10022. Tel. (212) 688-0188. Semiannual 24-page catalogue costs $3.*

Antique and contemporary Japanese prints, netsuke, pottery. Payment by check, money order, American Express, Visa, or Mastercard. Shipment by Postal Service or United Parcel. Refunds or credit for returned purchases.

L. H. SELMAN LTD. *Paperweights. See listing under* Cloissoné, Lacquerware, Paperweights, and Collector's Plates, *below.*

SQUAW ALLEY. *See listing under* Hardware for the Home.

STRIKE ONE (ISLINGTON) LTD., *51 Camden Passage, London, N1 8EA, England. Tel. (01) 226-9709. Free 12-page catalogue issued twice a year.*

Antique clocks, watches, and barometers. The shop will negotiate special prices with overseas buyers. Payment by check, money order, American Express, Visa, Mastercard, Diners Club, or Carte Blanche. Shipment by Postal Service or air freight. No returns.

See also ***Paintings, Prints, Posters, Maps, and Decorative Printed Matter*** **below, and** ***Rare and Finely Printed Books.***

Cloissoné, Lacquerware, Paperweights, and Collector's Plates

LIGHT OPERA GALLERY, *900 Northpoint No. 102, San Francisco, Calif. 94109. Tel. (415) 775-7665. Free 20- to 28-page catalogue issued 2 or 3 times a year.*

This company specializes in glass art, fine contemporary cloisoné, kaleidoscopes, and Russian lacquer boxes. The last named gets its own catalogue, with Light Opera saying it has the largest collection outside the Soviet Union. They are intricately painted, and the illustrations in the catalogue are fine. Payment by check, money order, Visa, or Mastercard. Shipment by United Parcel. Purchases may be returned within 60 days for refund or credit.

THE POST BOX EMPORIUM, *The Order Processing Center, Lake at Main Sts., Caledonia, Mich. 49316. Tel. (616) 891-9136. Free 20-page catalogue issued 4 times a year.*

Lyndon B. Johnson did not like his presidential portrait and told the artist so. "What do you like?" the artist wanted to know. "Norman Rockwell," the President answered. "Then hire Norman Rockwell," the artist said, or words to that effect. Some people love Norman Rockwell and some find him corny. People who like Norman Rockwell will like this catalogue of collector's plates, since that artist's works are featured among others'.

L. H. SELMAN LTD., *761 Chestnut St., Santa Cruz, Calif. 95060. Tel. (408) 417-1177 or (800) 538-0766 (except in California). The 120-page catalogue issued every other year costs $10, deductible against a purchase of $100 or more.*

Paperweights are usually thought of simply as heavy objects that keep papers in place, but "to a paperweight collector, they are works of art with rich simplicity that is crafted from the beauty and brilliance of glass." L. H. Selman has antique pieces from the French makers Baccarat, Clichy, and St. Louis, plus new works by American and British artists.

See also *Fine and Unusual Gifts* for such things as paperweights and thimbles.

Music Boxes

BORNAND MUSIC BOX CO., *139 Fourth Ave., Pelham, N.Y. 10803. Tel. (914) 738-1506. Brochure.*

Music boxes, recordings of the music, and books on the subject. Payment by check or money order. Delivery by Postal Service. No refunds on records or tapes.

KEITH HARDING, *Clocks and Musical Boxes, 93 Hornsey Rd., London, N7 6DJ, England. Tel. (01) 607-6181. Subject catalogues.*

This firm calls itself Europe's leading restorer of clocks and music boxes and has catalogues covering clocks, music boxes, spare parts, disks, and books. Payment by American Express, Visa, Mastercard, or Diners Club. Books are shipped by Postal Service, larger items by freight.

†*MUSIC BOX WORLD, *412 Main St., Avon, N.J. 07717. Tel. (201) 988-6600. Annual 32-page catalogue costs $1.*

This company claims to have the largest selection of tunes available anywhere. Some of the boxes are wood with inlays of wood or brass, and some are porcelain. Discounts of up to 60 percent occasionally available on discontinued items. A gift service is provided.

SAN FRANCISCO MUSIC BOX CO., *P.O. Box 26433, San Francisco, Calif. 94126. Tel. (415) 428-0194, (800) 227-2190 (except in California), or (800) 426-1400 (in California). Free 48-page catalogue issued twice a year.*

In addition to music boxes this company also sells other things with musical workings hidden inside them, including watches, tables, dolls, and even picture frames. These would make marvelous gifts.

Sculpture

ELEGANZA LTD., *1820 Magnolia Way West, Seattle, Wash. 98199. Tel. (206) 283-0609. Annual 32-page catalogue costs $3.*

Importers of fine statuary, including reproductions of classical Italian and Greek pieces, plus some Rodin copies and more modern pieces.

ERKINS, *604 Thames St., Newport, R.I. 02840. Tel. (401) 849-2660 or (401) 849-2665. Annual 36-page catalogue costs $4.*

Sculpted objects for the garden, including fountains, columns, planter pools, statues, planters, and benches. There is also a line of wooden outdoor furniture.

GIUST GALLERY, *1920 Washington St., Boston, Mass. 02118. Tel. (617) 445-3800. Annual 48-page catalogue costs $2.*

Reproductions of classical sculpture, including "Winged Victory" from the Louvre and Michelangelo's "David." The catalogue is well illustrated. Payment by check or money order. Delivery by United Parcel or air freight. Purchases may be returned for refund.

See also *Museum, Botanic Garden, and Public Radio Gift Catalogues* for reproductions of famous sculptures.

Paintings, Prints, Posters, Maps, and Decorative Printed Matter

†AIR MAPS DIVISION, *Ameropean Corp., 71 Hartford Turnpike South, Wallingford, Conn. 06492. Tel. (203) 265-4648. Free brochures.*

Aerial photos of many cities in the United States and Europe. They would make interesting decorations for the home, classroom, or office, and they would make memorable gifts. Payment by check, money order, American Express, Visa, Mastercard, or Diners Club. Shipment by Postal Service or United Parcel.

ART POSTER CO., *22255 Greenfield Rd., Suite 142, Southfield, Mich. 48075. Tel. (313) 559-1230 or (800) 521-8634 (except in Michigan). Annual 56-page catalogue costs $2.*

Attractive, colorful, and affordable art for the home, with the posters available framed or unframed. Payment by check, money order, American Express, Visa, Mastercard, Diners Club, Carte Blanche, or C.O.D. Delivery by Postal Service or United Parcel. Unframed posters can be exchanged or refunded; framed posters can be exchanged only.

AUDUBON PRINTS AND BOOKS, *9720 Spring Ridge Lane, Vienna, Va. 22180. Tel. (703) 528-4114 or (703) 759-5567. Free annual 18-page catalogue.*

Antique prints and books by John James Audubon and his contemporaries illustrating birds and animals. Payment by check. Delivery by Postal Service or United Parcel. Refunds for purchases returned within 10 days.

†**THE AUTHENTIC JOURNAL,** *3120 Via Mondo, Rancho Dominguez, Calif. 90221. Tel. (213) 537-8101, (800) 343-7488 (except in California), or (800) 343-7487 (in California). Brochure.*

Actual newspapers (not reproductions) available for special dates—historic events, birthdays, anniversaries—that make novel gifts. Payment by check, money order, Visa, or Mastercard. Shipment by United Parcel. Purchases may be returned within 2 days for refund.

CAHILL & COMPANY. *Old prints and photographs. See listing under* General Booksellers.

JOHN CAMPBELL FINE ART, *P.O. Box 22974, Nashville, Tenn. 37202. Tel. (615) 242-6773. Annual 10-page catalogue costs $4.50.*

Wonderful antique posters. In a recent catalogue the company listed a Toulouse-Lautrec from 1895 priced at $12,000. Payment by check or money order. Shipment by Postal Service. Purchases may be returned within 3 days for refund.

COLLECTOR'S GUILD, *601 W. 26th St., New York, N.Y. 10001. Tel. (212) 741-0400 or (800) 228-5454 (except in Nebraska). Free 40-page catalogue issued 12 times a year.*

Paintings, lithographs, and other fine arts by mail, plus jewelry and vases. Included are pieces from the Nelson Rockefeller Collection of fine art reproductions. Payment by check, money order, American Express, Visa, Mastercard, Diners Club, or Carte Blanche. Shipment by Postal Service, United Parcel, or truck. Purchases may be returned within 30 days for refund or exchange.

*****DECOR PRINTS,** *P.O. Box 502, 227 Main St., Noel, Mo. 64854. Tel. (417) 475-6367. Annual 16-page catalogue costs $3.*

Reproductions of antique lithographs at reasonable prices. The company will give a 50 percent discount on 20 or more prints.

ELIZABETH F. DUNLAP. *Maps. See listing under* Out-of-Print and Used Books.

FLORILEGIUM, *Box 157, Sneden's Landing, Palisades, N.Y. 10964. Tel. (914) 359-2926. Annual 52-page catalogue costs $3.*

This firm deals in antique prints, and, as the name suggests, the emphasis is on botanicals, but there are also some medical, landscape, and bird prints. Payment by check. Delivery by Postal Service. Purchases may be returned for refund within 10 days "or a reasonable time after notification."

HERITAGE EDITIONS, *P.O. Box 202, Continental Rd., Bellvale, N.Y. 10912. Tel. (914) 986-4870, (800) 654-5414 (except in New York), or (800) 832-3208 (in New York). Free 8- to 16-page catalogue.*

This company specializes in sports prints, executed by traditional methods (etching, lithography) rather than by photo-mechanical means. For those who do not subscribe to Red Smith's view that watching yacht racing is about as exciting as watching grass growing, there are some nice prints on the America's Cup.

JOAN HOULEHEN. *Abstract drawings and Christmas cards. See listing under* Crafts to Buy.

INSTITUT GEOGRAPHIQUE NATIONAL, *107 Rue le Boetie, 75008 Paris, France. Tel. (1) 225.87.90. Free annual 50-page catalogue.*

Reproductions of antique maps. Payment by check. Shipment by Postal Service. No returns.

ANNE KILHAM DESIGNS, *142 Russell Ave., Rockport, Me. 04856. Tel. (207) 236-8127. Annual brochure costs $1.*

Calendars and note and postcards with lovely drawings printed on them. Also, posters and prints.

JANET LIDLE, *P.O. Box 112, Clifton Heights, Pa. 19018. No telephone. Free brochure.*

This photographer specializes in pictures of wolves, which she sells in the form of prints and postcards. Payment by check or money order. Shipment by Postal Service. Refund, credit, or exchange for purchases returned within a month.

KAREN NELSON. *A set of 4 prints consisting of a windmill, a horse, a deer, and a bird. See listing under* Wall Coverings and Curtains.

OESTREICHER PRINT, *43 W. 46th St., New York, N.Y. 10036. Tel. (212) 719-1212. Annual catalogue costs $8.*

This company was started in 1898 and provides mail-order prints and fine art reproductions, many of them practically impossible to find elsewhere.

OLD HALL GALLERY LTD., *Crown Lodge, Crown Rd., Morden, Surrey, SM4 5BY, England. Tel. (01) 540-9918. The 6-page catalogue is free for the first issue but costs $2 for subsequent ones.*

Fine old paintings, mainly by English artists, are offered here, but there are also some by Dutch, German, and other European artists. Payment by check or bank draft. Shipment usually by air to nearest airport. Purchases may be returned for refund within 14 days.

ORIGINAL PRINT COLLECTORS GROUP, *215 Lexington Ave., New York, N.Y. 10016. Tel. (212) 685-9400. Free 16- to 24-page catalogue issued 6 times a year.*

Payment by check, money order, American Express, Visa, Mastercard, or Diners Club. Shipment by United Parcel. Purchases may be returned for refund within 30 days. There is a lifetime exchange privilege for members.

PROCREATIONS PUBLISHING CO., *8129 Earhart Blvd., New Orleans, La. 70118. Tel. (504) 486-7787 or (800) 245-8779. Annual 16-page catalogue costs $1.*

Silk-screen and offset prints of colorful posters on Mardi Gras, jazz, sports, etc. Payment by check, money order, American Express, Visa, or Mastercard.

PAUL PROUTE, *74 Rue de Seine, 75006 Paris, France. Tel. (1) 326.89.80. Annual 96-page catalogue costs $15 by air mail, and there are 2 free smaller issues.*

This place is known for its very large stock of art prints. Payment by check or money order. Shipment by Postal Service. "No return except on prior agreement and for important items only."

RONIN GALLERY. *Japanese prints. See listing under* Antiques, *above.*

THE SACRAMENTO CARD & GAME CO., *3403 Sacramento St., San Francisco, Calif. 94118. Tel. (415) 563-5244. No catalogue.*

Prints by the owner, who will send description of pieces available to anyone who asks and includes a first-class postage stamp. Payment by check or money order. Shipment by Postal Service. No returns except for items damaged in mail, which will be replaced.

STRATFORD BRASS RUBBINGS MUSEUM AND GALLERY, *Box 142, Stratford, Ont., Canada N5A 6S8. Tel. (519) 271-9333. Brochure price list.*

Handmade rubbings of brass memorials from churches and cathedrals in England. Payment by check, money order, American Express, Visa, or Mastercard. Shipment by Postal Service. No returns.

STURBRIDGE YANKEE WORKSHOP. *Reproductions of Early American art. See listing under* Furniture and Furnishings.

UCHIDA ART CO. LTD., *Kyoto Handicraft Center, Higashi, Kumanojinja, Sakyo-ku, Kyoto, 606, Japan. Tel. (075) 761-0345. Free 32-page catalogue.*

Woodblock prints. Payment by check or money order. Shipment by Postal Service. No returns.

WILD WINGS. *See listing under* Gifts for Nature Lovers.

WILLIAM WESTON GALLERY, *7 Royal Arcade, Albemarle St., London, W1X 3HD, England. Tel. (01) 493-0722. The 30- to 100-page catalogues are available on subscription at $20 a year.*

This is an internationally known specialist in 19th- and early 20th-century original European prints and drawings. Payment by check, money order, American Express, or Diners Club. Shipment by Postal Service or air freight. Refund or credit for returned purchases.

WINN GALLERIES, *P.O. Box 80096, Seattle, Wash. 98108. Tel. (206) 763-9544 or (800) 426-5589. The 72-page catalogue costs $3.*

This is a handsome catalogue of good-looking posters from museum and gallery shows and symphony performances. There are posters depicting flowers, postage stamps, animals, wineries, and landscapes. Payment by check, money order, American Express, Visa, Mastercard, Diners Club, or Carte Blanche. Shipment by United Parcel. Purchases may be returned within 30 days for credit.

YOSEIDO GALLERY, *5-5-15 Ginza, Chuo-ku, Tokyo, Japan. Tel. (03) 571-1312. Annual 100-page catalogue costs $10 by surface mail, $20 by air mail.*

This gallery, in business for more than 30 years, deals in contemporary Japanese limited edition prints. Payment by check or international money order. Shipment by Postal Service unless size or type of print requires another means. If damaged, prints may be returned for credit within 4 weeks.

See also *Art and Illustrated Books* and *Museum, Botanic Garden, and Public Radio Gift Catalogues* for prints, posters, maps, and note cards.

Movie and Fan Posters and Pictures

NANCY BARR, *c/o Mr. and Mrs. Max Barr, 506 Windermere Ave., Interlaken, N.J. 07712. Tel. (201) 531-2090. No catalogue; send list of desired photos with self-addressed envelope.*

Candid celebrity photos. Payment by check or money order. Shipment by Postal Service. No refunds.

S. CANDEL, *No. 9, 3600 21st St., Calgary, Alba., Canada T2E 6V6. Tel. (403) 245-3037. Price list.*

Here is a list of 2,000 posters, with 8,000 more in stock. Payment by check or money order. Shipment by Postal Service.

FLICKER ARTS, *7920 Chambersburg Rd., Suite 411, Huber Heights, Ohio 45424. Tel. (513) 236-3481. Price list issued 6 times a year costs $1.*

Original 1-sheet (27″ × 41″) posters, not reprints. Payment by check, money order, Visa, or Mastercad. Shipment by Postal Service or United Parcel. Purchases may be re-

turned, if in same condition as shipped, for refund.

FRONT ROW PHOTOS, *P.O. Box 484, Nesconset, N.Y. 11767. Tel. (516) 585-8297. Annual 36-page catalogue costs $2.*

Photos of rock stars.

*MISCELLANEOUS MAN, *George Theofiles, Box 1776, New Freedom, Pa. 17349. Tel. (717) 235-4766. Semi-annual 74- to-96 page catalogue costs $3 for 2 issues.*

Original movie posters and other graphics: John Wayne in *Rio Bravo,* Gary Cooper in a French version of *High Noon.* The company says it offers these at discount prices.

*MOVIE POSTER PLACE, *P.O. Box 309, Lansdowne, Pa. 19050. Tel. (215) 259-6592. Annual 32-page catalogue costs $1.*

Monthly list contains discount prices. There are thousands of lobby card reproductions (*The Wizard of Oz*), still photos, star portraits, pressbooks, 1-sheet posters, and some 3-sheet and 6-sheet versions. There are also video tapes and disks.

MOVIE POSTER WAREHOUSE, *1550 Westwood Blvd., Los Angeles, Calif. 90024. Tel. (213) 470-3050. Catalogue costs $1.*

Some very recent posters, plus reproductions of old classics (*Casablanca* and *Singin' in the Rain*). Payment by check or money order. Shipment by Postal Service or United Parcel. Purchases may be returned for credit.

PUBLISHERS CENTRAL BUREAU. *See listing under* General Booksellers.

ROCK TOPS, *Box D, Main St., Bloomington, N.Y. 12411. Tel. (914) 338-3344. Brochure price list.*

Scores of photos of rock stars and groups. There are other items, such as buttons and clothing.

Signs, Insignia, and Militaria

DER DIENST, *P.O. Box 211, Lowell, Mich. 49331. No telephone. Brochure price list costs 50 cents.*

Here are replicas of famous military decorations and related materials. This is your chance to receive the Croix de Guerre. Payment by check, money order, Visa, or Mastercard. Shipment by Postal Service or United Parcel. Purchases may be returned within 30 days for refund, credit, or exchange.

THE HEX BARN, *P.O. Box 57, Intercourse, Pa. 17534. Tel. (717) 768-8151. Brochure price list.*

Hex signs for outdoor or indoor hanging. This brouchure defines the designs, for example identifying a sign with 2 birds and a shamrock as Irish. The Double Distelfink brings double good luck. The signs are silkscreened by hand.

PETER HLINKA HISTORICAL AMERICANA, *P.O. Box 310, New York, N.Y. 10028. Tel. (212) 687-4055, ext. 446. Semiannual 24 page catalogue costs 50 cents.*

A marvelously wide variety of medals, from the City of Schenectady World War I service medal at $11 to several Legion of Honor medals from France at up to $400. There are also books and antique military

manuals and other war memorabilia. Payment by check or money order. Shipment by Postal Service or United Parcel. Purchases may be returned within 5 days for refund or credit.

MARTIN MARSH MILITARIA, *112 Buxton Rd., Whaley Bridge, Near Stockport, SK12 7JF, England. Tel. Whaley Bridge 3267. Catalogue costs $1 and must be in form of dollar bill.*

Here are hundreds of antique (and some more modern) military badges. There are many badges from World War I (such as the 11th Prince Albert's Own Hussars) and many earlier (such as the pre-1881 Royal Madras Fusiliers [23rd Regt. of Foot]). Payment by cash is requested for small orders, but checks or international money orders are o.k. for larger ones. Shipment by Postal Service. Refunds for purchases returned "promptly."

SARGENT-SOWELL INC., *1185 108th St., Grand Prairie, Tex. 75050. Tel. (214) 647-1525, (800) 527-2450 (except in Texas, Alaska, and Hawaii), or (800) 492-4200 (in Texas). Annual 416-page cataogue costs $5.*

This company sells law-enforcement supplies, such as speed-limit signs, highway and street signs, and decals for the doors of police cars.

SETON NAME PLATE CORP. *Signs and decals. See listing under* Stationery and Office Supplies.

See also *Army and Navy Goods.*

Railroadiana and Firehouse Memorabilia

B & O RAILROAD MUSEUM. *See listing under,* Museum, Botanical Garden, and Public Radio Gift Catalogues.

COLLECTION VENISE SIMPLON ORIENT-EXPRESS, *15 Rue Boissy d'Anglais, 75008 Paris, France. Tel. 742.24.45. Free 18-page catalogue issued twice a year.*

Mementoes of the fabled train—models, reproductions of china and tableware used on the train, copies of towels, etc. Payment by check, money order, American Express, Visa, or Diners Club. Shipment by Postal Service or air freight. Purchases may be returned for credit.

GRIFFITH POTTERY HOUSE, *100 Lorraine Ave., Oreland, Pa. 19075. Tel. (215) 887-2222 or (215) 885-5200. Free 36-page catalogue issued twice a year.*

This company describes itself as the world's largest supplier of "fine giftware and custom-decorated china and glassware to the firefighting service." I especially like the replicas in cast aluminum and iron of the old fire marks that people used to post on the sides of their houses and businesses noting which fire service protected their property. (The British office of this company is at 36 Edison Rd., Aylesbury, Buckinghamshire, England. Tel. Aylesbury 0296-82905.) Payment by check, money order, Visa, or Mastercard. Shipment by Postal Service or United Parcel. Purchases may be returned within 30 days for refund or credit.

Coins, Stamps, Sports Memorabilia, and Postcards

THE CARD MEMORABILLIA ASSOCIATES, *1000 N. Division St., Amawalk, N.Y. 10501. Tel. (914) 769-0161. Free 48-page catalogue issued 6 times a year.*

Baseball cards, some at discount prices.

STANLEY GIBBONS PUBLICATIONS LTD., *United 5, Parkside, Christchurch Rd., Ringwood, Hampshire, BH24 3SH, England. Tel. 042-54-2363. Free 16-page catalogue issued twice a year.*

"A complete range of philatelic books and accessories to suit every need—from the 7-year-old and his first tweezers to the veteran specialist and his gold-tooled album." Stanley Gibbons offers the widest range of philatelic books in the world. Payment by check, money order, American Express, Visa, Diners Club, Access, Canadian Chargex, and BankAmericard. Delivery by Postal Service. Refunds on returns made within a reasonable time.

JULES J. KARP., *110 Maiden Lane, New York, N.Y. 10269. Tel. (212) 943-5770. Free 52-page catalogue issued twice a year.*

Got some old pennies squirreled away somewhere? If they are valuable, you will probably find them in the fine print of this big catalogue.

THREE-STAR PRESS. *Car-oriented postcards. See listing under Automotive Needs.*

127

Fossils, Shells, and Minerals

DINOSAUR CATALOG, *P.O. Box 546, Tallman, N.Y. 10982. Tel. (212) 582-6343. Free semiannual 8- to 16-page catalogue; but they request a first-class postage stamp for mailing it.*

Here is a complete source of products related to dinosaurs and prehistoric artifacts. Payment by check, money order, Visa, or Mastercard. Shipment by United Parcel. Purchases may be returned for refund or credit.

DOVER SCIENTIFIC CO., *Box 6011, Long Island City, N.Y. 11106. Tel. (718) 721-0136. Annual 44-page catalogue costs $1; color portfolio of shells and minerals costs $2.*

Shells, fossils, minerals, Indian artifacts, and books on these subjects. Payment by check or money order. Delivery by Postal Service. Purchases may be returned within a week for exchange.

MALICK FOSSILS INC., *5514 Plymouth Rd., Baltimore, Md. 21214. Tel. (301) 426-2969. The 84-page catalogue costs $3.*

Fossils of animals and plants, plus ancient artifacts, meteorites, and minerals. Payment by check or money order. Delivery by Postal Service. Items broken in transit may be returned within 10 days for refund or credit.

Collectible Junque

ARCMAN CORP., *807 Center St., Throop, Pa. 18512. Tel. (717) 489-6402. Free 16-page catalogue.*

This company sells old electric meters as novel conversation pieces, fixed up as showpieces and in such forms as lamps, in which the electricity flows through the meter to light the light. It proves that people will collect anything.

DAIRY SERVICE INC., *P.O. Box 253, Bluffton, Ind. 46714. Tel. (219) 824-1100. Price list costs 25 cents.*

This company is "about the only retail or wholesale supplier of milk cans." These are not for gathering milk, I take it, but rather to be painted and decorated and used for ornamentation. There are also milk bottles for sale. Payment by check. Delivery by United Parcel or truck. Purchases may be returned within 10 days for refund.

Flags

*ACE FLAG & PENNANT FACTORY, *224 Haddon Rd., Woodmere, N.Y. 11598. Tel. (516) 295-2358. Annual 50-page catalogue costs $1.*

Discount prices on flags. For example, a 3′ × 5′ American flag, made of polyester with a list price of $10 sells for $8.50. Payment by check or money order. Shipment by Postal Service or United Parcel. Purchases may be returned, with written permission, within 1 week for refund or credit.

*CHRIS REID CO., *P.O. Box AA, Huntington, N.Y. 11743. Tel. (516) 421-0706. Free 8-page catalogue issued 3 times a year.*

Discount on flags and accessories. For example, a 6′ × 10′ nylon American flag sells for $67, compared with a regular price of $79. Payment by check, money order, American Express, Visa, or Mastercard. Shipment by United Parcel. Purchases may be returned, in original condition, within 10 days.

Floral and Fruit Decorations

ENGLISH HOLLY PACKERS OF OREGON, *14901 N.W. McNamee Rd., Portland, Ore. 97231. Tel. (503) 621-3486. Brochure price list.*

Holly sprays and wreaths for Christmas gifts and decorations. Payment by check, money order, Visa, or Mastercard. Shipment by Postal Service or United Parcel. Purchases may be returned within a year for refund or credit.

†GOLDEX-800, *Suite 204, 500 Gulfstream Blvd., Delray Beach, Fla. 33444. Tel. (305) 276-3905 or (800) 327-3729 (except in Florida). Several brochures, costing $2 each.*

Good-looking silk plants that are "always fresh. They can't die." Payment by check, money order, American Express, Visa, Mastercard, Diners Club, or Carte Blanche. Shipment by Postal Service, United Parcel, or courier. Purchases may be returned within 30 days of shipment for refund or credit.

PAYNE'S RISTRAS DE SANTA FE, *P.O. Box 4817, 715 St. Michael's Dr., Santa Fe, N.M. 87502. Tel. (505) 988-9626. Brochure price list.*

This company offers wall hangings of Indian corn, chilies, gourds, and other objects. Payment by check, money order, Visa, or Mastercard. Shipment by United Parcel. Purchases may be returned within 2 weeks for refund.

Accessories for Collectibles and Decorations

THE ART DISPLAY CO., *P.O. Box 880, Exmore, Va. 23350. Tel. (804) 442-2299. Brochure price list.*

This company makes display cases to protect and show off such valuable belongings as antique vases and ship models. It also has a line of silver polishes and tarnish preventives as well as polishes and preservatives for leather, paper, fabric, brass, and copper.

BAKER ENTERPRISES, *9441 Detwiler Rd., Canfield, Ohio 44406. Tel. (216) 549-5112. Free 16- to 20-page catalogue issued twice a year.*

Trays for floral arrangements, made of metal or wood. Payment by check or money order. Shipment by Postal Service or United Parcel. Credit for merchandise returned within 10 days in saleable condition.

CLASSIC FURNITURE, *P.O. Box 1544, Kansas City, Mo. 64141. Tel. (816) 461-6303. Brochure price list.*

The specialty here is wooden stands and other pieces for displaying plates, dolls, figurines, and toys. Payment by check, money order, Visa, or Mastercard. Shipment by United Parcel. Refunds for returns made within a reasonable time.

NEW ENGLAND FRAMEWORKS, *R.F.D. 1, Wilton N.H. 03086. Tel. (603) 878-1633 or (800) 258-5480 (except in New Hampshire). Free 16-page catalogue issued 4 times a year.*

Here are finely made frames to show off decorative plates.

❖8 Marvelous Machines

So many of the things that we take for granted today could not have been imagined just a few years ago. Inventions in this century have included not just the airplane and the ubiquitous radio and televison but also the computer, which, for good or bad, is changing our lives. Ninteenth-century inventions were rudimentary—like the motion picture, the phonograph, the camera, and the telephone—or available to only the well-to-do—like the automobile. Today, things are astonishingly different. What follows are some wonderful sources of marvelous machines. The great travel vehicles that changed the pace of our lives are covered in the Driving, Riding, and Flying Machines chapter.

One cautionary note: The purchase of computers and accessories for them by mail at the time of this writing is as unsettled as the computer industry itself. For the time being, I would approach this very carefully. Some of the costs are very high, and in a lot of cases you will not be able to sort out bargains from among the large number of products and packages available. A lot of homework should precede any computer purchase, and that becomes even more important when you are considering a mail-order computer purchase. You should read computer magazines for both their articles and their advertisements, ask your friends whether they recommend the computers they own, and be sure that any seller has a very good returns policy so that you can get your money back if you are not satisfied. Besides the computer magazines, you will find many ads in the Sunday issue of *The New York Times* (which most libraries across America carry), plus articles and advertising in the science section of that newspaper, which appears on Tuesdays. (You will also find many camera ads in the Sunday *Times*.) The Consumer Electronics Group of the Electronic Industries Association, in cooperation with the U.S. Office of Consumer Affairs, has prepared a buyer's guide on home computers, *How to Buy a Home Computer*. It can be obtained by sending 50 cents to the Consumer Information Center, Dept. 419M, Pueblo, Colo. 81009. Keep in mind, however, that whatever you read may already be out of date because the field is changing so quickly.

Prices in this area vary so greatly that it is important to shop around to get a really good buy. So many companies in this field offer discounts off list price that one wonders how meaningful the list price is.

Audio and Video Equipment, Computers, Electronics, Appliances, and Gadgets

*ALL ELECTRONICS CORP., *P.O. Box 20406, Los Angeles, Calif. 90006. Tel. (213) 380-8000, (800) 826-5432 (except in California, Alaska, and Hawaii), or (800) 258-6666 (in California). Free 48-page catalogue issued 3 or 4 times a year.*

Discount of 50 percent on new surplus electronics, including antennas, rechargeable batteries and battery chargers, capacitors, headphones, microphones, semiconductors, switches, and tools.

*AUDIOVISUAL SUPPLY CO., *P.O. Box 8277, Chattanooga, Tenn. 37411. Tel. (615) 894-9427 or (800) 251-7228. Free 16-page catalogue issued twice a year.*

A large line of tape cassettes, movie screens, and cassette recorders. Discount prices reported, including 30 percent off list price on high speed cassette duplicators.

*BONDY EXPORT CO., *40 Canal St., New York, N.Y. 10002. Tel. (212) 925-7785. No catalogue.*

Discount prices of 30 to 50 percent off list for cameras, movie and slide projectors, video recorders, microwave ovens, vacuum cleaners, typewriters, calculators, mixers, food processors, telephones, answering machines, and small appliances. There are also pens, luggage, and watches offered at discounts.

DON BRITTON ENTERPRISES, *P.O. Drawer G, Waikiki, Hawaii 96815. Tel. (808) 395-7458. Free 50-page catalogue issued 4 times a year.*

Plans for building radio transmitters, telephones, burglar alarms, satelite television receiving stations, TV sets, tape recorders, speakers, and many other interesting things. Payment by check, money order, Visa, or Mastercard. Shipment by Postal Service. No returns.

COMPUTER GAMES +. *Atari and Commodore computers. See listing under* Computer Software and Books.

*CRUTCHFIELD, *1 Crutchfield Park, Charlottesville, Va. 22906. Tel. (804) 973-1811, (800) 336-5566 (except in Virginia), or (800) 552-3961 (in Virginia). Free 92-page catalogue issued 3 times a year.*

Discount prices on car stereo radios, home stereo equipment, and telephones. An example, the Pioneer SX-303, which lists for $240, is available for $169. Payment by check, money order, American Express, Visa, Mastercard, Diners Club, or Carte Blanche. Shipment by Postal Service or United Parcel. Purchases may be returned, undamaged and with all packaging and parts, within 30 days for refund or credit.

*DAK INDUSTRIES, *10845 Vanowen St., North Hollywood, Calif. 91605. Tel. (818) 984-1559 or (800) DAK-0800. Free 70-page catalogue.*

Discount prices on stereo equipment, telephones, television sets, speakers, portable radios, and various gadgets. Payment by check, Visa, or Mastercard. Shipment by United Parcel. Purchases may be returned within 30 days, undamaged, with all parts, packaging, and invoice, for refund.

DECOURSEY ENGINEERING LABORATORIES, *11828 Jefferson Blvd., Culver City, Calif. 90230. Tel. (213) 397-9660. Brochures.*

High-quality electronic equipment. Payment by check or money order. Shipment by Postal Service or United Parcel. No returns.

*DIGI-KEY CORP., *P.O. Box 677, Thief River Falls, Minn. 56701. Tel. (218) 681-6674 or (800) 346-5144 (except in Minnesota, Alaska, and Hawaii). Free 76-page catalogue issued 6 times a year.*

Discounts of 10 to 25 percent on such electronics components as integrated circuits, transistors, capacitors, connectors, wire, diodes, and resistors.

*EDLIE ELECTRONICS, *2700 Hempstead Turnpike, Levittown, N.Y. 11756. Tel. (516) 735-3330 or (800) 645-4722 (except in New York State). Catalogues of 84 and 164 pages issued each year, priced at $1, refundable with order.*

Discount prices on electronic equipment, hardware, and tools. For example, the B & K oscilloscope model 1479BP, regular list price $795, is offered here at $617.

EDMUND CATALOGS, *101 E. Gloucester Pike, Barring-ton, N.J. 08007. Tel. (609) 547-3488; for orders only: (800) 232-6677 (except in New Jersey) or (800) 257-6173 (in New Jersey). Free 48- to 100-page catalogue.*

This company issues 15 different catalogues per year: *Edmund Scientific,* 7 catalogues; *Robert Edmund,* 6; and *Edmund Scientific, Industrial/Educational,* 2. My brother-in-law Frank bought a pair of binoculars for his son Keith at this place and was very pleased with them. In addition to binoculars, there are telescopes, microscopes, electronic equipment, tools, and projects, such as a build-your-own volcano. I wonder if Keith knows about this. Payment by check, money order, American Express, Visa, Mastercard, Diners Club, or Carte Blanche. Shipment by Postal Service or United Parcel. Purchases may be returned for refund or credit within 30 days.

*EDUCALC MAIL STORE, *27953 Cabot Rd., Laguna Niguel, Calif. 92677. Tel. (714) 831-2637. Free 56-page catalogue issued 6 times a year.*

Discounts of 15 to 30 percent on calculators, computers, and software. There is also a large section on books. Payment by check, money order, Visa, or Mastercard. Delivery by Postal Service, United Parcel, or air or truck freight. Purchases may be returned within 15 days for refund or credit.

EDUCATIONAL PRODUCTS, *P.O. Box 606, Mineola, N.Y. 11501. Tel. (516) 689-8409. Brochure price list.*

Books on electronics, including computers, robotics, and telephones. Payment by check, money order, Visa, or Mastercard. Shipment by Postal Service or United Parcel, Purchases may be returned for refund within 30 days.

*ETCO ELECTRONICS, *Route 9N, Plattsburgh, N.Y. 12901. Tel. (518) 561-8700. The 16- to-32-page catalogue issued 6 to 8 times a year costs $1.*

Discount prices on such things as electronics, cable television parts, video equipment, telephones.

*FOCUS ELECTRONICS, *4523 13th Ave., Brooklyn, N.Y. 11219. Tel. (718) 871-7600 or (800) 223-3411 (except in New York, Alaska, and Hawaii). The 96-page catalogue issued 2 to 3 times a year costs $2.*

Audio and video equipment, appliances, and electronics products at discount prices, including Sony Betamovie, Epson computer printer, and Panasonic color television. Purchases may be returned for exchange or credit.

*47TH ST. PHOTO, *67 W. 47th St., New York, N.Y. 10036. Tel. (212) 260-4410. Free 142-page catalogue.*

Discount prices on cameras, binoculars, computers and software, car stereos, radios, tape recorders, telephones, and many other products. Payment by check, money order, American Express, Visa, or Mastercard. Shipment by Postal Service or United Parcel. Purchases may be returned within 15 days for refund or exchange.

*GARDEN CAMERA, *135 W. 29th St., New York, N.Y. 10001. Tel. (212) 868-1420 or (800) 223-5830 (except in New York, Alaska, and Hawaii). The 32- or 100-page catalogues issued 2 to 4 times a year cost $2 or $3.*

Discount prices on cameras, video recorders, darkroom equipment and supplies, television sets, radios, computers, and typewriters.

*H. & A. DISTRIBUTORS, *Division of the Orlando Products Co., 6309 Elinore Ave., Baltimore, Md. 21206. Tel. (301) 254-0121. Free 16-page catalogue issued twice a year.*

Discount prices on computers, videotape recorders and cameras, stereos, tape decks, and speakers. Payment by check, money order, American Express, Visa, or Mastercard. Shipment by Postal Service, United Parcel, or freight. Purchases may be returned within 30 days for refund or credit.

†HAMMACHER SCHLEMMER, *147 E. 57th St., New York, N.Y. 10022. Tel. (212) 421-9000 or (800) 368-3584. Free 48- to 72-page catalogue issued 8 times a year.*

This marvelous store has thousands of interesting items. This is a place to find things not easily available elsewhere, like the professional chef's thermoprobe and the cordless electric blender—doesn't everyone need one? Or a pocket pepper mill? Other items include clocks, radios, televisions, cameras, phonographs, wine serving and storing equipment, an automatic bidet, exercise equipment, indoor and outdoor furniture, and telephones. Payment by check, money order, American Express, Visa, or Mastercard. Shipment by United Parcel. Unconditional guarantee; refunds upon return.

HOFFRITZ FOR CUTLERY. *Small appliances, scissors. See Cookware and Dinnerware.*

*ILLINOIS AUDIO, *12 E. Delaware Place, Chicago, Ill. 60611. Tel. (312) 664-0020 or (800) 621-8042 (except in Illinois). Brochure price list.*

Discount prices on stereo receivers, speakers, turntables, tape decks, car radios, and blank tapes. Payment by check, money order, Visa, or Mastercard. Shipment by United Parcel or motor freight. No returns without prior approval.

*J. & R. MUSIC WORLD, *23 Park Row, New York, N.Y. 10038. Tel. (212) 732-8600 or (800) 221-8180 (except in New York, Alaska, and Hawaii). The 298-page catalogue issued several times a year costs $2.95.*

More discount prices on computers, stereo equipment, video recorders, cameras and blank tapes, car stereos, and computer games, among many other things in this huge catalogue.

MARLIN P. JONES & ASSOC., *P.O. Box 12685, Lake Park, Fla. 33403. Tel. (305) 848-8236. Free 56-page catalogue issued 4 to 6 times a year.*

Electronic, photograhic, electrical, computer, and telephone equipment. Payment by check, money order, American Express, Visa, or Mastercard. Shipment by Postal Service or United Parcel. Purchases may be returned within 30 days for refund or credit.

J. S. & A. GROUP, *1 J.S.&A. Plaza, Northbrook, Ill. 60062. Tel. (312) 564-7000, (800) 323-6400, or (800) GAD-GETS. The 40- to 68-page catalogue issued about 6 times a year costs $2.50.*

Lots of high-tech things, including audio and video equipment, telephones with Mickey Mouse, Snoopy, or Kermit the Frog holding the receiver, a battery-powered scooter, a paper shredder, an ashtray that absorbs smoke, power "slugs" that are supposed to extend the life of a light bulb 100 times.

LYLE CARTRIDGES, *P.O. Box 69, 365 Dahill Rd, Brooklyn, N.Y. 11218. Tel. (718) 871-3303 or (800) 221-0906 (except in New York State, Hawaii, and Alaska). Brochure price list sent in return for self-addressed stamped envelope.*

This company offers discount prices and specializes in phonographic cartridges and diamond replacement needles. It also has replacement parts for Dual, Thorens, Garrard AR, B.I.C., and Empire turntables. Payment by check, money order, Visa, or Mastercard. Shipment by Postal Service or United Parcel. Defective merchandise replaced under manufacturer's warranty.

MISCO INC., *P.O. Box 399, Holmdel, N.J. 07733. Tel. (201) 946-3500 or (800) 631-2227 (except in New Jersey). Free 100-page catalogue issued 3 times a year.*

Computer supplies and accessories, including floppy disks, furniture, cables, daisy-wheels, and printwheels. Payment by check, money order, Visa, Mastercard, or Misco account. Shipment by United Parcel or courier service if requested. Purchases may be returned for refund or credit within 30 days, but authorization must be obtained first.

NEEDLE IN A HAYSTACK, *P.O. Box 17436, Washington, D.C. 20041. Tel. (703) 661-8868 or (800) 368-3506 (except in Virginia). Free 36-page catalogue issued twice a year.*

This company specializes in phonograph needles. The prices for the cartridges and needles are below list price, but the company does not want you to be misled into thinking that this represents a substantial discount. Payment by check, money order, American Express, Visa, Mastercard, Choice, or C.O.D.

Shipment by Postal Service or United Parcel. Purchases maybe returned within 30 days for refund or credit, but the customer must have the receipt and the original packaging, and the needle must not be broken.

PATENTED PRODUCTS CORP., *P.O. Box A, Danville, Ohio 43014. Tel. (614) 599-6842. Free annual 8- to 10-page catalogue.*

Electric bed-warmers, some for the home, some for vans and trucks using 12-volt current, even a pad for a pooch or other pet. This company is a manufacturer and says its prices are about 10 percent below retail.

ROBOT SHOP, *P.O. Box 582, El Toro, Calif. 92630. Tel. (714) 768-5798. Annual catalogue costs $5.*

A catchy song in the musical "A Funny Thing Happened on the Way to the Forum" insisted that everyone should have a maid. What fun Zero Mostel would have had with a robot! Here is a company that will bring a robot into your home, for as little as $20 for a start-up package. Fun and learning are supposed to be the immediate result here—build a robot that inflates balloons with its belly button and shoots a water pistol—but the long-term implications are clearly more than that.

S & S SOUND CITY, *58 W. 45th St., New York, N.Y. 10036. Tel. (212) 575-0210 or (800) 223-0360 (except in New York State). Brochure price list.*

Discount prices on video recorders, cameras, movies, blank tapes, disk players, televisions, home and car stereo systems, and video games, among other things. Payment by check, money order, American Express, Visa, Mastercard, or C.O.D. Delivery by Postal

Service or United Parcel. Purchases may be returned, with packaging materials and carton, for refund within 7 days.

*SAXITONE TAPE SALES, *1776 Columbia Rd., N.W., Washington, D.C. 20009. Tel. (202) 462-0800 or (800) 424-2490 (except in Washington metropolitan area). Free 32-page catalogue issued twice a year.*

This company offers discounts of 15 to 25 percent on all hardware in stock (video recorders, tape decks, and tape copiers) and software (the tapes). Payment by check, money order, Visa, Mastercard, or Choice. Shipment by Postal Service, United Parcel, Federal Express, or truck. If defective, purchases may be returned with all packing material within 7 days for credit.

THE SHARPER IMAGE, *650 Davis St., San Francisco, Calif. 94111. Tel. (415) 445-6000 or (800) 344-4444. Quarterly 60-page catalogue is sold for $2 on newsstands but is free on request by mail or phone.*

This company specializes in electronics and high technology merchandise. There is an ionizer that cleans the air in a room, an oxygen kit for the home, computers and computer accessories, an ultrasonic bug repeller, some really glitzy telephones. The company also puts out separate catalogues for gems and jewelry, exercise equipment, telephones, and watches. Payment by check, money order, American Express, Visa, Mastercard, Diners club, or Carte Blanche. Shipment by Postal Service, United Parcel, or Federal Express. Goods may be returned within 30 days for refund or credit.

†SHELBURNE INNOVATIONS, *100 Painters Mill Rd., Owings Mills, Md. 21117. Tel. (301) 363-4304 or (800) 638-6170. Free 32-page catalogue.*

All kinds of gadgets and high-tech products, including a timer for the garden hose, an ultrasonic humidifier, telephones, copiers, an electronic pulse taker, a pocket television set, wall stereos, an electronic pest chaser, and a pocket computer that has programmed into it vintage ratings of wines by year.

SPEAKERLAB, *735 No. Northlake Way, Seattle, Wash. 98103. Tel. (206) 633-5020 or (800) 426-7736 (except in Washington State, Alaska, and Hawaii). Free 32-page catalogue issued 3 or 4 times a year.*

A large selection of speakers, completed or in kits to be completed at home to save money.

*STEREO DISCOUNTERS ELECTRONIC WORLD, *6730 Santa Barbara Court, Baltimore, Md. 21227. Tel. (800) 638-3920 (in continental United States, Virgin Islands, and Puerto Rico). Free 132-page catalogue issued twice a year.*

This company offers discounts of 20 to 60 percent off suggested retail prices for computers, stereo equipment, television sets, tape decks, video cameras, recorders and tapes, speakers, amplifiers, and many other things. Payment by check, money order, American Express, Visa, Mastercard, or C.O.D. Delivery by United Parcel or truck freight.

SYNCHRONICS, *Unique Merchandise Mart, Building 42, Hanover, Pa. 17333. Tel. (717) 637-1600, (800) 621-5809 (except in Illinois), or (800) 972-5858 (in Illinois). Free 32-page catalogue.*

Telephones, calculators, computers, television sets, video recorders, stereo receivers and speakers, kerosene heaters, exercise equipment, a water massage device you can hook up to your bathtub, plus tools and other equipment. Payment by check, money order, American Express, Visa, Mastercard, Diners Club, Carte Blanche, or Synchronics account. Purchases may be returned within 30 days, in original condition, for refund.

TRIPLE A SCALE & MANUFACTURING CO., *2945 Southwide Dr., Memphis, Tenn. 38118. Tel. (901) 363-7040. Free catalogue.*

Large industrial scales and some smaller ones, including postal-package scales for the office.

See also *Musical Instruments* for synthesizers, amplifiers, speakers, and consoles and *Tools and Equipment for Craftspeople, Tinkerers, and Do-It-Yourselfers.*

Cameras and Optics, Photographic Supplies, and Photofinishing

*ADORAMA CAMERA, *138 W. 34th St., New York, N.Y. 10001. Tel. (212) 564-4465. Quarterly 32-page catalogue costs $1.95, which is deducted from your order.*

Discount prices on cameras. Payment by check, money order, American Express, Visa,

Mastercard, C.O.D., or corporate accounts. Delivery by Postal Service or United Parcel. Purchases may be returned within 14 days for refund.

BIRDING. *Optics for bird-watching. See listing under* Birding and Wildlife Supplies.

*CALUMET PHOTOGRAPHIC INC., *890 Supreme Dr., Bensenville, Ill. 60106. Tel. (312) 860-7447 or (800) 225-8638 (except in Illinois). Annual 128-page catalogue costs $3.*

This catalogue is designed for professional photographers and is not intended for the amateur market. For the pro, there are discounts such as a 210 mm. lens that lists for $862 offered by Calumet for $380.

CELESTRON INTERNATIONAL, *2835 Columbia St., Torrance, Calif. 90503. Tel. (213) 328-9560 or (800) 421-1526 (except in Hawaii and Alaska). The 32-page catalogue issued every 2 years costs $3.*

Precision optics, including telescopes, binoculars, telephoto lenses, and spotting scopes. Payment by check, money order, or Visa. Shipment by United Parcel. Purchases may be returned for refund within 30 days.

LIGHT IMPRESSIONS CORP., *P.O. Box 940, Rochester, N.Y. 14603. Tel. (716) 271-8960 or (800) 828-6216 (except in New York State). Free annual 64-page catalogue.*

Products for the conservation and preservation of photographs, and photographic acessories and books.

MIRAKEL OPTICAL CO., *331 Mansion St., West Coxsackie, N.Y. 12192. Tel. (518) 731-2610. Price list.*

Binoculars, telescopes, and scopes, plus accessories. The company has perhaps the largest binocular repair laboratory in the country. Payment by check or money order. Shipment by Postal Service or United Parcel. Purchases may be returned for refund.

MYSTIC COLOR LAB, *12 Roosevelt Ave., Mystic, Conn. 06355. Tel. (203) 536-4291. Free 16- to 32-page catalogue issued 3 times a year.*

The main business is photofinishing (1.5 million customers), but there is also a line of related products, including such things as frames and albums. Payment by check, money order, Visa, or Mastercard. Shipment by United Parcel. Purchases may be returned for refund within 14 days.

PHOTOGRAPHERS' FORMULARY, *P.O. Box 5105, Missoula, Mont. 59806. Tel. (406) 543-4534 or (800) 922-5255. Free 16-page catalogue.*

Chemicals for the darkroom.

*PORTER'S CAMERA STORE, *P.O. Box 628, Cedar Falls, Iowa 50613. Tel. (319) 268-0104 or (800) 553-2001; for orders only, (800) 553-2001 (except in Iowa) or (800) 772-7079 (in Iowa). Free 112-page catalogue issued twice a year.*

Cameras, lenses, and flash units available at what the company calls substantial discounts from manufacturers' list prices.

P.T.M. PRODUCTIONS, *46013 Clare Ave., Chilliwack, B.C., Canada V2P 6M9. Tel. (604) 795-5998. Brochure.*

The single product here is a tape cassette with instructions on photography.

ROCKLAND COLLOID, *302 Piermont Ave., Piermont, N.Y. 10968. Tel. (914) 359-5559. The 8-page catalogue costs 50 cents.*

Photographic chemicals.

*SOLAR CINE PRODUCTS, *4247 S. Kedzie Ave., Chicago, Ill. 60632. Tel. (312) 254-8310 or, for orders only, (800) 621-8796 (except in Illinois, Hawaii, and Alaska). Free 48-page catalogue issued 3 or 4 times a year.*

Discount prices on cameras, lenses, binoculars, and darkroom equipment and supplies. There are also many video films and books available, plus photo processing. Payment by check, money order, American Express, Visa, Mastercard, Diners Club, or Carte Blanche. Shipment by Postal Service or United Parcel. Purchases may be returned within 15 days for refund or credit.

ZONE VI STUDIOS, *Newfane, Vt. 05345. Tel. (802) 257-5161. Free 32-page catalogue issued 4 times a year.*

This is the designer and manufacturer of a line of fine cameras and equipment, including tripods, lenses, light meters, and enlargers.

See also *Audio and Video Equipment,* above.

Telephones and Telephone Equipment

BILLARD'S OLD TELEPHONES, *21710 Regnart Rd., Cupertino, Calif. 95014. Tel. (408)252-2104. The 16-page catalogue costs $1.*

Antique and rebuilt telephones and parts. Payment by check, money order, or C.O.D. Delivery by Postal Service or United Parcel. "All goods can be returned—no time limit!"

*PHONE CITY INC., *126 E. 57th St., New York, N.Y. 10022. Tel. (212) 644-6300. Free 26-page catalogue issued twice a year.*

Discount prices on telephones, answering machines, parts, and accessories.

PHONES FOR BUSINESS, *Division of Arcturus Co., 484 Tamarack Ave., Long Lake, Minn. 55356. Tel. (612) 473-1113 or (800) 328-5369 (except in Minnesota). Free 6-page catalogue.*

These are multiline telephone systems with many accessories available, including one that plays music when you press the "hold" button, which I could do very nicely without. If I wanted to listen to insipid music, I could turn on the radio. This company has a policy of allowing credit for old purchases toward new ones as the customer's business expands. The company believes telephone technology is simple enough to be mastered by anyone who is given clear directions.

TW COMMUNICATION CORP., *122 Cutter Mill Rd., Great Neck, N.Y. 11021. Tel. (516) 482-8100 or (800) 645-3363 (except in New York State). Free 16- to 20-page catalogue issued 3 times a year.*

Telephones, wire, cable, hardware, and plugs. Payment by check. Shipment by United Parcel or truck. Purchases may be returned within 7 days for refund.

See also *Audio and Video Equipment,* **above.**

Fire and Burglar Alarms, Security Equipment

CCS COMMUNICATION CONTROL, *633 Third Ave., New York, N.Y. 10017. Tel. (212) 697-8140. Annual 60- to 70-page catalogue costs 50 cents.*

"Is your phone tapped?" this company asks. This company will provide you with equipment to determine whether it is. The catalogue is in English, French, Spanish, and Arabic and also offers products to scramble communications, bullet-proof vests, and bomb detectors.

MOUNTAIN WEST ALARM SUPPLY, *P.O. Box 10780, Phoenix, Ariz. 85064. Tel. (602) 263-8831 or (800) 528-6169 (except in Arizona). Annual 64-page catalogue costs $1.*

This company is a distributor of crime and fire alarms for homes, schools, and businesses.

❖ 9 Marvelous Machine Accompaniments

By all accounts, the compact disk is supposed to represent a revolution in recorded music. Maybe so, but don't throw your record player or tape deck in the trash, because, for the immediate future, at least, not everything will be available on the new disks. If the compact disk is really as good as advertised, it may mean that music lovers ought to consider spending most of their budgets for recordings on compact disks instead of records and tapes. The time may come, indeed, when there will be no choice, the supposed merits of the disks being so great that they may very well pre-empt the field and lead manufacturers to discontinue their record and tape versions altogether.

In the meantime, selecting the kind of hardware you want poses difficult choices, but the purchase by mail of software—records, tapes, compact disks, and computer software—will probably prove an easier task than the buying by mail of the hardware.

Records, Audio Tapes, and Compact Disks

*ADVENTURES IN CASSETTES,** *1401-B W. River Rd. North, Minneapolis, Minn. 55411. Tel. (612) 588-2781 or (800) 328-0108 (except in Minnesota). Free 16- to 24-page catalogue issued 6 times a year.*

Discount prices on what the company calls quality tapes. An example: Books on tape that are said to cost $10 to $15 elsewhere are offered here at $7. Payment by check, money order, American Express, Visa, or Mastercard. Shipment by Postal Service or United Parcel. Purchases may be returned for refund or credit within 30 days.

*ANDY'S FRONT HALL,** *Drawer A, Voorheesville, N.Y. 12186. Tel. (518) 765-4193. Free annual 48-page catalogue.*

This is a mail-order folk music center. There are lots of records and tapes (both of performances and instructional) at discount prices, plus books on music and some instruments for sale, either complete or in kits, including autoharps, banjos, bodhrans (drums), bones, and bouzoukis, to mention the top of the alphabet alone.

ANIMAL TOWN GAME CO. *Old-time radio programs on tape. See listing under* Games and Toys.

AUDIO-FORUM AND VIDEO-FORUM, *Jeffrey Norton Publishers, On-the-Green, Guilford, Conn. 06437. Tel. (203) 453-9794 or (800) 243-1234 (except in Connecticut, Alaska, and Hawaii). Free 32-page catalogue issued once or twice a year.*

Courses in 32 languages are available on audio tapes; the selection on video tapes is limited.

*BARNES & NOBLE. *See listing under* General Booksellers.

BLACKHAWK FILMS. *See listing under* Films and Video Tapes, *below.*

BOOKS ON TAPE, *P.O. Box 7900, Newport Beach, Calif. 92660. Tel. (714) 548-5525 or (800) 626-3333. Annual 160-page catalogue costs $2.50.*

I wish I had thought to get some of these tapes for a long car trip through a part of the country whose music I didn't much care for. It looks like a fine idea, with tapes providing the contents of books to those unable to read because of physical condition, educational level, activity (commuting in a car, working on a repetitive job, exercising). There are lots of classics, including Tolstoy's *War and Peace.* Yes, it takes a long time to listen to it— 47 cassettes, each running an hour and a half. Tapes may be rented or purchased. Payment by check, money order, Visa, or Mastercard. Shipment by Postal Service. Cash refund or credit if returned within 30 days.

BORNAND MUSIC BOX CO. *See listing under* Music Boxes.

*BROTHER SLIM'S RECORD REVIVAL, *P.O. Box 12937, Fort Worth, Tex. 76121. Tel. (817) 731-7375. Free 56-page catalogue issued twice a year.*

Discount prices on banjo, bluegrass, Cajun, country western, and many other kinds of music. Several dozen related books and some instruments are also available.

Payment by money order, Visa, or Master-card. Shipment by Postal Service. Refunds only in event of incorrect shipment.

CAHILL & COMPANY. *See listing under* General Book-sellers.

CANYON RECORDS & INDIAN ARTS, *4143 N. 16th St., Phoenix, Ariz. 85016. Tel. (602) 266-4823. Annual 20-page catalogue costs 75 cents (with postage stamps suggested as means).*

The specialty is native American music, categorized by tribe. There are also record-ings of country, western, contemporary, rock, and gospel by Indian artists. Payment by check, money order, Visa, or Mastercard. Shipment by Postal Service or United Parcel. Refunds only on unopened records or tapes returned within 30 days; defective records or tapes may be returned within 30 days for re-placement.

*CHESTERFIELD MUSIC SHOPS, *226 Washington St., Mt. Vernon, N.Y. 10553. Tel. (914) 667-6200. Free 16-page catalogue issued 4 times a year.*

Big discounts on records and tapes—mostly classical in the catalogue they sent me but also some popular, folk, and jazz. Pay-ment by check, money order, American Express, Visa, Mastercard, or Diners Club. Shipment by Postal Service or United Parcel. Records may be returned after no more than 1 playing for credit or exchange less $1 per record.

CHILDREN'S BOOK & MUSIC CENTER. *See listing under* For Children.

*COLOSSEUM RECORDS, *P.O. Box 146, Croydon, Pa. 19020. Tel. (215) 785-1940. Brochure price list.*

Rock, popular, gospel, and soul records sold at big discounts. The company aims to sell new, unopened albums to people who will resell them at flea markets, from sidewalk stands, or as fundraising efforts by schools and churches. Payment by check or money order. Shipment by Postal Service, United Parcel, or truck. No returns without authori-zation.

*COUNTY SALES, *Box 191, Floyd, Va. 24091. Tel. (703) 745-2001. Free 8-page catalogue issued 7 times a year.*

This company claims to have the coun-try's largest selection of bluegrass and old-time music, over 3,000 titles, and also sells books. Everything at discount.

*COWBOY CARL RECORDS, *P.O. Box 116, Park For-est, Ill. 60466. Tel. (312) 481-7366. Brochure price list.*

Out-of-print, rare, imports, and 45's at "working man's prices." Payment by check or money order. Shipment by Postal Service or United Parcel. Returns accepted for defective merchandise only.

CREDENCE CASSETTES, *P.O. Box 281, Kansas City, Mo. 64141. Tel. (816) 531-0538 or (800)821-7926. Free 48-page catalogue.*

This catalogue is issued by The National Catholic Reporter Publishing Co.

CROSS-COUNTRY, *P.O. Box 50416, Washington, D.C. 20004. Tel. (202) 393-3660. Free monthly catalogue of 4 to 8 pages.*

Mostly rock and punk.

DOWN HOME MUSIC, *10341 San Pablo Ave., El Cerrito, Calif. 94530. Tel. (415) 525-1494. Subject catalogues cost $2 or $3, plus a free 16-page monthly newsletter.*

Blues, country, vintage rock and rock, and folk records listed in separate catalogues.

*FOLK-LEGACY RECORDS, *Sharon Mountain Rd., Sharon, Conn. 06069. Tel. (203) 364-5661. Free annual 16-page catalogue.*

Discount prices. Payment by check, money order, Visa, or Mastercard. Shipment by Postal Service or United Parcel. Returns accepted for exchange on defective records only.

*THE GOLD VAULT, *P.O. Box 202, Oshtemo, Mich. 49077. Tel. (616) 349-9413. Annual 70-page catalogue costs $2.*

This company has a large selection of hard-to-get and out-of-print records at discount prices, "specializing in oldies but goodies." Here's that Chubby Checker record you need to complete your collection.

HARVARD COOPERATIVE SOCIETY. *See listing under* Country and General Stores.

HOMESPUN TAPES, *Box 694, Woodstock, N.Y. 12498. Tel. (914) 679-7832. The 32-page catalogue costs $1.*

Here are instructional tapes for the guitar, mandolin, fiddle, piano, autoharp, dulcimer, and harmonica. Payment by check, money order, Visa, or Mastercard. Shipment by Postal Service or United Parcel. Purchases may be returned for credit within 7 days.

LYNN'S JAZZ AND THINGS, *P.O. Box 1704, Denver, Colo. 80201. Price list.*

Many discounts on jazz records, some costing as little as 99 cents or 3 for $2 for new disks that are missing their jackets.

LYRICHORD DISCS, *141 Perry St., New York, N.Y. 10014. Tel. (212) 929-8234. Brochure price list.*

This company has a long list of classical music and, in addition, stocks many albums of ethnic music from Afghanistan, Africa, Arab nations, Australia, Bali, Java, Latin America, China, Crete, Greece, Cyprus, Turkey, Yugoslavia, India, Nepal, Tibet, Iceland, Iran, Ireland, Japan, Korea, Morocco, the Philippines, Spain, Italy, Vietnam, and Thailand. Payment by check or money order. Shipment by Postal Service. Returns accepted for exchange on defective records only.

HUGH MACPHERSON (SCOTLAND) LTD. *Cassettes of Scottish music. See listing under* Men's Clothing.

*MIRO MUSIC, *P.O. Box 342, Old Chelsea Station, New York, N.Y. 10114. Tel. (212) 989-2323. Free 16-page catalogue.*

Classical and folk music, largely from Eastern Europe—especially the Soviet Union—but also from some Western European countries as well. The prices are discounted, and I have been pleased with my own purchases of some Mozart piano concertos from this company. The quality of the performances should not be surprising, since some of the artists who have recorded on the Monitor label from the Soviet Union are David Oistrakh, Emil Gilels, Sviatoslav Richter, Dinu Lipatti, Mstislav Rostropovich, Lili Kraus, and Galina Vishnevskaya. Some books available, including one on Russian folk music. Payment by check or money order. Shipment by Postal Service or United Parcel. Refunds for defective records.

DAVID MORGAN. *Music of Wales. See listing under* Men's and Women's Clothing.

*MUSICAL HERITAGE SOCIETY, *14 Park Rd., Tinton Falls, N.J. 07724. Recordings offered in a catalogue that is issued every 3 weeks. Substantial discounts reported. No phone.*

This is a well-regarded "negative-option" club, featuring classical music, with regular selection offers that you must turn down if you do not want each current one. It has issued all of Haydn's 107 symphonies on 49 records, which is quite an undertaking. When I finish this book, maybe I'll lock myself in a room and listen to all 107 (I think that's the correct number). A few years ago I heard perhaps a majority of them on Robert J. Lurtsema's public radio program from Boston which was retransmitted by a Connecticut station that we could receive on Long Island.

NATIONAL PUBLIC RADIO, *Publishing Dept., 2025 M St., N.W., Washington, D.C. 20036. Tel. (202) 822-2670 or (800) 253-0808. Free 96-page catalogue.*

More than 200 informative cassettes for use in secondary and post-secondary school courses. Included are recordings on the arts and humanities, education, culture, history, and psychology. Of course, the informative Susan Stamberg is to be heard on some of them. You don't know Susan Stamberg of N.P.R.? You should.

*PACK CENTRAL, *6745 Denny Ave., North Hollywood, Calif. 91606. Tel. (818) 760-2828. A 40-page catalogue issued 3 or 4 times a year, offered free in exchange for 2 first class stamps.*

Discount prices on records and cassettes of popular music from the 1950's, '60's, '70's, and '80's. LP's and cassettes with list prices of up to $9 are offered here for $4. There are also very pricey collections of such performers as the Beatles and Frank Sinatra. Payment by check, money order, Visa, or Mastercard. Shipment by Postal Service. Unopened and defective purchases can be returned for refunds.

POETS' AUDIO CENTER, *P.O. Box 50145, Washington, D.C. 20004. Tel. (202) 347-4823. Free catalogue.*

Many recordings of poets—famous, not too famous, avant-garde, and traditional.

PUBLISHERS CENTRAL BUREAU. *See listing under* General Booksellers.

RASHID SALES COMPANY, *191 Atlantic Ave., Brooklyn, N.Y. 11201. Tel. (718) 852-3295 or (718) 852-3298. Free annual 48- to 120-page catalogue.*

The catalogue is titled *Arabic Music* and includes music from much of the Middle East. There is a large section of religious recordings, one of which is Sheikh Mahmoud Khalil el-Hossary reciting the Holy Koran in a boxed set of 32 tape cassettes. The recordings are offered at discount. There are separate catalogues on belly-dance music, Greek music, and Arabic books and dictionaries.

RECORD EXCHANGER, *Box 6144, Orange, Calif. 92667. Tel. (714) 639-3383. Semiannual 64-page catalogue costs $4 for a 2-year subscription.*

This company conducts auctions by mail for buyers to bid on collector records from the 1950's and 1960's, especially rock 'n roll, rhythm and blues, rockabilly. Payment by check or money order. Shipment by Postal Service or United Parcel. Refunds made for records returned within 8 weeks of billing.

REGO RECORDS, *64 New Hyde Park Rd., Garden City, N.Y. 11530. Tel. (516) 328-7800 or (800) 856-3746 (except in New York State). Free catalogue.*

The catalogue, called *Memories of Ireland,* lists recordings of Irish songs and stories. Payment by check, money order, Visa, or Mastercard. Shipment by United Parcel. No returns.

*ROUNDUP RECORDS, *P.O. Box 154, North Cambridge, Mass. 02140. No telephone. For $1, they will send a 76-page master catalogue plus a copy of the 32- to 48-page Record Roundup.*

Discount prices on records ($6.50 instead of $9) for a wide range of country, western, old-timey, folk, jazz, and popular music. Payment by check, money order, Visa, or Mastercard. Shipment by Postal Service or United Parcel. Refund or credit for unopened or defective recordings.

THE SMITHSONIAN COLLECTION OF RECORDINGS. *For this marvelous selection of classical and jazz recordings see the Smithsonian Institution Press listing under* Selected University, Scholarly, and Small Presses.

SOUND TRACK ALBUM RETAILERS, *P.O. Box 7, Quarryville, Pa. 17566. Tel. (717) 284-2573. Free 10-page catalogue issued 12 times a year.*

This is a personal favorite that a colleague put me on to. The company says it is one of the largest retailers in the world specializing in sound tracks and original cast albums, plus out-of-print records. Indeed. When our daughter Michele went off to college, we made sure she had all the essentials—pens, pencils, notebooks, checkbook and, from Sound Track, an otherwise unavailable copy of Ella Fitzgerald singing the George and Ira Gershwin songbook. Payment by check, money order, American Express, Visa, or Mastercard. Shipment by Postal Service. Purchases may be returned for refund within 10 days.

TAFFY'S. *See listing under* Dance and Theater Supplies and Costumes.

*WORLDWIDE MUSIC, *P.O. Box 264, Hasbrouck Heights, N.J. 07604. Tel. (201) 487-4973. Free 24-page catalogue issued 6 times a year.*

This company never sells records or tapes "at manufacturer's suggested list price." There are rock and pop disks.

See also *Musical Instruments.*

Films and Video Tapes

*APPALSHOP FILMS, *Box 743, 306 Madison St., Whitesburg, Ky. 41858. Tel. (606) 633-0108. Free catalogue.*

These are films and filmstrips that might be considered more educational than entertaining, but one term does not necessarily exclude the other. A discount of 10 percent is offered when at least 3 films are purchased.

BARNES & NOBLE, *See listing under* General Booksellers.

BLACKHAWK FILMS, *1 Old Eagle Brewery, Davenport, Iowa 52802. Tel. (319) 323-9736. Free 48- to 80-page catalogue issued 12 times a year.*

Wonderful old classics, including Charlie Chaplin in *Easy Street* and *The Gold Rush,* Buster Keaton in *The General,* plus Laurel and Hardy, Gene Autry, Abbott and Costello, W.C. Fields, and many more—a real gold mine. The films are available on movie film, video cassette, and video disk, and there are some audio tapes as well. Payment by check, money order, Visa, Mastercard, or Blackhawk account. Shipment by Postal Service or

United Parcel. Purchases may be returned within 10 days for refund, credit, or exchange.

BULLFROG FILMS, *Oley, Pa. 19547. Tel. (215) 779-8226. Annual 40-page catalogue costs $2.*

This is a small company that specializes in films and video tapes on gardening, alternative technologies, and various forms of conservation. Included, for example, are 2 films of E.F. Schumacher.

THE COCKPIT/AVIREX LTD. *Video tapes on Air Force history and battles. See listing under* Aviation.

*DIRECT CINEMA LIMITED, *P.O. Box 69589, Los Angeles, Calif. 90069. Tel. (213) 656-4700. Free catalogue issued 24 times a year.*

Films and video tapes leased to schools, libraries, clubs, etc., and video tapes sold at discount for home use. For example, *Tootsie* is offered for $67.50 instead of the $80 list price. *Raiders of the Lost Ark,* $32.50 instead of $40. Payment by check. Shipment by United Parcel. Defective films and tapes may be returned for refund or credit.

FLOWER FILMS, *10341 San Pablo Ave., El Cerrito, Calif. 94530. Tel. (415) 525-0942. Annual catalogue costs $1.*

Films by Les Blank, who is described as "the down-home poet of regional cultures," including portraits of blues singers and Cajun musicians. Payment by check or money order. Shipment by Postal Service or United Parcel. Purchases may be returned within 30 days for refund or credit only if defective.

THE HARTLEY FILM FOUNDATION, *Cat Rock Rd., Cos Cob, Conn. 06807. Tel. (203) 869-1818. Free 14-page catalogue.*

Films on health and healing, psychic research, world religions, and Eastern philosophy.

KARTEMQUIN EDUCATIONAL FILMS, *1901 W. Wellington, Chicago, Ill. 60657. Tel. (312) 472-4366. Brochures.*

Films and video tapes on such topics as a maternity center in Chicago and a strike at a chain-making plant. Payment by check or money order. Shipment by Postal Service or United Parcel. No refunds; damage in transit is covered by insurance.

MERLIN MAIL, *Suite 7777, 12021 Wilshire Boulevard, Los Angeles, Calif. 90025. Tel. (213) 470-3597. Catalogue costs $1, deductible against first order.*

Video cassettes and disks of many movies, ranging from grade B Abbott and Costello to *Bonnie and Clyde* and *American Graffiti.* Payment by check, money order, Visa, or Mastercard. Shipment by Postal Service or United Parcel. Refund or credit for purchases returned within 1 month.

MOVIE POSTER PLACE. *See listing under* Movie and Fan Posters and Pictures.

PLAYINGS HARD TO GET, *P.O. Box 50493, Pasadena, Calif. 91105. Tel. (818) 795-4064. Catalogue costs $1.*

A varied assortment of video tapes is offered. There is a Julio Iglesias movie, plus foreign, silent, and classic films.

PUBLISHERS CENTRAL BUREAU. *See listing under* General Booksellers.

PYRAMID FILM & VIDEO CORP., *P.O. Box 1048, Santa Monica, Calif. 90406. Tel. (213) 828-7577 or (800) 421-2304 (except in California). Free 140-page catalogue issued every 2 years.*

More than 500 titles of educational, instructional, and self-help films and video cassettes.

SOLAR CINE PRODUCTS. *Video tapes. See listing under* Cameras and Optics, Photographic Supplies, and Photofinishing.

SPEEDIMPEX USA. *Video cassettes of Italian movies. See listing under* Foreign Books, Foreign Language and Culture, Travel Guides.

VIDEO-FORUM. *See listing for Audio-Forum and Video-Forum under* Records, Audio Tapes, and Compact Disks, *above.*

WORLD WIDE PICTURES, *The Billy Graham Film Ministry, 1201 Hennepin Ave. South, Minneapolis, Minn. 55403. Tel (612) 338-3335 or (800) 328-4318, (except in Minnesota). Free annual 12-page catalogue.*

This company is the producer and distributor of more than 100 Christian motion pictures. There are documentaries, dramatic films, so-called docu-dramas, and some films from Billy Graham crusades.

*WORLDWISE, *P.O. Box 41, Gays Mills, Wis. 54631. Tel. (608) 624-3466. Brochure.*

Some discounts offered on films and video tapes sold to churches and to purchasers of more than 1 film. These are films "with a sense of history," including pieces on Southern Africa, and political, civil rights, and governmental activities in the United States. Payment by check or money order. Shipment by Postal Service or United Parcel.

ZIPPORAH FILMS, *1 Richdale Ave., Unit 4, Cambridge, Mass. 02140. Tel. (617) 576-3603. Annual free 16-page catalogue.*

Distributed here are the marvelous documentary films of Frederick Wiseman, whose narration-free productions have had such a good reaction on public television. Among his most memorable films are *Titicut Follies, The Store,* and *Welfare.*

Computer Software and Books

BIRKHAUSER/BOSTON. *Books and software for computers. See listing under* Foreign Books, Foreign Language and Culture, Travel Guides.

*COMPUTER GAMES +, *Box 6144, Orange, Calif. 92667. Tel. (714) 639-8189. Free 6-page catalogue issued 4 times a year.*

Discount prices for computer games plus computer software and hardware for Atari and Commodore computers. Payment by check, money order, Visa, or Mastercard. Shipment by United Parcel. Purchases may be returned for credit.

*PAECO INDUSTRIES, *213 S. 21st St., Birmingham, Ala. 35233. Tel. (205) 323-8376. Free 50-page catalogue issued twice a year.*

Discounted computer software for the TRS-80, including word processor programs, payroll and other office functions, and video games.

PRELUDE PRESS, *944 N. Palm Ave., No. 5, Los Angeles, Calif. 90069. Tel. (213) 657-7714 or (800) 421-1809 (except in California). Free annual 14-page catalogue.*

A large line of computer books. Payment by check, money order, American Express, Visa, Mastercard, or C.O.D. Delivery by Postal Service, United Parcel, or Federal Express.

PUBLISHERS CENTRAL BUREAU. *Computer books. See listing under* General Booksellers.

*STRICTLY SOFTWARE, *28 Barrett Rd., Katonah, N.Y. 10536. Tel. (914) 232-4844 or (212) 734-SOFT. Free 3- to 70-page catalogue issued 12 times a year.*

Discount prices for computer software, including Apple, and several word processing and education programs. Payment by check, money order, Visa, Mastercard, or pre-arranged company purchase order agreement. Shipment by Postal Service or United Parcel. Purchases, if defective, may be returned within 30 days for refund, credit, or replacement.

❖ 10 Driving, Riding, and Flying Machines

We Americans consider ourselves to be authorities on cars, and for good reason: We certainly have enough problems with them. This is the most car-conscious country in the world; we feel deprived if we don't have a driver's license the day we reach legal age.

Driving through Austria once, my family got to a gasoline service station only to find it closed for lunch, with a line of motorists waiting patiently for it to reopen. Can you imagine that happening in this country?

In compiling this section, I was struck by the fact that Fords seem to be the favorites of collectors. This is something that goes back to the Model T and Model A and continues today with the Thunderbird and Mustang. My own nostalgic favorite is the line of Fords that came out in 1949, 1950, and 1951, although I never owned one. General Motors has various Chevies, such as the Corvette and the Corvair, that are coveted by collectors, but Chrysler does not appear to have any models that people look back on with fond memories. There seem to be a lot of companies doing a good business in selling copies of British cars, the M.G. in particular, which makes me wonder why the original car did not sell as well in the past decade. Perhaps the engineering people in Britain were not a match for the stylists.

Some of the companies listed here offer radar detectors, the use of which is illegal in some states. I am personally opposed to them; readers may make up their own minds.

It was hard to decide whether to include motorcycles with cars in the Automotive section (since they have engines) or with Bicycles (because they have two wheels). A case could be made for either; for absolutely no defensible reason, I have plopped them down in the Bicycles section.

Since the first viable plane was produced in the Wright brothers' bicycle shop, I think it's appropriate for the Aviation section to follow the Bicycles. The companies listed here also sell merchandise for the armchair pilot.

Automotive Needs

A & A FIBERGLASS, *1543 Nabell Ave., Atlanta, Ga. 30344. Tel. (404) 762-9631. Annual 28-page catalogue costs $3.*

This company makes fiberglass, urethane, and plastic components and accessories for cars (doors, hoods, fenders) and usually sells through wholesalers but is willing to sell direct to customers. It also offers a line of caps, jackets, and other clothing for the sporting driver, but do you really want to bear the A & A logo? Maybe you do. Payment by money order. Delivery by United Parcel or truck.

ADDCO INDUSTRIES, *700 East St., Lake Park, Fla. 33403. Tel. (305) 842-6065 or (305) 844-2531. Free annual 56-page catalogue.*

Antisway bars (stabilizers) for cars. Payment by check, money order, Visa, or Mastercard. Shipment by Postal Service or United Parcel. Purchases may be returned within 30 days for refund.

ANTIQUE & CLASSIC AUTOMOTIVE, *100 Sonwill Industrial Park, Buffalo, N.Y. 14225. Tel. (412) 283-4663 or (800) 245-1310 (except in Pennsylvania). The 12-page catalogue costs $3.*

This is for all those people who would like to own a 1937 Jaguar SS-100 and can't afford or even find one. This company offers the do-it-yourselfer a kit with fiberglass and steel components that are built over a VW Beetle or Ford Pinto chassis, but they don't list the price.

*AUTO ALARM SUPPLY CORP., *1814 Woodson Rd., St. Louis, Mo. 63114. Tel. (314) 428-7500 or (314) 868-5500. Catalogue costs $2.50, refundable with first order of $10 or more.*

A catalogue of devices to keep your car from being stolen or various parts from being ripped off. There are discounts for many items, including a hood lock that kills the starter if tampered with. Also available at discount is a radar detector.

*AUTO WORLD, *701 N. Keyser Ave., Scranton, Pa. 18508. Tel. (717) 344-7258 (for inquiries) or (800) 233-4673 (for orders only, except in Pennsylvania, Hawaii, and Alaska). Offers 2 catalogues—Fastcars: semiannual 132-page catalogue costs $2.95 but is free with an order; Modelcars: 84-page catalogue costs a model-sized $1.95.*

Fastcars. As the name suggests, this is for people who like to drive fast—on a race track, against which no one would argue, or on the highway, which is a dubious proposition. The Cobra RD-4000 radar detector was on sale at a discount in a recent catalogue, along with this quotation from the Cobra manual: "They should not be used to avoid legal enforcement of speed laws." That nonsense aside, and keeping in mind that their use is illegal in many states, the catalogue seems to have many parts, equipment, racing clothing, covers, wheels, scale model kits, books, how-to manuals, and such mysterious things as carburetors. A review of a book on do-it-yourself auto repair that appeared some years ago in *The New York Times* defined a carburetor as "A French word that means 'call a mechanic.' " Discounts of 30 percent or more are reported by this company.

Modelcars. I enjoyed this catalogue very much, especially when I saw a picture of the 1949 Ford model, but there are many others, and it is encouraging that there are enough people around who enjoy this craft to merit such a complete catalogue. No radar detectors.

AUTOMOD, *6477 Peachtree Industrial Blvd., Atlanta, Ga. 30360. Tel. (404) 458-6116. The 60-page catalogue costs $2, refundable on first order.*

A very complete listing of things for cars, including a radar detector (the description does not suggest that its purpose is to avoid getting nailed for speeding), parts, equipment, books, and accessories. Payment by check, money order, Visa, or Mastercard. Shipment by Postal Service or United Parcel, depending on weight. Refunds made.

AUTOMOTION, *3535 Kifer Rd., Santa Clara, Calif. 95051. Tel. (408) 736-9020. The approximately 128-page catalogue issued every 2 years costs $4, refundable against a purchase; for the years in which the catalogue is not issued, a supplement is issued.*

This company deals exclusively in Porsche products (which is probably why I am not personally acquainted with it) and claims to be the largest company in the world offering only Porsche parts via mail order. This is not a discount firm, as one can tell from its very thorough and handsome catalogues. Payment by check, money order, bank transfer, Visa, or Mastercard. Delivery by truck or air freight, especially overseas. Purchases may be returned for refunds within 30 days.

BAYLESS, *1377H Barclay Circle, Marietta, Ga. 30060. Tel. (404) 422-6274. Annual 116-page catalogue costs $5.50.*

This is a very nice, complete catalogue on improving the performance and appearance of Fiats and Lancias. If it were not for the fact that my own low-performance Fiat was destroyed by a drunk hit-and-run driver recently, I would buy a part. The drawing of the parts that can be bought for a carburetor looks as if it were taken from a manual on brain surgery. (I have this thing about carburetors.)

BEVERLY HILLS MOTORING ACCESSORIES, *200 S. Robertson Blvd., Beverly Hills, Calif. 90211. Tel. (213) 657-4800 (in California, Hawaii, Alaska, and foreign countries) or (800) 421-4513 (elsewhere). Semiannual 44-page catalogue costs $2, which is credited against purchases.*

Equipment and gadgets for such expensive cars as Porsches, Mercedes, Ferraris, and BMWs. The catalogue is a handsome one. Payment by check, money order, American Express, Visa, Mastercard, Diners Club, or Carte Blanche. Shipment by United Parcel. Refunds or credit for goods returned within 2 weeks.

B.G.W. LTD., *P.O. Box 498, Milwaukee, Wis. 53201. Tel. (414) 783-4550. Semiannual 28-page catalogue costs $2; there are additional free brochures.*

The catalogue offers kits that allow owners of Volkswagens to put bodies over their frames to make their cars look like old Fords and other nifty, low-tech cars.

BRITISH COACH WORKS LTD., *Arnold, Pa. 15068. Tel. (412) 339-3541 or (800) 245-1369. The 8-page catalogue costs $3.*

The product here is a replica (or "replicar," as they put it) of the 1952 M.G.-TD, and it looks great in the catalogue. Payment by money order, American Express, Visa, Mastercard, or Diners Club (this is such an expensive purchase to charge on a credit card

that I would suggest that a prospective buyer try to negotiate a discount for payment by other means). Customer pick-up or delivery by common carrier. Refunds only on deposits.

BRITISH MOTOR CARS LTD., *100 Sonwil Industrial Park, Buffalo, N.Y. 14225. Tel. (412) 285-1700 or (800) 222-9600 (except in Pennsylvania). The 8-page catalogue costs $3.*

This firm is an affiliate of Antique & Classic Automotive, listed above. It, too, sells something to remind you of the past, in this case the 1952 Jaguar. They offer bodies to plop over the frame of a Pinto, Mustang II, or Bobcat, which British Motors refers to as "the donor car." To use a 1950's word, this car is nifty. Payment by check, money order, American Express, Visa, Mastercard, or Diners Club. Shipment is by common carrier. Full refund within 30 days.

BROOKSTONE. *See listing under* Tools and Equipment for Craftspeople, Tinkerers, and Do-It-Yourselfers.

BURRO INC., *12775 County Road 43, Chaska, Minn. 55318. Tel. (612) 448-2700 or (800) 328-3592 (except in Minnesota, Hawaii, and Alaska). The 12-page catalogue costs $3.*

Small trailers for vacation travel. Payment by check, money order, Visa, or Mastercard. Delivery by company driver. There is a 2-year warranty.

CALIFORNIA MUSTANG, *1249 E. Holt, Pomona, Calif. 91767. Tel. (714) 623-6551, (213) 964-5110, or (800) 854-1737 (except in California). Quarterly 64-page catalogue costs $1.*

Hundreds of replacement and performance items for the excellent Mustang built by Ford. Payment by check, money order, Visa, or Mastercard. Shipment by United Parcel. Refund or credit for merchandise returned within 20 days of receipt.

CAPITAL CYCLE. *BMW auto parts. See listing under* Bicycles and Motorcycles, *below.*

*CAR BUILDER'S CATALOGUE, *H.C. Fastener Co., P.O. Box 900, Alvarado, Tex. 76009. Tel. (817) 783-8519. Annual 64-page catalogue costs $2.*

Equipment and materials to fix up and restore cars, many at discount prices. Door hinge pins that sell for $4.99 elsewhere are priced at 75 cents here. Payment by check, money order, or Mastercard. Shipment by Postal Service, United Parcel, or motor freight.

DICK CEPEK INC., *5302 Tweedy Blvd., South Gate, Calif. 90280. Tel. (213) 566-2131. Semiannual 132-page catalogue is free although it carries a $1 cover price.*

Driving sturdy cars onto beaches, deserts, valleys, hills, and meadows where there are no roads is becoming increasingly popular in this country. This catalogue helps the off-road driver find the right equipment, including heavy-duty tires. There is lots of camping equipment, too, including government surplus items and books on fixing up cars, camping, traveling, biking, etc. In all, this is a big catalogue for outdoor fun. Pay-

ment by money order, Visa, or Mastercard. Shipment by Postal Service, United Parcel, truck, or air freight. Refunds for goods returned within 30 days.

CLARK'S CORVAIR PARTS, *Route 2, Shelburne Falls, Mass. 01370. Tel. (413) 625-9776. Catalogue of over 350 pages costs $4.*

Only in America could there be such a fascination with a single car, in this case the Corvair, that an industry would be developed to deal with it. This company issues a huge catalogue that list 4,500 parts—just for Corvair cars.

CLASSIC MOTORBOOKS, *P.O. Box 1, Osceola, Wis. 54020. Tel. (715) 294-3345 or (800) 826-6600 (except in Wisconsin, Hawaii, Alaska, and Canada). Annual 136-page catalogue costs $2 but is free with an order.*

This company has the world's largest selection of automotive literature. There are thousands of entries listing how-to manuals, histories, etc. Payment by check, money order, American Express, Visa, or Mastercard. Delivery by Postal Service or United Parcel. Refund, replacement, or exchange for returns within 10 days.

DAYTONA COACH BUILDERS/DAYTONA AUTOMOTIVE FIBERGLASS, *819 Carswell Ave., Holly Hill, Fla. 32017. Tel. (904) 253-2575 or (800) 874-0138. Catalogue costs $3.*

Here is another copy of a classic car, in this case an MG, that is built upon the frame of a VW or a Chevette.

DUNE BUGGY SUPPLY, *717 E. Excelsior Ave., Hopkins, Minn. 55343. Tel. (612) 938-8877 or (800) 328-*

3992 (except in Minnesota). Annual 130-page catalogue costs $3.

Hundreds of parts to convert cars for use on the dunes. Payment by check, money order, Visa, or Mastercard. Delivery by United Parcel. Refund or credit for goods returned within 30 days, less 15 percent handling fee.

THE EASTWOOD CO., *15 Waterloo Ave., P.O. Box 524, Berwyn, Pa. 19312. Tel. (215) 644-4412. Catalogue costs $1.*

Auto restoration tools.

*EDGEWOOD NATIONAL TRUCK & EQUIPMENT, *6603 N. Meridian, Puyallup, Wash. 98371. Tel. (206) 927-3388. Annual 128-page catalogue costs $2.*

Wholesale and discount prices on thousands of parts from a "truck & 4x4 supermarket." An example is the steel running board on a Chevy pickup truck that lists for $175 and is available here for $140. Payment by check, money order, Visa, or Mastercard. Shipment by Postal Service, United Parcel or, of course, truck.

EGGE MACHINE CO., *8403 Allport Ave., Santa Fe Springs, Calif. 90670. Tel. (213) 945-3419. Annual 98-page catalogue costs $1.50.*

This is a no-nonsense list of thousands of parts for old cars. If I still had my 1948 Packard, I could buy an oil pump for it for $72. I wish I still had my old Packard.

GO CART, *9140 W. Dodge Rd., Omaha, Neb. 68114. Tel. (402) 397-3911. The 24-page catalogue costs $3.*

A factory direct source of bolt-together go-cart kits.

I.P.D., *2762 N.E. Broadway, Portland, Ore. 97232. Tel. (503) 287-1179. Annual 48-page catalogue costs $3.*

Parts and accessories for Volvos. Payment by money order, American Express, Visa, or Mastercard. Refund or credit for returns made within 30 days.

I.R.D., *1326 Santa Anita Ave., S. El Monte, Calif. 91733. Tel. (213) 575-3224. Free 32-page catalogue*

Utility trailers. Payment by check, money order, American Express, Visa, or Mastercard. Delivery by common carrier. Refunds for returns, less a 20 percent restocking fee.

JOBLOT AUTOMOTIVE INC., *98-11 211th St., P.O. Box 75, Queens Village, N.Y. 11429. Tel. (718) 468-8585 or (800) 221-0172 (except in New York). Free annual 148-page catalogue.*

This company specializes in supplying parts for antique and classic Fords and Ford products, 1909 to 1969, "including the Model T, Model A, Early Ford V-8, Nifty Fifties, Thunderbirds, Mustangs, Falcons and all other passenger cars, as well as trucks."

LARRY'S THUNDERBIRD & MUSTANG PARTS, *511 S. Raymond Ave., Fullerton, Calif. 92631. Tel. (714) 871-6432, (800) 854-0393 (except in California), or (800) 858-6125 (in California). Free 52-page catalogue issued twice a year.*

MALM CHEM CORP., *Box 300, Pound Ridge, N.Y. 10576. Tel. (914) 764-5775. Brochure price list.*

Products devoted to the care of auto paint surfaces, including waxes and cloths.

MASONVILLE GARAGE, *Box 57, Masonville, Iowa 50654. Tel. (319) 927-4290. Annual 96-page catalogue costs $2.*

Hundreds of parts for the 1928–31 Model A Fords. Payment by check, money order, Visa, or Mastercard. Delivery by Postal Service or United Parcel. Goods may be returned, with permisson, within 30 days for credit.

M. G. MITTEN MOTORING ACCESSORIES, *44 S. Chester Ave., Pasadena, Calif. 91106. Tel. (818) 681-4531, (800) 423-4517 (except in California), or (800) 821-1105 (in California). Annual 48-page catalogue costs $2.*

Besides mittens (that is, covers) for MGs, this place provides lots of other accessories for MGs and other sports and sporty cars.

*MIDAMERICA PARTS & EQUIPMENT CO., *1212 E. 19th St., Kansas City, Mo. 64108. Tel. (816) 221-4232 (office), (816) 471-2298 (parts), or (800) 821-5493 (except in Missouri). Annual 36-page catalogue costs $2.*

The speciality here is Jeep replacement parts. Their prices generally follow American Motors wholesale prices. Payment by check, money order, Visa, or Mastercard. Shipment by United Parcel or commercial truck. Refund or credit for returned goods.

MOSS MOTORS LTD., *P.O. Box MG, Goleta, Calif. 93116. Tel. (805) 968-1041, (800) 235-6954 (except in California), or (800) 322-6985 (in California only). The 40- to 104-page catalogue costs $2.*

This company describes itself as the largest supplier of parts for British sports cars in the world and publishes 7 separate catalogues—for MG (TC/TD/TF), MGA, MGB, Triumph (TR2/3/4/4A), Triumph TR 250/6, Austin-Healey (100/100-6/3000), and Jaguar XK (120/140/150).

MOTOR SHEEP, *5466 Complex Dr., Suite 203, San Diego, Calif. 92123. Tel. (619) 569-8111, (800) 854-1500 (except in California), or (800) 542-6300 (in California). Free 24-page catalogue.*

Mainly sheepskin seat covers, but also men's and women's sheepskin clothing and rugs and other accessories for the home.

MOTORBOOKS INTERNATIONAL. *Books on cars. See listing for Zenith Aviation Books under* Aviation, *below.*

NATIONAL AUTO PARTS DEPOT, *3101 S.W. 40th Blvd., Gainesville, Fla. 32607. Tel. (904) 378-2473 or (800) 874-7595 (except in Florida). Free catalogues, 64 pages for the Mustang, 48 for the Thunderbird.*

This company's catalogues of parts and acessories for the 1955–57 T-Bird and the 1965–73 Mustang are the most comprehensive available. Payment by check, money order, Visa, or Mastercard. Shipment by Postal Service, United Parcel, truck, or, if requested, overnight courier service. Refund or credit for returned parts, with 20 percent restocking fee charged if the return was caused by customer mistake.

PERFECT PLASTICS INDUSTRIES, *Schreiber Industrial Park No. 213, New Kensington, Pa. 15068. Tel. (412) 339-3568 or (800) 245-6520 (except in Pennsylvania). Annual 16-page catalogue costs $3,*

Fiberglass parts for imported cars and "fun" bodies to plop atop VW frames.

*PICKUP EQUIPMENT COMPANY, *P.O. Box 217, Hewitt, Tex. 76643. Tel. (817) 756-6221 or (800) 433-3323 (except in Texas). Free annual catalogue.*

This supplier offers equipment for pickups at discount prices.

PRINCESS AUTO & MACHINERY LTD., *P.O. Box 1005, Winnipeg, Man., Canada R3C 2W7. Tel. (204) 667-4630 or (800) 665-8685 (in Canada only). Free quarterly catalogue of 230 or 100 pages.*

Parts for cars and trucks, plus plenty of tools and machinery for use on farms and in factories. The company has a United States outlet for purchases south of the border: Northern Supply Co., Box 378, Walhalla, N.D. 58282; tel. (701) 549-2444. Payment by check, money order, Visa, or Mastercard. Shipment by Postal Service, truck, or rail transport. Refund, credit, or exchange for goods returned within 15 days.

PYRAMID PRODUCTS CO. *See listing under* Tools and Equipment for Craftspeople, Tinkerers, and Do-It-Yourselfers.

RACER WALSH CO., *Bel Ans Park, Orangeburg, N.Y. 10962. Tel. (914) 365-0500. The 78-page catalogue costs $3.*

Ford auto parts at competitive prices.

*RACING UNLIMITED, *2607 Hennepin Ave. South, Minneapolis, Minn. 55408. Tel. (612) 377-6707. Annual 48-page catalogue costs $2.*

Automotive products at discount prices. There are lots of things to make your fast car go faster plus a radar detector in case the products work and you do go faster. Also,

how-to books and clothes to wear while driving fast.

RAMS HEAD, *3070 Kerner Blvd., San Rafael, Calif. 94901. Tel. (415) 457-7180; for orders: (800) 227-2700 (except in California) or (800) 772-2648 (in California). Free 16-page catalogue.*

Sheepskin seatcovers are offered, along with some stuffed animals.

*R. C. CORVETTE MOTORCAR ACCESSORIES, *835 N. LaBrea Ave., Los Angeles, Calif. 90038. Tel. (213) 93-VETTE, (800) 42-VETTE (except in California, Hawaii, and Alaska), or (800) 428-3883 (in California). Semiannual 40-page catalogue costs $1.*

Corvette Accessories, some at discounts, such as doormats for $55 that list for $70. Some men's and women's clothing available, including panties and briefs with Corvette symbols. Payment by check, money order, American Express, Visa, or Mastercard. Shipment by United Parcel. Refunds for returns made within 10 days of shipment.

*RELIABLE TIRE DISTRIBUTORS, *P.O. Box 560, Camden, N.J. 08101. Tel. (609) 365-6500. Free 10-page catalogue issued once or twice a year.*

Discount prices on tires. Payment by check or money order. Shipment by United Parcel. No returns accepted.

*BOB SHARP RACING PARTS & ACCESSORIES, *21 South St., Danbury, Conn. 06801. Tel. (203) 743-4487. Annual 32-page catalogue costs $3.*

Here are parts and accessories for the BMW, Datsun, and Mazda, many at discounts. An example is a Z wing regularly $230, offered here for $200.

SKINNY'S DOWN UNDER, *1160 Industry Dr., P.O. Box 88067, Seattle, Wash. 98188. Tel. (206) 575-9128 or (800) 426-4626 (except in Washington State, Hawaii, and Alaska). Free catalogue of 16 to 24 pages issued twice a year.*

Sheepskin car seat covers are the speciality, and there are also sheepskin slippers and jackets. The name comes from the company's headquarters locations in New Zealand and Australia. Payment by check, money order, Visa, or Mastercard. Shipment by Postal Service or United Parcel. Refund or credit for returned goods.

*SPORTS & CLASSICS, *512 Boston Post Rd., Darien, Conn. 06820. Tel. (203) 655-8731 or (203) 655-8732. Annual 476-page catalogue costs $7.*

This company is an importer, exporter, distributor, and manufacturer of parts for British sports cars. Its products are available at a discount. Payment by check, money order, C.O.D., Visa, or Mastercard. Delivery usually by United Parcel. Returns may be made within 14 days with a 20 percent charge, but there are no cash refunds. Adjustments are made in credit against another purchase or exchange.

STULL INDUSTRIES, *1501 W. Pomona Rd., Corona, Calif. 91720. Tel. (714) 371-4561 or (800) 227-9206 (except in California). Annual 32-page catalogue costs $1.*

Custom steel grilles for vans and pickups, roll bars, and sway bars.

THREE-STAR PRESS, *Box 57, Masonville, Iowa 50654. Tel. (319) 927-4290. Annual 6-page brochure price list costs $1, including 3 sample postcards.*

Car-oriented collector of postcards from the turn of the century to more modern times.

*TROUTMAN LTD., *3198-L Airport Loop Dr., Costa Mesa, Calif. 92626. Tel. (714) 979-3295. Annual 8-page catalogue costs $5, refundable with any purchase.*

Discounts promised on virtually all items, which consist of Porsche parts and accessories. Payment by check, money order, C.O.D., Visa, or Mastercard. Shipment by Postal Service or United Parcel. Returns because of purchaser's error are subject to 15 percent handling charge and must be made within 30 days.

*VICTORIA BRITISH/SUNBEAM SPARES, *8609 Quivera Rd., Lenexa, Kan. 66215. Tel. (913) 541-8500 or (800) 255-0088 (except in Kansas). Catalogue costs $3 but is free with order.*

This company imports, distributes, and manufactures original equipment, reproduction parts, steel body panels, accessories, trim, tops, and interiors for British cars, especially MGs, Triumphs, and Sunbeams. Discounts of 10 to 30 percent are reported on the 5,000 parts carried. Payment by check, money order, C.O.D., American Express, Visa, or Mastercard. Shipment by Postal Service, United Parcel, or truck freight. Refund or replacement for purchases returned within 5 days of receipt.

*WESTERN TIRE CENTERS, *Arizona Desert Rat Off Road, 3705 S. Palo Verde, Tucson, Ariz. 85713. Tel. (602) 790-8502, (800) 528-3402 (except in Arizona), or (800)362-7006 (in Arizona). Free 44-page catalogue issued twice a year.*

Discount prices reported on a large number of auto and off-road vehicle equipment and accessories. An example is a Chevy Blazer tire carrier that retails for $121, on sale at $85.

WILCO SALES CORP., *P.O. Box 1128, Rochester, N.Y. 14603. Tel. (716) 442-7050. Annual 52-page catalogue costs $2 but is free with order.*

This company is one of the country's oldest distributors, manufacturers, and importers of accessories for sports cars.

Bicycles and Motorcycles

*BIKE NASHBAR, *10344 Youngstown-Pittsburgh Rd., New Middletown, Ohio 44442. Tel. (216) 542-3671 or (800) 345-BIKE (except in Ohio). The 56-page catalogue issued 4 or 5 times a year costs 50 cents.*

Discount prices on bike accessories, including a $12 pump for $7.50 and a $50 helmet for $36. There are also discounts on the bicycles themselves and lots of clothing, tools, parts, tents, and shoes.

CAMPMOR. *See listing under* Camping Equipment.

*CAPITAL CYCLE CORP., *2328 Champlain St., N.W., Washington, D.C. 20009. Tel. (202) 387-7360. Free 80-page annual catalogue.*

This company's prices are 20 percent below list for spare parts for BMW motorcycles.

*CLINTON CYCLE & SALVAGE, *6709 Old Branch Ave., Camp Springs, Md. 20748. Tel. (301) 449-3550 or* (800) 332-8264 (except in Maryland). Brochure price list.*

One of the largest suppliers of used motorcycle parts on the East Coast, with estimated savings of up to 60 percent over new parts prices. Payment by check, money order, American Express, Visa, Mastercard, or Choice. Shipment by Postal Service, United Parcel, or air freight. Purchases may be returned for refund within 14 days if a wrong or defective part was sent.

*CYCLE GOODS, *2735 Hennepin Ave. South, Minneapolis, Minn. 55408. Tel. (612) 872-7600 or (800) 328-5213 (except in Hawaii, Alaska, and Minnesota). Annual 180-page catalogue (called the* Handbook of Cycl-ology, *get it?) costs $3.*

Discounts of 10 to 40 percent off list for bicycles, accessories, tools, parts, and technical information needed by serious bikers.

CYCLO-PEDIA, *P.O. Box 427, Midland, Mich. 48640. Tel. (517) 835-2026 from 8 to 10 P.M. (Eastern time) on Mondays and Thursdays. The 72-page catalogue costs $2.*

The prices are "competitive," but not discount since there are no established retail prices for imported bike parts. Besides parts, accessories, and shoes, the catalogue also contains articles discussing the various aspects of biking that the serious biker might want to read. Payment by check, money order, Visa, or Mastercard. Shipment by Postal Service or United Parcel. Refund or credit for returns; no time limit, but goods may not be worn or scratched.

HINE/SNOWBRIDGE, *P.O. Box 4059, Boulder, Colo. 80306. Tel. (303) 530-1530. Free semiannual 16-page catalogue.*

Accessories, mostly for packing things on the bike.

MICHAEL'S CYCLERY, *233 Main St., Ames, Iowa 50010. Tel. (515) 232-7027. Monthly 4-page catalogue is free in exchange for a self-addressed stamped envelope.*

The specialty here is racing—frames, accessories, bicycles, parts, shoes. The owner is manager of a leading amateur bicycle racing team. Payment by check, money order, American Express, Visa, or Mastercard. Shipment by United Parcel. Refunds on unused purchases, less 15 percent restocking fee.

MIDVALE BOOKS, *155 S.W. Midvale Rd., Portland, Ore. 97219. Tel. (503) 636-7952. Catalogue issued 2 or 3 times a year costs $1.*

Talk of specialization, here is a catalogue devoted to books on bicycles and bicycling. It is not far-fetched. Some of the best writing I have seen is to be found in the section on the Tour de France in John Hess's book *Vanishing France* and in my friend George Vecsey's sports columns in *The New York Times* on bicycle races. I even covered a bicycle race once, in Baltimore. A bike race lacks the drama of a bullfight, but at least no animals are killed, at least not intentionally. Biking is good for you, it gets you where you want to go, and it doesn't burn any fossil fuel.

MOUNTAIN BIKES, *P.O. Box 405, Fairfax, Calif. 94930. Tel. (415) 459-2247. The 4- to 12-page catalogue issued once or twice a year costs $2.*

Bicycles, wheels, components, tools, and gears from a company that aims to "build a bicycle that feels like a natural extension of the rider." Payment by check, money order, Visa, or Mastercard. Delivery by Postal Service, United Parcel, truck, or Greyhound. Refund or credit for goods returned within 30 days, but no returns are accepted on tools.

PALO ALTO BICYCLES, *P.O. Box 1276, Palo Alto, Calif. 94302. Tel. (415) 328-0128 or (800) 227-8900 (except in California, Alaska, and Hawaii). Free annual 16- and 50-page catalogues.*

Everything for the biker, from clothes and shoes to frames, parts, and accessories to books. Prices are described as competitive but not discount. Payment by check, money order, Visa, or Mastercard. Shipment by Postal Service or United Parcel. Refunds for unused purchases returned within 30 days.

REI. *Bike equipment. See listing under* Camping Equipment.

Aviation

†THE COCKPIT/AVIREX LTD., *627 Broadway, New York, N.Y. 10012. Tel. (212) 420-1600. The 32-page catalogue issued 4 to 6 times a year costs $2.*

Clothing and accessories, much of it leather, for the well-dressed pilot or the deskbound who can only wish they were in the wide blue yonder. Also video tapes on Air Force history, great battles, and raids.

SKYCLONES, *2285 Oakvale Dr., Shingle Springs, Calif. 95682. Tel. (916) 677-2456. The 6-page catalogue costs $1.*

Accoutrements for flying buffs, including a line of rubber stamps depicting airplanes (one of them is the Sopwith Camel, Snoopy fans), stationery, books, and toys (there's Snoopy!). Payment by check or money order. Shipment by Postal Service or United Parcel. Purchases may be returned for refund or exchange.

ZENITH AVIATION BOOKS, *729 Prospect Ave., Osceola, Wis. 54020. Tel. (715) 294-3345 or (800) 826-6600 (except in Wisconsin, Hawaii, and Alaska). Free 36-page catalogue issued every 2 months.*

For hobbyists, enthusiasts, and professionals in aviation, a very large number of books on the subject. The same company publishes and distributes books about cars under the Motorbooks International name.

❖ 11 The Great Outdoors

Please go camping in the great outdoors while it is still there. My Boy Scout troop used to camp at Pine Hill, which used to be in the country outside Camden, N.J. Now it's being turned into a housing development.

When I was a youngster, I would take the bus to the ferry slip in Camden for the short ride across the Delaware River to Philadelphia. The waterfront area wasn't trendy in those days, but it had many small (barely profitable, I think) stores and two army-navy surplus stores that fascinated me. One of them was called Goldberg's (actually it was one of two places with similar names), and that is where I bought my sleeping bag, some bad-smelling insect repellent that didn't keep many bugs away but could make you unpopular among fellow Boy Scouts, a mess kit, and an ax.

One estimate puts the total sales relating to oudoor recreation at $244 billion a year. Of that, $40 billion is spent on recreation monitored by the Fish and Wildlife Service of the Department of the Interior. That includes hunting and fishing as well as what the government calls "nonconsumptive" activities, including bird watching, bird and animal photography, and bird feeding. The total fish and wildlife expenditure includes not only products that can be found in this part of the book, such as recreational equipment and clothing, but also such services as transportation and hotel accommodation.

According to the latest poll conducted by the Census Bureau on behalf of the Fish and Wildlife Service, in 1980, a total of 54 million Americans said they went fishing, 19 million said they were hunters, and 83 million said they were involved in "nonconsumptive" wildlife activities. There is, of course, a lot of overlapping, with many hunters also going fishing when that season rolls around.

These changes were noted in the poll: Hunting remains a largely male province, but more and more women are enjoying fishing. In addition, more residents of urban areas are joining the fishing corps, which the Fish and Wildlife Service believes is a result of the cleaning up of many rivers and streams near big cities. The biggest increase, according to the poll, has been the huge number of people watching, photographing, and feeding birds, and the annual bill for birdseed alone is now put at $517 million.

One of the few outdoor activities that this book can't help you with is the sale of firearms. Small weapons, such as pistols, cannot be purchased through the mail. Larger weapons, such as rifles and shotguns, may be purchased by mail, but only when the merchant and purchaser are in the same state. In that case, the chief law enforcement officer in the purchaser's home town is given prior notice and has seven days in which to object to the sale for any of a number of reasons. The National Rifle Association says that 5 million firearms are purchased in the United States each year; naturally, only a small fraction, perhaps a few hundred, are mail transactions.

When I was a boy, I also used to go fishing with my father. We would set out before dawn, take a long bus ride to Wildwood Crest, N.J., and there board a party boat for a day of fishing in the Atlantic, south of Cape May. (The best place was near the ruin of a concrete ship that sank many years ago; I remember thinking that even *I* could have told them a concrete ship was not a very good idea.) Our boat would find every bump in the ocean. I dropped my line over the side once, just before getting sick, and when a fish bit the hook my father had to pull it in. The fish was the largest caught that day, and we won the pool, which probably paid for our trip, but I was too young to notice and too sick to care. I should have quit while I was ahead, but I didn't. I went out with my father other times and even managed not to get sick sometimes, but we never won the pool again.

In recent years, I have been to many events at the Smithsonian Institution and few of them were as happy as the commemoration of the fiftieth anniversary of the publication of Roger Tory Peterson's classic field guide so essential to birdwatchers. Hardly the spacey little old ladies in tennis shoes celebrated in clichés, these are very nice people from just about every part of society, many of whom enjoyed watching birds as youngsters even before discovering that others were enjoying the same thing in a systematic way.

Sporting Goods

AKERS SKI, *Nordic Acres Way, Andover, Me. 04216. Tel. (207) 392-4582. Free annual 32-page catalogue, plus 2 or 3 sale catalogues.*

Skis, bindings, poles, boots, waxes, mittens, books, men's and women's clothing, children's equipment. Payment by check, money order, Visa, Mastercard, or C.O.D. Shipment by Postal Service or United Parcel. Refund or credit for returned purchases.

*AUSTAD'S, *4500 E. 10th St., P.O. Box 1428, Sioux Falls, S.D. 57101. Tel. (605) 336-3135. Free 32- to 64-page catalogue issued 4 times a year.*

The main interest here is golf. There are clubs, bags, carts, balls, shoes, and caps. In addition, there are sports shoes and clothing for men and women, baseball and softball gloves, exercise equipment, and tents and other outdoor equipment. The prices are below list, but the company doesn't like the label "discount house."

EDDIE BAUER, *15010 N.E. 36th St., Redmond, Wash. 98052. Tel. (206) 882-6100, (800) 426-8020 (except in Alaska, Hawaii, and Washington State), (800) 426-6363 (in Alaska and Hawaii), or (206) 885-3330 (in Washington State). Free 48- to 100-page catalogue issued 7 times a year.*

This is a class act. Imagine an 800 toll-free number just for Alaska and Hawaii. This is a place where I know I can go (they have a retail store near me in Washington, D.C.) for a piece of equipment that I can't find elsewhere. The main emphasis in the catalogue is on clothing for outdoor activities like boating, camping, golf, running, hiking, or just looking sharp. Also available are equipment for the above and for diving and exercising, plus bedding and shoes.

MOSS BROWN & CO., *5210 Eisenhower Ave., Alexandria, Va. 22304. Tel. (703) 751-0230 or (800) 424-2774. Free 40-page catalogue issued 12 to 24 times a year.*

Here is another place reluctant to be called "discount" but offering what it calls lower prices. It is the largest distributor of Gore-Tex running apparel and sells some $200 equipment for $129. The offerings include long underwear (Moss Brown Bodywear) and other cold weather gear, running wear, exercise equipment, shoes, and special support underwear (jock straps and bras) for athletes.

THE COMPETITIVE EDGE GOLF CATALOGUE, *39 W. 14th St., Suite 504, New York, N.Y. 10011. Tel. (212) 206-0760 or (800) 334-0854 (except in North Carolina). Free 8- to 16-page catalogue issued twice a year.*

Golf clubs and equipment. Payment by check, money order, American Express, Visa, or Mastercard. Shipment by Postal Service or United Parcel. Purchases may be returned within 30 days for refund or credit.

ENDURANCE SPORTS, *2206 S. 2000 West, Salt Lake City, Utah 84119. Tel. (801) 972-8740 or (800) 874-6740 (except in Utah). Quarterly 40-page catalogue costs $2.*

My daughter the runner (Ellen) gets this catalogue, which features running clothes and shoes plus bathing suits, bicycle clothing and shoes (and bicycles themselves), jewelry for athletes, watches, and rainwear.

†GOLF DAY PRODUCTS, *3015 Commercial Ave., Northbrook, Ill. 60062. Tel. (312) 498-1400 or (800) 433-4653 (except in Illinois). Quarterly 48-page catalogue costs 50 cents.*

Do-it-yourself golf supplies by mail, including golf grips and wood refinishing kits, plus gifts with a golfing flavor.

HIGHLANDER CO., *1072 Jacoby Rd., Akron, Ohio 44321. Tel. (216) 253-9524. Brochure price list.*

Men's and women's sports clothes, including sweaters and golf shirts, plus golf clubs and balls and other sports equipment.

HILLS' COURT, *100 Tennis Way, Manchester, Vt. 05254. Tel. (802) 362-1200. Free 40-page catalogue issued twice a year.*

Men's, women's, and children's tennis clothes, racquets, and balls, plus exercise and running togs.

PORT CANVAS, *P.O. Box H, Kennebunkport, Me. 04046. Tel. (207) 967-5570. Free 24-page catalogue issued 3 or 4 times a year.*

Duffles, handbags, beachcomber totes, seafaring shoulder bags, windsuits for wearing during sailing, slickers, and backpacks.

†*ROYAL GOLF PRODUCTS CORP., *P.O. Box C, Clarkson, Mich. 48016. Tel. (313) 625-1313. Free 32- to 48-page catalogue issued 4 times a year.*

Discounts of 35 to 45 percent off normal pro shop prices for golf clubs, balls, bags, gloves, men's and women's clothes, and shoes.

One of the catalogues contains gift suggestions.

SPORT ACESSORIES INTERNATIONAL. *Clothes, books, etc. This is actually the second part of the Racing Unlimited catalogue listed in* Automotive Needs.

†SPORTFOLIO, *7925 E. Harvard Ave., Suite F, Denver, Colo. 80231. Tel. (303) 750-4817. Free 28-page catalogue issued 4 times a year.*

Accessories for golfers and tennis players, many of them good ideas for gifts: a mounted gold-plated golf ball, stationery, watches with tennis or golf themes on the face, glassware.

SPORTS GIFT DIGEST, *1020 Church St., Evanston, Ill. 60201. Tel. (312) 491-6440. Semiannual 68-page catalogue costs $1.50.*

†TENNIS LADY, *9840 Monroe, Suite 116, Dallas, Tex. 75220. Tel. (214) 353-9631 or (800) 527-7523 (except in Texas). Free 32-page catalogue issued twice a year.*

Despite the name, this is for men as well as women, although the emphasis is by far on women. There are tennis clothes, ball machines, court dryers, gift items. Payment by check, money order, American Express, Visa, or Mastercard. Shipment by Postal Service or United Parcel. Refund or credit for purchases returned within 30 days.

See also *Casual and Sports Clothing.*

Boating and Fishing Supplies

AIRBORNE SALES CO. *See listing under* Tools and Equipment for Craftspeople, Tinkerers, and Do-It-Yourselfers.

ANGLING SPECIALTIES, *P.O. Box 6, Lethbridge, Alba., Canada T1J 3Y3. Tel. (403) 328-5252. Annual 40-page catalogue costs $1.*

Tools, hooks, accessories, and books for the angler, including equipment and materials for do-it-yourself lure-making and fly tying. A slightly smaller catalogue is issued under the name *Hook & Hackle*. Payment by check. Delivery by Postal Service, bus, or truck. Refund or credit for purchases returned within 5 days.

BASS PRO SHOPS, *1935 S. Campbell, Springfield, Mo. 65807. Tel. (417) 887-1915 or (800) 227-7776 (except in Missouri). Annual 400-page catalogue costs $2.*

This place calls itself the world's leading supplier of premium fishing tackle. There are boats, reels, line, rods, tackle boxes, plugs, spinners, lures, clothing, and safety equipment for fishermen. Perhaps on the theory that even the most devoted angler has to come ashore from time to time, there is also camping, archery, and hunting equipment.

BLUE HOLE CANOE CO., *Sunbright, Tenn. 37872. Tel. (615) 628-2116. Free 20-page catalogue.*

The catalogue contains a chatty account of how the company got started and how the owners chose the name, details of which I will permit the reader to discover. There are 6 models of canoes, from $775 to $1,025 (plus shipping, tax, etc.), in the catalogue in front of me, which strikes me as not unreasonable, but prices do have a tendency to rise, so these prices are not set in concrete (excuse the expression). There is also a line of safety equipment and repair material. Payment by check or money order. Delivery by United Parcel

for small things, commercial truck lines for canoes. Canoes may be returned for refunds at any time, but only if in unused condition.

*DEFENDER INDUSTRIES, *255 Main St., New Rochelle, N.Y. 10801. Tel. (914) 632-3001. Annual 200-page catalogue costs $1.25.*

This company has the most complete discount marine products catalogue in the U.S. and has been in business for 45 years. There are fiberglass, Styrofoam, polyurethane and such, plus less modern things like grommets, snaps, hooks, anchors, chains, compasses, knives, clothing, and equipment. Payment by check, money order, or C.O.D. Delivery by Postal Service, United Parcel, truck, bus, or air freight. Refund or credit for goods returned within 10 days.

*E. & B. MARINE, *980 Gladys Ct., P.O. Box 747, Edison, N.J. 08818. Tel. (201) 287-3900. Free 130-page catalogue.*

The catalogue lists many discounts, from simple pieces of hardware to sophisticated electronic gear. Payment by check, American Express, Visa, Mastercard, Diners Club, or Carte Blanche. Delivery by Postal Service (parcel post), United Parcel, or air courier services. Requests for refund, exchange, or credit must be made within 10 days of receipt.

FOLBOT INC., *P.O. Box 70877, Charleston, S.C. 29405. Tel. (803) 744-3483. The 20-page catalogue costs $1.*

Five models of lightweight, unsinkable boats are available. One model is a folding boat that can be stored in your closet or transported in your car trunk. They come al-

166

ready built or in kits. To a nonboater like me, they resemble canoes and kayaks, but anyone wanting a clearer description will have to send for the catalogue.

GLEN-L MARINE DESIGNS, *Box 756, Bellflower, Calif. 90706. Tel. (213) 630-6258. Annual 152-page catalogue costs $3.*

This is for the boater with another skill—building the boat itself. There are plans, patterns, and kits. According to the catalogue "anyone with average do-it-yourself abilities AND who can follow instructions can build his own boat when using our plans." A do-it-yourselfer could save 30 to 50 percent off the cost of a factory-built boat. Payment by check, money order, Visa, or Mastercard. Shipment by Postal Service, United Parcel, or common carrier.

*GOLDBERG'S MARINE, *202 Market St., Philadelphia, Pa. 19106. Tel. for orders only: (215) 627-3700 or (800) BOATING (except in Pennsylvania, Alaska, and Hawaii); for other things: (215) 627-3719 or (800) 523-2926. The 228-page catalogue costs $2.*

Many boating items offered at discount prices, including a large selection of clothing, electronic instruments, tools, hardware, ropes, radios, and lights. Payment by check, money order, American Express, Visa, or Mastercard. Delivery by Postal Service, United Parcel, air, or truck; a nice feature of the order form is a section where the customer can check off the preferred means of transportation. Merchandise may be returned within 10 days.

HOOK & HACKLE. *See listing for Angling Specialties, above.*

INTERNATIONAL MARINE PUBLISHING, *21 Elm St., Camden, Me. 04843. Tel. (207) 236-4837. Free 16-page catalogue issued monthly.*

Books for boaters, covering everything from navigation to cooking, including boat building, repairs, health, sailing, and fishing. Payment by check, money order, Visa, or Mastercard. Shipment by United Parcel. Books may be returned for refund or credit, but they must be in saleable conditon.

*M. & E. MARINE SUPPLY CO., *P.O. Box 601, Camden, N.J. 08101. Tel. (609) 858-1010. Annual 300-page catalogue costs $2; 4 sale flyers each year are free.*

This company offers substantial discounts off list prices and claims its boating supply catalogue is the most complete. It is very large and has lots of equipment, including 4 pages just on "heads," which I am given to understand has a meaning at sea entirely different from the one on land.

NAVAL INSTITUTE PRESS, *2062 Generals Highway, Annapolis, Md. 21401. Tel. (301) 268-6110. Free annual 24-page catalogue, plus 3-page springtime flyer with upcoming titles.*

This is in Annapolis but is not an arm of the United States Navy, although its books are used by students at the Naval, Coast Guard, and Merchant Marine Academies. The list includes how-to books on boating and navigation plus battle histories.

*NETCRAFT COMPANY, *2800 Tremainsville Rd., Toledo, Ohio 43613. Tel. (419) 472-9826. Free semiannual 162-page catalogue.*

Rods, reels, hooks, boxes, books, tools, lines, lures—just about anything an angler might want, all at prices said to be 25 to 40 percent below the suggested list prices. They also have crab traps, which are about my speed. As the catalogue notes, you don't have to be an expert to catch crabs. I am very good at it. When we used to visit our friends Liz and Artie, at their place on Oyster Creek in New Jersey, I would drop a trap in the water, come back a while later and pull it up, and sometimes there would be a crab inside.

*NEW ENGLAND DIVERS, *131 Rantoul St., Beverly, Mass. 01915. Tel. (617) 922-6951 or (800) 343-8122 (except in Massachusetts). Annual free 32-page catalogue.*

This company discounts all major brands of scuba diving equipment; for example, a single 80 cu. ft. aluminum tank with J-valve that lists for $236 is offered here for $145. Payment by check, money order, bank wire, American Express, Visa, Mastercard, or PADI Diver's Card. Shipment by Postal Service, United Parcel, motor freight, or whatever customer requests. Refunds for goods returned within 30 days, provided they have not been abused.

S. T. PRESTON & SON, *Main St. Wharf, Greenport, N.Y. 11944. Tel. (516) 477-1990. Free 112-page catalogue issued twice a year.*

This catalogue is crammed with nice things for sailors. There are nautical lamps, mugs, carvings, ships in bottles, ships outside bottles, clocks, barometers. Payment by check, money order, American Express, Visa, or Mastercard. Shipment by Postal Service, United Parcel, or motor freight. Refunds made for purchases returned within 30 days.

QUIK-N-EASY PRODUCTS LTD., *P.O. Box 878, Monrovia, Calif. 91016. Tel. (818) 358-0562. Free annual 4-page catalogue.*

Devices for getting a boat out of the water and onto the car. The company prefers to sell through dealers, but will sell by mail order if there is not a retailer near you or if you want replacement parts. Payment by check or money order. Delivery by Postal Service or United Parcel. Refunds will be made if goods are returned within 15 days and have not been assembled.

RUVEL & CO. *See listing under* Army and Navy Goods, *below.*

SAILRITE ENTERPRISES, *Rt. 1, Columbia City, Ind. 46725. Tel. (219) 244-6715 or (800) 348-2769 (except in Indiana). Annual 60-page catalogue costs $2.*

This is a catalogue of fabrics, tools, and instructions for the sailors who want to make their own sails. The catalogue says "making your own sails is one of life's satisfying experiences."

*THE TACKLE BOX, *303 Dillingham Ave., Falmouth, Mass. 02540. Tel. (617) 540-6800. Free catalogue.*

Discount prices on fishing equipment; one example is 2,400 yards of 20-pound test Stren fishing line, listed at $39.95, for $29.95. Payment by check, money order, Visa, or Mastercard. Shipment by Postal Service or

United Parcel. Refunds for goods returned within 15 days.

TUGON CHEMICAL CORP., *P.O. Box 31, Cross River, N.Y. 10518. Tel. (203) 762-3953. Brochure price list.*

Marine adhesives and coatings at factory prices.

*WAREHOUSE MARINE DISCOUNT, *4714 Ballard Ave. N.W., Seattle, Wash. 98107. Tel. (206) 789-3296 or (800) 426-8666 (except in Washington State). The 224-page catalogue costs $2, plus free 68-page fall and spring supplements.*

There are discounts reported here on clothing, electronics, hardware, equipment, lights, ladders, binoculars, not to mention blocks, booms, winches, pintles and gudgeons, boom vang and backstay systems, snatch blocks and fairleads. Great terms, aren't they?

THE WOODEN BOAT SHOP, *1007 N.E. Boat St., Seattle, Wash. 98105. Tel. (206) 634-3600. The 24-page catalogue costs $1.50.*

This is the most attractive catalogue I've seen in this category, although by its nature it must be more limited than the others listed here. There are many woodworking tools, plus hardware to install on boats, lamps, books, etc.

*YACHTMAIL CO., LTD., *5–7 Cornwall Crescent, London, W11 1PH, England. Tel. (01) 727-2373. Annual 22-page catalogue costs $2.*

Even with the cost of air freight, this company offers U.S. customers discounts on British-made items. For example, the Autohelm 3000 autopilot, which lists for $700 in the U.S., could be purchased for $500, including airmail charges. (These prices, of course, are approximate since they are affected by fluctuations in currency rates.) Payment by check, money order, Visa, or Mastercard. Shipment by Postal Service or air freight. Refunds for faulty goods returned within a year.

Camping Equipment

ADVENTURE 16 *(A16), 4620 Alvarado Canyon Rd., San Diego, Calif. 92120. Tel. (619) 283-2374. Free 20-page catalogue issued twice a year.*

A good-looking catalogue with backpacks (for people and dogs, too), clothing, tents, bags, and other things for the camper. Payment by check, money order, Visa, or Mastercard. Shipment usually by United Parcel but by Postal Service on request. This is one of the places, incidentally, that does not charge extra for shipping within the contiguous 48 states but includes it in the price. Refund or credit for returns within 20 days or after first use, which sounds like an excellent policy.

AIRBORNE SALES CO. *See listing under* Tools and Equipment for Craftspeople, Tinkerers, and Do-It-Yourselfers.

*BAILEY'S, *P.O. Box 550, Laytonville, Calif. 95494. Tel. (707) 984-6133, (800) 358-1661 (except in California), or (800) 356-1300 (except in Tennessee). Free 78-page catalogue issued 3 times a year.*

This is a catalogue aimed primarily at the professional logger, but I include it here because some of the equipment might be wanted by people reading this section of the book. There are tools for cutting trees, fire-fighting equipment, tree climbing equipment, boots, rain gear, shirts, safety equipment, and toys for little loggers. There are discount prices for, among other things, coats, chain saws, and chain saw accessories.

BIBLER TENTS, *954 A Pearl St., Boulder, Colo. 80302. Tel. (303) 449-7351. Brochure price list.*

These tents are lightweight and look a lot more roomy and colorful than the tents we used when I was a Boy Scout.

BIKE NASHBAR. *Camping equipment. See listing under* Bicycles and Motorcycles.

BRIGADE QUARTERMASTERS, *266 Roswell St., Marietta, Ga. 30060. Tel. (404) 428-1234. Free 48- to 96-page catalogue issued 4 to 6 times a year.*

Men's, women's, and children's outdoor clothing, such as sweaters, flight jackets, battle dress, trousers, hats, caps, and boots, plus military badges, humor and gifts, hunting accessories and knives, binoculars, books, and camping gear. Some of this stuff looks as if it is intended for use during Armageddon but actually would be helpful somewhere short of that. Payment by check, money order, American Express, Visa, Mastercard, or Diners Club. Shipment by Postal Service or

United Parcel. Refund or credit for unsatisfactory purchases returned.

*CAMPMOR, *810 Route 17 North, P.O. Box 999, Paramus, N.J. 07652. Tel. (201) 445-5500 or (800) 526-4784 (except in New Jersey). Free 88-page catalogue issued 5 times a year.*

Discount prices on tents, sleeping bags, and backpacks. There is a large line of camping equipment, including men's and women's clothing, boots, poles, stakes, accessories, plus biking equipment and clothing, special items for climbers, stoves, lamps, outdoor cooking equipment, and books. Payment by check, money order, Visa, or Mastercard. Shipment by Postal Service or United Parcel. Unused equipment may be returned within 6 months for refund.

DICK CEPEK INC. *Camping equipment. See listing under* Automotive Needs.

DAMART THERMAWEAR, *1811 Woodbury Ave., Portsmouth, N.H. 03805. Tel. (603) 431-4700 or (800) 258-7300 (except in New Hampshire). Free 48-page catalogue issued 3 times a year.*

Payment by check, money order, American Express, Visa, or Mastercard. Shipment by Postal Service or United Parcel. Purchases may be returned within 10 days for refund.

DRI-LITE FOODS. *See listing under* Grains and Vegetables, Natural and Freeze-Dried Foods.

*DUNNS, *Box 449, Grand Junction, Tenn. 38039. Tel. (901) 764-6901. Free 68-page catalogue issued 4 to 6 times a year.*

Some discounts, such as low prices on Browning boots; generally, their prices are 10 to 30 percent less than suggested retail. The specialty here is outfitting the waterfowler, hunter, and sporting dog owner. Other things in the big catalogue include binoculars, knives, rods and reels, long underwear, decoys, men's, women's, and children's clothing, lots of related books, saddles, and even a fancy shotgun.

EAGLE CREEK, *P.O. Box 651, Solana Beach, Calif. 92075. Tel. (619) 755-8931 or (800) 874-9925 (except in California). Free 16- to 32-page catalogue.*

Backpacks, soft luggage, sleeping bags, Swiss Army knives. (Can you imagine how many of us honorary Swiss soldiers there are by virtue of owning those knives?) Many of the offerings are directed more at those young people doing the youth hostel circuit in Europe than for those roughing it in the American woodlands. The excellent "Let's go" series of travel books is also available.

*ARTHUR ELLIS & CO., LTD., *Private Bag, Dunedin, New Zealand. Tel. (024) 67-284. Free annual 20-page catalogue.*

This is not a discount firm, but the goods are offered at factory wholesale prices and below normal American prices, even after the shipment costs are factored in. There are sleeping bags, packs, tents, and men's and women's outdoor clothing. Payment by check or money order. Shipment by air parcel post. Goods may be returned for credit within 12 weeks (but the owner said that no one had ever returned any purchase in 10 years of mail-order business).

FEATHERED FRIENDS. *Down-filled sleeping bags. See listing under* Bedding, Linens, and Towels.

C. C. FILSON CO., *205 Maritime Building, 911 Western Ave., Seattle, Wash. 98104. Tel. (206) 624-4437. Free annual 16-page catalogue.*

Better outdoor clothes since 1897.

DON GLEASON'S CAMPERS SUPPLY, *P.O. Box 87, Northampton, Mass. 01061. Tel. (413) 584-4895. Free annual 80-page catalogue.*

Payment by check, money order, Visa, or Mastercard. Shipment by Postal Service or United Parcel. Refund on nondefective goods within 30 days, on defective goods within a year.

BOB HINMAN OUTFITTERS, *1217 W. Glen, Peoria, Ill. 61614. Tel. (309) 691-8132. Free catalogue issued once or twice a year.*

This company has offered high-quality outdoor and hunting clothing and equipment for more than 25 years.

INDIANA CAMP SUPPLY, *P.O. Box 344, Pittsboro, Ind. 46167. Tel. (317) 892-3310. Free 72-page catalogue issued 6 times a year.*

Payment by check, American Express, Visa, or Mastercard. Delivery by Postal Service or United Parcel. Refunds for returned goods.

KREEGER & SONS, *16 W. 46th St., New York, N.Y. 10036. Tel. (212) 575-7825. Free catalogue issued 2 or 3 times a year.*

This company calls itself the "Outfitters for the Outdoors." Payment by check, money order, American Express, Visa, or Mastercard. Shipments usually by United Parcel. Prompt refund promised for any unsatisfactory purchase.

VICTOR LAURENCE. *Government surplus camping equipment. See listing under* Men's and Women's Clothing.

P. B. ENTERPRISES, *North Pomfret, Vt. 05053. Tel. (802) 763-8368. Brochure price list.*

Drinking water filter kits.

P. & S. SALES, *P.O. Box 1500, Chapel Hill, N.C. 27515. Tel. (919) 929-2183 or (800) 334-5476 (except in North Carolina, Alaska, and Hawaii). Free 48-page catalogue issued twice a year.*

Men's outdoor clothing, including jackets, hats, vests, ponchos, military fatigues and T-shirts, boots, gun accessories, fishing equipment, tents, knives, battle axes, swords, fake pistols, plus seemingly related books, such as one on Hitler. Payment by check, money order, Visa, or Mastercard. Shipment by Postal Service or United Parcel. Refund, credit, or replacement for goods returned within 90 days.

REI *(Recreational Equipment Inc.), P.O. Box C-88125, Seattle, Wash. 98188. Tel. (206) 575-3286, (800) 426-4840 (except in Washington State), or (800) 562-4894 (in Washington State). Free 48- to 96-page catalogue issued 4 times a year.*

This is a cooperative, with dividends paid based on annual purchases. Outdoor goods galore, including men's and women's clothing, long underwear, rainwear, women's jogging bras, shoes for men and women, back packs, climbing gear, cooking equipment, 9 kinds of Swiss Army knives, bike equipment, tents, and sleeping bags.

SIMS, *312½ Prickett Lane, P.O. Box 21405, Billings, Mont. 59104. Tel. (406) 259-5644. Free annual 24-page catalogue.*

The basic product here is a collapsible woodburning stove. Other products include cast iron pots and pans, saws and axes, tents, lanterns, and men's clothing. Payment by check or money order. Shipment by Postal Service, United Parcel, or truck. Refund or credit for returned goods.

SOUTHFIELD CO., *5725 Magazine St., New Orleans, La. 70115. Tel. (504) 891-8918 or (800) 824-0411 (except in Louisiana, Alaska, and Hawaii). Free 28-page catalogue issued 4 times a year.*

Men's and women's hunting clothes and casual wear. Payment by check, money order, American Express, Visa, or Mastercard. Shipment by Postal Service or United Parcel. Refund or credit for returned goods.

STEPHENSONS, *R.F.D. 4, Box 145, Gilford, N.H. 03246. Tel. (603) 293-8526. The 48-page catalogue issued every 6 years costs $3, and has annual supplements.*

Sleeping bags, tents, air mattresses, backpacks, and men's and women's outdoor clothing, much of it illustrated by seminude models.

*TAIGA WORKS, *1675 W. Second Ave., Vancouver, B.C., Canada V6J 1H3. Tel. (604) 731-2311 or (604) 731-0713. Free 50- to 60-page catalogue issued twice a year.*

Discount prices for outdoor clothing. For example, down vests that cost $60 to $70 elsewhere are sold for $48; alpaca sweaters that cost $60 elsewhere are sold for $37. Who should know better than Canadians how to keep warm outdoors in the winter? Payment by certified check or money order. Shipment by Postal Service. Unused goods may be returned for refund or exchange within 30 days, unless item is defective.

TWIN OAKS HAMMOCKS, *Route 4, Box 169, Louisa, Va. 23093. Tel. (703) 894-5125. Free 8-page catalogue.*

VERMONT TUBBS. *Snowshoes. See listing under* Furniture and Furnishings.

See also *Army and Navy Goods,* below.

Army and Navy Goods

THE ARMY AND NAVY STORE, VICTORIA, *105 Victoria St., London, SW1E 6QX, England. Tel. (01) 834-1234. No catalogue.*

This well-known store has no catalogue but is quite willing to sell any goods by mail order. This sounds like a difficult trick; perhaps if you write to them and tell them what you are interested in they will tell you if they have it or something like it. Payment by check, money order, American Express, Visa, Mastercard, Diners Club, or Army and Navy credit card. Shipment by Postal Service. Unused goods may be returned within 1 month for refund or credit.

JERRYCO. *Military surplus. See listing under* Sale and Surplus Goods.

*KAUFMAN'S WEST ARMY & NAVY GOODS, *1660 Eubank N.E., Albuquerque, N.M. 87112. Tel. (505) 265-7777 or (800) 545-0933 (except in New Mexico,* *Alaska, and Hawaii). Semiannual 60-page catalogue costs $1.*

Discount prices available, including 25 percent off for Ray Ban sunglasses and Victorinox Swiss knives. Products include such men's clothing as jackets, parkas, flight jackets, motorcycle jackets, peacoats, sweaters, trousers, and underwear; combat, survival, and diving knives; 34 kinds of Swiss Army knives, plus replacement parts for them; wool blankets, boots, backpacks, camping equipment, military books, T-shirts and sweatshirts. Payment by check, money order, American Express, Visa, Mastercard, or C.O.D. Shipment by Postal Service or United Parcel. Returns accepted for refund or credit at any time for any reason.

MASS. ARMY & NAVY STORE, *895 Boylston St., Boston, Mass. 02115. Tel. (617) 267-1692, (617) 267-1559, or (800) 343-7749 (except in Massachusetts). Free 32- or 36-page catalogue issued twice a year.*

Discount prices for men's and women's clothing (shirts, T-shirts, sweatshirts, hats, scarves, jackets), backpacks, shoes and boots, sleeping bags, handcuffs, Swiss Army knives, battle knives, insignia and patches, camp cooking gear.

S. J. PEDERGNANA JR., *Steve's Surplus & Medical Supply, P.O. Box 1062, Oak Park, Ill. 60304. No telephone. Annual 20-page catalogue costs $1.*

Military surplus, including men's and women's clothing (pants, caps, flight jackets, ponchos, shirts, jungle and Arctic gear), survival food, radios, backpacks, mess kits, canteens, parachute material, tents, sleeping bags, mine detectors, plus a separate section on medical and surgical equipment.

*RUVEL & CO., *3037 No. Clark St., Chicago, Ill. 60657. Tel. (312) 248-1922. Annual 64-page catalogue costs $2.*

Discount prices for camp stoves, lamps, men's outdoor clothing, backpacks, canteens, cooking equipment, sleeping bags, tents, cots and blankets, binoculars, inflatable boats, knives, hunting and camping equipment, handcuffs, mine detectors. Payment by check, money order, Visa, Mastercard, or C.O.D. Shipment by Postal Service, United Parcel, or truck. Refund for goods returned within 30 days.

U.S. CAVALRY STORE, *1375 N. Wilson Rd., Radcliff, Ky. 40160. Tel. (502) 351-1164 or (800) 626-6171 (except in Kentucky). Annual 100-page catalogue costs $3; monthly fliers sent to customers.*

This is military equipment, but it looks brand-new instead of surplus. Camping equipment, sleeping bags, tents, outdoor watches, knives, weapon replicas, police equipment (including handcuffs, flashlights, radios), boots and shoes, men's combat and fatigue clothing and military dress, military insignia, children's clothing and military toys, military books. Payment by check, money order, American Express, Visa, or Mastercard. Delivery by Postal Service or United Parcel. Refund for purchases returned within 30 days.

Birding and Wildlife Supplies

†AUDUBON WORKSHOP, *1501 Paddock, Northbrook, Ill. 60062. Tel. (312) 729-6660. Free 32-page catalogue issued 4 times a year.*

This is a private company unrelated to the nonprofit Audubon Society. It offers bird feeders, seeds, books, binoculars. We have stopped putting out seeds at our home because it gave our cat the equivalent of a free lunch, but my wife bought a feeder from this company for installation on the outside of her office window in downtown Washington, and it began attracting birds almost immediately. Somehow word gets around the bird community. Maybe that's what all the chirping is about. Payment by check, money order, American Express, Visa, Mastercard, or company account. Shipment by United Parcel. Refund or credit for purchases returned within a "reasonable" time.

BIRD IN HAND, *73 Sawyer Passway, Fitchburg, Mass. 01429. Tel. (617) 345-1000. The 16- to 24-page catalogue issued twice a year costs 50 cents.*

Wild bird seed and some bird feeders.

BIRDING, *P.O. Box 5, Amsterdam, N.Y. No telephone or catalogue.*

This company sells optics for watching birds. I would suggest that people interested in buying binoculars write to them and ask about their products and prices.

DUNCRAFT, *Penacock, N.H. 03303. Tel. (603) 224-0200. Free 32-page catalogue.*

Bird feeders, seeds, rubber snakes and owls for keeping birds away from gardens or other parts of the yard (they really work), books, bird houses, bird baths, bird bath heaters, and home furnishings with bird motifs. Payment by check, money order, American Express, Visa, or Mastercard. Delivery by United Parcel. Refund or exchange for returned purchases.

FEATHER FANCIER, *R5, Forest, Ont., Canada N0N 1J0. Tel. (519) 899-2364. Free catalogue; also, a 12-page newspaper issued 11 times a year cost $12 for annual subscription.*

The catalogue lists 100 books on birds. The newspaper deals with rearing poultry, pigeons, and pheasants.

*TOMAHAWK LIVE TRAP CO., *P.O. Box 323, Tomahawk, Wis. 54487. Tel. (715) 453-3550. Brochure price list.*

Discounts of up to 50 percent on traps designed to capture animals humanely. Various sizes are available, the most popular being the one designed for chipmunks or rats. Other traps catch, among other creatures, mice, beavers, raccoons, skunks, rabbits, cats, dogs, squirrels, turtles, pigeons, and fish.

WILDLIFE NURSERIES, *P.O. Box 2724, Oshkosh, Wis. 54903. Tel. (414) 231-3780. Annual 32-page catalogue costs $1.*

This company sells natural food plants, such as giant wild rice, Sago Pond plant, duck potatoes, and bur reed, intended to attract ducks, fish, and other wildlife. The stated reason for attracting the wildlife is so that hunters may shoot them, but people not interested in hunting might also be interested if they wish to attract wildlife to their property just for looking.

See also *Museum, Botanic Garden, and Public Radio Gift Catalogues* and *Gifts for Nature Lovers.*

❖ 12 For the Garden

Gardeners are special people. They enjoy working the soil; then they enjoy what springs from it. They can eat it, look at it, smell it, maybe even smoke it. Here is a hobby anyone can enjoy, even city dwellers— not just those with penthouse gardens, but also those living in places where local officials have set aside tiny plots for veggies and those with a sunny window. I have included everything for the garden here—the seeds and herbs, the gardening equipment, greenhouses. There are even some listings for farm equipment, particularly equipment designed for use on a smaller scale, including several foreign sources. Beekeeping equipment can also be found here because bees perform their pollination role in the garden before yielding their honey.

Here are catalogues that will help you get through the winter. Send for some of the seed or equipment catalogues in December or January, and in short order you will become convinced that spring will soon be here. It hasn't missed yet. Another source to check during those gray, chilly days is the Sunday Arts & Leisure section of *The New York Times,* where I first found many of the companies listed below. After trying their offerings, I became an enthusiastic (if not expert) gardener.

When our daughter Michele was about five years old, we tried to show her how to grow carrots. We had the right sandy soil, we planted the seeds properly, and we watered the garden, but the carrots grew for just a little bit and then withered away. One day, I discovered the reason. Michele was going out every day to check on her carrots' progress. To do this, she pulled them out of the ground, examined them, and put them back. That is not good for carrots.

Some of the gardening catalogues are beautiful, including Dutch Gardens, Wayside Gardens, and White Flower Farm, but some of the simple, unillustrated listings should not be overlooked. There are hundreds of varieties of fruits and vegetables available from these companies through plants and seeds that never, never will be found again in stores. There is a separate section for equipment, but some of the seed and plant catalogues also sell small garden tools and books.

Seeds and Plants

ABUNDANT LIFE SEED FOUNDATION, *P.O. Box 772, Port Townsend, Wash. 98368. Tel. (206) 385-5660. Annual 40-page catalogue costs $1.*

This is an interesting place. According to the catalogue, it is a nonprofit corporation whose purpose is to acquire, propagate, and preserve the plants and seeds of "the native and naturalized flora of the North Pacific Rim, with particular emphasis on those spe-cies not commercially available, including rare and endangered species." There are seeds for trees, shrubs, wildflowers, garden flowers, herbs, and vegetables, plus lots of books (some designed for children), tools, and even some taped music (to feed the soul of the gardener). Payment by check or money order. Shipment by Postal Service or United Parcel.

ALSTON SEED CO., *Box 266, Littleton, N.C. 27850. Free catalogue.*

Here is a company that wants to stress that it will sell only small amounts of seed and has no large amounts to sell to commercial growers. The specialty is research toward rediscovering the older plants that used to be widespread in the United States. One example of this is an old tomato variety that keeps coming back year after year from the seeds of the previous year's crop. Payment by check or money order. Shipment by Postal Service or United Parcel. No returns accepted, no guarantee given.

ALTMAN SPECIALTY PLANTS, *553 Buena Creek Rd., San Marcos, Calif. 92069. Tel. (619) 744-8191. Annual 40-page catalogue costs $1.*

Unusual succulent plants. Unusual? A recent cover included the Pachypodium lamerei (Madagascar palm), Aloe haworthioides, and Crassula (Ivory Pagoda), and a free offering of the Tanzanian zipper plant. There are also several books on growing cacti and succulents.

APPLEWOOD SEED CO., *5380 Vivian St., Arvada, Colo. 80002. Tel. (303) 431-6283. Free annual 24-page catalogue.*

The specialty here is an excellent one— wildflowers. Our next trend? That would be nice. There are also herbs, seeds for sprouts, and potpourri.

*THE BANANA TREE, *715 Northampton St., Easton, Pa. 18042. Tel. (215) 253-9589. Annual 16-page catalogue costs 50 cents.*

While this company does not describe itself as a "discount" firm, it does offer reduced prices for quantity purchases. Their clientele includes botanists, botanical garden managers, and serious hobbyists. The no-nonsense catalogue lists 30 varieties of namesake bananas, plus many rare and uncommon plants, bulbs, and seeds. Payment by check or money order. Shipment by Postal Service or United Parcel. Refund or credit for returned merchandise.

BEAR CREEK NURSERY, *P.O. Box 411, Northport, Wash. 99157. No telephone. Price list.*

This nursery offers cold- and drought-hardy antique varieties of apples, plus nuts, pears, multiple-use trees and shrubs for wildlife, windbreaks, hedges, timber, and beauty.

BORCHELT HERB GARDENS, *474 Carriage Shop Rd., East Falmouth, Mass. Tel. (617) 548-4571. Brochure price list free for self-addressed stamped envelope.*

Herbs for cooking, healing, smelling.

*BOUNTIFUL RIDGE NURSERIES. *P.O. Box 250, Princess Anne, Md. 21853. Tel. (301) 651-0400 or (800) 638-9356. Free annual 48-page catalogue.*

There are lots of reduced-price specials on fruit and nut trees, grape vines, and strawberry, raspberry, blueberry, and blackberry plants. Payment by check, money order, American Express, Visa, or Mastercard. Shipment by Postal Service, United Parcel, air freight, or commercial carrier.

BRECK'S, *6523 N. Galena Rd., Peoria, Ill. 61632. Tel. (309) 691-4616. Free 60-page catalogue.*

Bulbs, imported from Holland, for great looking tulips and daffodils.

JOHN BRUDY EXOTICS, *Route 1, Box 190, Dover, Fla. 33527. Tel. (813) 752-2590. Annual catalogue costs $1.*

Uncommon seeds and ornamental trees, such as the bat-wing coral tree, African wisteria tree, and the Australian hibiscus. Payment by check or money order. Shipment by Postal Service. Seeds are not returnable; other purchases may be returned for refund or credit.

BUELL'S GREENHOUSES, *P.O. Box 218, Eastford, Conn. 06242. Tel. (203) 974-0623. The 32-page catalogue costs 25 cents plus self-addressed long envelope with enough postage for 2 ounces.*

This company specializes in the Gesneriad family of plants—African violets and their exotic relatives. Albert H. Buell is said to have a large following for his hybrid gloxinias.

BURGESS SEED & PLANT CO., *905 Four Seasons Rd., Bloomington, Ill. 61701. Tel. (309) 663-9551. Free annual 48-page catalogue.*

This is one of 4 related gardening companies, the others, listed below, being Farmer

Seed & Nursery, House of Wesley, and Owen Nursery. Burgess specializes in vegetable and flower seeds, but it also has many fruit and nut trees. I once ordered a dozen trees by mail order (not from Burgess) and was surprised when they arrived in a small package that the letter carrier was able to deliver to me with one hand. The trees were about the width of a pencil and 2 to 3 feet tall, but they were hardy and they grew well. When you grow trees you must set aside a certain amount of time, measured in years. Payment by check, money order, Visa, or Mastercard. Shipment by Postal Service or United Parcel. Purchases may be returned within a year for refund or replacement.

W. ATLEE BURPEE CO., *300 Park Ave., Warminster, Pa. 18974. Tel. (215) 674-4900. Free annual 184-page catalogue.*

This has got to be the best known seed company in the United States, and for good reason besides its being over 100 years old. My own earliest recollection of it is from planting seeds in a Victory garden during World War II when I was a little boy, and later in driving past its huge headquarters in North Philadelphia. They have since moved to the suburbs, but their reputation carries on with them, and we grew big crops of Burpee cucumbers at our home on Long Island. Cucumbers are good crops to start children with: They are easy to grow, the kids have fun training them up the string, and they are fun to eat. Payment by check, money order, American Express, Visa, or Mastercard. Shipment by Postal Service or United Parcel. Refunds for purchases returned within a year.

D. V. BURRELL SEED GROWERS CO., *P.O. Box 150, Rocky Ford, Colo. 81067. Tel. (303) 254-3318. Free 96-page catalogue.*

This is another old firm, more than 80 years old. The catalogue is crammed with lists of seeds and information on cultivation.

*BUTTERBROOKE FARM, *78 Barry Rd., Oxford, Conn. 06483. Tel. (203) 888-2000. Annual brochure price list.*

Discount prices for seeds, plus additional discounts for members of Butterbrooke cooperative. These are chemically untreated seeds. Payment by check or money order. Delivery by Postal Service or United Parcel. Purchases may be returned for refund within 30 days.

CALIFORNIA SEED CO., *904 Silver Spur Rd., Suite 414, Rolling Hills Estates, Calif. 90274. Tel. (213) 375-4356. Free annual 36-page catalogue.*

This company specializes in seeds for home gardeners in Southern and Central California. Maybe that means that people not actually living in lotusland but having a similar climate might be able to grow California produce.

†CAPRILANDS HERB FARM, *Silver St., Coventry, Conn. 06238. Tel. (203) 742-7244. Annual 4-page catalogue free for self-addressed stamped envelope.*

Plants and seeds (from 300 varieties grown at the farm), books, gifts, and old-fashioned dolls. Payment by check or money order. Shipment by Postal Service or United Parcel. No returns allowed.

CASA YERBA GARDENS, *Star Route 2, Box 21, Days Creek, Ore. 97429. Tel. (503) 835-3534. The 18- to 24-page catalogue issued every two years costs $1.*

This is a small, family-owned farm that uses organic methods to raise a variety of unusual herb seeds and plants. Payment by check or money order. Shipment by United Parcel. No returns.

COMSTOCK, FERRE & CO., *263 Main St., Wethersfield, Conn. 06109. Tel. (203) 529-3319. Free annual 32- to 40-page catalogue.*

This place was established in 1820. How many businesses that you can think of go back that far? The company offers lawn, garden, herb, and flower seeds of old, new, and ethnic varieties, onion sets, and garden supplies.

CONVERSE NURSERY, *Amherst, N.H. 03031. Tel. (617) 354-3424. Price list.*

Here are more than 150 apple trees from which to select, starting with Adam's Peramain and going on until York Imperial, including in between the Black Gilliflower (Sheepnose), the Calville Rouge d'Automne (Roter Herbstkalwil), and the Westfield Seek-No-Further. Isn't it marvelous that there are so many varieties available beyond Red and Golden Delicious (also available here)? Payment by check or money order. Shipment by Postal Service or United Parcel.

DE GIORGI COMPANY, *P.O. Box 413, Council Bluffs, Iowa 51502. Tel. (712) 328-2372. Annual 120-page catalogue costs $1.*

Flower seeds, mostly imported from Europe, but some also brought in from Japan, and lots of vegetable seeds not available elsewhere. This is an old-fashioned encyclopedic catalogue with no glossy color photographs, from a company started in 1905. Payment by check or money order. Shipment by Postal Service. Refund or credit for returned purchases.

J. A. DEMONCHAUX CO. *See listing for Herb Gathering, below.*

EARL DOUGLAS, *R.D. 1, Box 38, Red Creek, N.Y. 13143. Tel. (315) 754-6621. Brochure price list costs 25 cents.*

Mr. Douglas offers a hybrid chestnut tree resistant to the blight that has wiped out most American chestnuts.

*DUTCH GARDENS, *P.O. Box 30, Lisse, Holland. Tel. 02521-1 4648. But you are encouraged to use the U.S. address: P.O. Box 400, Montvale, N.J. 07645. Tel. (201) 391-4366. Free 128-page annual catalogue.*

The catalogue's color illustrations of the flowers are gorgeous. There is a large selection of bulbs, corms, and tubers for such plants as begonias, dahlias, gladioli, lilies, and peonies, but, curiously, no tulips. The company says its prices are 50 percent below others'. Payment by check, Visa, or Mastercard.

DUTCH MOUNTAIN NURSERY, *7984 N. 48th St., Augusta, Mich. 49012. Tel. (616) 731-5232. Semiannual brochure price list costs 50 cents.*

Plants, trees, and shrubs, many of them rare, intended to attract birds. Payment by check. Delivery by United Parcel. Refund or credit for purchases returned after one season if they have been given proper care.

*EMLONG NURSERIES, *2671 W. Marquette Woods Rd., Stevensville, Mich. 49127. Tel. (616) 429-3612, (800) 225-0002 (except in Michigan), or (800) 225-0005 (in Michigan). A free 40- to 50-page catalogue is issued every spring.*

Fruit, shade, and ornamental trees, berry bushes, strawberries, raspberries, grapes, and many flowers, some of them offered at discount prices. Payment by check, money order, Visa, or Mastercard. Shipment by Postal Service or United Parcel. Credit for purchases returned within 5 days.

ESP WILDFLOWERS (*Environmental Seed Producers*), *P.O. Box 5125, El Monte, Calif. 91734. No telephone. Free annual 6-page catalogue.*

Sixty popular wildflowers, the seed sold by the pound for mixtures and by the half-pound for separate species.

EXOTICA SEED CO. & RARE FRUIT NURSERY, *8033 Sunset Blvd., Suite 125, Los Angeles, Calif. 90046. Tel. (213) 851-0990. The 24-page catalogue costs $2.*

Many foreign plants propagated in California, including figs, cactus, gingers, mango, and various beans. There are also books on how to grow things.

FAR NORTH GARDENS, *16785 Harrison, Livonia, Mich. 48154. Tel. (313) 422-0747. A 3-year subscription to 48-page annual catalogue costs $2.*

Rare flowers and seeds, with a specialty in the Barnhaven silver dollar primrose. There also are some books on growing these unusual flowers.

FARMER SEED & NURSERY, *2207 E. Oakland Ave., Bloomington, Ill. 61701. Tel. (309) 663-9551. Free annual 64-page catalogue.*

Not a discount place, but they say they have "special" prices on certain items. There are fruit trees, vegetable seeds, berry bushes, flower seeds, roots, and bulbs—a broad selection. Payment by check, money order, Visa, or Mastercard. Shipment by Postal Service or United Parcel. There is a good returns policy, offering refund or replacement within a year if dissatisfied.

HENRY FIELD SEED & NURSERY CO., *407 Sycamore St., Shenandoah, Iowa 51602. Tel. (712) 246-2110. Free annual 100-page catalogue.*

This is a real old-fashioned catalogue crammed with color photos of the vegetables as you hope they will look under your loving care. One double-page spread, for example, has pictures of 17 different ears of corn. There are vegetables, fruits, and flowers.

†DEAN FOSTER NURSERIES, *Hartford, Mich. 49057. Tel. (616) 621-2419. Free annual 32-page catalogue.*

This is another long-established business, having been started in 1837. The specialty is fruits—strawberries (93 varieties!), raspberries, blackberries, boysenberries, grapes, and fruit trees. There are several food gift items offered. Payment by check, money order, Visa, or Mastercard. Delivery by Postal Service or United Parcel. Purchases may be returned within 10 days for refund, credit, or exchange.

181

FRIENDS OF THE TREES SEED SERVICE, *P.O. Box 1064, Tonasket, Wash. 98855. Tel. (509) 485-3643. The 8-page catalogue issued twice a year costs $1.*

This company specializes in seeds of fruit and nut trees, native Indian foods, medicinal herbs, Pacific Northwest wildflowers, plants to keep honeybees filled up with nectar, and ornamental trees and shrubs. This catalogue, printed on tabloid-sized sheets, is crammed with information and products. Payment by check, money order, or—and what a marvelous idea—barter. Shipment by Postal Service. Purchases may be returned for refund or credit.

G. SEED CO., *P.O. Box 702, Tonasket, Wash. 98855. No telephone. Annual 52-page catalogue costs 50 cents.*

Lots of ethnic, bio-regional, and heirloom seeds in an eclectic combination catalogue and how-to guide. Payment by check, money order, or barter. Shipment by Postal Service or United Parcel. Refund or credit for returned goods.

GARDEN IMPORTS INC., *545 Pine Top Trail, Bethlehem, Pa. 18017. Tel. (215) 868-8225. Brochure price list.*

This company specializes in lettuce and salad greens from England and other countries. Payment by check. Delivery by Postal Service or United Parcel. Refunds for purchases returned within 10 days.

GARDENS OF THE BLUE RIDGE, *P.O. Box 10, Pineola, N.C. 28662. Tel. (704) 733-2417. Annual 32-page catalogue costs $2.*

"Answering the wildflower desires and needs of the U.S., Canada, and all parts of the world since 1892," the catalogue proclaims. There are also ferns, bushes, and trees.

*GIRARD NURSERIES, *Box 428, Geneva, Ohio 44041. Tel. (216) 466-2881 or (216) 969-1636. Free annual 20- and 6-page catalogues.*

This company has specials at discount prices. Payment by check, money order, Visa, or Mastercard. Shipment by Postal Service, United Parcel, or commercial truck. Purchases may be returned within 30 days for refund or credit.

GOD'S LITTLE ACRE NURSERY, *13131 Allison Ranch Rd., Grass Valley, Calif. 95945. Tel. (916) 273-9420. Brochure price list.*

This new company specializes in selling tree seedlings, most of them unique to the Western U.S. For example, you can plant a giant Sequoia seedling in New Jersey and amaze your friends' descendants when it grows, some years hence, to 300 feet. Payment by check or money order. Shipment by Postal Service. Refund or replacement for returned purchases.

*GREENLAND FLOWER SHOP, *R.D. 1, Box 52, Port Matilda, Pa. 16870. Tel. (814) 692-8308. Annual 16-page catalogue costs 50 cents.*

Discounts of 50 percent on the purchase of house plants and perennials, with shrubs, evergreens, and bulbs due next.

GRIMO NUT NURSERY, *R.R. 2, Lakeshore Rd., Niagara-on-the-Lake, Ont., Canada L0S 1J0. Tel. (416) 935-9773. Annual 10-page catalogue costs $1, redeemable when ordering.*

The benefits of raising nut trees are put quite clearly in this catalogue: "Not only do they make fine shade and ornamental trees, but they also provide timber and a crop of valuable nuts." The trees offered here are hardy in Canada, so most of them ought to thrive in colder United States areas as well as in much of Canada. Payment by check or money order. Shipment by Postal Service, United Parcel, or CanPar. If the customer notifies the nursery by July 1 of a tree's failure to grow, the nursery will provide a refund, credit, or replacement. That seems fair. I once planted 3 black walnut trees (not from Grimo) and one of them failed to grow, but the nursey refused to give me any credit for it, so I stopped doing business with that company.

GURNEY SEED & NURSERY CO., *Yankton, S.D. 57079. Tel. (605) 665-4451. Free 64-page catalogue issued twice a year.*

This is one of my favorite mail-order companies. I figured that anything that they could grow in South Dakota should be a breeze to grow in New York. There are 4,000 items in the catalogue—vegetables seeds, plants, sets and tubers, standard and dwarf fruit trees, shade and ornamental trees, flower bulbs and seeds, rose bushes, on and on—but the item I remember with fondness is the 1-cent offer of a package of mixed seeds for children. The children's seed package is unlabeled, so you and the children don't know what to expect, the result being a nice anticipation for the whole family to share.

HALCYON GARDENS HERBS, *P.O. Box 124, Gibsonia, Pa. 15044. Tel. (412) 443-5544. The 28-page catalogue costs $1, refundable with order.*

This is a small but handsome catalogue with a very nice selection of herbs for cooking and admiring the looks and aroma of, and they are also suggested for medicinal use and herbal teas. Halcyon suggests that city dwellers grow their herbs in window boxes, a suggestion we may take up some day. Payment by check, money order, Visa, or Mastercard. Shipment by Postal Service or United Parcel. Unused portion of purchase may be returned for refund or replacement if seeds fail to germinate.

HANA GARDENLAND, *P.O. Box 248, Hana, Maui, Hawaii 96713. Brochure price list costs 50 cents.*

Plants and seeds for Hawaiian plants, including many orchids. "Our plants can grow and thrive as house plants anywhere," the brochure declares. Payment by check, money order, Visa, or Mastercard. Shipment by airmail Postal Service. Plants and seeds are guaranteed to arrive in perfect condition.

JOSEPH HARRIS CO. *(Harris Seeds), 3670 Buffalo Rd., Rochester, N.Y. 14624. Tel. (716) 594-9411. Free annual 96-page catalogue.*

Here is another long-established company, founded in 1879. This catalogue will warm up a cold winter day, with pictures of tomatoes, carrots, cucumbers, zucchini, corn, peppers, beans, squash, pumpkins, radishes (start your children on radishes, there's never been a failure yet), peas, and many other veggies, plus lots of flowers.

HARTMANN'S PLANTATION, *310 60th St., Grand Junction, Mich. 49056. Tel. (616) 253-4281. Free annual 18-page catalogue.*

Several dozen varieties of blueberry plants suitable for various climates.

HEIRLOOM GARDEN SEEDS, *Division of Abracadabra, P.O. Box 138, Guerneville, Calif. 95446. Tel. (707) 869-0961. The 34-page catalogue issued every two years costs $2.*

This company specializes in culinary, historic, and rare plant seeds. There are 9 kinds of basil alone. Payment by check or money order. Shipment by Postal Service.

*HERB GATHERING *(formerly J.A. Demonchaux Seeds), 5742 Kenwood, Kansas City, Mo. 64110. Tel. (816) 523-2653. Annual 10-page catalogue costs 50 cents.*

Seeds with a special appeal to the gourmet cook, with seeds for vegetables and herbs that one might expect to find in France. There are some fraises des bois, the tiny, tasty strawberries that are available all summer. The company offers wholesale prices with reduced per unit costs as the quantity increases. Payment by check, money order, or United Parcel C.O.D. Shipment by Postal Service or United Parcel. Credit for goods returned in the season purchased.

HILLIER NURSERIES (WINCHESTER) LTD., *Ampfield House, Ampfield, Romsey, Hampshire, SO5 9PA, England. Tel. (0794) 68733. Free annual 100-page catalogue.*

The English are the busiest gardeners in the world. Any empty patch of land is soon home to a rose bush, a thin strip between railroad tracks on a right of way becomes a gera-nium bed. Here, in a huge catalogue, are hundreds, perhaps thousands, of the plants, trees, and shrubs the English love to plant. There is information on import restrictions to the United States and Canada. Payment by check, money order, Visa, or Mastercard. Shipment by Postal Service or air freight. No returns.

HILLTOP HERB FARM, *P.O. Box 1734, Cleveland, Tex. 47327. Tel. (713) 592-5859. Brochure price list costs 50 cents.*

Lots of herb plants and dried herbs and botanicals for flavoring and cooking, plus books, herbal vinegars, and gift baskets.

HORIZON SEEDS, *P.O. Box 81823, Lincoln, Neb. 68501. Tel. (402) 475-1232. Or: P.O. Box 886, Hereford, Tex. 79045. Tel. (806) 364-5250. Brochures and price lists.*

This company is a family-operated business that offers many kinds of agricultural seeds, especially those for grass and corn, as well as a grass drill.

HOUSE OF WESLEY, *Nursery Division, 2200 E. Oakland Ave., Bloomington, Ill. 61701. Tel. (309) 663-9551. Free annual 32-page catalogue.*

Ornamental, nut, and fruit trees, roses, strawberries, elderberries, blackberries, raspberries, and seeds for vegetables and flowers.

J. L. HUDSON, SEEDSMAN, *P.O. Box 1058, Redwood City, Calif. 94064. No telephone. Annual 100-page catalogue costs $1.*

This is a no-nonsense listing, with line drawings that look like old woodcuts, of the thousands of seeds available, many of them rarities. There are flowers, fruits, vegetables, and herbs.

INTER-STATE NURSERIES, *504 E St., Hamburg, Iowa 51640. Tel. (712) 382-2411 or (800) 831-4104 (except in Iowa). Free 24- to 56-page catalogue issued 4 times a year.*

Some sale catalogues sent out with savings of 25 percent on certain items. Payment by check, money order, American Express, Visa, or Mastercard. Shipment by Postal Service, United Parcel, or truck freight. Unsatisfactory goods must be returned promptly for credit as nursery stock is perishable.

ISBS INC. *Books on gardening and horticulture. See listing under* Foreign Books, Foreign Language and Culture, Travel Guides.

ISON'S NURSERY AND VINEYARDS, *Route 1, Box 191, Brooks, Ga. 30205. Tel. (404) 599-6970. Free 16-page catalogue.*

This is the biggest producer of scuppernong-muscadine grape plants in the United States and also offers blackberries, blueberries, and fruit and nut trees. Payment by check or money order. Shipment by Postal Service or United Parcel. Purchases may be returned for refund, but must be sent back immediately.

JACKSON & PERKINS, *1 Rose Lane, Medford, Ore. 97501. Tel. (503) 776-2400. A free annual 40-page catalogue is published in the fall for delivery of plants the following spring.*

This is the best known grower of roses in the U.S., and probably the world's largest. The company was started in 1872 and has been brightening gardens and lives ever

since. The refund policy is a good one: "We will replace, prepaid and free of charge, any rose which does not perform according to this guarantee, or we will refund its cost, whichever you prefer, providing your report is filed with us by Aug. 1 of this year." Payment by check, money order, Visa, or Mastercard. Delivery by U.S. Postal Service or United Parcel. Plants may be returned for credit or refund, but roses are not guaranteed over the winter.

LE JARDIN, *West Danville, Vt. 05873. No telephone. Semiannual 16-page catalogue costs 50 cents.*

Bulbs, plants, and seeds to grow things that will make French food taste like French food—shallots, garlic, leeks, and many others. Payment by check or money order. Shipment by Postal Service or United Parcel. Refund for unsatisfactory purchases.

JOHNNY'S SELECTED SEEDS, *Foss Hill Rd., Albion, Me. 04910. Tel. (207) 437-9294. Free annual 84-page catalogue.*

Here is an interesting, informative catalogue of flower, vegetable, herb, and grain seeds, including several varieties of strawberries, which I have never tried to grow from seed but perhaps will be encouraged to by this catalogue.

JOHNSON NURSERY, *Rt. 5, Box 29J, Ellijay, Ga. 30540. Tel. (404) 273-3187. Free annual 16-page catalogue.*

Here are fruit trees, especially apples, and especially varieties that go beyond the Delicious—such as Granny Smith, Ozark Gold, and Jerseymac. Payment by check, money order, Visa, or Mastercard. Shipment by Postal Service, United Parcel, or motor freight. Replacement for any trees that fail to leaf out by July 1 of year of planting.

J. W. JUNG SEED CO., *335 S. High, Randolph, Wis. 53956. Tel. (414) 326-3121. Free catalogue issued twice a year.*

This company was started in 1907 and produces a large catalogue of seeds and plants for flowers, tomatoes and other vegetables, strawberries, raspberries, blueberries, plums, cherries, apples, roses, and shade and ornamental trees.

KALMIA FARM, *P.O. Box 3881, Charlottesville, Va. 22903. No telephone. Free 16-page annual catalogue.*

Here is a catalogue of oddities that seem to have been popular at the turn of the century and are the subject of an effort by this concern to repopularize them. They include "multiplier" perennial onions that grow in bunches and do not need to be reseeded, plus various other onions, shallots, garlic, and books on onions and garlic. Payment by check or money order. Shipment by Postal Service. Refunds or replacements of unsatisfactory purchases, with returns not necessary.

KELLY BROTHERS NURSERIES, *23 Maple St., Dansville, N.Y. 14437. Tel. (716) 335-2211. Free 56-page catalogue issued twice a year.*

This is another catalogue that I have ordered from in the past, with success and satisfaction. There are many flowers, fruits, vegetables, and trees in seeds or plants to be purchased through this fine company. Especially for the young and the patient, it is a source of good stock for such trees as the English walnut, which are sent out when they are 1 foot to 1½ feet tall. You, like the Kelly Brothers, ought to take the long view of things. (I would like to think that someone will get some satisfaction 100 years from now from those black walnut trees I planted at a house we used to own on Long Island. Take a walk through Washington Square in New York City or Hyde Park in London or the Tuileries in Paris—somebody had to plant those trees very long ago, and you could do it today. But I digress.) This is a company with a well-earned good reputation. Payment by check, money order, American Express, Visa, Mastercard, or Diners Club. Shipment by Postal Service or United Parcel. Unsatisfactory goods will be replaced, and the returns policy is a very good one.

KERNCRAFT, *434 W. Main St., Kutztown, Pa. 19530. Tel. (215) 683-6335. Price list.*

Here are vegetable seeds that should appeal to the gourmet; they produce plants that reflect the gardening and culinary practices of France, Germany, and Italy. Payment by check or money order. Shipment by Postal Service. Purchases may be returned for refund.

KESTER'S WILD GAME FOOD NURSERIES, *P.O. Box V, Omro, Wis. 54963. Tel. (414) 685-2929 or (800) 588-8815 (except in Wisconsin). Annual 36-page catalogue costs $2.*

Plants that are designed to attract wildlife—deer, ducks, quail, pheasant, partidge, doves, turkeys, etc.—for hunting, but they can be used by nonhunters as well to help the same creatures. Payment by check, money order, Visa, or Mastercard. Shipment by United Parcel. No returns accepted.

KITAZAWA SEED CO., *356 W. Taylor St., San Jose, Calif. 95110. Tel. (408) 292-4420. Price list.*

Seeds for Japanese, Chinese, and Indian vegetables.

THE KRIDER NURSERIES, *P.O. Box 29, Middlebury, Ind. 46540. Tel. (219) 825-5714. Free 32-page catalogue issued twice a year.*

Evergreen, hardwood, and ornamental trees, blooming shrubs, and roses.

LANDS-END SEEDS, *Crawford, Colo. 81415. Tel. (303) 921-5331. Brochure.*

Available are "souper beans," white Jerusalem artichokes, comfrey, horseradish, and sweet peas.

LAWSON'S NURSERY, *Route 1, Box 294, Ball Ground, Ga. 30107. Tel. (404) 893-2141. Free 28-page catalogue.*

This is a specialist in old-fashioned and unusual fruit trees. I counted 89 apple varieties alone, including the familiar McIntosh and Delicious and, to me, the unfamiliar Arkansas Black, Blue Pearmaine, Limbertwig, and Maden Blush, the last "described in 1817 by Coxe as being very popular in the Philadelphia market." (I wonder if "Maden" wasn't misspelled some time in the past century or is this a pre-Webster spelling?) There

are some books available. Payment by check, money order, Visa, or Mastercard. Shipment by Postal Service or United Parcel.

OROL LEDDER & SONS, *P.O. Box 7, Sewell, N.J. 08080. Tel. (609) 468-1000 or (800) 257-6272 (except in New Jersey). Free annual 32-page catalogue.*

Plants, bulbs, and seeds for flowers, vegetables, and herbs from a company established in 1864. Also available are tools, supplies, equipment, fertilizers, and insecticides. Payment by check, money order, Visa, or Mastercard. Shipment by Postal Service or United Parcel. Purchases may be returned within 30 days for credit.

HENRY LEUTHARDT NURSERIES, *Montauk Highway, Box 666, East Moriches, N.Y. 11940. Tel. (516) 878-1387. Brochure price list.*

This is one of the finest nurseries in the New York–Long Island area, offering many dwarf and semi-dwarf fruit trees. Payment by check or money order. Shipment by Postal Service. No returns.

LIBERTY SEED CO., *128 First Dr., S.E., Box 806, New Philadelphia, Ohio 44663. Tel. (216) 364-1611. Free annual 56-page catalogue.*

This is described as Ohio's only family owned and operated flower and vegetable seed company. There are hundreds of kinds of plants and seeds, plus equipment, sprays, and books.

†**LILYPONS WATER GARDENS,** *6800 Lilypons Rd., P.O. Box 10, Lilypons, Md. 21717. Tel. (301) 874-5133. Annual 68-page catalogue costs $3.50.*

Newsletters with discounts of 20 to 50 percent are sent to purchasers of the catalogue. Payment by check, money order, American Express, Visa, Mastercard, Diners Club, Carte Blanche, or Choice. Delivery by Postal Service or United Parcel. Refund or credit for purchases returned within a year after permission is obtained.

LIVING TREE CENTRE, *P.O. Box 797, Bolinas, Calif. 94924. Tel. (415) 868-1786. Annual 16-page catalogue costs $2.*

Here is a company devoted to the proposition that Delicious apples should not be the country's national fruit. There are many other, older varieties that people can plant as a protest against conformity and uniformity, including 2 dozen varieties that most Americans have never heard of—Irish Peach, Red Astrachan, Red Gravenstein, just to list the midsummer harvest varieties. Payment by check or money order. Shipment by Postal Service or United Parcel. Replacement for any trees that fail to grow within a "specified time."

LONG ISLAND SEED AND PLANT, *P.O. Box 1285, Riverhead, N.Y. 11901. No telephone. Annual 8-page catalogue in return for a first-class postage stamp.*

I always like to call attention to Long Island companies, and this one is a special pleasure because it is primarily a collector of rare and unusual vegetable seeds. The company also works on breeding tomatoes, and a recent catalogue had 100 varieties listed.

MAKIELSKI BERRY FARM AND NURSERY, *7130 Platt Rd., Ypsilanti, Mich. 48197. Tel. (313) 343-3673 or (313) 429-9355. Free 14-page catalogue.*

The specialty is raspberry plants, and there are also blackberries, strawberries, rhubarb, currants, gooseberries, blueberries, and asparagus. Payment by check or money order. Shipment by United Parcel. Plants may be returned within 6 weeks for refund or replacement if the company is notified first.

EARL MAY SEED & NURSERY CO., *Shenandoah, Iowa 51603. Tel. (712) 246-1020, (800) 831-4193 (except in Iowa), or (800) 432-5858 (in Iowa). Free catalogue.*

MCFAYDEN, *P.O. Box 1800, 30 Ninth St., Brandon, Man., Canada R7A 6N4. Tel. (204) 727-0766, (1-800) 665-2790 (in all of Canada except British Columbia and Manitoba), or (112-800) 665-2790 (in British Columbia only). Free 96-page spring catalogue and 20-page fall catalogue.*

Many seeds for vegetables, flowers, herbs, fruit and ornamental trees, bulbs, perennials, roses, roots, and garden supplies. Payment by check, money order, Visa, or Mastercard. Shipment by Postal Service. Refund or credit for goods returned within a year.

MERRY GARDENS, *P.O. Box 595, Camden, Me. 04843. Tel. (207) 236-9046. Annual 12-page catalogue costs $1, and there are 2 free newsletters.*

This company specializes in rare house plants, including herbs, ivies, fuchsias, geraniums, hederas, cacti, and ferns.

MIDWEST WILDFLOWERS, *P.O. Box 64, Rockton, Ill. 61072. No telephone. The annual catalogue costs 50 cents.*

Featured here are wildflowers native to the Midwest. The seed has been collected, with permission, from private meadows and woodlots. Some examples are wild columbine, wild Canadian ginger, and bloodroot. There are some books on recognizing and raising wildflowers. Payment by check or money order. Shipment by Postal Service. Refund for returned goods.

J. E. MILLER NURSERIES, *5060 W. Lake Rd., Canandaigua, N.Y. 14424. Tel. (716) 396-2647, (800) 828-9630 (except in New York), or (800) 462-9601 (in New York). Free 64-page catalogue issued twice a year.*

Fruit trees (including dozens of apples), nut, ornamental, and shade trees, grape vines, blueberries, raspberries, blackberries, strawberries, and asparagus. Payment by check, money order, American Express, Visa, or Mastercard. Shipment by Postal Service or United Parcel. Good return policy: refund or replacement for plants that fail to grow.

MOON MOUNTAIN WILDFLOWERS, *P.O. Box 34, Morro Bay, Calif. 93442. Tel. (805) 772-2473. Annual catalogue costs 75 cents.*

Specialties of California, plus seeds for wildflowers native throughout North America.

NEW YORK STATE FRUIT TESTING ASSOCIATION, *P.O. Box 462, Geneva, N.Y. 14456. Tel. (315) 787-2205. Free annual 40-page catalogue.*

New fruits developed by this nonprofit association, including apples, apricots, blackberries, grapes, peaches, raspberries, strawberries, and ornamental cherry and apple trees. Payment by check or money order. Delivery by Postal Service. Refunds for returned purchases.

NICHOLS GARDEN NURSERY, *1190 North Pacific Highway, Albany, Ore. 97321. Tel. (503) 928-9280. Free annual 76-page catalogue.*

Some of the specialties are rare seeds, gourmet vegetable seeds, elephant garlic, saffron crocus bulbs for making your own saffron, and wine-making supplies. There are also many herbs and spices available. Payment by check, money order, Visa, or Mastercard. Delivery by Postal Service or United Parcel. Purchases may be returned for refund, credit, or replacement.

NORTHPLAN SEED PRODUCERS, *P.O. Box 9107, Moscow, Idaho 83843. Price list costs $1, returnable with purchase.*

Here are seeds for wildflowers, trees, berries, and other vegetation suitable for land restoration after such disturbances as mining, construction of transmission rights of way, drillings.

L. L. OLDS SEED CO., *Box 7790, Madison, Wis. 53707. Tel. (608) 249-9291. Annual free 80-page catalogue*

This company was founded in 1888 and has a large number of seeds for vegetables and flowers, and many fruit trees, plus books, grass seed, and garden equipment.

RICHARD OWEN NURSERY, *2300 E. Lincoln St., Bloomington, Ill. 61701. Tel. (309) 663-9551. Free 48-page catalogue issued 3 times a year.*

Flower and fruit plants and trees for the garden. Payment by check, money order, Visa, or Mastercard. Shipment by Postal Service or United Parcel. Refund or replacement of purchases returned within a year.

GEORGE W. PARK SEED CO., *P.O. Box 31, Greenwood, S.C. 29647. Tel. (803) 374-3341. Free 132-page catalogue issued 4 times a year.*

This company has 3,000 varieties of flower and vegetable seeds, bulbs, and plants. Payment by check, money order, American Express, Visa, Mastercard, or Diners Club. Shipment by Postal Service. Refund or credit for purchases returned within a year.

PETER PAULS NURSERIES, *R.D. 4, Canandaigua, N.Y. 14424. Tel. (716) 394-7397. Annual 4-page price list costs 25 cents.*

Terrarium plant kits, including carnivorous plants, several kinds of pitcher plants, and many kinds of rare plants and seeds. Also available is a book about carnivorous plants. Payment by check, money order, Visa, or Mastercard. Shipment by Postal Service. Refund for purchases returned immediately.

PEACE SEEDS, *1130 Tetherow Rd., Williams, Ore. 97544. Tel. (503) 846-7173. Brochure price list.*

This is a primary source of organically grown seeds for rare and heirloom plants. Payment by check or money order. Shipment by Postal Service or United Parcel. Refund or credit for purchases returned "promptly."

PETER PEPPER SEEDS, *H. W. Alfrey, Box 415, Knoxville, Tenn. 37901. Tel. (615) 524-5965. Brochure price list.*

As the name suggests, the specialty here is peppers, including some that grow into curious shapes.

PLANTS OF THE SOUTHWEST, *1812 Second St., Santa Fe., N.M. 87501. Tel. (505) 982-0450. Annual 32-page catalogue costs $1.*

Colorful flowers, vegetables, and grasses especially tolerant of the arid Southwest, plus a dozen books.

PRAIRIE STATE COMMODITIES. *Agricultural grain. See listing under* Gardening Tools, Equipment, and Furniture, *below.*

PUTNEY NURSERY, *Putney, Vt. 05346. Tel. (802) 387-5577. Free 8- to 16-page catalogue issued twice a year.*

RAINTREE NURSERY, *391 Butts Rd., Morton, Wash. 98356. Tel. (206) 496-5410. Free annual 42-page catalogue.*

Fruit and nut trees suited to the Pacific Northwest. This catalogue also includes the Willapa Hills Hatchery catalogue, which offers select breeds of poultry for gardens or small farms. Payment by check or money order. Shipment by Postal Service or United Parcel. New tree or plant will be provided to replace failed plants within 6 months.

REDWOOD CITY SEED CO., *P.O. Box 361, Redwood City, Calif. 94064. Tel. (415) 325-SEED. Annual 28-page catalogue costs 50 cents.*

This is a "catalogue of useful plants," which takes in quite a broad swath. The most useful, I'd guess, are plants you can eat, and there are seeds for lots of them in lists of tiny type. There are, for example, 10 varieties of oriental cabbage alone, while I have never seen gardening stores with seeds for more than one, bok choi (rendered in this catalogue as "pak-choi"). Payment by check or money order. Shipment by Postal Service. If unsatisfied, it is not necessary to return the seeds (they are, after all, in the ground, the company notes), but a letter will bring a refund or replacement.

RICHTERS, *Box 26, Goodwood, Ont., Canada L0C 1A0. Tel. (416) 640-6677. The 64-page catalogue issued every two years costs $2.*

Seeds for scores of herbs and some vegetables and wild flowers, plus books, dried herbs and spices, and posters. Payment by check, money order, Visa, or Mastercard. Shipment by Postal Service. Credit given for returns by customers who have legitimate complaints.

RINGER RESEARCH, *6860 Flying Cloud Rd., Eden Prairie, Minn. 55344. Tel. (612) 941-4180. Free 16- to 32-page catalogue issued 3 times a year.*

The emphasis here is on organic products for natural lawn and garden care, plus gardening tools and equipment.

†CLYDE ROBIN SEED CO., *P.O. Box 2366, Castro Valley, Calif. 94546. Tel. (415) 581-3468. The 52-page catalogue costs $2.*

This company says its prices are considerably lower than other seed suppliers'. Available are seeds for herbs, wild flowers, shrubs, and trees, plus books, fertilizers, and gift items, such as Meadow-in-a-Can. Payment by check, money order, Visa, Mastercard, or C.O.D. Delivery by Postal Service or United Parcel. Refund or credit for returned purchases.

S. & H. ORGANIC ACRES. *See listing under* Grains and Vegetables, Natural and Freeze-Dried Foods.

SAGINAW VALLEY NUT NURSERY, *8285 Dixie Highway, Birch Run, Mich. 48415. Tel. (517) 652-8552. Price list.*

Dozens of nut trees from a nursery whose owner provides a list of other places that have other nut trees you may want. That is some gesture; Macy's would not send a customer to Gimbels. Payment by check or money order. Shipment by Postal Service or United Parcel. No returns.

SANCTUARY SEEDS, *2388 W. Fourth Ave., Vancouver, B.C., Canada V6K 1P1. Tel. (604) 733-4724. Annual 40-page catalogue costs $1.*

Seeds for vegetables, culinary and medicinal herbs, plus large lists of herbs, spices, dried fruits, and nuts. Payment by check, money order, Visa, or Mastercard. Delivery by Postal Service. Credit for purchases returned.

SHARP BROS. SEED CO., *P.O. Box 140, Healy, Kans. 67850. Tel. (316) 398-2231. Brochure.*

Seeds for native grasses, flowers, and other products suitable for use on the Great Plains. Payment by check or money order. Shipment by United Parcel. No returns.

SISKIYOU RARE PLANT NURSERY, *2825 Cummings Rd., Medford, Ore. 97501. Tel. (503) 772-6846. Annual 60-page catalogue costs $1.50.*

Here is a very large list of alpine, dwarf hardy plants for woodland and rock gardens, plants for use in climates that have cold winters. Payment by check or money order. Shipment by Postal Service or United Parcel. Refund, credit, or replacement for plants that do not arrive in satisfactory condition.

SOUTHERN EXPOSURE SEED EXCHANGE, *P.O. Box 158, North Garden, Va. 22959. No telephone. Annual 36-page catalogue costs $1.*

This is a new company offering seeds for new varieties and historic ones, including various beans, melons, herbs, squash, and tomatoes. They are interested also in obtaining seeds from others.

*SOUTHMEADOW FRUIT GARDENS, *Lakeside, Mich. 49116. Tel. (616) 469-2065. Large illustrated catalogue costs $8; price list is free.*

Here is a very long list of what the company calls choice and unusual fruit varieties for the connoisseur and home gardener. There are some discounts available, for example, a free tree for 6 trees purchased. There is an emphasis on older American and foreign varieties, with about 100 unusual apples and 20 more popular ones, like Red Delicious.

STARK BROS. NURSERIES & ORCHARDS CO., *Highway 54 West, Louisiana, Mo. 63353. Tel. (314) 754-5511. Free 60-page catalogue issued twice a year.*

This company has been selling fruit trees since 1816. Luther Burbank, the pioneer horticulturalist and plant breeder, worked with this company, which developed the Stark Red Delicious apple tree in 1893 and has since then sold 10 million trees of this variety alone. Besides fruit trees, the company also grows grapevines and ornamental shrubs. Payment by check, money order, Visa, Mastercard, or Stark deferred-payment plan. Shipment by Postal Service, United Parcel, or truck freight. Refund or credit for unsatisfactory purchases, but the company usually does not ask for returns.

STOCK SEED FARMS, *R.R. 1, Box 112, Murdock, Neb. 68407. Tel. (402) 867-3771. Annual price list.*

This company is dedicated to the preservation and duplication of the original prairie, selling deep-rooted perennial prairie grasses and wild flowers. Payment by check or money order. Shipment by Postal Service or United Parcel. Refunds for purchases returned immediately, but no return permitted if seed has not been mixed according to specifications.

STOKES SEEDS INC., *P.O. Box 548, Buffalo, N.Y. 14240. Tel. (416) 688-4300. Free annual 164-page catalogue.*

Another long-established company, this one begun in 1881. There are hundreds of kinds of seeds for vegetables, herbs, flowers, and Chinese vegetables and also gardening equipment.

TATER MATER SEEDS, *R.R. 2, 22 Evergreen, Wathena, Kans. 66090. Tel. (913) 989-3520. Free annual 8- to 10-page catalogue.*

Many varieties of tomatoes, potatoes, and corn.

TAYLOR'S HERB GARDEN, *1535 Lone Oak Rd., Vista, Calif. 92083. Tel. (619) 727-3485. Annual 32-page catalogue costs $1.*

TERRITORIAL SEED CO., *P.O. Box 27, Lorane, Ore. 97451. Tel. (503) 942-9547. Free annual 56-page catalogue.*

This is a regional company whose seeds are developed in, and are most suitable for, the Cascade Mountains in Oregon and Washington, southern British Columbia, and Northern California. Too bad for the rest of the country, since the catalogue carries some very interesting vegetable seeds. Lucky people in the Pacific Northwest can buy these seeds with check or money order. Delivery by Postal Service or United Parcel. In case of unsatisfactory results, the package and any remaining seeds should be returned for credit or exchange.

THOMPSON & MORGAN, *P.O. Box 100, Farmingdale, N.J. 07727. Tel. (201) 363-2225 or (800) 367-7333. Free annual 200-page catalogue.*

This company issues the world's largest seed catalogue. There are hundreds of varieties of seeds for flowers, grass, vegetables, fruits, trees, and shrubs in this encyclopedic catalogue.

†URBAN HERBS HYDROPONICS, *P.O. Box 19044, Washington, D.C. 20036. Tel. (202) 462-2720. Free flyer issued 3 times a year.*

Cultivate basil, oregano, thyme, rosemary, marjoram, and sorrel in your kitchen, growing them in a water solution that is supposed to contain all the nutrients they need. This is suggested as a novel gift for friends who like to cook and would enjoy having fresh herbs at their fingertips.

VERMONT BEAN SEED CO., *Garden Lane, Bomoseen, Vt. 05732. Tel. (802) 265-4212. Free 96-page catalogue issued twice a year.*

This company has the largest selection of bean, pea, and corn seeds in the world, over 140 varieties, and also issues a bulb catalogue. Payment by check, money order, American Express, Visa, or Mastercard. Purchases may be returned within 90 days for refund or credit.

WAYSIDE GARDENS, *Hodges, S.C. 29695. Tel. (803) 374-3341 or (800) 845-1124 (except in South Carolina). The 132-page catalogue issued twice a year, costs $1, refundable against first purchase.*

The cover on the catalogue before me, showing the Princess of Monaco rose, is among the most beautiful I have seen in the preparation of this book. Beside roses, this company also offers flower bulbs, shrubs, and other hardy plants. Payment by American Express, Visa, Mastercard, or Diners Club. Shipment by Postal Service or United Parcel. Refund or credit for merchandise returned within 3 months.

WELL-SWEEP HERB FARM, *317 Mt. Bethel Rd., Port Murray, N.J. 07865. Tel. (201) 852-5390. Annual 32-page catalogue costs 75 cents.*

Besides herb seeds and plants, there are dried flowers, flowering perennials, and geraniums. Payment by check or money order. Shipment by United Parcel. Credit for unsatisfactory purchases, but returns are not necessary.

WESTERN MAINE NURSERIES, *1 Evergreen Dr., Frye-burg, Me. 04037. Tel. (207) 935-2161. Free semian-nual 16-page catalogue.*

This company grows conifer seedlings and transplants, selling primarily to Christmas tree growers, nursery operators, and landowners for reforestation.

WHITE FLOWER FARM, *Litchfield, Conn. 06759. Tel. (203) 567-0801 (for customer service or to speak with a staff horticulturalist), or (800) 243-2853 for orders only, (except in Connecticut, Alaska, and Hawaii). The approximately 124-page catalogue costs $5 for a one-year subscription of 3 issues, with the $5 good toward a purchase over $25. Active customers get free catalogues.*

This is another very handsome catalogue, with excellent color photographs of flowers and garden settings. Besides flower plants and shrubs, there are garden tools and books. Payment by check, money order, Visa, or Mastercard. Shipment by Postal Service, United Parcel, or truck. Unsatisfactory purchases may be returned for refund or credit within 30 days.

LESLIE H. WILMOTH NURSERY, *Route 2, Box 469, Elizabethtown, Ky. 42701. Tel. (502) 369-7493. Price list.*

More than 100 varieties of nut trees, one of the largest selections in the United States. There are, for example, 23 varieties of pecan trees alone. Payment by check or money order. Shipment by United Parcel. Refund or credit for returned purchases.

WILSON PLANT SALES, *Box 188, Roachdale, Ind. 46172. Tel. (317) 522-1320. Annual 16-page catalogue costs 25 cents.*

Indoor and outdoor house flowers, including African violets, geraniums, begonias, and fuchsias.

WOODLAND ACRES NURSERY *(Sperka's), Rt. 2, Crivitz, Wis. 54114. Tel. (715) 757-3853. Annual brochure costs 25 cents.*

Hardy, northern-grown wild flowers such as bleeding heart, anemone, and bugle-flower. The owner, Marie Sperka, also sells autographed copies of her book, *Growing Wildflowers: A Gardener's Guide.*

WYATT-QUARLES SEED CO., *Box 739, Garner, N.C. 27529. Tel. (919) 832-0551. Free 32-page catalogue.*

Vegetable seeds (from asparagus to zucchini), strawberry plants, flower bulbs, plants, herbs, and grass seed. Payment by check or money order. Shipment by Postal Service or United Parcel. Refund or credit for purchases returned within 10 days.

Garden Tools, Equipment, and Furniture

ALUMINUM GREENHOUSES, *Everlite, 14605 Lorain Ave., P.O. Box 11087, Cleveland, Ohio 44111. Tel. (216) 251-6100. Annual 44-page catalogue costs $2.*

Prefabricated aluminum greenhouses. Payment by check, Visa, Mastercard, or C.O.D. Delivery by United Parcel or common carrier. Purchases may be returned within a year for refunds.

AMERICAN SPRING & PRESSING WORKS, *Post Box 7602, Adarsh Housing Society Road, Malad, Bombay 400 064, India. Tel. 692331. Free 12-page catalogue.*

Sprayers for pesticides, threshers, weeders, seeders, and hoes. This company sells in India and exports to East Africa and the Middle East as well as to other Asian countries. Payment by letter of credit. Shipment by ocean freight, air freight, or air parcel post.

AUTO HOE INC., *P.O. Box W121, Lost Dauphin Dr., DePere, Wis. 54115. Tel. (414) 336-4753. Brochure price list.*

This company makes the only auto hoe that is both a tiller and a hoe.

BERRY-HILL LTD., *75 Burwell Rd., St. Thomas, Ont., Canada N5P 3R5. Tel. (519) 631-0480. Free catalogue.*

Equipment for the hobby farmer, plus gardening tools, cultivators, and the like. There are also specialty kitchen utensils, such as a grindstone for making flour. Payment by check, money order, Visa, or Mastercard. Shipment by Postal Service or United Parcel. Refund or credit for purchases returned within 30 days.

BRAMEN CO., *P.O. Box 70, Salem, Mass. 01970. Tel. (617) 745-7765. Free 8-page catalogue issued twice a year.*

Greenhouse equipment, cold frames, and gardening tools. Payment by check or money order. Shipment by Postal Service or United Parcel. Purchases may be returned for refund within 30 days.

CENTRE FOR AGRICULTURAL MECHANIZATION AND RURAL TECHNOLOGY, *P.O. Box 764, Arusha, Tanzania. Tel. 3594. Brochure.*

Planters, cultivators, plows, and ground nut (peanut) shellers, plus other equipment for rural life, such as ox carts. Payment by check.

†**THE CLAPPER COMPANY,** *P.O. Box A, 1121 Washington St., West Newton, Mass. 02165. Tel. (617) 244-7900. Brochure.*

Books, tools, toys, and furniture for the garden, for yourself or for gifts. Payment by check, money order, American Express, Visa, or Mastercard. The return policy is a good one: Purchases may be returned within a year for refund, credit, exchange, or repair.

†**CORSICANA FARM EQUIPMENT, DIRECT,** *P.O. Box 1699-D, Corsicana, Tex. 75110. Tel. (214) 874-3254 or (800) 527-6454. Free 16-page catalogue issued twice a year.*

Discount prices on farm equipment, tractor-mounted attachments such as 3-point hitch blades, mowers, plows, seeders, and post-hole diggers.

ELFENCE WHOLESALE LTD, *R.R. 1, Belwood, Ont., Canada N0B 1J0. Tel. (519) 843-5817. The 12-page catalogue costs $1.*

This company makes electrified fences "to keep dogs from sheep, goats in, bears from beehives." Payment by check, money order, Visa, or C.O.D. Shipment by Postal Service or United Parcel. Purchases may be returned, with permission, for exchange.

ERKINS. *Garden ornaments. See listing under* Sculpture.

FARNAM FARM EQUIPMENT. *See listing under* Horse Supplies and Riding Equipment.

†GARDENER'S EDEN, *P.O. Box 7307, San Francisco, Calif. 94120. Tel. (415) 428-9292. Free 48-page catalogue issued several times a year.*

Nice tools for gardening, equipment, garden furniture, gift suggestions, and a small number of wildflower and herbs seeds.

GREEN RIVER TOOLS, *5 Cotton Mill Hill, P.O. Box 1919, Brattleboro, Vt. 05301. Tel. (802) 254-2388. Free 20-page catalogue issued twice a year.*

A handsome catalogue that offers "the highest quality tools for garden, field, and forest."

BERNARD D. GREESON, *3548 N. Cramer St., Milwaukee, Wis. 53211. Annual 6-page catalogue costs 50 cents, refundable against first order.*

Horticultural supplies, such as plant food, special plant food for African violets, potting soil, insecticides, fungicides, plastic labels, and pots. Payment by check or money order. Shipment by Postal Service, United Parcel, or motor freight. Goods may not be returned unless prior approval is obtained.

DAVID KAY GARDEN & GIFT CATALOGUE, *26055-D Emery Rd., Cleveland, Ohio 44128. Tel. (216) 464-5125, (800) 621-5199 (except in Illinois), or (800) 972-5855 (in Illinois). Free 24- to 32-page catalogue issued 4 times a year.*

There are many items here that would appeal to the genteel weekend gardener, and even more that would make nice gifts for such a person.

*A. M. LEONARD, *P.O. Box 816, 6665 Spiker Rd., Piqua, Ohio 45356. Tel. (513) 773-2694, (800) 543-* 8955 *(except in Ohio), or (800) 762-8922 (in Ohio). Free 80-page catalogue issued twice a year.*

Discounts of 10 to 25 percent on horticultural and gardening tools and supplies. Payment by check, money order, Visa, or Mastercard. Shipment by Postal Service or United Parcel. Refunds or credit for merchandise returned after approval and less a 5 percent restocking fee, with minimum of $4.

MELLINGER'S, *2310 W. South Range Rd., North Lima, Ohio 44452. Tel. (216) 549-9861 or (800) 321-7444 (except in Ohio). Free annual 112-page catalogue.*

Lots of gardening equipment and tools, chemical pest killers and natural things used by organic gardeners (the latter includes praying mantises and inflatable owls and snakes), nut, fruit, and ornamental trees, roses, vegetable, flower, and herb seeds, books and berries.

PRAIRIE STATE COMMODITIES, *P.O. Box 6, Trilla, Ill. 62469. Tel. (617) 235-4322. Free 6- to 8-page catalogue.*

One catalogue of this company offers new and used equipment for handling seeds and grain, and another has agricultural seeds. Payment by check, money order, or C.O.D. Delivery by Postal Service, United Parcel, or commercial truck. Refunds for defective goods returned within 30 days.

RURAL ADVANCEMENT FUND, *P.O. Box 1029, Pittsboro, N.C. 27312. Tel. (919) 542-5292. The 24-page directory costs $2.*

This is not quite a catalogue, but rather a source of other catalogues as part of an interesting and worthwhile nonprofit effort to revive the use of older American fruit and vegetable varieties. Many of the catalogue companies listed by Rural Advancement are also in this book, but the directory also includes essays and advice and is well worth reading. Payment by check or money order. Delivery by Postal Service.

SELF-SUFFICIENCY & SMALLHOLDING SUPPLIES, *The Old Palace, Priory Rd., Wells, Somerset, BA5 1SY, England. Tel. 0749-72127. The 68-page catalogue costs $4.*

Here are tools, equipment, and other supplies for backyard gardeners and owners of small farms. There is a separate catalogue of books on growing food and raising cattle, sheep, goats, pigs, dogs, rabbits, horses, poultry, fish, and bees, among other things. Payment by check, money order, or Visa. Shipment by Postal Service or air freight. Goods in saleable condition may be returned for credit within a month.

SMITH & HAWKEN, *25 Corte Madera, Mill Valley, Calif. 94941. Tel. (415) 383-4415. Free 32-page catalogue issued 3 times a year.*

Fine tools. Payment by check, money order, American Express, Visa, or Mastercard. Shipment by Postal Service or United Parcel. Refund or credit for returned purchases.

UNION TRACTOR WORKSHOP, *8-B, Phase-II, Mayapuri Industrial Area, New Delhi 110 064, India. Tel. 504615. Brochure.*

Tractor equipment made in India and available for export to half a dozen countries. Payment by letter of credit. Shipment by air or sea freight. No returns accepted.

*WHOLESALE AMERICA, *4777 Menard Dr., Eau Claire, Wis. 54703. Tel. (715) 874-5000 or (800) 826-3403 (except in Wisconsin). The 16- to 20-page catalogue issued 9 times a year costs $1.*

Here are discount prices on milling and drilling machines and tractors. The company offers a 46.5-horsepower tractor for $6,000, compared with the $15,000 list price. Payment by check, money order, Visa, or Mastercard. Shipment by Postal Service, United Parcel, or freight. Purchases may be returned within 10 days for refund or credit.

See also *Seeds and Plants,* above, for small garden tools, fertilizers, insecticides, books, and gifts.

Beekeeping Supplies

*BETTERBEE, *P.O. Box 37, Route 29, Greenwich, N.Y. 12834. Tel. (518) 692-9669. Free annual 40-page catalogue.*

Discount prices for beekeeping supplies, including a beginner's kit, regularly $79, offered for $62. Could I have your attention, please? You can order bees by mail. By the pound. I didn't know that. The queen bee costs extra, naturally. Payment by check, money order, Visa, or Mastercard. Shipment by United Parcel. Purchases may be returned within 30 days for refund. I wonder how many requests for refunds they get. How you return 3 pounds of bees is not explained. Very carefully.

DADANT & SONS INC., *Second St. and Broadway, Hamilton, Ill. 62341. Tel. (217) 847-3324. Free annual 40-to 60-page catalogue.*

Beekeeping equipment, honey removing devices, and special supplies for raising queens, plus the bees themselves and some queens, and everything you will need to make honey. Payment by check, money order, Visa, or Mastercard. Shipment by Postal Service, United Parcel, or commercial freight.

†*GLORYBEE HONEY & SUPPLIES, *1006 Arrowsmith St., Eugene, Ore. 97402. Tel. (503) 485-1649. Free 16-page annual catalogue.*

Discount prices for beehive equipment and for honey gifts. Payment by check, Visa, or Mastercard. Shipment by United Parcel. Refund for defective merchandise.

WALTER T. KELLEY CO., *Clarkson, Ky. 42726. Tel. (502) 242-2012. Free annual 64-page catalogue.*

The catalogue of beekeeping equipment is chatty and informative; the owner occasionally states that a particular product is not his preference, but he will sell it to you if you insist. There is a lot of equipment and many bees: "We are passing all of our bees through an excluder so that you will not receive any drones"—lots of bosses would like to know how to buy a big enough excluder, I'm sure. Payment by check or money order. Delivery by Postal Service, United Parcel, or truck. Purchases may be returned within 10 days for refund or credit.

†A. I. ROOT CO., *P.O. Box 706, Medina, Ohio 44258. Tel. (216) 725-6677. Free annual 48-page catalogue.*

Beekeeping equipment, bees, and gifts and books related to bees.

SELF-SUFFICIENCY AND SMALLHOLDING SUPPLIES. *Books on beekeeping. See listing under* Gardening Tools, Equipment, and Furniture, *above.*

❖ 13 For Horses and Other Pets

According to the Pet Industry Joint Advisory Council, there has been a surge in recent years in mail-order sales for pet care. Items being newly sold by mail include over-the-counter medicines and ointments and special shampoos, plus the old standbys of cages, toys, water bowls, leashes, training devices, and coats. Excluding the huge person-to-person market in pets, which cannot even be guessed at, pet industry sales are running at about $10 billion a year.

Dogs have long been America's favorite, but cats are gaining. The American Veteri-nary Medical Association estimates that there are 55 million dogs in the United States and almost as many cats. The figures on dogs are pretty much what they've been, but the number of cats has leaped from 38 million just a few years ago to 52 million today. Why is that? The veterinary association attributes it to changing life-styles, especially the rise of two-income families. If both a husband and wife work and they want a pet, a cat is the logical choice because it can be left alone all day in a home.

When it comes to large numbers,

though, tropical fish are way out in front, with an estimated 1 billion of them in American homes at one time of the year or another. One reason for this large number is the brief lives of many of the fish, which, as many parents will attest, need to be replaced with some frequency as predecessors are flushed down the toilet. Or, in the words of the veterinary association, it is an "expendable" item.

Once cars replaced horses as the primary means of transportation, horses rose on the scale of things to be owned by people who still have lots of money after the landlord and grocer have been paid. In recent years, I have lived near the North Shore of Long island, noted for its fine horses, and not far from the horsey set in the Virginia countryside near Washington, D.C. The closest we have ever come to this kind of thing was when our daughter Ellen went horseback riding in Hyde Park during a visit to London. I am not now, nor have I ever been, a horse owner, but I have paid the landlord and grocer. Just barely.

There are an estimated 8 million horses in the country, including an unknown but large and increasing number used as pets. There are also race horses, work horses, and police horses.

There are 45 million caged birds and an estimated 15 million in a catch-all category that includes rabbits, hamsters, white mice, gerbils, and snakes. If that strikes you as an odd categorization, keep in mind that a lot of the white mice are raised by people to feed their pet snakes.

The American Veterinary Medical Association does not support the keeping of snakes as household pets on the grounds that they are considered wild animals. Also in the category that the association advises against bringing into the home are lions, tigers, monkeys and apes, ferrets, skunks, and raccoons. The association acknowledges, however, that ferrets are enjoying increasing popularity. The larger animals are opposed by the association because they are dangerous, and all these animals are opposed because they can bring dangerous diseases into the house, especially rabies. In addition, they can never be housebroken, and who would want to clean up after a lion or a gorilla?

Pet Supplies

ANIMAL VETERINARY PRODUCTS, *P.O. Box 1267, Galesburg, Ill. 61401. Tel. (309) 342-9511, (800) 447-8192 (except in Illinois), or (800) 322-8183 (in Illinois). Free annual 80-page catalogue.*

Health care products for cats and dogs, including furniture and toys for cats, medicines, grooming aids, and books.

*ECHO PET SUPPLIES, *335 Mill St., Ortonville, Mich. 48462. Tel. (313) 627-2877. The 40-page catalogue issued twice a year costs $1 but will be sent free if you telephone for it.*

Lots of equipment for dogs, cats, birds, fish, hamsters, and guinea pigs. Discount prices on pet supplies, such as a bamboo bird cage for $13 instead of the $18.50 list.

ELGIN ENGRAVING CO. *Dog tags. See* Hardware for the Home.

FARNHAM COMPANIES. *Dog care products. See listing under* Horse Supplies and Riding Equipment, *below.*

†**FRIENDS OF ANIMALS,** *1 Pine St., Neptune, N.J. 07753. Tel. (201) 922-2600. Annual 32-page catalogue costs $1.*

Here are things for pets and their owners, mostly the latter, and they would make nice gifts. Payment by check, money order, Visa, or Mastercard. Shipment by Postal Service or United Parcel. Purchases may be returned for refund or credit within 30 days.

JIM & BARBARA OLSEN, *Box 796A, Fairview, Alba., Canada T0H 1L0. Tel. (403) 835-4851. Price list.*

Live rabbits and rabbit wool. Payment by check or money order. Shipment by air freight. Purchases may be returned for refund.

PATENTED PRODUCTS. *Electrically heated pads for pets. See listing under* Audio and Video Equipment.

PET COMPANY OF AMERICA, *465 Furnace St., Marshfield, Mass. 02050. Tel. (617) 834-7814 or (800) 343-3383 (except in Massachusetts). Free 16-page catalogue issued twice a year.*

Pet accessories, including a dog's brass bed with plush cushion. Payment by check, money order, Visa, or Mastercard. Shipment by Postal Service or United Parcel. Purchases may be returned for refund or credit.

†**PETCO ANIMAL SUPPLIES,** *P.O. Box 1076, 8500 Alvarado Rd., La Mesa, Calif. 92014. Tel. (619) 469-2111. Free annual 128-page catalogue.*

Discounts on animal and pet supplies, including things for horses, dogs, cats, birds, and fish. There are hundreds of items offered. Payment by check, money order, Visa, Mastercard, or C.O.D. Shipment by Postal Service or United Parcel. Purchases (except vaccines and instruments) may be returned within 15 days of invoice date for refund or credit.

RAINTREE NURSERY. *Live poultry and birds for the garden. See listing under* Seeds and Plants.

TUREN INC., *Flexport, Etna Rd., P.O. Box 270, Lebanon, N.H. 03766. Tel. (603) 448-2990. Brochure.*

The main product is a molded "flexport" that allows a dog or cat to go in and out of a house without a door having to be opened for it. Other products include an automatic outdoor drinking fountain and monogrammed collars.

†**WAGGIN' TAILS,** *2001 Holland Ave., P.O. Box 5019, Port Huron, Mich. 48061. Tel. (313) 987-2000 or (800) 882-1273 (except in Michigan). Free 32-page catalogue issued twice a year.*

Things for cats and dogs, including beds, baskets, gadgets to let pets enter and leave the house, and an awful lot of things with animal motifs for animal lovers, many of which are suggested as gifts.

Horse Supplies and Riding Equipment

COUNTRYSIDE GENERAL STORE. *How-to books on raising livestock and poultry. See listing under* Country and General Stores.

DAIRY ASSOCIATION CO., *Lyndonville, Vt. 05851. Tel. (802) 626-3610. Brochure price list.*

Although, as the name suggests, there are cow-care products available from this company, the emphasis appears to be on horses. This manufacturer prefers to sell through retailers, but will sell directly to customers if no retail store is in the area. Among the products are conditioners and preservatives for saddles and other leather goods, and hoof softeners. Payment by check. Shipment by Postal Service.

FARNAM EQUIPMENT CO., *6847 N. 16th St., Omaha, Neb. 68112. Tel. (800) 528-1378. Free 72-page catalogue.*

Many supplies and pieces of equipment for raising and riding horses, including stalls, saddles, and books. This company issues 2 other free catalogues besides the one for horses; one is on farm equipment (88 pages) and the other is a products catalogue (30 pages) that includes some horse care items but also has things for dogs.

†H. KAUFFMAN & SONS SADDLERY CO., *141 E. 24th St., New York, N.Y. 10010. Tel. (212) 684-6060. The 72-page catalogue issued twice a year costs $2.*

This firm has been in business since 1875, which means it has been around longer then the automobile. If you are going to go riding, you have to be properly turned out, and here is a place where you can get the accoutrements. There are lots of men's, women's, and children's riding clothes, shoes and boots, helmets and other things listed under 2 headings: English Riding Attire and Western Wear. There are polo outfits and jockeys' riding silks, plus many saddles and bridle parts. This very nice catalogue also offers gifts, artwork (by artists who seem to be familiar with Frederic Remington), and books.

LIBERTYVILLE SADDLE SHOP, *P.O. Box M, 306 Peterson Rd., Libertyville, Ill. 60048. Tel. (312) 362-0570 or (800) 323-0570 (except in Illinois). The 192-page catalogue issued 3 times a year costs $3.*

Here is another big catalogue for the horse owner, and it claims to have the country's most complete saddlery offerings. There are English and Western saddles, bridles and crops, shoes and boots, and men's, women's and children's riding clothes. Payment by check, money order, American Express, Visa, Mastercard, Diners Club, or Libertyville charge. Shipment by Postal Service or United Parcel. Refund or credit for purchases returned within 15 days.

MILLER'S, *123 E. 24th St., New York, N.Y. 10010. Tel. (212) 673-1400. The 118-page spring catalogue costs $2; The 32-page Christmas catalogue is free.*

This is the official saddler to the United States Equestrian Team.

SWAINE ADENEY BRIGG & SON LTD. *Saddles and clothing. See* Luggage, Handbags, Briefcases, Canes and Umbrellas, Travel Clocks.

❖ 14 Crafts and Hobbies

I n reaction to our mass-produced, look-alike world—where everything from clothing to furniture and homes comes out of a package—there has been increasing interest in crafts and handmade and custom-made products, both to buy and to make. All over the country, craftsmen, artisans, and businesses that promote and sell local crafts seem to be thriving again. The surge of interest in hand- and custom-made products also extends to do-it-yourselfers, who have taken up hobbies like weaving, silkscreening, and calligraphy.

In this chapter you'll find a wide range of items to buy and make in the area of crafts: needlecraft patterns, fabrics, looms, sewing accessories, leather-crafting kits and tools, wool yarns and rug-hooking supplies, artists' paints, brushes and pens, pottery-making equipment, jewelers equipment and gem-stones, bookbinding supplies, etching and lithography equipment, glass-working supplies and equipment, model-making kits and tools, and all kinds of tools and equipment for sculptors, tinkerers, and do-it-yourselfers. Several of the listings here are suppliers to professional users who will sell to individuals in the arts and crafts fields.

Some of the companies in the *Crafts to Buy* section also provide supplies for people who want to make their own things, especially fabrics. Many of the other chapters also list places that sell kits for things you can make, including furniture, clocks, cars, boats, and even houses.

Many of the entries in the *Crafts to Buy* section could also be listed in the Clothing and Accessories chapter of this book. I have made something of an arbitrary decision to separate crafted clothing from the clothing noted elsewhere, primarily because I have perceived a real attempt to keep crafts alive in the United States as well as a desire to use crafts as an important part of the economy in some foreign countries. In addition to the sources of handmade items noted here, there are others listed elsewhere in the book, such as fine handmade woolen Irish sweaters in the Clothes chapter. Just about every one of these entries includes gift ideas, so I have called attention to gift services only for those catalogues that point it out themselves.

General Craft Supplies

AMERICAN HANDICRAFTS. *Kits and tools for many crafts. See listing for Merribee Needlearts under* Needlecrafts, *below.*

BERMAN LEATHERCRAFT, *145 South St., Boston, Mass. 02111. Tel. (617) 426-0870 or (800) 341-FAST (except in Massachusetts). Semiannual 32-page catalogue costs $1.*

Here are leather-crafting kits, hardware, accessories, brass buckles, and tools.

BOURGET BROS., *1626 11th St., Santa Monica, Calif. 90404. Tel. (213) 450-7407. The 250-page catalogue costs $3.*

Jewelers tools, casting supplies, wax patterns, lapidary supplies, gemstones, sterling silver castings, and books.

***BOYCAN'S CRAFT & ART SUPPLIES,** P.O. Box 897, Sharon, Pa. 16146. Tel. (412) 346-5534. The 96-page catalogue costs $2.*

Discount prices offered.

CEDAR CAVE CRAFTS, *185A Avenue Rd., Toronto, Ont., Canada M5R 2J2. Tel. (416) 964-7883. Annual 14-page catalogue costs $1.*

Off-beat and hard-to-find craft supplies and kits. Payment by check or money order. Shipment by Postal Service, United Parcel, or CanPar. Purchases may be returned for refund within 7 days if in saleable condition.

CRAFT PRODUCTS CO. *Quarterly 64- to 100-page catalogue costs $2. See listing for Craft Patterns Co. under Plans and Patterns for Do-It-Yourselfers, below.*

DEL TRADING POST, *Box 248, Mission, S.Dak. 57555. Tel. (605) 856-4817. The 24-page catalogue costs $1.*

A large selection of hard-to-get items, including Indian-tanned hides, sinew, and rawhide. Other items include Indian seed beads and many other kinds of beads, bone, horn, bells, shells, and shawl fringe. Among the completed craft items for sale are shawls and wool blankets in old Indian designs. Payment by check or money order. Shipment by Postal Service or United Parcel. Purchases may be returned within 10 days for refund or credit.

DERBY LANE SHELL CENTER, *10515 Gandy Blvd., St. Petersburg, Fla. 33702. Tel. (813) 576-1131. Annual 36-page catalogue costs $2.*

All you need to make crafts out of sea shells. There are the shells themselves, some domestic and some imported, plus coral, craft supplies, books, and glue.

THE FREED COMPANY. *Assorted leathers. See listing under* Men's and Women's Clothing.

HANDS MAGAZINE, *Box 867, Station F, Toronto,Ont., Canada M4Y 2N7. Tel. (416) 964-8705.*

Hands Books by Mail ($3) and *Hands Magizine* ($3 per copy), the latter a bimonthly crafts magazine offering a limited number of kits and craft items. Payment by check, money order, Visa, or Mastercard. Shipment by Postal Service, United Parcel, or CanPar. Purchases may be returned within 7 days if in saleable condition for refund or credit.

*HOUSE OF ORANGE LTD., *553 Hillside Ave., Victoria, B.C., Canada V8T IY8. Tel. (604) 384-1117. The 30-page catalogue costs $5.*

Glass and wooden beads, mother of pearl designs, plated and sterling silver ornaments for jewelry and other crafts. There are discounts for larger purchases, ranging to 50 percent off on an order of over $100 (Canadian). Payment by check, money order, Visa, or Mastercard. Shipment by Postal Service or CanPar. Purchases may be returned for refund within 10 days, but prior notification is required.

*NERVO INTERNATIONAL, *4365-C Arnold Ave., Naples, Fla. 33942. Tel. (813) 775-8336; for orders only and using I.D. No. 2897: (800) 325-6000 (except in Missouri) or (800) 342-6700 (in Missouri). Quarterly 18-page catalogue costs $3.*

Wholesale prices for tools and glaziers' supplies, cut glass, and glass jewels.

POURETTE, *P.O. Box 15220, 6910 Roosevelt Way, N.E., Seattle, Wash. 98115. The 70-page catalogue issued 3 times a year costs $1.*

Candle-making supplies. Payment by check, money order, Visa, or Mastercard. Shipment by Postal Service, United Parcel, or truck freight. Purchases, may be returned within 20 days for refund or credit.

QUILL ART, *11762-A Westline Dr., St. Louis, Mo. 63146. Tel. (314) 872-3181 or (800) 325-4116. The 14-page catalogue costs $1.*

Quilling is the art of rolling, gluing, and shaping narrow strips of paper into beautiful designs, and it is said to have begun during the Renaissance. This company is a supplier of the paper, kits, and accessories. Payment by check, money order, Visa, or Mastercard. Shipment by Postal Service or United Parcel. Purchases may be returned, if unopened and in good condition, for refund or credit.

ROBERTS INDIAN CRAFTS & SUPPLIES, *404 West Virginia St., Anadarko, Okla. 73005. Tel. (405) 247-3301. Price list is free in exchange for first-class postage stamp.*

Here are Indian crafts and supplies, including beads from Czechoslovakia, mother of pearl, and abalone shells. Payment by money order or C.O.D. Shipment by United Parcel. Purchases may be returned for refund or exchange within 5 days.

*SAX ARTS & CRAFTS, *P.O. Box 2002, Milwaukee, Wis. 53201. Tel. (414) 272-4900, (800) 558-6696 (except in Wisconsin), (800) 242-4911 (in Wisconsin). Annual 400-page catalogue costs $3.*

A discounted Sax price is shown on many items and there are quantity discounts on most items.

C. W. SOMERS & CO., *387 Washington St., Boston, Mass. 02108. Tel. (617) 426-6880 or (800) 462-8803 (in Massachusetts only). Annual 56-page catalogue costs $1.50.*

Jewelers' and metalcraft supplies. Payment by check or money order. Shipment by Postal Service or United Parcel. Purchases may be returned, with authorization, within 15 days for credit.

UNICORN BOOKS FOR CRAFTSMEN. *See listing under* Needlecrafts, *below.*

UNITED ART GLASS, *1032 E. Ogden Ave., Naperville, Ill. 60540. Tel. (312) 369-8168 or (800) 323-9760. Annual 100-page catalogue costs $3, refundable with purchase.*

Many pieces of glass, framing, tools, and wires for creating artworks using glass. Pay-

ment by check, money order, Visa, Mastercard, or C.O.D. Shipment by Postal Service, United Parcel, or truck. Purchases may be returned for refund or credit (although lead, zinc, and glass are not returnable).

*VETERAN LEATHER CO., *204 25th St., Brooklyn, N.Y. 11232. Tel. (718) 768-0300. Annual 56-page catalogue costs $2.*

Leather craft equipment, including some kits. Available are leather, tools, and lacing, to make such products as wallets, purses, and handbags. Discount prices.

WHITTEMORE-DURGIN GLASS CO., *P.O. Box 2065, Hanover, Mass. 02339. Tel. (617) 871-1790. The 76-page catalogue costs $1.*

Hundreds of glass projects to be made at home, including lamps, lampshades, and windows. There are tools, glass, lead, and many books. Payment by check, money order, American Express, Visa, or Mastercard. Shipment by Postal Service, United Parcel, or truck. Return of goods for refund or credit is subject to condition of purchases.

Needlecrafts, Weaving, and Textile Dyeing, Fabrics and Yarns

A. N. I. (*Art Needlework Industries*), *7 St. Michael's Mansions, Ship St., Oxford, OX1 3DG, England. Tel. (in Oxford) 247-566. Annual 20-page catalogue costs $4.50.*

Payment by check or money order. Shipment by Postal Service.

ANNIE'S ATTIC, *Route 2, Box 212-B, Big Sandy, Tex. 75755. Tel. (214) 636-4353 or (800) 527-8452 (except in Texas, Alaska, and Hawaii). Quarterly 40-page catalogue costs $2.*

This is a needlecraft catalogue with hundreds of patterns and kits offered. Payment by check, money order, Visa, or Mastercard. Shipment by Postal Service or United Parcel. Purchases may be returned for refund or credit.

A. V. L. LOOMS *(Ahrens & Violette Looms), 601 Orange St., Chico, Calif. 95926. Tel. (916) 345-2811. Annual 12-page catalogue costs $1.*

This company builds fine hand looms and production weaving machines.

DOROTHY H. BECKER, *1378 E. Eighth St., Brooklyn, N.Y. 11230. No telephone. Brochure.*

Accessories for home sewing, including cutters and dress maker's graph paper. Payment by check or money order. Shipment by Postal Service or United Parcel. Purchases may be returned for refund.

BETTER HOMES & GARDENS CRAFTS CATALOGUE, *P.O. Box 374, Des Moines, Iowa 50336. Tel. (800) 247-5099 (except in Iowa) or (800) 532-1526 (in Iowa). The 60-page catalogue costs $1.25.*

This is a huge catalogue for people interested in needlecrafts. It includes embroidery, crewel, needlepoint, sewing, quilting, and many other crafts. Payment by check, money order, American Express, Visa, or Mastercard. Shipment by Postal Service or United Parcel. Purchases may be returned for refund or credit.

BRAID-AID FABRICS, *466 Washington St., Pembroke, Mass. 02359. Tel. (617) 826-6091. The 96-page catalogue costs $2.*

The specialty here is braiding and hooking to produce rugs of diverse designs and shapes, plus some things for shirret, quilts, spinning, and weaving. Payment by check, money order, Visa, or Mastercard. Shipment by Postal Service or United Parcel. Purchases may be returned, with written permission, for refund or credit within 2 weeks.

BRIGGS & LITTLE WOOLEN MILLS LTD., *York Mills, Harvey Station, N. B., Canada E0H 1H0. Tel. (506) 366-5438.*

Wool yarns and rug-hooking supplies. Payment by check or money order. Shipment by Postal Service. Purchases may be returned for refund, with no time limit as long as skeins are unopened.

BRITEX FABRICS—BRITEX-BY-MAIL, *146 Geary St., San Francisco, Calif. 94108. Tel. (415) 392-2910. No catalogue, but there is a swatch service that costs $2.*

Fabrics by mail from a huge assortment.

CABIN FEVER CALICOS, *P.O. Box 6256, Northwest Station, Washington, D.C. 20015. Tel. (202) 686-0767. Catalogue costs $2.75, including swatches.*

Quilting supplies, books, fabrics, and notions. Payment by check, Visa, or Mastercard. Shipment by United Parcel. Purchases may be returned for refund or credit, within 10 days.

CALICO 'N THINGS, *P.O. Box 265, Marquette, Mich. 49855. Tel. (906) 228-7145. The 20-page catalogue costs $1.25, or $3 with 250 fabric swatches.*

This company specializes in quilting fabrics, patterns, kits, and designs. Payment by check, money order, Visa, or Mastercard. Shipment by Postal Service or United Parcel. Purchases may be returned for refund.

*CAMBRIDGE WOOLS LTD., *P.O. Box 2572, Auckland, New Zealand. Tel. 30-769. Brochure costs $1.*

Spinning wheels, sheepskin rugs, Aran sweaters, natural wools for spinning, weaving, and knitting. All prices are equivalent to wholesale. Payment by money order. Shipment by Postal Service. Purchases may be returned for refund.

CERULEAN BLUE LTD., *P.O. Box 21168, Seattle, Wash. 98111. Tel. (206) 625-9647. Annual 48-page catalogue costs $3.25.*

Textile art supplies, including dyes, tools, chemicals, printing devices, and fabrics.

CHARING CROSS KITS, *Main St., P.O. Box 79832, Meredith N.H. 03253. Tel. (603) 279-8449. Semiannual 44-page catalogues costs $2.00.*

Kits for children's clothes; for example, $11.50 for a kit with which one can make a pinafore worth $30. Payment by check, money order, Visa, or Mastercard. Shipment by Postal Service or United Parcel. Full refund or credit for kits within 30 days, even if partly sewn.

CONDON'S YARNS, *P.O. Box 129, Charlottetown, P.E.I., Canada C1A 7K3. Tel. (902) 892-7995 or (902) 894-8712. Annual catalogue costs $1.*

Wool yarns, mohair yarns, and accessories, and they include a handy conversion chart for metric, Canadian, and American sizes for knitting needles, plus instructions for washing woolen garments. Payment by check, money order; American Express, Visa, or Mastercard. Shipment by Postal Service. Purchases may be returned for refund within 60 days.

CR'S CRAFTS, *P.O. Box 8, Leland, Iowa 50453. Tel. (515) 567-3652. Annual 36-page catalogue costs $2.*

Here are cute toys available ready-made or in kits to do it yourself. There are stuffed animals, clowns, baby dolls, and dolls' clothing.

FABDEC, *3553 Old Post Rd., San Angelo, Tex. 76904. Tel. (915) 944-1031. Brochure price list costs $1.*

Procion fiber reactive dyes and chemicals are available here.

FIRESIDE LOOMS & WEAVING, *91600 W. Fork Rd., Deadwood, Ore. 97430. Tel. (503) 964-3771. Brochure costs $1.*

Foot-powered weaving looms that, in the brochure photos, look as handsome as a spinet piano in a living room. Payment by check. Shipment by United Parcel or truck freight. Defective parts may be returned for replacement at any time.

GINGER SNAP STATION, *P.O. Box 81086, Atlanta, Ga. 30366. Tel. (404) 455-8227. The 40-page catalogue issued 2 or 3 times a year costs $1.*

This is a colorful catalogue of kits and patterns for quilts, pillow covers, stuffed animals, and wall hangings. Payment by check, money order, Visa, or American Express. Shipment by Postal Service or United Parcel. Purchases may be returned within a "reasonable time" for refund.

GLIMAKRA LOOMS 'N YARNS, *P.O. Box 16157, Rocky River, Ohio 44116. Tel. (216) 333-7595 or (800) 843-9276 (except in Ohio). The 22-page catalogue costs $2.50.*

The catalogue on looms is nicely photographed and shows off good-looking equipment that looks like it would fit into any home. Payment by check or money order. Shipment by United Parcel. Returns not accepted unless equipment arrives damaged.

GOHN BROS. *Fabrics. See listing under* Men's and Women's Clothing.

THE GREEN PEPPER, *941 Olive St., Eugene, Ore. 97401. Tel. (503) 345-6665. Annual 20-page catalogue costs $1.*

Here are otherwise hard-to-find patterns and fabrics. The patterns include those for back-packs, round cargo bags, ski suits, warmup and running suits.

*GURIAN'S, *276 Fifth Ave., New York, N.Y. 10001. Tel. (212) 689-9696 or (800) 221-3477 (except in New York State). Annual 16-page catalogue costs $1.*

Hand-embroidered crewel, made of wool embroidered onto cotton, with the suggestion that the fabrics be used for upholstery, draperies, bedspreads, slipcovers, and clothing. The company says its prices are 50 percent below those charged by department stores and decorators.

GUTCHEON PATCHWORKS, *P.O. Box 57, Prince St. Station, New York, N.Y. 10012. Tel. (212) 505-0305. For $2, they will send 150 to 200 swatches of cloth, an order form, and a list of books.*

HEARTHSIDE QUILTS, *P.O. Box 27, Charlotte, Vt. 05445. Tel. (802) 425-2164 or (800) 451-3533 (except in Vermont, Alaska, and Hawaii). Semiannual 20-page catalogue costs $2.*

This company calls itself the complete quilter's store. There are precut kits for quilts, pillows, and the like, plus quilting frames, needles, and other equipment. Payment by check, money order, American Express, Visa, or Mastercard. Shipment by Postal Service or United Parcel. Purchases maybe returned for refund.

HEARTHSIDE CRAFTS CALICO COUNTRY STORE, *P.O. Box 71, Endwell, N.Y. 13760 or P.O. Box 9120, Stn. E, Edmonton, Alba., Canada T5P 4K2. Tel. (403) 454-2601. No U.S. phone number. The 60-page catalogue issued 3 times a year costs $3.*

Patterns, templates, tools, and ideas for quilting and crafts.

HERRSCHINERS INC., *Hoover Rd., Stevens Point, Wis. 54481. Tel. (715) 341-0604. Free catalogue.*

Herrschiners, which deals in needlecrafts, was established in 1899 and considers itself No. 1 in the United States and Canada in mail-order crafts.

HOMECOMER WOOL FARM. *See listing under* Crafts to Buy, *below.*

*HOME-SEW, *Bethlehem, Pa. 18018. Tel. (215) 867-3833. Annual 24-page catalogue costs 25 cents.*

A very large selection of sewing and craft supplies, many at discount prices, such as $1.30 for 9 yards of ribbon instead of the 50 cents a yard you might pay in a crafts store. Payment by check or money order. Shipment by Postal Service or United Parcel. Refund or credit for purchases returned same day as received.

ICELANDIC WOOLENS, *Box 3418, Halifax, N.S., Canada B3J 1H1. Tel. (902) 425-6048. Annual brochure.*

Several lines of yarns and hundreds of patterns. Payment by check, money order, American Express, Visa, or Mastercard. Shipment by Postal Service. Purchases may be returned for credit.

KASURI DYEWORKS. *See listing under* Crafts to Buy, *below.*

LACIS, *2982 Adeline St., Berkeley, Calif. 94703. Tel. (415) 843-7178. The 16-page catalogue issued 5 times a year costs $1.*

Antique textiles and laces, plus supplies. Payment by check, money order, Visa, or Mastercard. Shipment by Postal service or United Parcel. Purchases may be returned within 30 days for refund, less 10 percent restocking-handling fee.

THE MANNINGS CREATIVE CRAFTS, *R.D. 1, East Berlin, Pa. 17316. Tel. (717) 624-2223 or (800) 233-7166 (for orders only, except in Pennsylvania). Annual 28-page catalogue costs 50 cents.*

Looms, spinning equipment, yarns, and a very large list of books on the subject.

MARY MAXIM, *2001 Holland Ave., Port Huron, Mich. 48060. Tel. (313) 987-2000. Free 64-page catalogue issued 4 times a year.*

Needlecraft kits for sweaters, afghans, quilting, latch-hook rugs, plus a large selection of yarns.

JEAN MCINTOSH LTD., *P.O. Box 478, Pembina, N.Dak. 58271. Tel. (204) 772-6058. The 30-page catalogue costs $2.50.*

Intricate and attractive designs for needlepoint.

MERRIBEE NEEDLEARTS & CRAFTS, *P.O. Box 3387, Fort Worth, Tex. 76113. Tel. (817) 265-9142 or (800) 433-2924 (except in Texas). The 48- to 72-page catalogue issued 3 to 5 times a year costs 50 cents.*

Kits and yarns for making afghans, tablecloths, and quilts, and there are many non-needlecraft items, such as candle-making, clock-making, and wood-burning supplies. Payment by check, money order, Visa, or Mastercard. Shipment by Postal Service or United Parcel. Purchases may be returned within 30 days for refund or credit.

THE PENDLETON SHOP, *P.O. Box 233, Sedona, Ariz. 86336. Tel. (602) 282-3671. A packet of information sheets on looms and yarn samples costs $1.*

The company has a large selection of looms, loom equipment, and Navajo rug weaving supplies, including yarn. Payment by check or money order. Shipment by United Parcel. Purchases may be returned within 10 days, with permission, for refund or credit.

*PRO CHEMICAL & DYE INC., *P.O. Box 14, Somerset, Mass. 02726. Tel. (617) 676-3838. Free annual 12-page catalogue.*

This company offers a complete line of supplies for the surface coloration of fabrics and says its prices are 25 to 30 percent lower than any other supplier's.

QUILTS, *Leman Publications, 6700 W. 44th Ave., Wheatridge, Colo. 80033. Tel. (303) 420-4272. Annual 40-page catalogue costs $1.25.*

Scores of patterns for quilts.

RAINBOW GALLERY TAPESTRIES, *13615 Victory Blvd., Van Nuys, Calif. 91401. Tel. (818) 787-3542. The 32-page catalogue costs $1.*

This company specializes in needlepoint versions of European tapestries. The canvases may be purchased alone, but kits are also sold. Payment by check, money order, Visa, or Mastercard. Shipment by Postal Service or United Parcel. Purchases may be returned within 14 days for refund.

RAMMAGERDIN. *Woolen yarns from Iceland. See listing under* Crafts to Buy, *below.*

SHILLCRAFT, *500 N. Calvert St., Baltimore, Md. 21202. Tel. (301) 539-0430 or (800) 638-1544 (except in Maryland, Alaska and Hawaii). The 48-page catalogue costs $1.*

Here are designs for rugs, wall hangings, and pillow covers to be made by hooking yarns. Payment by check, money order, Visa, Mastercard, or C.O.D. Purchases may be returned for refund.

JANE SNEAD SAMPLERS, *Box 4909, Philadelphia, Pa. 19119. Tel. (215) 848-1577. Annual 48-page catalogue costs 50 cents.*

Hundreds of samplers awaiting embroidery stitches and depicting flowers, animals, and such sayings, as "God Bless Our Home." Payment by check or money order. Shipment by Postal Service or United Parcel. Purchases may be returned for refund or credit within 15 days.

THE STITCHERY, *204 Worcester St., Wellesley, Mass. 02181. Tel. (617) 237-7554 or (800) 225-4127 (except in Massachusetts). Free 80-page catalogue.*

Scores of needlecraft projects, including needlepoint rugs, samplers, and Christmas tree ornaments. Payment by check, money order, American Express, Visa, or Mastercard. Delivery by Postal Service or United Parcel. Purchases may be returned unused within 2 weeks for refund.

STRAW INTO GOLD, *3006 San Pablo Ave., Berkeley, Calif. 94702. Tel. (415) 548-5247. Brochure price list is free in exchange for self-addressed stamped envelope.*

Weaving and knitting supplies, including silk and blended silk fibers, spinning wheels, and dyes. Payment by check, money order, Visa, or Mastercard. Shipment by Postal Service or United Parcel. Purchases may be returned for credit within 1 year, "with explanation."

SWALLOWHILL. *Doll-making kits. See listing under* For Children.

CAROL THOMAS QUILTING, *P.O. Box 2101, Stn. B, Scarborough, Ont., Canada M1N 2E5. Tel. (416) 261-4819. Semiannual 22-page catalogue costs $1.*

Quilting kits and supplies. Payment by check, money order, or Visa. Shipment by Postal Service. Refund or credit for returned gifts.

THE UNICORN BOOKS FOR CRAFTSMEN, *Box 645, Rockville, Md. 20851. Tel. (301) 933-5497. The 8-page catalogue issued twice a year costs 50 cents.*

This company puts out 2 book catalogues, one on needlework and the other on weaving, and plans to issue others on pottery and woodworking books. They offer a 10 percent discount on orders of $50 or more and 15 percent over $100. Payment by check, money order, Visa, or Mastercard. Shipment by Postal Service or United Parcel. Purchases may be returned within 10 days of receipt for refund.

WINDSOR FARMS, *Route 1, Box 76, Amesville, Ohio 45711. Tel. (614) 448-2771. Catalogue is free without samples or $1 with them.*

Wool for handspinners or prepared as yarn in natural colors—white, gray, brown, or black (this place specializes in black sheep)—plus live sheep for breeding stock and slaughtered lamb in halves or whole, packaged and frozen. There are discounts for quantity purchases of wool, yarns, and sheepskins. Payment by check or money order. Shipment by United Parcel. Purchases may be returned for refund, if undamaged, within 10 days.

WOOL DESIGN, *8916 York Rd., Charlotte, N.C. 28210. Tel. (704) 588-3128 or (800) 438-3118 (except in North Carolina, Hawaii, and Alaska). Annual 64-page catalogue costs $1.*

Rug-making kits, including canvas and yarn. Payment by check, money order, American Express, Visa, or Mastercard. Shipment by Postal Service or United Parcel. Purchases may be returned for refund within 30 days.

Art Supplies

*DICK BLICK CREATIVE MATERIALS, *P.O. Box 1267, Galesburg, Ill. 61401. Tel. (309) 343-6181, (800) 447-8192 (except in Illinois), or (800) 322-8183 (in Illinois). Annual 384-page catalogue costs $2.*

Discount prices on 20,000 items for the artist—brushes, paints, pens, pencils, tables, easels, crayons, knives, and many books on art. Payment by check, money order, Visa, Mastercard, or C.O.D. Delivery by Postal Service, United Parcel, or truck. Purchases may be returned for refund or credit within 10 days.

THE FLAX COMPANY, *180 N. Wabash Ave., Chicago, Ill. 60601. Tel. (312) 346-5100. The 200-page catalogue costs $3.*

A very large selection of art and drafting supplies, plus a separate free catalogue on pens and writing equipment.

*GRAPHIC CHEMICAL & INK CO., *728 N. Yale Ave., P.O. Box 27, Villa Park, Ill. 60181. Tel. (312) 832-6004. Free 54-page catalogue issued every 9 months or so.*

This company offers a complete line of materials for artists working in etching, lithography, block printing, and silk screening. Many are at discount, with zinc plates at 25 to 40 percent below competitors'.

HEARLIHY & CO. *Drawing supplies and equipment. See listing under* Stationery and Office Supplies.

S. & C. HUBER, *Stenciling supplies. See listing under* Furniture and Furnishings.

T. N. LAWRENCE & SON LTD., *2–4 Bleeding Heart Yard, Greville St., London, EC1N 8SL, England. Tel. (01) 242-3534. Free 8-page catalogue.*

Supplies for artists, including special paper, engraving tools, wood and linoleum cutters, Japanese and English brushes, and various inks. Payment by money order. Shipment by Postal Service.

NAZ-DAZ/KC INC., *1087 N. Branch St., Chicago, Ill. 60622. Tel. (312) 943-8338. Free annual 130-page catalogue.*

This company supplies ink for silkscreen printing. Payment by check or money order. Shipment by Postal Service or United Parcel. Purchases may be returned, with prior authorization, for refund or credit.

*NEW YORK CENTRAL ART SUPPLY INC., *62 Third Ave., New York, N.Y. 10003. Tel. (212) 473-7705 or (800) 242-2408 (except in New York State). Five catalogues:* Air Brush, *20 pages, $1;* Color, Canvas, & Easel, *40 pages, $2;* Fine Papers, *60 pages, $2;* Printmaking Supplies, *30 pages, $2;* General Supply, *226 pages, $3. Catalogue costs are refundable against orders.*

Prices for colors, canvas, easels, and airbrushes represent a discount of 20 percent

and quantity discounts are available for paper and print-making supplies. This is quite an operation.

THE OLD-FASHIONED MILK PAINT CO., *Box 222, Groton, Mass. 01450. Tel. (617) 448-6336. Brochure free in exchange for self-addressed stamped envelope.*

"The only manufacturer of real milk paint in the United States."

Skimmed cow's milk and buttermilk have been used as a vehicle and binder in paints for thousands of years. The company supplies a chip card with 8 colors that would be valued by people painting antique items or trying to give an old appearance to new pieces. Payment by check or money order. Shipment by Postal Service or United Parcel. Purchases may be returned within 90 days for refund or replacement.

SCREEN PROCESS SUPPLIES MFG. CO., *1199 E. 12th St., Oakland, Calif. 94606. Tel. (415) 451-1048. Annual free 14-page price list.*

Equipment and ink for silkscreen printing.

*DANIEL SMITH INC., *4130 First Ave. South, Seattle, Wash. 98134. Tel. (206) 223-9599 or (800) 462-6740 (except in Washington State, Alaska and Hawaii). Free annual 100-page catalogue, plus free 24-page sale catalogue issued 3 times a year.*

The covers on these art supplies catalogues are handsome and tasteful, and the lists inside are encyclopedic, taking in paints and pastels, canvas and papers, brushes, calligraphy, Oriental art supplies, and print-making equipment. Prices are 25 to 50 percent below list. Payment by check, money order, Visa, or Mastercard. Shipment by United Parcel or truck freight. Purchases may be returned for refund.

*STU-ART SUPPLIES, *2045 Grand Ave., Baldwin, N.Y. 11510. No telephone. Free 16-page catalogue.*

Discount prices of 50 percent on such things as Nielson metal frame sections.

Calligraphy, Bookbinding, Paper-Making, and Art Preservation

CALPEN, *176 W. Jaxine Dr., Altadena, Calif. 91001. Tel. (818) 794-4927. Free catalogue.*

Quill and reed pens made of turkey quill, bamboo, or reeds favored by calligraphers.

COIT CALLIGRAPHICS, *Old Mill Rd., P.O. Box 239, Georgetown, Conn. 06829. Tel. (203) 544-9140. Brochure.*

Here are pens that the company says are "exciting calligraphers, designers, school teachers and artists everywhere."

COLOPHON HAND BINDERY, *1902 N. 44th St., Seattle, Wash. 98103. Tel. (206) 633-1759. Free 16-page catalogue.*

This shop sells marbled paper for use in end papers of fine books and also the equipment for making the marbled paper yourself. My family and I once saw a display of this being done at Colonial Williamsburg, and the results are frequently beautiful enough to frame, as we have done.

GANE BROTHERS & LANE, *1400 Greenleaf, Elk Grove Village, Ill. 60007. Tel. (312) 437-4880. Free annual 12-page catalogue.*

This company, which sells equipment and materials in the graphic arts, has been in business for more than 150 years and has recently begun a mail-order division. The specialty here is bookbinding, an old and admired craft.

ITALMUSE INC., *Route 3, Box 90, Colfax, Wis. 54730. Tel. (715) 962-3085. Free annual catalogue.*

This company is a supplier of things needed for calligraphy—pens, nibs, instructional books, paper, and ink.

TALAS, *Division of Technical Library Service, 213 W. 35th St., New York, N.Y. 10001. Tel. (212) 736-7744. The 100-page catalogue costs $5.*

This is a source of supplies for people involved in book and art conservation. There are entries on tools, bookbinding, marbling, paper-making, calligraphy, art conservation, and photograph conservation, among other things. Payment by check or money order. Shipment by Postal Service or United Parcel. Purchases may be returned within 30 days for refund, but a 15 percent charge is imposed.

TWINROCKER HANDMADE PAPER, *R.R.2, Brookston, Ind. 47923. Tel. (317) 563-3210. Free 5-page catalogue.*

This company supplies pulp for people who want to make their own paper, or they will supply the handmade paper itself. I love the touch of handmade paper, and I like the idea of properly made paper lasting a long, long time.

Ceramics and Sculpture Supplies

BLUEBIRD MANUFACTURING CO., *P.O. Box 96, Livermore, Colo. 80536. Tel. (303) 484-3243. Brochure.*

This company manufactures clay processing equipment used by schools, private studios, and potteries. Payment by check or money order. Shipment by common carrier. No returns.

CUTTER CERAMICS, *P.O. Box 151, Waltham, Mass. 02154. Tel. (617) 893-1202. Free annual 70-page catalogue.*

Lots of clay, potter's wheels, kilns, and the like to set up a pottery shop. It appears to be a very complete catalogue. Payment by check, Visa, or Mastercard. Shipment by United Parcel or common carrier. Purchases may be returned within 10 days, with receipt, for credit.

EAGLE CERAMICS, *12266 Wilkins Ave., Rockville, Md. 20852. Tel. (301) 881-2253. Free annual 70-page catalogue.*

Here is another very inclusive listing of things for the potter—several kinds of clay, lead-free glazes, potter's wheels, and kilns. Payment by check, Visa, or Mastercard. Shipment by Postal Service, United Parcel, or common carrier. Credit for purchases returned within 10 days of receipt.

POTTERYCRAFTS LTD., *Campbell Rd., Stoke-on-Trent, ST4 4ET, England. Tel. 782-272444. Free annual 84-page catalogue.*

This is a handsome catalogue of potter's equipment, including clay, coloring oxides, glazes and colors, wheels, kilns, and other equipment. Payment by check, money order, Visa, Mastercard, or letter of credit. Delivery by Postal Service, United Parcel, or air or sea freight. Goods damaged in transit will be replaced.

QUYLE KILNS, *3353 East Highway 4, Murphys, Calif. 95247. Tel. (209) 728-3562. Annual 10-page catalogue costs $1, refundable with first order.*

This is a supplier of several types of clay for potters.

SCULPTURE HOUSE, *38 E. 30th St., New York, N.Y. 10016. Tel. (212) 679-7474. Annual 86-page catalogue costs $2.*

A large catalogue offering clay, kilns, knives for carving wood, and pneumatic tools for working with stone.

SOLDNER POTTERY EQUIPMENT, *P.O. Box 428, Silt, Colo. 81652. Tel. (303) 787-5834 or (800) 525-3459 (except in Colorado). Free brochure price list.*

Potter's equipment, including clay mixers, kick wheels, and electric wheels.

THORLEY'S POTTERY SUPPLY, *P.O. Box 2156, Hollydale Station, South Gate, Calif. 90280. Tel. (213) 633-2647 or (213) 636-6683. Price list.*

This company makes kiln furniture that is said to be highly resistant to thermal shock, with shelving sent to buyers all over the country. Payment by check or money order. Shipment by common carrier. Refunds or credit for returned goods, but only on account of manufacturer's defect or error in shipment.

WESTWOOD CERAMIC SUPPLY CO., *14400 Lomitas Ave., City of Industry, Calif. 91744. Tel. (818) 330-0631. Annual 196-page catalogue costs $3.*

This is a very large book with supplies for the potter. There are clays, glazes, clay mixers, wheels, tools, kilns, and a very large section on books.

Woodworking Tools and Lumber

CONOVER WOODCRAFT SPECIALTIES INC., *18125 Madison Rd., Parkman, Ohio 44062. Tel. (216) 548-3481. The 48-page catalogue costs $1.*

Joiners, bits, drills, planers, sanders, and saws are among the many pieces of equipment, and there also is a large number of books on woodworking. Payment by check, money order, Visa, or Mastercard. Shipment by Postal Service, United Parcel, or common carrier. Refunds for returns, but time limit was given as "whenever."

CRAFTSMAN LUMBER CO., *Box 222, Groton, Mass. 01450. Tel. (617) 448-6336. Free catalogue in exchange for self-addressed stamped envelope.*

This company specializes in wide pine boards for flooring and paneling. Also offered are old-fashioned cut nails and Watco Danish oil products. Payment by check or money order. Shipment by motor freight. Refund or credit for purchases returned within 30 days.

*CRAFTSMAN WOOD SERVICE CO., *1735 W. Cortland Ct., Addison, Ill. 60101. Tel. (312) 629-3100. Annual 148-page catalogue costs $1.*

Hundreds of tools and things for wood hobbyists, many at discount prices. For example, the Dremel Deluxe Moto Shop, which lists for $130, is offered here for $104. Also available are domestic and imported hardwoods with sanded finishes and many how-to books. Payment by check, money order, Visa, or Mastercard. Shipment by Postal Service,

United Parcel, or truck. Purchases may be returned within 30 days for refund.

GILLIOM MANUFACTURING, *1700 Scherer Parkway, St. Charles, Mo. 63301. Tel. (314) 724-1812. Catalogue costs $1.*

Kits for the construction of woodworking machines, such as a 12-inch bandsaw, with the promise that you will save a lot of money by putting it together yourself.

W. S. JENKS & SON. *Woodworking tools. See listing under* Tools and Equipment for Craftspeople, Tinkerers, and Do-It-Yourselfers, *below.*

SCULPTURE HOUSE. *See listing under* Ceramics and Sculpture Supplies, *above.*

SHOPSMITH INC., *6640 Poe Ave., Dayton, Ohio 45414. Tel. (513) 898-6070, (800) 543-7586 (except in Ohio, Alaska, and Hawaii), or (800) 762-7555 (in Ohio). Free catalogues of 48- to 64-pages issued 6 times a year.*

The publication is called the *Better Woodworking Catalog and Guide,* and it offers drilling tools, saws, turning tools, picture framing supplies, screwdrivers, hammers, and power tools, among other things.

TASHIRO'S, *P.O. Box 3409, Seattle, Wash. 98114. Tel. (206) 622-8452. Brochure price list.*

Japanese and Western tools and knives, much of it woodworking equipment. Payment by check, money order, Visa, Mastercard, or C.O.D. Shipment by Postal Service or United Parcel. Purchases may be returned for refund within 10 days.

GARRETT WADE CO. *161 Avenue of the Americas, New York, N.Y. 10013. Tel. (212) 807-1155 or (800) 221-2942 (except in New York, Alaska, and Hawaii). Annual 230-page catalogue costs $3.*

This catalogue, illustrated with exceptionally good photographs, contains hundreds of woodworking tools, accessories, and books. There is a large section devoted to Japanese woodworking tools. Payment by check, money order, American Express, Visa, or Mastercard. Shipment by Postal Service, United Parcel, or truck. Purchases may be returned within 14 days for refund.

WOODCRAFT SUPPLY CORP., *41 Atlantic Ave., P.O. Box 4000, Woburn, Mass. Tel. (617) 935-5860 or (800) 225-1153. The 88-page catalogue issued 5 times a year costs $2.*

Lots of handsomely designed woodworking tools, including a large number of Japanese tools, and there are many books available. The company is affiliated with Winstead (see listing under *Tools and Equipment for Craftspeople, Tinkerers, and Do-It-Yourselfers,* below) and was established in 1928.

THE WOODEN BOAT SHOP. *Woodworking tools. See listing under* Boating and Fishing Supplies.

WOODLINE THE JAPAN WOODWORKER, *1731 Clement Ave., Alameda, Calif. 94501. Tel. (415) 521-1810. Annual 50-page catalogue costs $1.50.*

So many woodworking catalogues listed above have sections on Japanese tools that it is fitting that the last entry be for a company that makes this a specialty. There are many carving tools, chisels, hammers, knives, saws, and other tools, plus books. Payment by check, money order, American Express, Visa, or Mastercard. Shipment by Postal Service or United Parcel. Refund or exchange for tools as long as they have not been used or damaged.

Basket-Making, Caning, and Furniture Webbing

CANE & BASKET SUPPLY CO., *1283 S. Cochran Ave., Los Angeles, Calif. 90019. Tel. (213) 939-9644. Annual 16-page catalogue costs $1.*

This company offers cane and other supplies and tools for making cane chairs, baskets, and the like.

CANER'S CORNER, *4413 John St., Niagara Falls, Ont., Canada L2E 1A4. Tel. (416) 356-6978. Brochure price list.*

Furniture kits, including hardwood frames and caning. Payment by check or money order. Shipment by Postal Service, United Parcel, or bus express. Purchases may be returned for refund or credit within 30 days.

THE CANING SHOP, *926 Gilman St., Berkeley, Calif. 94710. Tel. (415) 527-5010. Annual 20-page catalogue costs $1, refundable with order.*

This shop offers tools and supplies for the construction of chairs and other things of cane. Payment by check, money order, Visa, or Mastercard. Shipment by United Parcel. Purchases may be returned for refund.

E. J. EVANS, *P.O. Box 988, Venice, Calif. 90294. Tel. (213) 821-6400. Brochure costs 50 cents.*

This company sells fabric coverings for cushions on Danish modern chairs and sofas, plus those rubberized straps and webbing that are used to support the cushions and are always so difficult to find. Payment by check or money order. Shipment by United Parcel. Goods may be returned within 10 days for refund.

FRANK'S CANE & RUSH SUPPLY, *7244 Heil Ave., Huntington Beach, Calif. 92647. Tel. (714) 847-0707. Free 12-page catalogue issued 6 times a year.*

Canes, fibers, webbing, reeds, rattans, tools, books, and instructions.

*PEERLESS RATTAN & REED MFG. CO., *P.O. Box 636, Yonkers, N.Y. 10702. Tel. (914) 968-4046. Free annual 12-page catalogue.*

Discount prices for multiple orders of strand cane; binding; flat, flat oval, and round reeds; basket reeds, and hoops.

See also *Furniture and Furnishings* and *Clocks* for kits to make furniture and clocks.

Plans and Patterns for Do-It-Yourselfers

A. B. ENTERPRISES, *P.O. Box 856, Peoria, Ill. 61652. Tel. (309) 673-1777. The 400-page catalogue costs $2.*

This huge catalogue is called *A. Brill's Bible of Building Plans,* and it contains plans for carnivals and midways (funhouse, mirror house, miniature golf), illusions, rides, games, and shows. Step right up! Learn to pull a rabbit out of a hat! Mr. Brill says it is the only publication of its kind. Payment by money order. Shipment by Postal Service. No returns accepted.

CRAFT PATTERNS CO., *2200 Dean St., Charles, Ill. 60174. Tel. (312) 584-9600. Annual catalogue costs $1.50.*

Hundreds of home workshop plans for indoor and outdoor furniture, clocks, gifts, toys, home additions, and recreational items. Payment by check, money order, Visa, Mastercard, or Diners Club. Shipment by Postal Service or United Parcel. Purchases may be returned for refund within 30 days.

U-BILD, *Box 2383, Van Nuys, Calif. 91409. Tel. (818) 785-6368. Annual 112-page catalogue costs $1.95.*

Patterns for 700 projects for do-it-yourselfers to make for the house, including furniture, house additions, and toys. Payment by check or money order. Shipment by Postal Service.

See also *Building and Architectural Supplies.*

Model and Hobby Kits and Supplies

*AMERICA'S HOBBY CENTER, *146 W. 22nd St., New York, N.Y., 10011. Tel. (212) 675-8922. Free 20-page tabloid catalogue.*

In addition to the tabloid-sized catalogue listed above, America's Hobby Center offers these specialized catalogues: *Model Airplanes, Boats, Cars,* $2; *Model Railroad, H-O and N gauge,* $2; *Model Ships (wood hulls),* $1.50; *Model Cars (radio control),* $1.50; *Plastic Display Models, Boats, Planes, Cars,* 50 cents; *Model Airplanes, Boats, Cars, Plastics,* bulletin, 54 cents; and *Model H-O and N Railroad Cars,* bulletin, 54 cents.

Hundreds of model trains—N and H-O gauge—buildings, equipment, track, and books. Many items are sold at discount. Payment by check, money order, or C.O.D. Delivery by Postal Service or United Parcel. Purchases may be returned for refund or credit within 10 days if unused and permission has been given.

CHERRY'S (SURREY) LTD., *62 Sheen Rd., Richmond, Surrey, TW9 1UF, England. Tel. (01) 940-2454. The 30- to 40-page catalogue issued twice a year costs $4.*

This company makes working steam models—locomotives, stationary engines, traction engines, etc. Payment by check, money order, or banker's draft. Shipment by Postal Service or specialist packers. Purchases may be returned for refund within 7 days.

CLASSICS GUILD, *9903 Santa Monica Blvd., No. 119, Beverly Hills, Calif. 90212. Tel. (213) 559-3627. Semiannual 32-page catalogue costs $2.*

Plastic model kits for boats, cars, airplanes, and ships, plus paint and accessories.

ESTES INDUSTRIES, *P.O. Box 227, Penrose, Colo. 81240. Tel. (303) 372-6565. Annual 72-page catalogue costs $1.*

Kits to build your own rockets that really fly and then parachute back to earth. Payment by check, money order, Visa, or Mastercard. Shipment by Postal Service or United Parcel. Purchases may be returned for refund or credit within 1 year.

H–O RACING SPECIALTIES, *4708 W. Compton Blvd., Lawndale, Calif. 90260. Tel. (213) 973-7073. Annual 48-page catalogue costs $5.*

Payment by check, money order, Visa, Mastercard, or C.O.D. Shipment by Postal Service or United Parcel. Purchases may be returned within 90 days for credit, less a 15 percent restocking fee.

*HOBBY SHACK, *18480 Bandilier Circle, Fountain Valley, Calif. 92708. Tel. (714) 963-9881, (800) 854-8471 (except in California), or (800) 472-8456 (in California). Free 32-page catalogue issued 6 times a year.*

This "supermarket of hobby goods," has discount prices on things for hobbyists, such as the Futaba radio control system for $105 instead of the list of $200.

KIT KRAFT, *Box 1086, 12109 Ventura Pl., Studio City, Calif. 91604. Tel. (213) 877-5001 or (818) 984-0780. Free 18-page catalogue.*

Plastic model cars, planes, and boats, plus wooden ship models, are available, as are hobby and craft paints and books, brass tubing, beads, glitter, and art supplies.

SCIENTIFIC MODELS, *340 Snyder Ave., Berkeley Heights, N.J. 07922. Tel. (201) 464-7070. Annual 16-page catalogue costs $1.*

This company offers tiny replicas of furniture for construction and placing in doll houses or on curio shelves. Payment by check, money order, American Express, Visa, Mastercard, or Diners Club. Shipment by Postal Service or United Parcel. Purchases may be returned within 30 days for refund.

STOCK DRIVE PRODUCTS. *See listing under* Tools and Equipment for Craftspeople, Tinkerers, and Do-It-Yourselfers, *below.*

WARNER SCIENTIFIC, *The Franklin Mint, Franklin Center, Pa. 19091. Tel (215) 459-6000, (800) 523-0267 (except in Arizona), or (800) 523-0695 (in Arizona). Free 32-page catalogue issued 3 to 4 times a year.*

Robots, weather forecasting, rocketry, telescopes, computer programming, and photography are among the wonders young people can be introduced to.

See also *Audio and Video Equipment.*

Tools and Equipment for Craftspeople, Tinkerers, and Do-It-Yourselfers

*AIRBORNE SALES CO., *P.O. Box 2727, Culver City, Calif. 90230. Tel. (213) 870-4687. Semiannual 92-page catalogue costs $1.*

Surplus equipment, such as fans and blowers, electric motors, MK14 gun sights (I don't know what you would use it for, but at $90 it's a terrific bargain for something for which the Pentagon paid $3,510, although just because the Pentagon paid that much for it doesn't mean it's really worth that), winches, magnets, hand tools, and drill bits. There are also lots of pieces of marine equipment, backpacks, and aircraft instruments. Payment by check, money order, Visa, or Mastercard. Shipment by Postal Service or United Parcel. Purchases may be returned within 60 days for refund.

*AMERICAN MACHINE & TOOL CO., *Fourth Ave. and Spring St., P.O. Box 70, Royersford, Pa. 19468. Tel. (215) 948-0400. Free 20-page catalogue.*

Discount prices on power and hand tools and pumps.

ANCHOR TOOLS & WOODSTOVES. *See listing under* Wood Stoves.

BAILEY'S. *See listing under* Camping Equipment.

BROOKSTONE, *1053 Vose Farm Rd., Peterborough, N.H. 03458. Tel. (603) 924-7181 or (603) 924-9511. Free 68-page* Tools *catalogue issued 3 times a year.*

Lots of tools and energy-saving devices, locks, gadgets, painting equipment, many things for the garden, framing materials, and automobile accessories. Brookstone issues other catalogues, including one listed under *Cookware and Dinnerware.* Payment by check, money order, American Express, Visa, or Mastercard. Shipment by United Parcel. Goods may be returned for refund with no time limit.

CARACAL ENTERPRISE CO., *P.O. Box 59442, Taipei, Taiwan. Tel. (02) 752-2284. Free 32-page catalogue.*

This company sells a large line of tools and also produces a catalogue for its locks under the name Yesk Enterprise Co.

CHARRETTE CORP., *31 Olympia Ave., P.O. Box 4010, Woburn, Mass. 01888. Tel. (617) 935-6010 or (800) 242-7738 (except in Massachusetts). Annual 284-page catalogue costs $3.50.*

Architectural, engineering, and art supplies.

COPE PLASTICS, *4441 Industrial Dr., P.O. Box 529, Godfrey, Ill. 62035. Tel. (800) 851-5510 (except in Illinois, Alaska, and Hawaii), or (800) 642-1792 in Illinois).*

Plastic sheets, rods, tubes, liquids, and films, plus related supplies, equipment, and power tools.

GEODE INDUSTRIES, *P.O. Box 158, 108 W. Main St., New London, Iowa 52645. Tel. (319) 367-2256. Several catalogues, some free; a 180-page catalogue for craftsmen and technicians costs $1.*

The large catalogue has tools, supplies, and equipment for such technicians and craftsmen as jewelers, watchmakers, clock repairers, silversmiths, opticians, engravers, and metal workers. There are other catalogues, including one on lapidary equipment made by the Imahashi Mfg. Co. of Japan.

GREEN RIVER TOOLS, *5 Cotton Mill Hill, P.O. Box 1919, Brattleboro, Vt. 05301. Tel. (802) 254-2388. Free 20- to 24-page catalogue issued twice a year.*

The company offers a line of high-quality tools. Payment by check, money order, Visa, or Mastercard. Shipment by United Parcel unless Postal Service is requested. Purchases may be returned, with written explanation, for refund or credit.

CARL HEALD INC., *P.O. Box 1148, Benton Harbor, Mich. 49022. Tel. (616) 849-3400 or (800) 253-1030 (except in Michigan). Free 8- to 16-page catalogue issued 6 times a year.*

Many tools for the home (band saws), the garden (tillers), and the neighborhood (motorized carts). Payment by check or money order. Shipment by Postal Service, United Parcel, or motor freight. A 90-day warranty on parts, a 1-year warranty on engines, refunds for returns.

W. S. JENKS & SON, *2024 West Virginia Ave., N.E., Washington, D.C. 20002. Tel. (202) 529-6020, (202) 737-7490, or (800) 638-6405 (except in Washington, D.C.). Free annual 100-page catalogue on electronics and*

communications tools; also, free annual 124-page catalogue on woodworking tools.

This company has been supplying tools in Washington since 1866, and its selection is enormous. Payment by check, money order, American Express, Visa, Mastercard, or Choice. Delivery by Postal Service, United Parcel, or common carrier.

JENSEN TOOLS INC., *7815 S. 46th St., Phoenix, Ariz. 85040. Tel. (602) 968-6231. Free 80- to 160-page catalogue issued 4 times a year.*

There are hundreds of tools and devices, some made by Jensen, others by such companies as Stanley and Skil. Payment by check, money order, American Express, Visa, or Mastercard. Shipment by Postal Service or United Parcel. Purchases may be returned for refund or credit within 30 days.

*KELLYCO METAL DETECTOR DISTRIBUTORS, *1441 S. Orlando Ave., Maitland, Fla. 32751. Tel. (305) 645-1332. Free 150-page catalogue issued 6 times a year.*

Discount prices on metal detectors, such as $490 for a Whites electronics model that costs $600 elsewhere.

LEHMAN HARDWARE & APPLIANCES, *Box 41, Kidron, Ohio 44636. Tel. (216) 857-5441. Annual 80-page catalogue costs $2.*

Popular Science said this was "like looking through an old catalogue, except that you can buy all of the items shown." Nothing offered here runs by electricity, so this catalogue would be helpful for people with vacation cabins as well as those choosing to live without such power. Available are grist mills, pumps, self-heating irons, gasoline and kerosene lamps, refrigerators run by kerosene, fruit presses, corn huskers, wind mills, sausage stuffers, noodle-makers, hand tools, pumps, wood and coal stoves, and cast iron pots and pans.

LEICHTUNG, *4944 Commerce Parkway, Cleveland, Ohio 44128. Tel. (216) 831-6191 or (800) 321-6840 (except in Ohio, Alaska, and Hawaii). The 96- to 112-page catalogue issued 8 times a year costs $1.*

Power saws and other tools, many of them available in money-saving kits, and workshop accessories. Payment by check, money order, Visa, or Mastercard. Payment by Postal Service or United Parcel. Purchases may be returned for refund within 90 days.

MASON & SULLIVAN. *Clock-making tools. See listing under* Clocks.

MASONRY SPECIALTY CO., *4430 Gibsonia Rd., Gibsonia, Pa. 15044. Tel. (412) 443-7080. Free 92-page catalogue issued twice a year.*

More than 2,500 tools and pieces of equipment for use in the "trowel trades" such as masonry, cement finishing, plastering, tile-setting, and drywall construction.

MASTER MECHANIC MFG. CO., *P.O. Box A, 280 S. Pine St., Burlington, Wis. 53105. Tel. (414) 763-2428 or (800) 558-9444. Free 68-page catalogue.*

Gasoline engines, lathes, bandsaws, drill presses, hand tools, pumps, and many other things. Payment by check, money order, American Express, Visa, or Mastercard. Shipment by Postal Service, United Parcel, or truck or air freight. Refund or credit for purchases returned within 10 days.

MATERIAL FLOW, *Centex Industrial Park, Box 69, Elk Grove Village, Ill. 60007. Tel. (312) 421-7111 or (800) 962-7100. Free 132-page catalogue issued twice a year.*

Storage bins, cabinets and shelves, hand trucks, hydraulic lift platforms and jacks, welding helmets, goggles and gloves, ladders, wheels, and casters.

MICRO-MARK, *P.O. Box 5112, 24 E. Main St., Clinton, N.J. 08809. Tel. (201) 464-6764. Semiannual 48-page catalogue costs $1.*

Precision miniature tools, some of them offered at discount; for example, a $40 X-Acto knife is offered for $30.

PARKER'S, *Box 241, Wellesley Hills, Mass. 02181. No telephone. Brochure price list.*

Whetstone sharpeners for knives and scissors, and other sharpening and smoothing devices.

PRINCESS AUTO & MACHINERY LTD. *Car tools. See listing under* Automotive Needs.

PUTNAM ROLLING LADDER CO., *32 Howard St., New York, N.Y. 10013. Tel. (212) 226-5147. Annual 28-page catalogue costs $1.*

This company was founded in 1905 and calls itself the leading manufacturer of custom oak ladders in the United States. It also makes aluminum ladders and oak outdoor furniture for the patio and garden. Payment by check or money order. Shipment by United Parcel or common carrier. Purchases may be returned for refund or credit within 30 days.

PYRAMID PRODUCTS CO., *3736 S. Seventh Ave., Phoenix, Ariz. 85041. Tel. (602) 276-5365. Brochure price list.*

Gas and propane melting furnaces for hobbyists, sculptors, miners of precious metals, and car restorers. Payment by check or money order. Shipment by Postal Service, United Parcel, or truck freight. Refunds for purchases returned within a "reasonable" time.

*****I. D. RATHERBY,** *18480 Bandilier Circle, Fountain Valley, Calif. 92728. Tel. (714) 963-6480, (800) 854-8471 (except in California), or (800) 472-8456 (in California). Free catalogue issued 5 times a year.*

Discount prices for tools and equipment, such as a 100-ft. extension cord that lists for $33 and is offered for $21.50.

STOCK DRIVE PRODUCTS, *55 S. Denton Ave., New Hyde Park, N.Y. 11040. Tel. (516) 328-3330. The 768-page catalogue costs $5.95.*

This encyclopedic catalogue lists 24,000 (I took their word for the total) hard-to-find small mechanical parts for engineers, inventors, machinists, and hobbyists who are trying to build, repair, or invent various models and machines. Payment by check or money order. Shipment by Postal Service or United Parcel. Purchases may be returned for refund within 30 days.

*****U. S. GENERAL SUPPLY CORP.,** *100 Commercial St., Plainview, N.Y. 11803. Tel. (516) 576-9100 or (800) 645-7077. Semiannual 196-page catalogue costs $1.*

Discount prices on tools; for example, a Skil saw Model 576, list price $89, U.S. General asks $50. Payment by check, money order, Visa, or Mastercard. Shipment by Postal Service, United Parcel, or truck. Refund or credit for returned purchases.

WINSTEAD, *41 Atlantic Ave., P.O. Box 4024, Woburn, Mass. 01888. Tel. (617) 935-9278. Free 40-page catalogue issued twice a year.*

Tools, equipment, and gadgets for the home and workshop.

See also *Sales and Surplus Goods* and *Audio and Video Equipment* for electronic parts, tools, and supplies.

Crafts to Buy

ANDEAN PRODUCTS, *Box 472, Cuenca, Ecuador. Free 32-page catalogue and price list.*

There are a lot of good-looking pieces here, including sweaters, handwoven straw figures, jewelry, tapestries, furniture, embroidered blouses and dresses, and leather goods. Payment by letter of credit or certified check. Shipment by air freight or air parcel post.

APPLE VALLEY STORE. *Montana crafts. See listing under* Gourmet, Ethnic, and Special Foods.

†ARTISANS COOPERATIVE, *Box 216, Chadds Ford, Pa. 19317. Tel. (215) 388-1433. Free 24-page catalogue.*

This is a cooperative that encourages and preserves old American rural crafts, at the same time providing an opportunity for the participants to work in their own homes. "Women who used to regard their fine hand skills as a way of passing the time of day," the co-op says, "now realize those skills are valuable." Available are clothing, jewelry, bedding, toys, porcelain, stoneware, clocks, rugs, woodcuts, and numerous other things, many of which would make good gifts.

JAMES AVERY CRAFTSMAN INC., *P.O. Box 1367, Kerrville, Tex. 78028. Tel. (512) 895-1122, (800) 531-7198 (except in Texas), or (800) 292-7059 (in Texas). Free 24-page catalogue of secular objects issued 3 times a year; also a 72-page catalogue of religious objects that costs $1.*

Here is jewelry displayed in catalogues that show to advantage the designs' intent: simplicity and cleanliness.

BATIKS BY ZANDRIA, *346 North Fourth West, Logan, Utah 84321. Tel. (801) 752-6025. The 4 different annual brochures cost 50 cents.*

There are 2 brochures on batik clothing and 2 on wall decor. The pieces are by Zandria Merrill, an artist working in the batik medium, which is an ancient technique of resist-dyeing of fabric. The designs on the brochures she sent me were very nice, and most of them depicted nature scenes.

BENNINGTON POTTERS, *P.O. Box 199, 324 County St., Bennington, Vt. 05201. Tel. (802) 447-7531. The 10-page catalogue costs $1.*

†CHATHAM FIELDS, *550 Warren St., Hudson, N.Y. 12534. Tel. (518) 828-9427, (800) 621-5559 (except in Illinois), or (800) 972-5858 (in Illinois). Quarterly 12- to 48-page catalogue costs $1.50.*

Handcrafted glassware, jewelry, pottery, woven goods, silver, pewter, and women's clothing. A gift service is available.

CLYMER'S OF BUCKS COUNTY. *See listing under* Fine and Unusual Gifts.

COLONIAL CASTING CO., *443 S. Colony St., Meriden, Conn. 06450. Tel. (203) 235-5189. The 14-page catalogue costs $1.*

Handcrafted pewter in Colonial reproductions. There are candlesticks, plates, and assorted ornaments, and they are lead-free. Purchases may be returned for refund or exchange within 7 days of receipt.

THE CRAFT SHOP AT MOLLY'S POND, *Route 2, Cabot, Vt. 05647. No telephone. The 14-page catalogue issued about once every 2 years costs $1.*

This shop offers jewelry designs by Luella Schroeder, who calls attention to her "polliwog" pieces and also to 2 designs based on objects in nature—beechnuts and wild strawberries—made using the lost-wax casting process. Payment by check, money order, Visa, or Mastercard. Shipment by Postal Service. Purchases may be returned for refund or credit.

DEL TRADING POST. *See listing under* General Craft Supplies, *above.*

DEVA, *303 E. Main St., Burkittsville, Md. 21718. Tel. (301) 473-4900. Free 12-page catalogue issued twice a year.*

Handmade casual clothing—shorts, overalls, pants, jackets, kimonos, shirts, skirts, and women's underwear. Payment by check, money order, Visa, or Mastercard. Shipment by Postal Service or United Parcel. Purchases may be returned at any time for refund or credit.

ELVETTE HANDBAG CO., *Box 3542, 1048 Main St., Winnipeg, Man., Canada R2W 3R4. Free catalogue.*

Custom-assembled needlepoint handbags. Payment by check or money order. Shipment by Postal Service. Purchases may be returned within 2 weeks for refund.

EMGEE CORP., *3210 Koapaka St., Honolulu, Hawaii 96819. Tel. (808) 836-0988 or (800) 367-2666 (except in Hawaii). Free annual 12-page catalogue.*

Handpainted wooden Christmas tree ornaments in old European style. Payment by check, money order, Visa, or Mastercard. Shipment by Postal Service or United Parcel. Refunds for purchases returned within 30 days, but personalized items are not returnable.

FAITH MOUTAIN HERBS, *Box 199, Main St., Sperryville, Va. 22740. Tel. (703) 987-8824. Semiannual 16-page catalogue costs $2.*

Candles, hanging herb bundles, handmade teddy bears and other toys, hearth brooms, baskets, and rugs. Payment by check, money order, American Express, Visa, or Mastercard. Shipment by United Parcel. Purchases may be returned within 20 days for refund.

GATHERINGS (AT THE OLD PARSONAGE), *R.F.D. 9, Box 2H, Concord, N.H. 03301. No telephone. Annual 36-page catalogue costs $4.*

Handmade shirts, dresses, scarves, sweaters, handmirrors, toys, stuffed bears, and dolls. Payment by check, money order, Visa, or Mastercard. Shipment by United Parcel. Purchases may be returned within 10 days for refund.

GERANIUMS 'N SUNSHINE, *Box G, Aspen, Colo. 81612. Tel. (303) 925-8348. Annual 4-page catalogue costs $1.*

"Aspen's artisan boutique," this place offers handmade handbags, jewelry, women's clothing, and accessories.

GOODFELLOW CATALOGUE PRESS, *P.O. Box 4520, Berkeley, Calif. 94704. Tel. (415) 428-0142. The 250- to 300-page catalogue costs 12.95.*

You cannot order crafts through this catalogue, called *The Goodfellow Catalogue of Wonderful Things,* but instead this book will allow you to gain direct access to the artisans creating the things you want. Their catalogues, the Goodfellow people say, provide a living history of American crafts.

GREY OWL INDIAN CRAFT CO., *113–15 Springfield Blvd., Queens Village, N.Y. 11429. Tel. (718) 464-9300. Annual 188-page catalogue costs $1.*

Payment by check, money order, Visa, or Mastercard. Shipment by Postal Service or United Parcel. Purchases may be returned for refund or credit within 30 days of receipt.

*HANDART EMBROIDERIES, *Room 106, Hing Wai Building, 36 Queen's Road Central, Hong Kong. Tel. (5) 235744. Free annual 10-page catalogue.*

Discounts based on quantity purchased. Embroidered tablecloths, pajamas, beaded slippers, kimonos, jackets, housecoats, dresses, silk blouses, and many other articles made by Chinese craftspeople. Payment by check, money order, American Express, Visa, or Mastercard. Shipment by Postal Service. Purchases may be returned for refunds.

†**HAPPI FACES,** *P.O. Box 2087, West Peabody, Mass. 01960. Tel. (617) 535-5277. Annual 16-page catalogue costs $1.*

Handpainted remembrances that put real people in the picture. A nice gift idea for birthdays, graduations, weddings, and the like.

HOMECOMER WOOL FARM, *Windham Hill Rd., Windham, Vt. 05359. Annual 8-page catalogue costs $1; the sample card of yarns costs $1 more.*

This company, which has no phone (At the spot on my questionnaire where I asked for the telephone number, one of the Homecomer people wrote, "None!" There are a few other people in this country without telephones, but only New Englanders are enthusiastic about it. Maybe they are right), is a small sheep farm. It produces knitting yarns and hand-knitted garments that are high-quality approximations of designs from the British Isles, and the catalogue shows off some handsome things, particularly the Aran sweaters. Payment by check, money order, American Express, Visa, or Mastercard. Shipment by Postal Service or United Parcel. Purchases may be returned within 30 days for refund, credit, or exchange.

JOAN HOULEHEN, *4045 E. Bottsford Ave., Cudahy, Wis. 53110. Tel. (414) 481-6265. No catalogue.*

This artist offers several of her works in various media. She has Christmas cards, she reproduces children's drawings onto rugs, and produces wall hangings, rugs, and abstract drawings. She sent me some photos of her work that I liked a lot. Payment by check or money order. Shipment by Postal Service or United Parcel. Purchases may be returned within 10 days for replacement.

ICEMART, *Keflavik International Airport, Iceland. Tel. (800) 431-9003. The 36-page catalogue costs $1.*

Hand-knitted sweaters, lava ceramic ware that "borrows its themes and materials from the molton core of Iceland," handcrafted silver jewelry, sheepskin rugs, and woven blankets. Payment by check, money order, American Express, Visa, Mastercard, or Diners Club. Shipment by United Parcel. Purchases may be returned within 2 weeks for refund.

IRISH COTTAGE INDUSTRIES LTD., *44 Dawson St., Dublin 2, Ireland. Tel. 713039 or 713224. Annual brochure costs $1.*

Here are hand-knitted garments, including Aran designs, and tweed suits, coats, skirts, hats, and caps. Payment by check, American Express, Visa, Mastercard, or Diners Club. Shipment by Postal Service. Purchases may be returned within 3 months for refund.

IROQRAFTS LTD., *R.R. 2, Ohsweken, Ont., Canada N0A 1M0. Tel. (416) 765-4206. Annual 50-page catalogue costs $1, refundable with first order.*

Traditional and ceremonial Iroquois arts and crafts from the Six Nations reservation. The offerings include ceremonial masks, carvings, pipes, and snowshoes, and there are many books available on Indian history and tradition. Payment by money order. Shipment by Postal Service. No cash refunds; some exchanges may be arranged within 5 days of receipt.

*KARNATAKA STATE HANDICRAFTS DEVELOPMENT CORP. LTD., *Webb's Complex, 26, Mahatma Gandhi Rd., Bangalore 560 001, India. Tel. 52317. Free 8-page catalogue.*

Handicrafts sold at discount when purchases exceed 10,000 rupees—20 percent off on sandalwood and rosewood, 15 percent on lacquerware, textiles, leather, and brassware, 12 percent on agarbathis, 10 percent on bronze articles. Payment by check, money order, American Express, Visa, Diners Club, or irrevocable letter of credit. Delivery by Postal Service or air or sea freight. No returns.

†KASURI DYEWORKS, *1959 Shattuck Ave., Berkeley, Calif. 94704. Tel. (415) 841-4509. The 20-page catalogue costs $5, refundable on initial order of $25 or more.*

This shop specializes in Japanese textiles, crafts, and gift items.

KENNEDY OF ARDARA. *See listing under* Men's and Women's Clothing.

D. MACGILLIVARY. *See listing under* Men's and Women's Clothing.

DON MILLER, PEWTERSMITH, *P.O. Box 141, Harpers Ferry, W. Va. 25425. Tel. (304) 535-6508. Price list.*

Handmade pewter pieces. Payment by check, money order, Visa, or Mastercard. Shipment by United Parcel. An official of the shop said returns would be accepted but that there never had been one.

MOUNTAIN CRAFT SHOP, *American Ridge Rd., Route 1, New Martinsville, W.Va. 26155. Tel. (304) 455-3570. Free annual 8-page catalogue.*

"Today's largest and best source of authentic American folk toys—reproductions of the toys once made at home and handed down from one generation to another."

*NARAYANA PHAND, *Thai Handicrafts Center, 275/2, Larn Luang Rd., Pomprab, Bangkok, Thailand. Tel. 2813180. Free catalogue.*

Here are crafts made in various parts of Thailand, including clothing, toys, tableware, pewter, carved teak furniture, bronze and brass ware, and mother of pearl. A discount of 20 percent is offered on purchases of $2,500. Payment by check, American Express, or irrevocable letter of credit. Shipment by Postal Service or air or sea freight.

NATURALLY BRITISH, *148 High St., Boston, Mass. 02110. Tel. (617) 426-9333. Annual 24-page catalogue costs $1.50.*

The company's London store is at 13 New Row, Covent Garden, WC2N 4LF. My wife and I looked it over during a recent visit to England, and it is very nice, although there did not seem to be any bargains the day we were there. It offers handmade articles from Britain, including great-looking cotton lace blouses, girls' dresses, Welsh tweed coats, sweaters, and a large assortment of gifts. Payment by check, money order, American Express, Visa, or Mastercard. Delivery by United Parcel. Purchases may be returned, with "no time limit, within reason," for refund or credit.

OKLAHOMA INDIAN ARTS & CRAFTS COOPERATIVE, *P.O. Box 966, Anadarko, Okla. 73005. Tel. (405) 247-3486. Brochure.*

Moccasins, belts, handbags, ties, aprons, shirts, dolls, and featherwork—all genuine handicrafts. Payment by check or money order. Shipment by Postal Service. Purchases may be returned within 10 days for refund.

THE PERUVIAN CONNECTION LTD. *See listing under* Men's and Women's Clothing.

PIPESTONE INDIAN SHRINE ASSOCIATION, *Pipestone National Monument, P.O. Box 727, Pipestone, Minn. 56164. Tel. (507) 825-5463, ext. 2. Brochure price list costs $1, refundable with first purchase.*

Pipestone from the local quarries hand-carved by Indians. Pipestone is a reddish stone that Indians have used for centuries to carve ceremonial objects such as pipes and turtles (the latter considered a fertility symbol by the Sioux). Payment by check, money order, Visa, or Mastercard. Shipment by Postal Service or United Parcel.

PLUMB HILL STUDIO, *Priscilla M. Porter, Plumb Hill Rd., Washington, Conn. 06793. Tel. (203) 868-2938. Brochure price list.*

Miss Porter is a noted artist-craftswoman working in fused glass. Some pieces are ornamental and are designed to be displayed like sculpture; others are functional, such as bowls and plates. Payment by check or money order. Shipment by United Parcel. Broken objects may be returned for replacement, otherwise no returns.

PRAIRIE EDGE, *P.O. Box 8303, Rapid City, S.D. 57709. Tel. (605) 341-4525. Free annual 32-page catalogue.*

Handmade Indian crafts, including necklaces, beads, buffalo robes, and war bonnets. Payment by check, money order, American Express, Visa, or Mastercard. Shipment by Postal Service or United Parcel. Purchases may be returned for refund within 10 days of receipt.

THE QUILTERY, *P.O. Box 337, R.D. 4, Boyertown, Pa. 19512. Tel. (215) 845-3129. Annual brochure price list costs $1, refundable with purchase.*

The work of 40 women who make quilts as a cottage industry and sell them through The Quiltery. Payment by check or money order. Shipment by United Parcel. Stock quilts may be returned within 10 days for refund or credit; custom quilts returnable only if workmanship is unsatisfactory.

RAMMAGERDIN, *P.O. Box 751, 121 Reykjvik, Iceland. Tel. 91-11122. Annual 24-page catalogue costs $1.*

Icelandic woolen handicrafts, including knitted sweaters, dresses, shawls, and other garments. Wool from Icelandic mountain sheep is also sold. Payment by check, money order, American Express, Visa, Mastercard, or Diners Club. Shipment by Postal Service. Purchases may be returned within 10 days after receipt for refund.

ROWANTREES POTTERY, *Box C, Blue Hill, Me. 04614. Tel. (207) 374-5535. Brochure price list costs $1.*

Handmade pottery by local craftsmen—mostly tableware, but other pieces as well, including bud vases, soap dishes, etc. Payment by check, money order, American Express, Visa, or Mastercard. Shipment by Postal Service or United Parcel.

TIBETAN REFUGEE SELF-HELP CENTRE, *Havelock Villa, 65, Gandhi Rd., Darjeeling, West Bengal, 734 101, India. Tel. 2346. The 40-page catalogue costs $1.50.*

This organization was formed in 1959 to help Tibetan refugees, giving them a chance to support themselves with their crafts and, at the same time, allowing them to keep their cultural heritage alive. The specialty is handmade carpets with Tibetan designs featured on 3′ x 6′ rugs. Other products include shawls, shirts, caps, gloves, socks, and boots. Payment by check or money order. Shipment by Postal Service or air or sea freight. Purchases may be returned for replacement.

TIPI SHOP INC., *P.O. Box 1542, Rapid City, S.D. 57709. Tel. (605) 343-8128. Brochure free with self-addressed stamped envelope.*

Indian arts and crafts, beaded craftwork, some replicas of antiques. Payment by money order. Shipment by Postal Service or United Parcel. Refund or credit for purchases returned in new condition within 5 days.

TOUCHING LEAVES INDIAN CRAFTS, *927 Portland Ave., Dewey, Okla., 74029. Annual 24-page catalogue costs $1.*

Beadwork includes chokers, necklaces, and bracelets, and there are German silver earrings and bracelets. Among the other crafts is a blanket in the Catawba pattern made of 50 percent acrylic and 50 percent polyester. Payment by check. Shipment by Postal Service. Purchases may be returned for refund within 10 days.

TRADE EXCHANGE (CEYLON) LTD., *72 Chatham St., Colombo 1, Sri Lanka. Tel. 25521. Catalogue costs $2.50.*

Handmade dresses in handsome Ceylonese fabrics, plus brass objects that include pots, pitchers, candle holders, trays, and lamps. Payment by American Express, bank draft, or letter of credit. Shipment by air parcel post or air or sea freight. No returns.

WELFARE HANDICRAFTS, *15/16 Lower Ground Floor, Connaught Centre, Hong Kong. Tel. 5-243356. Brochure price list.*

These are handicrafts made by handicapped and needy people in Hong Kong. The articles include brocade and Thai cotton, embroidery and patchwork, dolls, teakwood objects, and pieces in silver, pewter, bronze, and brass. Payment by check or international money order. Shipment by Postal Service. No returns.

❖ 15 The Performing Arts

Here is an area of widening interest in the United States. There has been a surge in people attending dance, instrumental, and vocal performances, and this has been accompanied by an increase in people participating in the arts themselves.

When so many companies say they offer discounts off the list price, it makes you wonder just how often anybody pays the list price for a musical instrument. This is an area where it is important to shop around for a good buy. Some of the instruments come in the form of kits that you must complete. Here also are places that sell books to help you learn to play some of these instruments as well as books on the history and theory of music and on great composers and musicians.

Musical Instruments

ANDY'S FRONT HALL. *See listing under* Records, Audio Tapes, and Compact Disks.

*MIKE BAILEY MUSIC CO. *See listing under* Music Books and Fan Accessories, *below.*

*EDDIE BELL GUITAR/JAN MAR INC., *P.O. Box 314, Hillsdale, N.J. 07642. Tel. (201) 664-3930. Annual 72-page catalogue costs $1, deductible from first order.*

This company offers discounts on all standard-priced fretted instrument parts and accessories. Payment by check, money order, Visa, or Mastercard. Shipment by United Parcel. Refund or credit for goods returned within 14 days.

BLACK MOUNTAIN INSTRUMENTS, *P.O. Box 779, Lower Lake, Calif. 95457. Tel. (707) 994-9315. Brochure.*

This company sells dulcimer kits and accessories. Payment by check, money order, or C.O.D. Delivery by Postal Service or United Parcel. Refunds for purchases returned within 30 days.

BROTHER SLIM'S RECORD REVIVAL. *See listing under* Records, Audio Tapes, and Compact Disks.

R. G. BRUNE, LUTHIER, *800 Greenwood St., Evanston, Ill. 60201. Tel. (312) 864-7730. Free 16-page catalogue.*

Harpsichords, lutes, and guitars (baroque and classical) from a small workshop where hand work is the rule. There are also 2 phonograph records of music played by Roger Goodman on a Brune harpsichord.

*BUCK MUSICAL INSTRUMENT PRODUCTS, *40 Sand Rd., New Britain, Pa. 18901. Tel. (215) 345-9442. The old 44-page catalogue costs $3.50, of which $3 was refundable toward an initial order of $15 or more; a new catalogue is on the way.*

Banjos, dulcimers, guitars, harmonicas, jaw harps, mandolins, recorders, violins, and zithers, plus parts and acessories for them. Special discounts offered from time to time on such things as Martin guitars, violin cases, and recorders. There is a separate list for records that seem to be heavily folk and bluegrass.

*CAPRITAURUS FOLK MUSIC, *P.O. Box 153, Felton, Calif. 95018. Tel. (408) 335-4478. Annual 66-page catalogue costs $4.50; there are smaller free catalogues.*

Discounts of 10 to 40 percent are reported for such instruments as harps, dulcimers, Autoharps, bowed psalteries, hurdy-gurdies, zithers, guitars, ukeleles, mandolins, banjos, flutes, recorders, bagpipes, concertinas, harmonicas, and drums. Record albums and books are also discounted. Payment by check, money order, Visa, or Mastercard. Shipment by Postal Service or United Parcel. Purchases may be returned within 10 days for refund or credit.

CARVIN, *Dept. 84, 1155 Industrial Ave., Escondido, Calif. 92025. Tel. (619) 747-1710, (800) 854-2235 (except in California), or (800) 542-6070 (in California). Free annual 84-page catalogue.*

This handsome catalogue quotes approvingly the biblical demand "Make a joyful noise unto the Lord, all the earth; make a loud noise." Here are guitars and basses and equipment to amplify and project them, mixers, amps, crossovers, equalizers, and speakers. The psalmist could not have meant *this* much noise, from enought watts to shake the fillings from your teeth. The consoles of the equipment are so high-tech that they look like they came out of a space ship. Payment by certified check, bank check, money order, Visa, Mastercard, or C.O.D.

*CHACEY-BUILT, *Route 1, Box 76, Amesville, Ohio 45711. Tel. (614) 448-2771. The brochure is free, but there is a $1 charge for additional color photos.*

This company offers discounts of 20 to 30 percent on banjos, guitars, and mandolins. Payment by check or money order. Delivery by United Parcel, with a 50 percent advance payment required; the balance and shipping fees can be paid C.O.D. Instruments may be returned within 14 days, but custom-decorated items are not returnable.

*CITY LIGHTS, *P.O. Box 2436, Elizabeth, N.J. 07207. Tel.(201) 351-3330. The 6- to 10-page catalogue issued 8 times a year costs $1 each or $3 for a year's subscription.*

This firm caters to guitar collectors, repairers, dealers, and those interested in restoring fine old instruments. Discounts are offered on both instruments and parts.

THE DULCIMER SHOPPE, *McSpadden Musical Instruments, P.O. Drawer EZ, Mountain View, Ark. 72560. Tel. (501) 269-4313. The 20-page catalogue costs $1.25: there is also a free brochure.*

This company makes dulcimers; it sells the completed instruments and also kits for do-it-yourselfers, books, music, and records. Payment by check, money order, Visa, or Mastercard. Shipment by Postal Service or United Parcel.

*FIDDLEPICKER, *P.O. Box 1033, Mountainside, N.J. 07092. Tel. (201) 379-9034 or (201) 223-0751. Free 8-page catalogue issued 3 or 4 times a year.*

Violins at a discount. For example, a Barcus-Berry violin that lists for $675 is on sale here for $575. There are lots of used, inexpensive violins. Payment by money order, bank check, Visa, or Mastercard. Shipment by United Parcel or air express. Refund or exchange for purchases returned within 10 days.

*FRED'S STRING WAREHOUSE, *P.O. Box 7, Temple, Pa. 19560. Tel. (215) 373-4545. Annual 24-page catalogue costs $2.*

Discounts of 40 percent on instrument strings. There are also guitar accessories, harmonicas, books, and amplifier equipment. Payment by check, money order, Visa, Mastercard, or Choice. Delivery by Postal Service or United Parcel. Unopened merchandise may be returned for credit.

GREVEN GUITAR COMPANY, *Route 3, Box 289, Nashville, Ind. 47448. Tel. (812) 988-6725. Free 12-page catalogue issued semiannually.*

This company specializes in mail-order custom-built instruments, all one-of-a-kind, made at the rate of 30 to 60 a year.

*GRUHN GUITARS, *410 Broadway, Nashville, Tenn. 37203. Tel. (615) 256-2033. Free catalogue, but a 1-year subscription of 18 issues costs $10.*

"One of the largest inventories in the world of fine vintage instruments at competitive prices." Discounts of 35 percent off list offered on Gibson guitars. Besides guitars, there are violins, violas, cellos, basses, banjos, and mandolins, plus books. They have a special section for southpaws, with a recent issue offering a 12-string guitar for lefties.

GUITAR EMPORIUM, *104 Brighton Ave., West End, N.J. 07740. Tel. (201) 571-0038. Monthly catalogues.*

This company buys and sells vintage guitars and accessories. Why are there so many guitar dealers in New Jersey?

*GUITAR TRADER, *12 Broad St., Red Bank, N.J. 07701. Tel. (201) 741-0771. The 24-page catalogue issued 12 times a year costs $20 for a year's subscription, refundable with a guitar purchase of more than $200.*

Mostly electric guitars, but also some vintage acoustical guitars and banjos. Its prices are 40 to 70 percent below suggested list.

*GUITARS FRIEND, *1810 S. Woodward Ave., Birmingham, Mich. 48011. Tel. (313) 540-8037. The 120-page catalogue costs $3, but there are also free price lists.*

This place offers discounts of 40 percent off list price on Martin and Guild guitars. They are planning to change their name to Musicians Friend because they also sell other stringed instruments. Payment by check, money order, Visa, or Mastercard. Shipment by United Parcel. Refund or credit for instruments returned within 24 hours.

GURIAN INSTRUMENTS, *R.F.D. 2, Richmond, N.H. 03470. Tel. (603) 239-4080. Brochure price list.*

Parts, accessories, and cleaners for fretted instruments.

*HOBGOBLIN MUSIC, *659 El Camino Real, South San Francisco, Calif. 94080. Tel. (415) 872-1388. Free annual 16- to 24-page catalogue.*

Discounts on new and used concertinas, bagpipes, flutes, flageolets, krummhorns, re-corders, mandolins, mandolas, citterns, bouzoukis, violins, balalaikas, lutes, dulcimers, and other instruments, plus books and records. Payment by check, money order, Visa, or Mastercard. Delivery by Postal Service or United Parcel. Refund or credit for returned purchases, but only if authorized on day of delivery.

HUBBARD HARPSICHORDS, *144 Moody St., Waltham, Mass. 02154. Tel. (617) 894-3238. Annual 20-page catalogue costs $1.*

For years I was struck by tiny ads I saw in smallish magazines offering harpsichord kits, and I always wondered how many people undertook the daunting task of building a keyboard instrument. Once, while wearing an editor's hat, I asked a reporter to do a piece on it, and she found that a surprising number of people did buy the kits and actually put them together. Here is one of the leading suppliers of harpsichord kits and of the completed instruments themselves. The completed harpsichords, clavichords, virginals, and fortepianos, beautifully decorated, cost upward of $14,000, while the kits can be a quarter or a half of that, depending on the extent of the assembly to be done by the purchaser. Payment by check or money order. Shipment of kits and instruments by truck or air freight, parts by Postal Service or United Parcel. Defective parts will be replace within 90 days; instruments may not be returned.

M. B. HUGHES DULCIMER CO., *4419 W. Colfax Ave., Denver, Colo. 80204. Tel. (303) 572-3753. Free 6- to 8-page catalogue issued 3 times a year.*

More kits and completed instruments—harpsichords, harps, lutes, guitars, hammered dulcimers, mandolins, balalaikas, bowed psalteries, hurdy-gurdies—plus books, records and tapes, and accessories. Payment by check, money order, Visa, Mastercard, or C.O.D. Shipment by United Parcel. Purchases may be returned for refund or credit within 30 days.

KOCH RECORDERS, *Haverhill, N.H. 03765. Tel. (603) 989-5620. Brochure price list.*

Handsome soprano, alto, and tenor recorders made of cherry, maple, or cocobolo (you may have to look up the last named, as I did).

*JAPANESE SHAKUHACHI, *P.O. Box 294, Willits, Calif. 95490. No telephone. The 14-page catalogue costs $1.*

This flute, the informative catalogue tells us, is thought to have originated in ancient Egypt and then to have migrated through India and China, finally reaching Japan in the 6th century A.D. It is tuned to a 5-note (pentatonic) scale, but Western music can be played on it by employing various tricks with the mouthpiece. Other flutes are also available, as are music and records. Discounts are offered.

*LARK IN THE MORNING, *P.O. Box 1176, Mendocino, Calif. 95460. Tel. (707) 964-5569. Semiannual 104-page catalogue costs $2.50, and there are free supplements.*

An enormous range of instruments are offered, from accordion to zither and embracing most other plucked, strummed, squeezed, and woodwind instruments in between, plus books, music, and records. Moeck recorders are offered at a 25 percent discount, and there are other discounts on mandolins and records. Payment by check, money order, Visa, or Mastercard. Shipment by Postal Service, United Parcel, or freight. Purchases may be returned for refund or credit within 3 days of receipt, except special orders.

THE LIBERTY BANJO COMPANY, *2472 Main St., Bridgeport, Conn. 06606. Tel. (203) 368-1176. Annual 20-page catalogue costs $4.*

This company makes and sells banjos and their parts and accessories. Payment by check or money order. Shipment by Postal Service, United Parcel, or common carrier. Refunds or credit for purchases returned within 90 days.

*MANDOLIN BROS. LTD., *629 Forest Ave., Staten Island, N.Y. 10310. Tel. (718) 981-3226. Free 80-page catalogue issued twice a year.*

New and vintage fretted instruments (guitars, banjos, mandolins), many at discounts. An example: Dobro guitar Model 60-D-S, list price $597, offered here at $418, including hard case. There are also electronic gadgets, amplifiers, and multitrack dubbers without which a rock band would be incomplete (or at least not as loud). Payment by check, money order, bank wire transfer, American Express, Visa, or Mastercard. Shipment by United Parcel. Refund or credit for purchases returned after a 48-hour approval period.

*THE MARTIN GUITAR CO., *(1833 Shop)*, P.O. Box 329, Nazareth, Pa. 18064. Tel. (215) 759-2837 or (800) 345-3103 (except in Pennsylvania). Free 16-page catalogue.*

Discounts of 10 to 50 percent available on guitars, kits, parts, accessories, and books.

HUGH MACPHERSON (SCOTLAND) LTD. *Bagpipes. See listing under* Men's Clothing.

*MOGISH STRING CO., *P.O. Box 493, Chesterland, Ohio 44026. Tel. (216) 729-3470. Free 20-page catalogue.*

Guitars and other fretted instruments and accessories, with discounts for strings, microphones, guitars, and the like. The Yamaha FG345 guitar is said to list for $305 and be available here for $179. Payment by check. Shipment by Postal Service or United Parcel. Refund or credit for purchases returned within 3 days.

*MORGAN COMPANY, *Route 3, Box 204, Dayton, Tenn. 37321. Tel. (615) 775-2996. Brochure price list.*

Discounts of 25 percent off list on banjos, mandolins, Autoharps, and guitars. Repairs also available.

DAVID JOHN MORSE GUITARS, *1825 Soquel Ave., Santa Cruz, Calif. 95062. Tel. (408) 426-4745. The 4-page catalogue costs $3.*

Guitars that are handmade with the same care associated with violins.

MUSICAL INSTRUMENTS OF THE ANDES, *P.O. Box 55, Hayfork, Calif. 96041. Tel. (916) 628-4384. Catalogue sent in exchange for a first-class stamp.*

Wind (quena, sikus or zamponas, and antara), percussion (bombo), and string instruments (charango and harp) from the Chilean Andes. Payment by money order. Delivery by Postal Service or United Parcel. Instruments may be returned within 20 days for an exchange.

MUSICIANS FRIEND. *See listing for Guitars Friend, above.*

PLAYER PIANO COMPANY, *704 E. Douglas, Wichita, Kans. 67202. Tel. (316) 263-3241. The 160-page catalogue issued every 3 years costs $3.50 for the most recent issue.*

Parts for player pianos, music rolls, glue, tools, and books. Payment by check, money order, Visa, or Mastercard. Delivery by Postal Service or United Parcel. Purchases may be returned for refund or credit, but restocking fee is charged.

ROBINSON'S HARP SHOP, *P.O. Box 161, Mount Laguna, Calif. 92048. Tel. (619) 473-8556. Free annual 8-page catalogue.*

Harp blueprints, strings, hardware, books, and records. Payment by check or money order. Shipment by Postal Service or United Parcel. Refund or credit for goods returned within 30 days.

SANTA CRUZ GUITAR CO., *328 Ingalls St., Santa Cruz, Calif. 95060. Tel. (408) 425-0999. Catalogue costs $2.*

Acoustical guitars of classic design that are sold in Europe and Japan as well the in the U.S.

*SILVER & HORLAND, *170 W. 48th St., New York, N.Y. 10036. Tel. (212) 869-3870. No catalogue.*

This is a 50-year-old company offering new musical instruments at discounts of 30 to 50 percent, plus used and vintage instruments. They have guitars, mandolins, banjos, violins, keyboard instruments, synthesizers, saxophones, trumpets, trombones, and other band instruments, plus amplifiers. Payment by check, money order, American Express, Visa, or Mastercard. Delivery by United Parcel or truck. Purchases may be returned within 24 hours for refund or credit.

STEWART-MACDONALD, *P.O. Box 900, 21 N. Shafer St., Athens, Ohio. 45701. Tel. (614) 592-3021 or (800) 848-2273 (except in Ohio). Semiannual 32-page catalogue costs $1.*

Kits and parts to make banjos, mandolins, and violins. A kit to make guitars is under development.

SULTAN'S DELIGHT. *Instruments for middle Eastern Music. See listing under* Gourmet, Ethnic, and Special Foods.

ROBERT S. TAYLOR *(Harpsichords by Sperrhake), 8710 Garfield St., Bethesda, Md. 20817. Tel. (301) 530-4480. Free 12-page catalogue.*

Harpsichords, spinets, and clavichords made in Germany in several finishes and ranges. Payment by check or money order. Shipment by motor freight. Returns are "negotiable."

MATT UMANOV GUITARS, *273 Bleecker St., New York, N.Y. 10014. Tel. (212) 675-2157. Free brochure price list.*

Guitars, banjos, mandolins, amplifiers, books, and accessories. Payment by check, money order, American Express, Visa, or Mastercard. Shipment by United Parcel. Purchases may be returned for credit within 5 days.

*PHILIP H. WEINKRANTZ MUSICAL SUPPLY CO., *2519 Bomar Ave., Dallas, Tex. 75235. Tel. (214) 350-4883. Free 40-page catalogue issued twice a year.*

Discount prices on violins and cellos, and on parts, strings, and cases for them.

RAPHAEL WEISMAN, *Lorien Woodcrafts, 737 N. Star Route, Questa, N.M. 87556. Tel. (505) 586-1307. Free brochure.*

This is a small company turning out handmade instruments, including renaissance and baroque fretted instruments. Payment by check or money order. Shipment by United Parcel. Instruments may be returned within 30 days for refund or credit.

THE WILLIAMS WORKSHOP, *1229 Olancha Dr., Los Angeles, Calif. 90065. Tel. (213) 258-1626. Brochure price lists cost $1.*

Kits to make harpsichords, clavicords, spinets, and virginals.

THE WORLD OF PERIPOLE, *Browns Mills, N.J. 08015. Tel. (609) 893-9111. Free annual 32-page catalogue.*

This company manufactures some of those musical instruments so loved by children—tambourines, triangles, drums, rhythm bells—and there are also some instruments imported from France. Payment by check or money order. Shipment by Postal Service, United Parcel, or truck. Refund or credit for purchases returned within 30 days.

Music Books and Fan Accessories

*MIKE BAILEY MUSIC CO., *8937 Drake Parkway Rd., Chattanooga, Tenn. 37416. Tel. (615) 344-2290. Free annual 24-page catalogue.*

Instructions (some with tapes) on how to play the banjo, mandolin, and guitar. There are also accessories, instruments, and kits to make them, and discounts are reported for all goods. The emphasis is on bluegrass. Payment by check under $50 or money order above that amount. Instruments by United Parcel, other things by Postal Service. Refund or credit for purchases returned within 10 days.

B. H. BLACKWELL. *See listing under* General Booksellers.

THE GOLDMINE BOOKSHELF, *P.O. Box 187, Fraser, Mich. 48026. Tel. (313) 776-0540. Free 24-page catalogue issued 4 times a year.*

This place calls itself the "world's largest mail-order music book company." It offers mostly rock histories and stories about musicians—*Boy George in His Own Words,* for example—and 2 full pages on books about the Beatles.

*MUSICADE, *19777 W. 12-Mile Rd., Southfield, Mich. 48076. Tel. (313) 968-1987. Monthly 12-page catalogue costs 50 cents.*

Rock accoutrements at discount prices, including such needs as The Who buttons, Led Zeppelin painter's hats, Grateful Dead bandanas, lots of photos, T-shirts, posters, bumper stickers. Payment by check, money order, Visa, or Mastercard. Shipment by Postal Service or United Parcel. Purchases may be returned within 30 days for exchange.

THE OPERA BOX, *Box 48, Homecrest Station, Brooklyn, N.Y. 11229. Tel. (718) 627-0477. Free 16- to 24-page catalogue issued twice a year.*

Histories, biographies, criticism, and analysis in opera, such as Milton Cross's two volumes of complete stories of the great operas, still interesting to read after 30 years. Payment by check or money order. Delivery by Postal Service or United Parcel. Returns are not accepted.

TAFFY'S CATALOGUE OF RECORDS AND BOOKS. *See listing for Taffy's under* Dance and Theater Supplies and Costumes, *below.*

TIMBERWOOD INDUSTRIES, *Marlin Brinser Books on Music Division, P.O. Box 82, South Salem, N.Y. 10590. Tel. (914) 533-2020. Brochure price list.*

Over 1,200 titles, with prices 50 cents to $3 below list, on such things as music theory, composition, harmony, singing, conducting, performing. There are also histories, criticism, dictionaries, and guides. Payment by check or money order. Shipment by Postal Service or United Parcel. Refund for books returned within 30 days.

See also *Musical Instruments,* above, and *Records, Audio Tapes, and Compact Disks* for music instruction books.

Dance and Theater Supplies and Costumes

ALCONE CO., *5-49 49th Ave., Long Island City, N.Y. 11101. Tel. (718) 361-8373. The 150-page catalogue costs $1.50 but is free to schools and other nonprofit institutions.*

Paramount theatrical supplies at discount prices. Payment by check, money order, Visa, or Mastercard. Shipment by United Parcel. Authorization must be obtained to return purchases.

ALGY DANCE COSTUMES, *440 N.E. First Ave., Hallandale, Fla. 33009. Tel. (305) 457-8100. Semiannual catalogue costs $2.*

Payment by check, Visa, or Mastercard. Delivery by United Parcel. No returns on custom-made items; refunds for others.

ARABESQUE DANCE SUPPLIES, *113 Bank St., Waterbury, Conn. 06702. Tel. (203) 754-2260. Annual 36-page catalogue costs $1.*

Payment by money order or bank check. Shipment by United Parcel. No returns since all costumes are made to order.

THE DANCE MART, *Box 48, Homecrest Station, Brooklyn, N.Y. 11229. Tel. (718) 627-0477. Free 16- to 24-page catalogue issued twice a year.*

Discounted books on all aspects of dance—history, biography, guides, and anthropology. Payment by check or money order. Delivery by Postal Service or United Parcel. Returns are not accepted.

VICTOR LAURENCE LTD. *Theatrical costumes. See listing under* Men's and Women's Clothing.

NORCOSTCO, *3203 N. Highway 100, Minneapolis, Minn. 55422. Tel. (612) 533-2791. Free annual 72-page catalogue.*

This catalogue for the performing arts permits you to costume, stage, and light a production, from medieval madrigals to modern Broadway shows. There are costumes, wigs, make-up, props, a fog machine, lights, paint, and sound systems.

SULTAN'S DELIGHT. *Belly dancer and musical items. See listing under* Gourmet, Ethnic, and Special Foods.

TAFFY'S, *701 Beta Dr., Cleveland, Ohio 44143. Tel. (216) 461-3360. Four separate catalogues.*

Showstoppers, 86 pages, costs $3. Theatrical costumes for children, outfits for dancers, and shoes.

Catalogue for Dance and Gymnastics, 114 pages, costs $3. A very large selection of dance and gymnastic clothes.

Taffy's on Parade, 66 pages, costs $3. Costumes for marching, prancing, and dancing on parade.

Taffy's Catalogue of Records and Books, 118 pages, costs $2. An enormous listing of music and instruction for all of the above.

Payment by check, American Express, Visa, Mastercard, or C.O.D.

THEATRE HOUSE, *P.O. Box 2090, Covington, Ky. 41012. Tel. (606) 431-2414. Annual 50-page catalogue costs $2.*

Available from this theatrical supply house are costumes, stage drapes, backdrops, Halloween items, make-up, lighting, fabrics, sequin goods, rhinestones, sound effects records, mirrored balls, paint, and other items. Payment by check, money order, Visa, or Mastercard. Shipment by United Parcel. Purchases may be returned, with authorization, for refund within 5 days.

❖ 16 Amusements and Vices

The companies listed here sell things that people don't necessarily need but which may provide them with some fun or perhaps satisfy some craving.

There are some interesting doodads available here, and I call your attention to one, Think Big, which has supersized novelties.

I have a section on fireworks, but I really cannot encourage untrained people to get involved in this. I like nothing better than watching the fireworks go off above the Washington Monument on the Fourth of July, and I am very willing to leave that to people who know something about it. Note that you should check first with local authorities to be sure fireworks are legal in your area.

Lastly, a word on smoking. You are aware, I am sure, that the Surgeon General of the United States has declared that cigarette smoking is a major cause of death—the latest estimate is that 350,000 people a year die from heart disease, cancer, and pulmonary lung disease associated with cigarettes—and that people may be harmed by other people's smoke. You also should know that many people find smoke offensive. I quit smoking on October 27, 1969, and do not recommend that anyone smoke.

Games and Toys

ANIMAL TOWN GAME CO., *P.O. Box 2002, Santa Barbara, Calif. 93120. Tel. (805) 962-8368. Free annual 64-page catalogue.*

Unusual boardgames, such as "Back to the Farm," "Save the Whales," and "Dam Builders," plus books on games, and old-time radio programs on tape cassettes. Payment by check or money order. Shipment by United Parcel. Refund or credit for purchases returned within a few weeks (preferably unused).

COMPUTER GAMES +. *See listing under* Computer Software and Books.

FAMILY PASTIMES. *R.R. 4, Perth, Ont., Canada K7H 3C6. Tel. (613) 267-4819. The 16-page catalogue costs 25 cents and is issued twice a year.*

Games that encourage cooperation.

GAMES CATALOGUE, *P.O. Box 5357, F.D.R. Station, New York, N.Y. 10150. Tel. (212) 421-5984 or (800) 852-5200 (except in New Jersey). The 16-page catalogue costs $1.*

A Sherlock Holmes mystery game, chess, and other board games, many of which would make nice gifts. Payment by check, money order, Visa, or Mastercard. Shipment by Postal Service or United Parcel. Purchases may be returned within 30 days for refund.

THE ISHIPRESS, *C.P.O. Box 2126, Tokyo, Japan. Tel. 0467-83-4369. Brochure price list.*

Books and equipment for the game "Go". There is also a helpful list in the catalogue of where you might go in the U.S. and elsewhere to try and get a "Go" game started.

THE JUGGLING ARTS, *612 Calpella Dr., San Jose, Calif. 95136. Tel. (408) 267-8237. The 12-page catalogue costs $1.*

Beginners' equipment (cloth balls so you can learn to juggle without hurting your hands) and assorted clubs, torches, cigar boxes, and other devices—the object being to keep all these things in the air at the same time. Corny, old-fashioned, and lots of fun. Payment by check or money order. Shipment by Postal Service or United Parcel. Purchases may be returned for refund or replacement only if they break in normal use.

KENDAL PLAYING CARD SALES, *3 Oakbank House, Skelsmergh, Kendal, Cumbria, LA8 9AJ, England. Tel. Kendal 22055. Annual 14-page catalogue costs 50 cents (for which the proprietors request a $1 bill, allowing a 50-cent credit against your purchase).*

This is a concern that specializes in beautiful and unusual playing cards not normally found in shops. Besides dealing in cards still in production, the proprietors also sell old and antique cards as well as books about cards. Payment by check or money order. Shipment by Postal Service. Purchases may be returned for credit against future purchase or for refund, less money-transfer costs.

KITES ON A STRING, *3098-A Fuller St., Coconut Grove, Fla. 33133. Tel. (305) 447-9616. Free annual 18-page catalogue.*

Lots of kites in various designs, some of them very expensive, but they presumably will last long and bring lots of pleasure.

HANK LEE'S MAGIC FACTORY, *24 Lincoln St., Boston, Mass. 02111. Tel. (617) 482-8749. The main 250-page catalogue costs $5; there are 4 additional free 16-page supplements for people on the mailing list.*

Professional magic equipment.

SCHUBEL & SON, *P.O. Box 214848, Sacramento, Calif. 95821. Tel. (916) 483-1944. The 44-page catalogue costs $1, which is refunded when one sends in a coupon from the catalogue.*

Here are games that people play against one another by mail, which is said to be a rapidly growing pastime. The company acts as the games master and the customers are the contestants. The games are computerized, and as few as 10 people or as many as 2,000 may be playing in a game at the same time. Payment by check, money order, Visa, or Mastercard. Shipment by Postal Service. A refund of the unused portion of a person's account is sent within 30 days of notification of quitting.

WORLD WIDE GAMES, *Box 450, Delaware, Ohio 43015. Tel. (614) 369-9631. Annual 24-page catalogue costs $1.*

Handmade wooden games, including pool-type tables, shuffleboard, and the like. There are also some books on recreation and games. Payment by check, money order, Visa, or Mastercard. Shipment by Postal Ser-

vice, United Parcel, or motor freight. Purchases may be returned for refund.

Fireworks

BLUE ANGEL, *P.O. Box 26, Columbiana, Ohio, 44408. Tel. (216) 482-5595, (800) 321-9071 (except in Ohio, Alaska, and Hawaii), or (800) 362-1034 (in Ohio). The 24-page catalogue costs approximately $2.*

Here is a source of fireworks. Payment by check, money order, Visa, or Mastercard. Shipment by United Parcel or truck. United Parcel cannot deliver fireworks to California, Massachusetts, Connecticut, New Jersey, New Hampshire, or Rhode Island. Purchases may be returned for refund within 14 days.

BUCK PYROTECHNICS, *P.O. Box 71, New Britain, Pa. 18901. Tel. (215) 345-6477. A price list is available.*

This company is available to set off fireworks displays for huge community gatherings or small private events. It will provide the bangs and glares, the people to set them off, and the insurance policies. No returns.

Novelty Items and Gag Gadgets

ANYTHING LEFT HANDED, *65 Beak St., London, W1R 3LF, England. Tel. 01-437-3910. Free 6-page catalogue issued 4 times a year.*

This specialty shop stocks 100 items for people like my daughter Ellen: left-handed scissors, pens (pens?), kitchen gadgets, and literature for teaching left-handed children. The store also stocks scissors designed for the disabled and the elderly.

BOREAL ARTIFACTS. *Beaver Totems. See listing under* Furs.

FUNNY SIDE UP, *425 Stump Rd., North Wales, Pa. 19454. Tel. (215) 368-8911. Free 64-page catalogue issued twice a year.*

Slightly silly novelties that could make good-natured gifts. There is an electric hammer, a tuxedo T-shirt, and an executive bib. Payment by check, money order, American Express, Visa, or Mastercard. Shipment by Postal Service or United Parcel. Purchases may be returned for refund, credit, or exchange.

ROBERT D. GRIMM MARKETING. *Giant cookies, balloons. See listing under* Baked Goods, Sweets, and Snacks.

JOHNSON SMITH CO., *35075 Automation Dr., Mt. Clemens, Mich. 48043. Tel. (313) 791-2800. Three free 48-page catalogues—* The Lighter Side, *the* Johnson Smith Co. *catalogue, and* The Old Catalogue Book—*issued each year.*

The Lighter Side catalogue provides, well, lighter gifts and novelties. There is, for example, a musical dustpan that plays "Born Free."

The *Johnson Smith Co.* catalogue has unusual items—a deck of cards with the clubs and spades in red and the hearts and diamonds in black, for example.

My favorite is *The Old Catalogue Book,* which is filled with reminiscences of my own youth—those cheap ads for cheap products that used to be printed in the back of cheap magazines. Remember the joy buzzer for shocking someone when shaking hands, sneezing powder, exploding matches and loaded cigarettes ("Positively No End of Fun")? Payment by check, money order, American Express, Visa, or Mastercard. Shipment by Postal Service or United Parcel. Purchases may be returned for refund or credit.

WILLIAM H. SPRAGUE COLLECTION, *P.O. Box 412, New York, N.Y. 10024. Tel. (212) 438-1043. Brochure.*

Custom-printed ribbons with your message on them.

THINK BIG, *390 West Broadway, New York, NY 10012. Tel. (212) 925-7300 or (800) 221-7019 (except in New York State). Annual 16-page catalogue costs $1.*

These are terrific gags, gifts, and fun home furnishings—everyday objects made in gargantuan models. There are Crayola crayons 56 inches long, a 70-inch Ticonderoga pencil, a 57-inch toothbrush, a 71-inch artist's paint brush. I thank my brother-in-law Frank for bringing this nifty store to my attention. Payment by check, money order, American Express, Visa, or Mastercard. Shipment by United Parcel. Purchases may be returned within 30 days for refund.

WORLDWIDE CURIO SHOP. *See listing under* Occult, Meditation, Self-Help, Astrology.

See also *Casual and Sports Clothing* for novelty T-shirts.

Novelty Rubber Stamps

FUNNY BUSINESS, *2129 Second Ave., Seattle, Wash. 98121. Tel. (206) 623-7842. The 30-page catalogue issued twice a year costs $2*

Some very pretty, some very clever, and a few slightly scatological rubber stamps. Payment by check, money order, Visa, or Mastercard. Shipment by Postal Service or United Parcel. Damaged goods only may be returned within 7 days for exchange; no refunds.

LETTERS, *Suite 555, 429 W. Ohio, Chicago, Ill. 60610. Tel. (312) 644-4616. Catalogue costs $2.*

Very nice, almost sweet and gentle, rubber stamps. Payment by check or money order. Shipment by United Parcel. Purchases may be returned within 30 days for refund if there is an error.

NATURE IMPRESSIONS, *1007 Leneve Place., El Cerrito, Calif. 94530. Tel. (415) 527-9622. The 20-page catalogue issued twice a year costs $1.70.*

Here are stamps of finely drawn things, largely animals and objects related to nature. Payment by check or money order. Shipment by Postal Service or United Parcel. Purchases may be returned for credit.

SKYCLONES. *See listing under* Aviation.

UPTOWN RUBBER STAMPS, *P.O. Box 2147, Fort Collins, Colo. 80522. Tel. (303) 493-3212 or (800) 621-4322 (except in Colorado). The 16-page catalogue costs $2.*

Here are some stamps of an anti-establishment mood, plus some of the Beatles, movie stars (Groucho, Marilyn Monroe), and cartoon characters. Payment by check, money order, Visa, or Mastercard. Shipment by Postal Service. Purchases may be returned for refund.

Erotica and Far-Out Amusements

ADAM & EVE, *P.O. Box 800, Carrboro, N.C. 27510. Tel. (919) 929-2143 or (800) 334-5474 (except in North Carolina). The 48-page catalogue costs $2.50 for a year's subscription to 6 issues.*

Kinky clothes, devices, and books.

BIZARRE VIDEO PRODUCTIONS; CENTURIAN INTERNATIONAL DISTRIBUTING; CUSTOM SHOE COMPANY; LEATHER UNLIMITED; AND PLEASURE TIME, *12812 Garden Grove Blvd., Garden Grove, Calif. 92643. Tel. (714) 534-5336 or (800) 854-7119 (except in California).*

The above catalogues are very expensive, ranging from $3 to $29, and offer accoutrements, video tapes, and books on sexual fantasies and fetishes.

KRUPP'S FANTASY EXPRESS, *P.O. Box 9090, Boulder Colo. 80301. Tel. (303) 443-8700. Free 48-page catalogue.*

T-shirts with sexually provocative and obscene slogans that you may find humorous or sophomoric; couture jock straps; indoor gardening equipment, tobacco and smoking accessories, and books on growing marijuana.

MELLOW MAIL, *Box 811, New York, N.Y. 10276. Tel. (212) 475-1876. Free 48-page catalogue issued 12 times a year.*

Some naughty negligees, underwear, bathing suits, smoking equipment, and some mildly provocative (or corny) T-shirts.

*C. J. SCHIENER, BOOKS, *275 Linden Blvd., Brooklyn, N.Y. 11226. Tel. (718) 469-1089. The 64-page catalogue issued once or twice a year costs $2.*

This is a specialist in "erotica, curiosa and sexology," some of it quite old. What many would call "dirty books" evidently is not such a new phenomenon. There is one book, for example, on anecdotes, letters, and cases of sexual flagellation published in 1885. Lots of books on the Marquis de Sade. Payment by check or money order. Shipment by

Postal Service or United Parcel. Refund or credit for books returned within a week.

Tobacco and Smoking Equipment

GREEN RIVER TOBACCO CO., *P.O. Box 1313, Owensboro, Ky. 42302. Tel. (502) 684-4737. Free annual 10-page catalogue.*

This company has been selling tobacco by mail order for more than 70 years. It offers discount prices on tobacco for rolling your own cigarettes, and its prices for pipe tobacco are below retail. There are also smoking accessories, pen knives, and Famous Amos chocolate chip cookies. I don't understand that at all.

MELLOW MAIL. *See listing under* Erotica and Far-Out Amusements, *above.*

*NURHAN CEVAHIR, *Bekar Sokak No. 12/4, Beyoglu, Istanbul, Turkey. Tel. 144 41 23. Price list.*

The shop offers discounts of 10 percent on meerschaum pipes, which it manufactures and exports. Payment by check or money order. Delivery by Postal Service. No returns.

WALLY FRANK LTD., *63-25 69th St., Middle Village, N.Y. 11379. Tel. (718) 326-2233. Annual 48-page catalogue costs $1.*

Cigars, pipes, tobacco, and smokers' supplies. Payment by check, money order, American Express, Visa, Mastercard, Diners Club, or Carte Blanche. Shipment by United Parcel. Purchases may be returned within 30 days for refund.

KRUPP'S FANTASY EXPRESS. *See listing under* Erotica and Far-Out Amusements, *above.*

*HAYIM PINHAS, *Tahtakale, Kristal Han 312, Istanbul, Turkey. Tel. 522 93 02. Free 24-page catalogue.*

Discounts offered for quantity purchases of meerschaum pipes, some of them quite elaborate, like the "Picasso style saxaphone." Payment by check. Shipment by Postal Service. No returns.

NAT SHERMAN, *711 Fifth Ave., New York, N.Y. 10022. Tel. (212) 751-9100 or (800) 221-1690 (except in New York State). The 52-page catalogue costs $3.*

This is one of New York City's best-known sellers of fine cigars. There are cigars for new fathers and other happy people to hand out.

G. SMITH & SONS, *74 Charing Cross Rd., London, WC2H OBG, England. Tel. (01) 836-7422. Brochure price list.*

Choice snuffs and smoking tobacco. "Make friends with snuff," the brochure demands. Payment by check (in sterling drawn on a British bank), American Express, Visa, Mastercard, Diners Club, or Carte Blanche. Shipment by Postal Service. Purchases may be returned, by next post, for credit.

*FRED STOKER, *P.O. Box 707, Dresden, Tenn. 38225. Tel. (901) 364-5419. Brochure price list.*

Discount prices on tobacco for chewing or smoking. Payment by check, money order, or C.O.D.. Shipment by Postal Service or United Parcel. Purchases may be returned for refund or credit.

THOMPSON CIGAR CO. *5401 Hangar Court, Tampa, Fla. 33614. Tel. (813) 884-6344, (800) 237-2559 (except in Florida), or (800) 282-0646 (in Florida). Free 32-page catalogue issued 2 to 4 times a year.*

Cigars made from tobacco grown from seed from Cuba.

❖17 Religious and Spiritual Needs

Since the Puritans came here seeking religious freedom, perhaps it isn't surprising that America is one of the most religious countries in the world—at least if one goes by the number of people affiliated with churches and synagogues. It is almost impossible to say how many people in the United States are members of religions, partly because churches and synagogues count their members differently. Some count everyone who has ever been a member and some count only those who attend services on a regular basis. Some observers believe that interest in religion has been increasing recently, while others assert that it is on the decline.

In any event, the National Council of Churches says that the 1984 figures for American membership in churches and synagogues was 77,253,700 for Protestants, 52,392,934 among Catholics, and 5,728,075 among Jews. (If Protestants are divided among their 186 denominations, this makes Roman Catholics by far the largest single religious group. Members of the Southern Baptist Convention come in second at 14,178,051, and the United Methodist Church third at

9,405,164.) But there are, of course, many Americans whose spiritual or religious satisfactions are found in nontraditional ways—meditation, the occult, and sensitivity groups, to name only a few that have been increasingly popular since the turbulence and change of the sixties and seventies.

In this section you will find catalogues that cater to the religious, spiritual, and psychological needs of these different and disparate groups.

Religious Articles and Books

ABBEY PRESS, *Christian Family Catalogue, Hill Dr., St. Meinrad, Ind. 47577. Tel. (812) 357-8011. The 36- to 60-page catalogue issued 9 times a year costs $1.*

Nativity scenes, a calendar that provides a daily Bible verse, and Christmas cards, plus some nonreligious gift items, such as a left-handed coffee mug.

GEORGE T. ABU-AITA & BROTHERS, *Manger St., Box 96, Bethlehem, Israel. Tel. 2249. Free 16-page catalogue.*

This is a manufacturer and exporter of religious souvenirs and jewelry made of mother of pearl, olive wood, and other materials. There are hand-carved depictions of Moses, Jesus, and the Virgin Mary.

JAMES AVERY CRAFTSMAN INC. *See listing under* Crafts to Buy.

COMMUNITY PLAYTHINGS, *Books for children with a religious or inspirational theme. See listing under* For Children.

CONCORDIA PUBLISHING HOUSE, *3558 S. Jefferson Ave., St. Louis, Mo. 63118. Tel. (314) 664-7000, (800) 325-3040 (except in Missouri), or (800) 392-9031 (in Missouri). Free 350-page catalogue issued once a year.*

Books on subjects related to Protestantism, including theology, fiction, and music.

FORTRESS CHURCH SUPPLY STORES/FORTRESS PRESS, *2900 Queen Lane, Philadelphia, Pa. 19129. Tel. (800) FORTRESS. Free 114-page catalogue.*

These are the merchandising and publishing arms of the Lutheran Church of America, but they supply Roman Catholic as well as Protestant churches. There are vestments and such objects as chalices, crosses, communion vessels, and candles.

HAMAKER JUDAICA, *P.O. Box 59453, Chicago, Ill. 60659. Tel. (312) 463-6186, (800) 423-2567 (except in Illinois), or (800) 228-5000 (in Illinois). The 56-page catalogue issued twice a year costs $2.*

This is "the Source for Everything Jewish." There are many gift items in this big catalogue: mezuzzahs to be placed on doorposts, a Wedgwood seder plate and other Wedgwood religious objects, menorahs, even a teddy bear dressed up for a bar mitzvah. Payment by check, money order, American Express, Visa, Mastercard, Diners Club, or Carte Blanche. Shipment by United Parcel. Purchases may be returned within 30 days for refund.

LEANIN' TREE PUBLISHING CO. *Cards, stationery, and prints. See listing under* Stationery and Office Supplies.

Occult, Meditation, Self-Help, Astrology

THE ADVOCATES, *P.O. Box 143, Sandy Hook, Conn. 06482. No telephone or catalogue.*

"An organization based on occult knowledge" that sells "power-charged pendants." Payment by check or money order. Shipment by Postal Service or teleportation. No returns.

ASSOCIATION FOR RESEARCH & ENLIGHTENMENT, *67th St. and Atlantic Ave., P.O.Box 595, Virginia Beach, Va. 23451. Tel. (804) 428-3588 or (800) 368-2727 (except in Virginia, Alaska, and Hawaii). Free annual 56-page catalogue.*

Books, tapes, and educational material on self-help and healing, and on Edgar Cayce. Payment by check, money order, Visa, or Mastercard. Shipment by Postal Service or United Parcel. Refund or credit if not satisfied.

HELIOS BOOKS, *2 High St., Glastonbury, Somerset, BA6 9DU England. Tel. 0458-34184. The 20-page catalogue costs $5 for a year's subscription of 10 issues, but a single sample copy is free.*

Specialists in books on the mind, religion, meditation, psychology, astrology, the occult, and the psychic, with a worldwide following. Payment by check, money order, American Express, Visa, or Mastercard. Shipment by Postal Service. Refund or credit if book is returned within 7 days of receipt.

HERITAGE BOOK STORE, *P.O. Box 71, Virginia Beach, Va. 23458. Tel. 428-0400. Free annual 22-page catalogue, plus sale leaflets. Also, free annual 32-page Edgar Cayce catalogue.*

Books on diet, nutrition, health, healing, metaphysics, inspiration, astrology, tarot, I Ching, and Edgar Cayce. The Cayce catalogue is a source of hard-to-find items mentioned in the writings of Edgar Cayce, the late psychic who has a large following in the United States to this day. Payment by check, money order, Visa, or Mastercard. Shipment by Postal Service or United Parcel. Purchases may be returned for refund or credit.

THE HUG FACTORY, *P.O.Box 4353, Louisville, Ky. 40204. Tel. (502) 459-9398. The 16- to 20-page catalogue issued twice a year costs $1.*

This company is "high-touch" and offers products that "support people in embracing life—feeling good about themselves and being successful in reaching their goals." One way of doing this, it seems is by wearing a Hug Therapist T-shirt. There are also hug mugs, sweatshirts, children's clothing, buttons, and bumper stickers.

INSTITUTE FOR RATIONAL-EMOTIVE THERAPY, *45 E. 65th St., New York, N.Y. 10021. Free 24- to 32-page catalogue issued twice a year.*

The institute offers therapy sessions, workshops, and courses. For people who cannot get to the institute, there are books, films, and audio and video tapes.

MANI TRADING CO., *Box 607, Spencer, W.Va. 25276. Tel. (304) 927-5686. The 4-page catalogue costs $1.*

This company primarily sells meditation-related supplies, including Buddhist and Hindu religious articles, and Tibetan handicrafts. Payment by check or money order. Shipment by Postal Service or United Parcel. Purchases may be returned within 30 days for refund or credit.

UNIQUITY, *P.O. Box 6, Galt, Calif. 95632. Tel. (209) 745-2111. Annual 32-page catalogue costs 25 cents.*

Games, devices, books, tapes, posters, and other things to help people deal with their psychological problems. Payment by check, money order, Visa, or Mastercard. Shipment by Postal Service, United Parcel, or freight. Purchases may be returned, in good condition, within 30 days for refund.

WORLDWIDE CURIO SHOP, *P.O. Box 17095, Minneapolis, Minn. 55417. No telephone. Three-catalogue set*—Worldwide Curio Shop, Tyrad Co., *and* Marlar Publishing Co.—*issued twice a year costs $1.*

The *Worldwide* catalogue lists curios such as pencil sharpeners in the shape of cannons, boats, cars, and sewing machines; magic tricks, novelties, and gags; incense; herbs, roots, barks, and berries for culinary use; and balms. Also, books on which herbal remedies are supposed to work on which problems.

The *Tyrad* catalogue is said to contain the world's largest selection of occult curios. It has books on casting spells, jade dragon and Hotai God of Luck statues, jewelry with occult symbols, voodoo dolls, and, these being modern times, aerosol cans with incense, such as that favored by St. Jude Thaddeus, "patron saint of difficult cases."

Marlar offers hundreds of books on astrology, cookery and herbs, gambling, hypnotism, metaphysics, the occult, self-help, and inspiration, plus contract bridge, calligraphy, and humor. I found nothing on St. Jude Thaddeus.

See also *Vitamins, Herbs, and Health Guides.*

❖18 Health Care and Beauty Aids

Here are some things intended to help the healthy stay healthy, as well as some health aids for the ill and elderly. Among the former are some herbal remedies about which I remain skeptical, but these things do have a large following. Besides the herbs listed here, others are to be found in the Food and For the Garden chapters. There are also sources for vitamin supplements, about which I also have doubts, but a lot of readers of this book probably use them, and the prices by mail order are said to be substantially lower than in stores. You will also find aids for those with vision and hearing problems, as well as eye and ear protectors.

In addition, there are firms that sell merchandise designed specifically for the comfort and interests of basically healthy people with special needs, including large print and braille books, easy-to-put-on clothing for the handicapped, and special telephones and scissors.

Finally, I have included cosmetics, beauty supplies, and fragrances here, along with health aids. Perhaps this is because looking good helps to make you feel better.

Vitamins, Herbs, and Health Guides

*AURORA BOOK COMPANIONS, *P.O. Box 5852, Denver, Colo. 80217. No telephone. Free catalogue issued 3 to 6 times a year.*

Books on good health—how to lose weight, get healthy, quit smoking, have a happier cat, a happier dog, and a happier sex life. A discount is offered on all orders over $10, and many books are regularly offered at a 50 percent discount.

BARTH'S OF LONG ISLAND, *270 W. Merrick Rd., Valley Stream, N.Y. 11582. Tel. (516) 561-8800 or (800) 645-2328. Monthly 48-page catalogue costs $1.50 but is sent free to customers.*

Vitamins, "protein powder," brewers yeast, sleep aids, herb teas, peanut butter, skin lotions. Payment by check, money order, Visa, or Mastercard. Shipment by Postal Service or United Parcel. Purchases may be returned for refund or credit.

CATHAY OF BOURNEMOUTH, *32 Cleveland Rd., Bournemouth, BH1 4QG, England. Tel. 0202-37178. Catalogue costs $3 by airmail.*

Herbs, soaps, tablets, capsules, ointments from the largest retail herbalists in Britain. Of the offerings, 150 are put forward for their medicinal value and 90 are listed as cosmetics. Payment by check, money order, Visa, or Access. Shipment by Postal Service. Purchases may be returned for credit.

EFFECTIVE LEARNING SYSTEMS, *6950 France Ave. South, Suite 14, Edina, Minn. 55435. Tel. (612) 927-4171. Free 32-page catalogue.*

"Love Tapes" to help you lose weight, reduce blood pressure, stop smoking, control stress, study better, and feel good, plus vitamins, exercise equipment, and Oriental weight-loss tea.

EREWHON. *See listing under* Grains and Vegetables, Natural and Freeze-Dried Foods.

FLOWER ESSENCE SERVICES, *P.O. Box 586, Nevada City, Calif. 95959. Tel. (916) 273-6363. Several free catalogues.*

Flower essences to stimulate consciousness and assist in communing with nature. This is a business, but the principals also run a nonprofit educational organization, the Flower Essence Society, (P.O. Box 459, Nevada City, Calif. 95959).

GENSALAY SKIN CARE, *225 W. 35th St., New York, N.Y. 10001. Tel. (212) 489-0729 or (212) 947-5525. Annual 20-page catalogue costs $2.*

Their products are supposed to make you look younger by removing wrinkles. Payment by check or money order. Shipment by United Parcel. Refunds for purchases returned within 7 business days.

INDIANA BOTANIC GARDENS, *P.O. Box 5, Hammond, Ind. 46325. Tel. (219) 931-2480 or (800) 348-6434 (except in Indiana). The 64-page catalogue costs 50 cents.*

Herbs and teas for health care and cosmetic use, and also a lot of fresh herbs for cooking. Payment by check, money order, Visa, or Mastercard. Shipment by Postal Service or United Parcel. Purchases may be returned for refund.

KINGSMILLE FOODS CO. *Special-diet foods. See listing under* Gourmet, Ethnic, and Special Foods.

L. & H. VITAMINS, *38-01 35th Ave., Long Island City, N.Y. 11101. Tel. (718) 937-7400 or (800) 221-1152 (except in New York). Free 48- to 64-page catalogue issued 4 times a year.*

Vitamins, minerals, herbs, oils, bee pollen.

LIFE-RENEWAL INC., *Box 92, Highway 18, Garrison, Minn. 56450. Tel. (612) 692-4498. Catalogue costs $2.*

Herbs for health care, weight loss, virility (the last called "Resurrection Herbs"), and other nifty things. Payment by check or money order. Shipment by Postal Service, United Parcel, or truck. Purchases may be returned, upon getting approval, for refund or credit within 30 days.

THE LIVIA COLLECTION, *Livia Sylva, 111 E. 56th St., New York, N.Y. 10022. Tel. (212) 759-9797 or (800) 221-4978 (except in New York). Free 24-page catalogue.*

This modest catalogue offers you nothing less than the secret to the restoration and preservation of the radiance of youth. Available here in face creams and the like is a substance, bee pollen, which no less an authority than Hippocrates urged women to use.

MIRACLE OF ALOE, *530 Westport Ave., Norwalk, Conn. 06851. Tel. (203) 846-1617. Free 12- to 24-page catalogue issued 4 times a year.*

Health and beauty products made with aloe gel, including a rub for muscles, a shampoo, moisturizer, night cream, facial gel and ointment for burns, bites, and rashes.

STAR PHARMACEUTICAL, *11 Basin St., Plainview, N.Y. 11803. Tel. (516) 938-9220, (800) 262-STAR (except in New York), or (800) 645-7197 (in Kentucky). Free 48-page catalogue issued 4 times a year.*

Discount prices for vitamins, minerals, and food supplements from a company that has been in business 30 years.

STUR-DEE HEALTH PRODUCTS, *Austin Blvd., Island Park, N.Y. 11558. Tel. (516) 889-0640, (800) 645-2638 (except in New York), or (800) 632-2592 (in New York). Free 88-page catalogue issued 8 times a year.*

This company, which is more than 50 years old, sells vitamins, herbal cold tablets, garlic capsules, desiccated beef liver (imported from Argentina! it is noted with exclamation), amino acids, lecithin, minerals, sunflower and pumpkin seeds, and other things.

*SUNBURST BIORGANICS, *P.O. Box 607, Rockville Centre, N.Y. 11571. Tel. (516) 623-8478 or (800) 645-8448 (except in New York). Free 48-page catalogue issued 6 times a year.*

Discount prices of up to 70 percent off prices of vitamins, minerals, and other health related products. For example, 100 capsules of vitamin E costs $4 instead of the $8.50 usually charged in stores. Payment by check, money order, Visa, or Mastercard. Shipment by United Parcel unless Postal Service is requested. Refund or credit for products returned within 30 days.

*VITAMIN SPECIALTIES, *8200 Ogontz Ave., Wyncote, Pa. 19095. Tel. (215) 885-3800, (800) 523-3658 (except in Pennsylvania), or (800) 822-3972 (in Pennsylvania). Free 84-page catalogue issued twice a year.*

This company offers its own line of vitamins, minerals, and the like at a significant savings over comparable brand-name products. For example, it sells 100 capsules of its Centrex for $3.45; this product is comparable to Lederle's Centrum, which costs $7 for the same quantity. Payment by check, money order, Visa, or Mastercard. Shipment by United Parcel unless Postal Service is requested. Refund or credit for purchases returned within 30 days if container is still sealed.

WESTERN NATURAL PRODUCTS, *P.O. Box 284, South Pasadena, Calif. 91030. Tel. (818) 441-3447. Free annual 24-page catalogue.*

Discounts of 30 to 50 percent off on products that are the equivalent of such things as Z-Bex and Stress Tabs.

WORLDWIDE CURIO SHOP. *Herbal remedies. See listing* under Occult, Meditation, Self-Help, Astrology.

See Also *Herbs and Spices.*

Cosmetics and Perfume

*BEAUTY BUY BOOK, *65 E. Southwater, Chicago, Ill. 60601. No telephone. Free 32-page catalogue.*

Discount prices on brand-name cosmetics, such as Halston, Elizabeth Arden, and Max Factor.

CASWELL-MASSEY CO., *111 Eighth Ave., New York, N.Y. 10011. Tel. (212) 620-0900. Free annual 84-page catalogue.*

Another of New York's wonders, this shop was established in 1752, making it "the country's oldest chemists and perfumers." Their No. 6 cologne is supposed to have been a favorite of George Washington, who gave some as a gift to the Marquis de Lafayette. Other notable customers have included John Quincy Adams, Dolley Madison, Edwin Booth, Lillian Russell, P. T. Barnum, Jenny Lind, Sarah Bernhardt, and Edgar Allan Poe (Caswell-Massey is among the 99.99 percent of the population that misspells Poe's middle name). Among the products available in this nifty catalogue illustrated with woodcuts are soaps, cucumber products, shaving supplies, perfumes, oils, and herbs.

*ESSENTIAL PRODUCTS CO., *90 Water St., New York, N.Y. 10005. Tel. (212) 344-4288. Brochure price list.*

This company has created "interpretations" (read that "copies") of expensive women's perfumes and men's colognes that provide savings over the cost of name-brand products of up to 90 percent on perfumes and 70 percent on colognes. Genuine Opium perfume costs $160 an ounce, but their "interpretation" costs only $17 for the same amount.

*VITTORIA GENTILLE COSMETICS, *41 Adams Ave., Short Hills, N.J. 07078. Tel. (201) 376-7029. Brochure price list.*

Discount prices on cosmetics and on perfumes that are versions of more expensive ones, such as $20 for a quarter-ounce of their version of Opium, while genuine Opium perfume costs $50 for the same amount. Payment by check or money order. Shipment by United Parcel. Purchases may be returned within 2 weeks for refund or credit.

*GRILLOT, *10 rue Cambon, 75001 Paris France. Tel. 260-73-62 or 260-76-35. Free price list.*

Perfumes and toilet water at discount prices.

HOVE PARFUMEUR LTD., *824 Royal St., New Orleans, La. 70116. Tel. (504) 525-7827. Free annual 20-page catalogue.*

Standard and luxury fragrances for women, plus imported crystal atomizers and some luxury colognes for men.

MAY COVE, *P.O. Box 327, Colonial Heights, Va. 23834. Tel. (804) 526-7410. Brochure price list.*

There is a large "library" of perfume fragrances available, starting with apple blossom and ending with wisteria. Purchases may be returned within 30 days for refund or credit.

See also *Vitamins, Herbs, and Health Guides,* above, for cosmetics and soaps.

Medical Supplies and Physical Aids

BETTER SLEEP. *Bedboards and special pillows. See listing under* Bedding, Linens, and Towels.

BLAINE HARDWARE INTERNATIONAL. *Grab bars for the handicapped. See listing under* Hardware for the Home.

*BURKE INC., *P.O. Box 1064, Mission, Kans. 66202. Tel. (913) 772-5658 or (800) 255-4147 (except in Kansas). Annual 12-page catalogue costs 25 cents.*

Elevating chairs at discount prices; for example, the company has a power recliner at $950 that sells for $1,200 to $1,300 elsewhere.

CLEO LIVING AIDS, *3957 Mayfield Rd., Cleveland, Ohio 44121. Tel. (216) 382-9700. Free 276-page catalogue.*

Thousands of items of health and rehabilitative equipment. Just a brief listing includes tilt tables, home whirlpool baths, exercise equipment, braces, crutches, commodes, shower chairs, and recreational therapy equipment. Payment by check, money order, Visa, or Mastercard. Shipment by Postal Service or United Parcel. Purchases may be returned only after receiving authorization; a 15 percent restocking fee may be charged against refund.

COMFORTABLY YOURS, *52 W. Hunter Ave., Maywood, N.J. 07607. Tel. (201) 368-0400. Free 48-page catalogue issued 4 times a year.*

Products for the ill, including absorbent pants, smocks, a combination knife and fork, pillows, cups, commodes. Payment by check, money order, American Express, Visa, Mastercard, Diners Club, or Carte Blanche. Shipment by Postal Service or United Parcel. Refund or credit for purchases returned.

LE GUARD CORP., *P.O. Box 18652, Raleigh, N.C. 27619. Tel. (919) 876-2454.*

This company makes a sanitary kit for travelers to take with them to restrooms. It includes such things as folding toilet seat covers and toilet tissue. Payment by check, money order, Visa, or Mastercard. Shipment by United Parcel. Purchases may be returned within 20 days for refund.

S. J. PEDERGNANA JR. *Medical equipment. See listing under Army and Navy Goods.*

ROCKFORD MEDICAL & SAFETY CO., *4620 Hydraulic Rd., Rockford, Ill. 61109. Tel. (815) 874-7891, (800) 435-9451 (except in Illinois), or (800) 892-9435 (in Illinois). Free 180-page catalogue issued twice a year.*

Equipment for emergency medical care and training, oxygen kits, stethoscopes, first aid kits, cervical collars, and stretchers, among many other items. Payment by check,

money order, American Express, Visa, or Mastercard. Shipment by Postal Service, United Parcel or truck. Purchases may be returned within 30 days for refund.

SEARS HOME HEALTH CARE SPECIALOG, *Chicago, Ill. 60607. Tel. (800) 323-3274 (except in Illinois) or (800) 942-7446 (in Illinois), or call your local Sears store. Free 88-page catalogue.*

Wheelchairs, some powered by electric motors, hospital beds, lift chairs, absorbent bedding and undergarments, lots of clothing with Velcro closures, whirlpool bath attachments. Payment by check, money order or Sears charge. Delivery by truck. Purchases may be returned for refund or credit.

*SIMMONS COMPANY, *P.O. Box 3193, Chattanooga, Tenn. 37404. Tel. (615) 622-1308. Free 4- to 8-page catalogue issued twice a year.*

Discount prices on fitness and health products. A Maxi-Power adjustable pneumatic exerciser that normally sells for $30 is offered here for $25. Payment by check or money order. Shipment by Postal Service or United Parcel. Refunds for purchases returned within 30 days.

Eyeglasses, Hearing Aids, Eye and Ear Protectors

*DUK KWONG OPTICAL CENTRE, *27 Cameron Rd., 4th Floor, Tsimshatsui, Kowloon, Hong Kong. Tel. 3-668019. Brochure price list.*

Discount prices on eyeglasses in a very wide selection of fashion frames. Payment by check, money order, American Express, Visa, or Mastercard. Shipment by Postal Service. Purchases may be returned for refund.

FLENTS PRODUCTS CO., *Box 2109, Norwalk, Conn. 06852. Tel. (203) 866-2581. Free annual 12-page catalogue.*

Ear stopples to help in sleeping, plus other ear and eye protection for swimming, shooting, and safety.

*RIC CLARK CO., *9530 Langdon Ave., Sepulveda, Calif. 91343. Tel. (818) 892-6636. Free annual 16-page catalogue.*

Discounts of about 50 percent for a national brand of hearing aids sold under the Ric Clark label. Payment by check or money order. Shipment by Postal Service. Purchases may be returned for refund within 30 days.

RITE-WAY HEARING AID CO., *P.O. Box 59451, 6041 N. St. Louis Ave., Chicago, Ill. 60659. Tel. (312) 539-6620. Brochure price list.*

Hearing aids and batteries, with sharp discounts reported for the latter. Payment by check or money order. Shipment by Postal Service. Purchases may be returned within 30 days for refund.

Supplies and Services for the Physically and Visually Handicapped

AMERICAN FOUNDATION FOR THE BLIND, *15 W. 16th St., New York, N.Y. 10011. Tel. (212) 620-2172. Several free catalogues.*

One catalogue lists products for people with vision problems, such as watches and clocks with braille faces, canes, board games (such as Monopoly, Scrabble, backgammon), playing cards in large print and braille, sports equipment, telephones with extra large push-buttons, and a talking calculator.

Another catalogue offers publications aimed at people involved in the treatment of the blind and also at people concerned about their own sight or that of their relatives or friends. Much of the material is available in books, on tape cassettes, and in braille.

G. K. HALL & CO., *70 Lincoln St., Boston, Mass. 02111. Tel. (617) 423-3990 or (800) 343-2806 (except in Massachusetts, Alaska, and Hawaii). Free annual 48-page catalogue, plus 9 additional brochures.*

Large-Print-Books-by-Mail is the name of the catalogue, and that well describes the books available. Payment by check, money order, American Express, Visa, or Mastercard. Delivery by Postal Service or United Parcel. Refund or credit if not satisfied and books are returned within 10 days; defective books may be returned at any time.

NATIONAL LIBRARY SERVICE FOR THE BLIND AND PHYSICALLY HANDICAPPED, *Library of Congress,*

1291 Taylor St., N.W., Washington, D.C. 20542. Tel. (202) 287-5100; TWX 710-822-1969.

This is a Federal agency that provides a free library service to handicapped people.

PIRCA FASHIONS INC., *901 Third Ave., Sacramento, Calif. 95818. Tel. (916) 443-1060. Annual 16-page catalogue costs $1.*

Here's a terrific idea—clothing for people confined to wheelchairs, requiring the use of crutches, or with other handicaps who will not allow that handicap to keep them from leading a full and creative life. The company was started by Hollynn Fuller Boies, who uses a wheelchair and says she started developing these clothes when she discovered that traditional off-the-rack clothing was often unsuitable for people with handicaps. Payment by check, money order, Visa, Mastercard, or C.O.D. Shipment by Postal Service or United Parcel. Purchases may be returned within 60 days for refund.

ULVERSCROFT AND CHARNWOOD LARGE PRINT BOOKS, *279 Boston St., Guilford, Conn. 06437. Tel. (203) 453-2080, telex 4993674 ACTPC. Free catalogue issued 5 times a year.*

Even the catalogues are in large type. There are some modern classics, such as *Catch-22* by Joseph Heller and *Lost Horizon* by James Hilton, plus a lot of romance novels ("When Sarah marries television star Niall Rhodes she has no reason to believe that the rich full life she had led in her family's home in Guinever, a lovely old castle on the English coast, will not continue." Watch out, Sarah! Don't do it! Drat. Too late.) Payment by check or money order. Shipment by United Parcel. Refunds for returns made within a year.

VOCATIONAL GUIDANCE & REHABILITATION SERVICES, *2239 E. 55th St., Cleveland, Ohio 44103. Tel. (216) 431-7800. Annual catalogue costs $1.*

Here is a very worthwhile place, an organization that makes clothing for the physically handicapped, infirm, and others who want attractive, noninstitutional-looking clothing that is easy to put on and take off. Payment by check or money order. Shipment by United Parcel. Purchases may be returned for refund.

See also *Medical Supplies and Physical Aids,* above.

❖ 19 Stationery and Business and Social Needs

We must do something to preserve the art of letter writing, or there will be no collections of the correspondence of notable or interesting people in the future. A telephone call, after all, leaves no record (unless, of course, someone is improperly recording it). Here is everything you need to write to a favorite uncle, the kids at camp, your editor, or a potential customer, including paper, pen (or typewriter element), and desk.

This chapter lists sources that will interest business people, social secretaries, organizational activists (P.T.A. members, political activists, volunteer workers), among others. The products they offer are suitable for homes, businesses, and schools and other institutions.

Stationery and Office Supplies

AJAX EDITIONS, *1142 Manhattan Ave., C. P. 108, Manhattan Beach, Calif. 90266. Tel. (213) 376-3026. No catalogue, but samples of cards will be sent on request.*

This company offers a very nice line of note cards. Payment by check or money order. Shipment by Postal Service. Purchases may be returned within 30 days for refund.

AMERICAN STATIONERY CO., *P.O. Box 207, Peru, Ind. 46970. Tel. (317) 473-4438. Free 16-page catalogue issued twice a year.*

A large line of personalized stationery for the home and office. Payment by check, money order, Visa, or Mastercard. Shipment by Postal Service or United Parcel. Purchases may be returned within 60 days for refund or credit.

ANITA BECK CARDS, *3409 W. 44th St., Minneapolis, Minn. 55410. Tel. (612) 920-4741 or (800) 328-3894 (except in Minneapolis). The 32-page catalogue costs $1.*

This is a catalogue of very nice note cards and other stationery. Payment by check, Visa, or Mastercard. Shipment by Postal Service or United Parcel. Refund or credit for purchases returned promptly.

BENTON ANNOUNCEMENTS, *3006 Bailey Ave., Buffalo, N.Y. 14215. Tel. (716) 836-4100. Free 36-page catalogue issued twice a year.*

A large assortment of wedding invitations.

*BROWNCOR INTERNATIONAL, *3251 S.W. 11th Ave., Ft. Lauderdale, Fla. 33315. Tel. (305) 463-9400, (800) 327-2278 (except in Florida), or (800) 346-6666 (in Florida). Free 66-page catalogue.*

You could set up an office shipping department with things from this catalogue. There are shipping equipment and tape,

mailing envelopes and tubes, shipping labels, storage files, bins and shelving. The company offers discounts of up to 40 percent.

CENTURY FAMILY PRODUCTS. *Appointment books, inventory registers. See listing under* Cookware and Dinnerware.

*COPEN PRESS, *100 Berriman St., Brooklyn, N.Y. 11208. Tel. (718) 235-4270. Free annual 16-page catalogue.*

This company prints catalogues, stationery, and mailing pieces and offers discounts on catalogues and business return envelopes. Other services include binding and mailing catalogues and brochures. Payment by check. Shipment by United Parcel.

†*CURRENT, *Express Processing Center, Colorado Springs, Colo. 80941. Tel. (303) 594-4100. Free 48-page catalogue issued 6 to 8 times a year.*

Discount prices on greeting cards; for example, cards costing $1 each in retail stores are 19 cents each. There is also note paper, cards, memo sheets, gift wrapping paper, and some stationery with attractive designs. Payment by check or money order. Shipment by United Parcel. Purchases may be returned for refund or credit.

DAY-TIMERS INC., *P.O. Box 2368, Allentown, Pa. 18001. Tel. (215) 395-5884. Free annual 112-page catalogue.*

Pocket and office desk planners; business stationery, memos, forms, and supplies; binders and report covers; business gifts and promotional ideas. Payment by check, money order, American Express, Visa, Mastercard, Diners Club, or Day-Timers account. Shipment by Postal Service, United Parcel, or truck. Purchases may be returned within 30 days for refund, credit, or exchange.

DEMCO INC., *P.O. Box 7488, Madison, Wis. 53707. Tel. (608) 241-1201; for orders: (800) 356-1200 (except in Wisconsin) or (800) 362-3311 (in Wisconsin); for inquiries: (800) 356-8394 (except in Wisconsin) or (800) 362-4007 (in Wisconsin). Annual 300-page catalogue costs $2; there are also 6 free 72-page specialized catalogues.*

Here are products to deal with just about every piece of paper in an office, library, school, or home. There are binders, files, labeling devices, pens, book and record shelves, desks, world globes, and many other things. Payment by check, money order, American Express, Visa, Mastercard, or Diners Club. Shipment by Postal Service, United Parcel, or truck. Purchases may be returned within 30 days for refund or credit.

*FIDELITY PRODUCTS, *5601 International Parkway, New Hope, Minn. 55428. Tel. (612) 536-6500, (800) 328-3034 (except in Minnesota), or (800) 862-3765 (in Minnesota). Free 120-page catalogue issued twice a year.*

Discount prices on office supplies and equipment, such as Bic Biro pens, 99 cents a dozen instead of the $1.49 list price, and typ-

ing elements for IBM typewriters, $11.88 instead of $16.95 list. Payment by check, money order, American Express, Visa, Mastercard, Diners Club, or Carte Blanche. Shipment by Postal Service, United Parcel, or truck. Refund or credit for purchases returned within 30 days, but imprinted orders are not returnable.

HEARLIHY & CO., *714 W. Columbia St., Springfield, Ohio 45501. Tel. (513) 324-5721 or (800) 622-1000 (except in Ohio). Free annual catalogue.*

This company makes drawing supplies and equipment for the office, shop, and classroom. Payment by check, money order, Visa, or Mastercard. Shipment by United Parcel or freight. Purchases may be returned, for any reason, within 30 days of receipt for refund, credit, or exchange.

HISTACOUNT, *965 Walt Whitman Rd., Melville, N.Y. 11747. Tel. (516) 351-4900 or (800) 645-5220 (except in Alaska and Hawaii). Free quarterly 92-page catalogues issued in 9 separate professional areas.*

Here are catalogues for accountants, lawyers, osteopaths, podiatrists, optometrists, chiropractors, veterinarians, dentists, and physicians offering personal and professional stationery, business cards, memo pads, drug envelopes and labels, prescription pads, and billing and insurance forms.

I-Z INDUSTRIES, *Box 735, Acton, Mass. 01720. No telephone. Brochure price list.*

This company makes stickers in the form of owls, frogs, and turtles with your name (or company name), address, and telephone number printed on them. Payment by check or money order. Shipment by Postal Service. Purchases may be returned for refund within 30 days.

LEANIN' TREE PUBLISHING CO., *P.O. Box 9500, Boulder, Colo. 80301. Tel. (303) 530-1442 or (800) 525-0656 (except in Colorado). Two free semiannual catalogues.*

Cards, stationery, and prints in 2 separate catalogues, one Christian and one Western/wildlife, each issued both at Christmas and in the spring. Payment by check, money order, Visa, or Mastercard. Shipment by Postal Service or United Parcel. Returns accepted for refund.

LETTER BOX, *P.O. Box 371, Woodbury, N.Y. 11797. Tel. (516) 367-4234. Annual catalogue costs $1.*

A line of stationery. Payment by check, money order, Visa, or Mastercard. Shipment by Postal Service or United Parcel. Nonpersonalized items are returnable, if in good condition, for refund.

SETON NAME PLATE CORP., *P.O. Drawer 1331, New Haven, Conn. 06505. Tel. (203) 488-0085. Free annual 68-page catalogue.*

This company sells primarily to other companies, its products being such things as no-smoking signs, warnings of high voltage, truck signs, hardhat decals with your company logo, door signs (I like "Not an Exit" especially; it reminds me of the sign P. T. Barnum was supposed to have had in his midway tents; "This Way to the Egress"). Payment by check or Seton account. Shipment by United Parcel. No returns.

STATIONERY HOUSE, *1000 Florida Ave., P.O. Box 1393, Hagerstown, Md. 21740. Tel. (301) 739-4487 or (800) 638-3033. Free 64-page catalogue.*

My wife, Iris, bought stationery from this company and was quite pleased with it. Available are letterhead stationery, envelopes, snap-out and continuous forms, memo pads, and rolls of labels, among many other things for the office or home. Payment by check, American Express, Visa, Mastercard, Diners Club, or Carte Blanche. Purchases may be returned—even if imprinted—for credit within 30 days.

20TH CENTURY PLASTICS, *3628 Crenshaw Blvd., Los Angeles, Calif. 90030. Tel. (213) 731-0900, (800) 421-4662 (except in California), or (800) 252-4631 (in California). Free 48-page catalogue issued twice a year.*

Supplies for the office, industry, and home, including vinyl sheet protectors for papers in notebooks, binders, hanging folders, portfolios, albums and sheets for holding slides and stamp collections, floppy disk storage units.

VULCAN BINDER & COVER, *Division of EBSCO Industries, Box 29, Vincent, Ala. 35178. Tel. (205) 672-2241 or (800) 633-4526 (except in Alabama). Free 48-page catalogue issued 4 times a year.*

This company manufactures ring binders and claims to have the largest selection sold by direct mail. It also sells other office supplies, including units for storing floppy disks. Payment by check, money order, Visa, or Mastercard. Shipment by United Parcel or truck. Purchases may be returned within 15 days for refund on nonimprinted products.

Wedding Stationery and Supplies

BENTON ANNOUNCEMENTS. *See* Stationery and Office Supplies, *above.*

*EVANGEL WEDDING SERVICE, *P.O. Box 366, Harrison, Ohio 45030. Tel. (812) 623-2509 or (800) 457-9774 (except in Indiana, Alaska, and Hawaii). Free 36-page catalogue.*

Discount prices for wedding invitations with religious themes and illustrations. There are also napkins, programs, thank you notes, gifts for attendants, and other accessories, all maintaining the religious theme.

*NOW AND FOREVER WEDDING STATIONERY, *P.O. Box 1009, Fullerton, Calif., 92632. Tel. (800) 451-0610 (except in California) or (800) 321-0584 (in California). Free 36-page catalogue.*

Discount prices on a full line of wedding stationery, from the invitations to the thank you notes, gifts for members of the wedding party, reception decorations, and other things.

VILLARI HANDKERCHIEF CO., *30 W. 54th St., New York, N.Y. 10019. Tel. (212) 586-2991. Brochure costs 50 cents.*

This company specializes in wedding handkerchiefs for every member of the wedding party—bride, groom, bridesmaids, flower girls, ushers, and mothers.

*WEDDING INVITATIONS AND ACCESSORIES BY DAWN, *P.O. Box 100, Lumberton, N.J. 08048. Tel.*

(609) 267-6020, (800) 257-9567 *(except in New Jersey, Alaska, and Hawaii), or (800) 665-0353 (in Canada). Free annual 56-page catalogue.*

Discount prices on contemporary and traditional invitations, printed using the thermography (raised letters) method. There are also matching accessory cards, accessories for wedding receptions, and gifts for the bride, groom, and bridal party.

Party Supplies

ANDERSON'S, *5350 North Highway 61, White Bear Lake, Minn. 55110. Tel. (612) 426-1667 or (800) 328-9640 (except in Minnesota). Free annual 68-page catalogue.*

This company is a leader in prom decorations and supplies, and it also makes school spirit products for cheerleaders and fans. Payment by check, money order, Visa, Mastercard, or Anderson's account. Shipment by Postal Service or United Parcel. Purchases may be returned for refund or credit.

PARADISE PRODUCTS, *P.O. Box 568, El Cerrito, Calif. 94530. Tel. (415) 524-8300. Annual 72-page catalogue costs $2.*

Theme party supplies—what to do at a party for the Kentucky Derby, the World Series, the Super Bowl, holidays, honoring a couple dozen countries, and sundry other excuses. Payment by check, money order, Visa, or Mastercard. Shipment by Postal Service, United Parcel, or Federal Express. Returns accepted only on defective merchandise.

See Also *Fireworks.*

Office Furnishings and Equipment

AMERICAN FURNITURE SYSTEMS. *See listing under* Furniture and Furnishings.

FOSTER MANUFACTURING CO., *414 N. 13th St., Philadelphia, Pa. 19108. Tel. (215) 625-0500 or (800) 523-4855 (except in Pennsylvania). Free 24-page catalogue.*

Furniture and equipment for the office, art studio, or publishing house, including light tables and accessories for them.

*A. LISS & CO., *35-03 Bradley Ave., Long Island City, N.Y. 11101. Tel. (718) 392-8484, (800) 221-0938 (except in New Jersey), or (800) 221-2352 (in New Jersey). The 146-page catalogue issued twice a year costs $3.*

This company offers discounts off list prices and reduced prices on quantity purchases. It has a very large number of products for the office and factory, including shelving, folding chairs, ladders, storage cabinets, desks, lockers, casters and wheels, hand trucks, executive chairs, filing cabinets, and conference tables.

MONDRIAN CUSTOM CABINETRY. *See listing under* Furniture and Furnishings.

NATIONAL BUSINESS FURNITURE, *222 E. Michigan St., Milwaukee, Wis. 53202. Tel. (414) 276-8511, (800) 558-1010 (except in Wisconsin), or (800) 242-0030 (in Wisconsin). Free 48-page catalogue issued twice a year.*

Discount prices on such office furniture as computer tables, desks, chairs, shelving, filing cabinets, and conference tables. Payment by check, money order, Visa, or Mastercard. Shipment by United Parcel or common carrier. "If there are any problems with quality or workmanship, NBF will adjust, repair, or replace to customer' satisfaction."

THE OFFICE WORKS, *97-06 Queens Blvd., Forest Hills, N.Y. 11374. Tel. (718) 459-2875. The 6-page catalogue issued 2 to 4 times a year costs $1.*

This company scouts Europe and the United States for well-designed items for the office and home. Some of the pieces are indeed good-looking, and I especially admired the clocks.

See also *Stationery and Office Supplies,* above, for shelving and desks and *Audio and Video Equipment, Computers, Electronics, Appliances, and Gadgets* for calculators, typewriters, postage scales, and other business machines.

Clip Art, Printing, and Promotional Services

COPEN PRESS. *Printing, binding, and mailing of catalogues and brochures. See listing under* Stationery and Office Supplies *above.*

NORMAN H. LUDLOW, *516 Arnett Blvd., Rochester, N.Y. 14619. Tel. (716) 235-0951. Free 24-page catalogue.*

Clip art is a service that provides illustrations which you can put on newsletters or sales sheets and avoid the expense of hiring an artist. Mr. Ludlow has a large selection of pictures, including one grouping that illustrates "Disabled People at Work and Play." His clip art service is available to anyone who wants to buy it, but he is particularly interested in reaching nonprofit agencies, such as churches, recreational, service, and educational institutions, hospitals, and parks.

PACKAGE PUBLICITY SERVICE, *1501 Broadway, Room 1314, New York, N.Y. 10036. Tel. (212) 354-1840. Free annual 12-page catalogue.*

This company supplies amateur and professional theater groups with such aids as prewritten articles and feature stories, artwork for use in paste-ups for advertisements, posters, flyers, and programs. Payment by check or established account. Shipment by Postal Service, United Parcel, or courier services. Purchases may be returned, with prior authorization, for credit.

Promotional Gifts and Premiums

DENCO INTERNATIONAL, *5499 N. Federal Highway, Suite A, Boca Raton, Fla. 33431. Tel. (305) 994-4400 or 426-6400.*

This company markets a small number of educational products to be used as fund-raisers, such as a spelling-helper dictionary that carries a $5.95 cover price and is available to groups for $3.95.

ELECTION IDEAS CAMPAIGN GUIDE, *P.O. Box 946, Naperville, Ill. 60566. Tel. (312) 357-7522 or (800) 323-5656 (except in Illinois). Free annual 32-page catalogue.*

Bumper stickers (with American flags, donkeys, elephants, eagles, sheriff badges, and the like), match books, campaign buttons, sponges, flower seeds, first aid kits, T-shirts, painter's caps, skimmers, etc. Payment by check, money order, Visa, or Mastercard. Shipment by Postal Service, United Parcel, or air freight. Purchases may be returned, "if error or product not as advertised," for refund, credit, or replacement.

EQUALITY PRODUCTS, *1554 Bardstown Rd., Louisville, Ky. 40205. Tel. (502) 459-8755. Free 32-page catalogue issued once or twice a year.*

This catalogue offers 240 buttons, bumper stickers, posters, T-shirts, post cards, calendars, and the like, with feminist slogans promoting equality for women. Payment by check, money order, Visa, or Mastercard. Shipment by Postal Service or United Parcel. Purchases may be returned for refund or credit.

PRAIRITOPIAN ENTERPRISES, *Box 116, Cochin, Saskatchewan, Canada SOM 0L0. Tel. (306) 386-2532. Brochure price list.*

This organization combines a small business enterprise with advocacy of nuclear disarmament. Its products include cookbooks, greeting cards, potpourris, and T-shirts that say "People for Peace" and show a dove carrying an olive branch.

REVERE, *North South Rd., Scranton, Pa. 18505. Tel. (800) 233-4193 (except in Pennsylvania) or (800) 248-3200 (in Pennsylvania). Free 16-page catalogue.*

Here are gifts to be sold by organizations in fund-raising efforts. The products include sculpted candles, candies, stuffed animals, tools, light bulbs, first-aid kits, etc. Except for candy, unsold merchandise may be returned within 30 days for refund.

UPSTART LIBRARY PROMOTIONS, *Box 889, Hagerstown, Md. 21741. Tel. (301) 797-9689. Free 24-page catalogue issued twice a year.*

Here are promotional items to encourage people, especially children, to use the library. One item is an emblem that describes a person as a member of the U.S.A. Reading Team. Payment by check, money order, Visa, or Mastercard. Shipment by United Parcel. Purchases may be returned, with no time limit, for refund or credit.

❖20 Reading Matter

Many thousands of different books are published in this country every year. But only a small portion of these—mainly the products of major trade publishing houses, such as the publisher of this book—are to be found in general bookshops around the country.

The vast majority of other books are those geared to a specific and often very limited audience. Many of these books—largely the products of univeristy presses, specialty publishers, and small publishing firms—are sold primarily to libraries and by direct mail to a known audience. The bookstores that stock these books are usually special-interest shops that frequently do most of their selling through mail-order catalogues.

University press books often reflect the nature of the colleges that publish them. One should not be surprised to find Catholicism and theology on the Notre Dame list, and a couple of Nebraskans—Willa Cather and Wright Morris—are well represented in the University of Nebraska Press catalogue. But there are also surprises, since a college or university may find a specialty, for whatever reason, in a subject that has nothing to do with its religious foundation or its location.

Although most university press books are nonfiction, these houses occasionally take a chance on works of fiction that are thought to have great merit even if they are not expected to have large sales. One example of such a book, although a tragic one, is *A Confederacy of Dunces* by John Kennedy Toole, who committed suicide after having failed to see his book published. His mother got the Louisiana State University Press to publish it, and it won the 1980 Pulitzer Prize for fiction.

At times, the university press functions as sort of a farm system for the large publishing houses. . . . *And the Ladies of the Club*, written over a fifty-year period by Helen Hooven Santmyer, was published by the Ohio State University Press. It then came to the attention of G. P. Putnam's Sons, which published it and made it more widely available. After the Book-of-the-Month Club made it a main selection, it became a bestseller. Who knows what might have happened to the manuscript if the book had not been published by the Ohio State University Press during the author's lifetime.

The following section includes a selected list of university presses and scholarly publishers; my apologies if I left out any reader's alma mater or favorite press, university or otherwise. Unlike major trade publishing companies, many university presses remainder their overstocked titles direct and issue special sales catalogues, so you will find many of them marked with an asterisk (*).

I have also included some special-interest book shops that deal in old, rare, and out-of-print books, first editions, even some anti-quarian pornography—the kinds of books that are easy to find in big cities like New York and London but are not widely available elsewhere. I also list some big mail-order companies that do a nationwide business. Specialty book sellers are listed in the appropriate chapters—such as Food Companions (for cookbooks), For the Garden (for gardening books), and the Performing Arts (for music and dance books).

General Booksellers

*BARNES & NOBLE BOOKSTORES, *126 Fifth Ave., New York, N.Y. 10011. Tel. (201) 440-3336 (but no phone orders accepted.)*

The *Guinness Book of World Records* says this is the largest bookstore in the world, which may be argued by Foyle's in London and a few other shops, but there probably would be no dispute to its claim to be the world's largest discount bookstore. I used to browse through this marvelous place when I lived in New York; now I have to content myself with browsing through the catalogues. A recent catalogue offered *Six Armies in Normandy*, by John Keegan, published at $17.95, for $4.98; a study of the French painter David by Antoine Schnapper, with 40 color plates, published at $75, for $29.95; *American Journey*, in which Richard Reeves retraced the steps of Alexis de Tocqueville, published at $15.95, for $3.98. Besides books, there are art prints, records, audio and video tapes, and movies. Payment by check, money order, American Express, Visa, or Mastercard. Full refund or credit for merchandise returned within 30 days.

269

*BETTER BOOKS CO., *Dept. 818, P.O. Box 9770, Fort Worth, Tex. 76107. Tel. (817) 335-1853. Free 68-page catalogue.*

Some big discounts: *Art of Maurice Sendak* by Selma G. Lanes, with 94 color plates, published at $60, for $24.95; *Richard Simmons Never-Say-Diet Book*, published at $14.95, for $7.98, *The World According to Garp* by John Irving, published at $10.95, for $4.98.

B. H. BLACKWELL, *48-51 Broad St., Oxford, England. Tel. 0865-49111, telex 83118. Twenty free subject catalogues, ranging from 20 to 120 pages.*

Blackwell's describes itself as a mail-order bookseller with one of the world's largest stocks of books, sheet music, and rare books, also offering bibliographic service and special order procurement. Payment by check, money order, Visa, Mastercard, Access, Mastercharge Group, and charge account for regular customers. Delivery by Postal Service, air freight, or accelerated surface post. No returns except on books supplied incorrectly.

†BOOK CALL, *59 Elm St., New Canaan, Conn. 06840. Tel. (203) 966-5470 or (800) 255-2665 (except in Connecticut). Free annual catalogue plus bimonthly newsletters.*

If you read about a book in *The New York Times Book Review*, in another newspaper or newsmagazine, or hear about it on radio or television, you are encouraged to telephone Book Call, which promises to zip it to you. A recent catalogue of gift books had some nice offerings, such as *Great Hollywood Movies* by Ted Sennett, Yousuf Karsh's 50-year retrospective (with 188 photographs), and the paintings from the labels of Chateau Mouton Rothschild (125 color plates, including works by Dali, Motherwell, Miro, Braque, and Picasso).

†CAHILL & COMPANY, *145 Palisade St., Dobbs Ferry, N.Y. 10522. Tel. (914) 693-3600. Free 56-page catalogue.*

Children's books (*Wynken, Blynken and Nod*), fantasy (*The Lord of the Rings*), humor (lots of P. G. Wodehouse), and music (recordings of Gilbert and Sullivan with librettos). There are also calendars, cards, prints and photographs, and gifts. Payment by check, money order, American Express, Visa, or Mastercard. Shipment by United Parcel whenever possible. Any item may be returned for refund or credit if it is in saleable condition and was not a personalized order.

*B. DALTON BOOKSELLER, *P.O. Box 1403, Minneapolis, Minn. Tel. (612) 922-6699, (800) 328-3890 (except in Minnesota, Alaska, and Hawaii), (800) 682-3816 (in Minnesota), (907) 276-3242 (in Alaska), or (809) 752-1275 (in Puerto Rico). Free 36- to 48-page catalogue.*

This chain of book stores also has a large mail-order business. The front of the catalogue has popular titles while the back has bargain books. In the latter category (and this is offered as an example only, since chances are slim that these titles are still available), a recent catalogue offered a book of 332 Norman Rockwell covers that had been published at $85 with its price reduced to $39.95, while *Eric Sloane's America*, published at $31.85, was selling for $7.98. Payment by check, money order, American Express, Visa, Mastercard, Dayton's, or Hudson's.

*EDWARD HAMILTON, *Rt. 7, Falls Village, Conn. 06031. Tel. (203) 824-0628. Free 12- to 24-page catalogue issued 5 times a year.*

This mail-order company has a huge selection of publishers remainders and overstock books, both paperback and hardcover.

HARVARD COOPERATIVE SOCIETY. *Current books and scholarly remainders. See listing under* Country and General Stores.

HATCHARDS, *187 Piccadilly, London W1V 9DA, England. Tel. (01) 439-9921, telex 8953970. Free 26-page catalogue issued twice a year.*

Large selection in the arts, humanities, biography, gardening, with the physical sciences not included. Under children's literature a book on animal puns, *Otter Nonsense* by Norton Juster, caught me eye: "Humor takes a 'tern' for the worse," the entry says. Oh well. Payment by check, money order, American Express, Visa, Master Card, Diners Club, Carte Blanche, or Access. Shipment by Postal Service. Refunds in cash or credit.

HEFFERS BOOKSELLERS, *20 Trinity St., Cambridge, CB2 3NG, England. Tel. 0223-358351, telex 81298. Free subject catalogues.*

Heffers offers a large number of books in several catalogues. A suggestion would be to write for some of their flyers and check off the subjects you are interested in. One flyer lists catalogues in academic areas and the other in medicine. The catalogues sent to me (1,677 titles in the history and philosophy of science and 1,498 in children's books and videotapes, ending with a Woody Woodpecker cartoon) had a wide breadth. Payment by check,

money order, Visa, or Heffers charge account, or through American Express in New York or the Royal Bank of Canada in Toronto. Delivery by Postal Service or air parcel service. Returns accepted only if damaged or faulty.

*LANDMARK BOOK COMPANY, *260 Fifth Avenue, New York, N.Y. 10001. Tel (212) 696-5430. Free subject catalogues of 4 to 64 pages.*

Uncommon books in many fields, including art, orientalia, natural history and science, the performing arts, Americana, books about books (this is the company's specialty, and the selection in this area is one of the largest in the world), philosophy and religion, and numismatics, most of them offered at big discounts off the published price. There are also rare books and fine editions. Payment by check or money order. Delivery by Postal Service or parcel post. No returns unless the shipment is damaged or faulty.

MOTHER'S BOOKSHELF, *105 Stoney Mountain Rd., Hendersonville, N.C. 28791. Tel. (704) 693-0211 or (800) 438-0238 (except in North Carolina). Annual 32-page catalogue costs $1.*

ORANGE CAT GOES TO MARKET, *442 Church St., Garberville, Calif. 95440. Tel. (707) 923-9960. Free 48- to 56- page catalogue issued 3 or 4 times a year.*

This company puts out attractive and descriptive catalogues offering books on birth and parenting, general adult reading, and children's books. Payment by check, money order, Visa, or Mastercard. Shipment by Postal Service. Refund, credit, or exchange for purchases returned in new condition at any time.

271

*PUBLISHERS CENTRAL BUREAU, *1 Champion Ave., Avenel, N.J. 07001. Tel. (201) 382-7600. Free 64-page catalogues published from time to time.*

Books and records at discounts of up to 85 percent. A recent catalogue had the *Guinness Book of World Records*, published at $12.95, for $5.95. The mix is varied, on one page there is a collection of Beatrix Potter's stories for $3.98 and on the next a book of dirty limericks. The series of excellent Fodor guides is discounted, apparently to make way for the next year's batch. There are also video cassettes, records and tapes, movie posters, and a growing section on computer programming. Payment by check, money order, American Express, Visa, or Mastercard. Delivery by Postal Service or United Parcel. Refund or credit with no time limit on returns.

REFERENCE BOOK CENTER, *175 Fifth Ave., New York, N.Y. 10010. Tel. (212) 677-2160. Semiannual 16-page catalogue costs 50 cents but is free to libraries.*

New books at list price but used books at bargain prices. They sell dictionaries, encyclopedias, and basic reference books in every field including literature, music, and science. Payment by check or money order. Delivery by Postal Service. No refunds unless books are received damaged or are not what was ordered.

*THE SCHOLAR'S BOOKSHELF, *51 Everett Dr., Princeton Junction, N.J. 08550. Tel. (609) 799-7233. Free 48-page catalogues issued 4 times each year.*

Discounts on 1,100 titles from 200 publishers in the arts, literature, humanities, and science. Discounts ranged up to 75 percent.

HENRY SOTHERAN LTD, *2, 3, 4 and 5 Sackville St., Piccadilly, London, W1X 2DP, England. Tel. (01) 734-1150 or (01) 734-0308. The 32-page catalogue costs $1 and is issued 3 or 4 times a year.*

This is a dealer in new, second-hand, out-of-print, remaindered, and rare books, which leaves little out. Excellently printed catalogues, including one devoted entirely to an exhibition at Southeran's on *Watership Down* by Richard Adams. Payment by check, money order, American Express, Visa, Diners Club, or Access. Shipment by air parcel or surface mail printed paper rate. Credit for returns made within 10 days.

Out-of-Print and Used Books and Modern First Editions

ARGOSY BOOK STORE, *116 E. 59th St., New York, N.Y. 10022. Tel. (212)753-4455. Free subject catalogues of about 36 pages issued 10 times a year.*

Catalogues issued in such subject categories as rare books, first editions, autographs, rare medical books, Americana, art, English literature. Payment by check, money order, Visa, Mastercard, or Argosy charge account. Cash or credit refund for returns made within 5 days of receipt.

AUSTIN BOOK SHOP, *Box 36, Kew Gardens, N.Y. 11415. Tel. (212) 441-1199. Subject catalogues issued 4 to 6 times a year, each about 32 pages; they cost $3 but are sent free after initial book purchase.*

Rare, old, and out-of-print books. A recent handful of catalogues illustrates the range of topics: "Immigration and Ethnic

Studies," "The Jews: Culture and History," "The Law," and "Woman, With Special Emphasis on Immigrant and Ethnic Women." The catalogues on the law and immigration and ethnic studies are "unique in the antiquarian world."

BELL, BOOK & RADMALL, *4 Cecil Court, London, WC2N 4HE, England. Tel. (01) 240-2161. Free 32-page catalogue issued 4 times a year.*

First editions of English and American literature, including selections of detective, science fiction, and fantasy. Payment by check, money order, American Express, Visa or Mastercard. Delivery by Postal Service. Credit or bank draft refund for books returned within 7 days of receipt.

BOLERIUM BOOKS, *2141 Mission, Suite 300, San Francisco, Calif. 94110. The 20- to 32-page subject catalogue cost $1.*

This concern handles rare and out-of-print books in classical studies, medieval history, women's studies, labor history, linguistics, economics, and Latin American affairs. Inquiries must specify an area of interest, since no general catalogues are issued. Payment by check or money order. Delivery by Postal Service. Refunds for books returned within 2 weeks.

BOSTON BOOK ANNEX, *906 Beacon St., Boston, Mass. 02215. Tel. (617) 266-1090. Free annual 100-page catalogue.*

Lots of affordable first editions. One recent catalogue had a pageful of Evelyn Waugh, another of Kurt Vonnegut Jr., another of Ezra Pound. Books to read and hold on to.

EL CASCAJERO (*The Old Spanish Book Mine*), *506 W. Broadway, New York, N.Y. 10012. Tel. (212) 254-0905. Free subject catalogue.*

The range of books in this shop is broader than its name would indicate. One recent catalogue dealt with economics, Wall Street, and labor, and another dealt with English translations and criticism of Balkan, French, German, Greek, Latin, Medieval, Oriental, Russian, Spanish, and Yiddish literature.

*WALT CHADDE, BOOKSELLER, *Rt. 3, Box 629, Grand Marais, Minn. 55604. Tel. (218) 387-2220. The 20-page catalogue costs $1.*

The shop lists about 18,000 used novels each year, both paper and hardcover, many of them out of print and hard to find. The two lists sent to me—H to R and S to Z—contained works by hundreds of authors, many of whom I had never heard (but might be known to aficionados) and some who are more familiar, like Kafka, Hardy, Hemingway, London, Saroyan, Sartre, Sayres, Tolstoy, Twain. There are many bargains to be had.

ELIZABETH F. DUNLAP, *Books & Maps, 6063 Westminster Place, St. Louis, Mo. 63112. Tel. (314) 863-5068. Free 10-page catalogue issued 3 or 4 times a year.*

Antique books and maps. The catalogue I received had several 18th-century maps of the world as it was then known and many more 19th-century maps of parts of the U.S.

EDITIONS, *Boiceville, N.Y. 12412. Tel. (914) 657-7000. The 40-page catalogue costs $1 and is issued 24 times a year.*

Used books, most of them in very good to fine condition. There are some older, out-of-print books available here that will not cost you a fortune. A wide range of interests is represented.

PRINCETON ANTIQUES BOOKSERVICE, *2915 Atlantic Ave., Atlantic City, N.J. 08401. Tel. (609) 344-1943.*

You may be as surprised as I was to find an antiquarian bookshop in a seaside resort that was called "The Nation's Playground" in my youth and now enjoys the distinction of being the center of legalized gambling in the East. And so, in what is now "The Nation's Blackjack Table," we find a store calling itself "The Servants of Knowledge." Good for them. The store has 175,000 out-of-print volumes and will find whatever you need, even searching elsewhere if that is called for. Instead of going through a long catalogue, you are asked to write or telephone and say what you need, and they will see if they have it or if they can get it for you.

HENRY SOTHERAN LTD. *See listing under* General Booksellers, *above.*

***STRAND BOOK STORE,** 828 Broadway, New York, N.Y. 10003. Tel. (212) 473-1452. Free 36-page catalogue issued 7 times a year.*

Many books that publishers send to critics are never read by the recipients. Instead, they are sold, often to stores like Strand. A typical arrangement that I am aware of called for the critic to get 1/3 of the cover price for new books and 1/4 for books out for 3 months or more. Right or wrong, this makes the books available at Strand for 50 percent off list price. There are also some remaindered books at up to 90 percent discounts. Strand is probably the largest second-hand book store in the country, with 2 million books on 8 miles of shelves. Refunds or credit for returned books.

THE TYPOGRAPHEUM BOOKSHOP, *The Stone Cottage, Bennington Rd., Francestown, N.H. 03043. No telephone. Free catalogue issued 4 times a year.*

Discovering this bookshop alone would have been sufficient justification for my undertaking this book. The store sells old and recent good books, such as a tribute to the late South African poet Roy Campbell by his friends, who included Dylan Thomas, Wyndham Lewis, Richard Aldington, and Alister Kershaw. I bought a 29-volume set of the *Encyclopedia Brittanica* for 1903 for $25 plus postage (the postage cost more than the encyclopedia). The catalogue is hand-set and beautifully printed by the owner, whose real love is printing books. I am so used to modern, high-speed offset printing that I had forgotten the wonderful look of hand-set type run off on a good letterpress. Hooray for R. T. Risk! Payment by check or money order. Delivery by Postal Service.

Rare and Finely Printed Books, Juvenalia

ALEPH-BET BOOKS, *670 Waters Edge, Valley Cottage, N.Y. 10989. Tel. (914) 268-7410. The 24-page catalogue issued 3 or 4 times a year costs $2.*

Antiquarian and collectible children's and illustrated books. Here is an example: a 1926 copy of Lewis Carroll's *Alice's Adventures in Wonderland*, illustrated by Ada Bowley with four color plates plus cover plate as well as many black and whites in text, for $35. Check or credit card for payment. Postal Service or United Parcel for delivery. Full refund for purchases returned within 10 days of delivery.

APPELFELD GALLERY, *1372 York Ave., New York, N.Y. 10021. Tel. (212) 988-7835. Quarterly 26-page catalogue costs $5.*

Rare books. Payment by check or money order. Shipment by United Parcel. Purchases maybe returned within 10 days for refund or credit.

J. N. BARTFIELD, *45 W. 57th St., New York, N.Y. 10019. Tel. (212) 753-1830. The 36-page catalogue costs $1.*

This firm has been described as "New York's most fascinating book shop." Some of the illustrated and leather-bound books, mostly first editions that it sells, such as a recently advertised 64-volume set of Dickens, can run into the thousands of dollars. In a recent catalogue, there was a 51-volume first edition of the works of Thomas Hardy and a copy of the edition of James Joyce's *Ulysses* published by the Paris bookstore Shakespeare & Co., its original publisher.

BATTLEDORE BOOKS, *36 E. 61st St., New York, N.Y. 10021. Tel. (212) 832-8232. Free catalogue issued 4 times a year.*

This shop, a subsidiary of Justin G. Schiller Ltd., (listed below), specializes in rare and unusual 18th- to 20th-century children's books with emphasis placed on those that help to educate the reader.

†**BOOKS OF WONDER,** *464 Hudson St., New York, N.Y. 10014. Tel. (212) 989-3270. Quarterly catalogue costs about $5; also, free newsletter issued twice a year.*

A specialist in old and rare children's and illustrated books, with a collection that includes the largest stock in the world of Oz books and other works of L. Frank Baum. There is also a large stock of unusual new children's books. One entire catalogue is given over to Oz, and reading it makes you want to take up their offer to visit the shop in lower Manhattan. Some are priced in the thousands, but others, especially non-Oz, are within reach of most people looking for a gift for a special child. Payment by check, money order, American Express, Visa, or Mastercard. Delivery inside U.S. by United Parcel, outside by Postal Service. Returns for credit or exchange only.

PHILIP C. DUSCHNES, *699 Madison Ave., New York, N.Y. 10021. Tel. (212) 838-2635. The 20-page catalogue is issued 4 or 5 times a year.*

Rare books and first editions. A recent catalogue had one of the 150 copies of the 1922 Shakespeare & Co. edition of James Joyce's *Ulysses*, priced at $1,750. Many first editions at affordable prices, including several Graham Greene novels.

KIM KAUFMAN, BOOKSELLER, *1370 Lexington Ave., Suite 2F, New York, N.Y. 10128. Tel. (212) 369-3384. Free quarterly catalogues of varying length.*

The proprietor, a rare-book dealer with a specialty in children's 19th- and early 20th-century books, also carries some used and new titles as well. One recent catalogue had lots of Twain, including an 1882 first American edition of *The Prince and the Pauper.* Payment by check or money order. Delivery by Postal Service or United Parcel. Refunds for books returned with 7 days.

EDWARD D. NUDELMAN, BOOKSELLER, *P.O. Box 20704, Broadway Station, Seattle, Wash. 98102. Tel. (206) 782-2930. Semiannual 50-page catalogue costs $4 but is sent free with purchase of books.*

Antiquarian books, 1700 to 1920. The firm's specialties are illustrated books, signed copies, and limited editions. A recent catalogue had a 1910 edition of Beatrix Potter's *The Tale of Mrs. Tittlemouse,* with the author's color illustrations, for $75. Payment by check. Delivery by Postal service. Refunds for books returned in 7 to 10 days.

PHILLIP J. PIRAGES, *315 N. Prospect, Kalamazoo, Mich. 49007. Tel. (616) 345-7220. Semiannual 100-page catalogue costs $5 but is free to regular customers.*

This shop deals in very fine books and manuscript material. Nothing is under $50, and just a few books are under $100. One item is pegged at $20,000. A recent catalogue offered a 1758 copy of Milton's *Paradise Regain'd.* There is even some incunabula, including a pair of books by Thomas Aquinas (c. 1500).

JUSTIN G. SCHILLER, *36 E. 61st St., New York, N.Y. 10021. Tel. (212) 832-8231. Catalogues issued of varying size.*

One recent catalogue listed hundreds of illustrated art and children's books, but also included titles for adults. The line between the two is often difficult to draw anyway. For example, is *The Count and the Cobbler* by Ludwig Bemelmans, which includes 25 original ink drawings, for children or adults? Payment by check, Visa, or Mastercard. Shipment by Postal Service, United Parcel or, on request, other couriers. Books may be returned for refund or credit within 10 days only if catalogued incorrectly.

W. THOMAS TAYLOR, *708 Colorado, Suite 704, Austin, Tex. 78701. Tel. (512) 478-7628. Free catalogues issued 3 to 5 times each year.*

This is a catalogue of fine books and manuscripts "in all periods and fields, with a particular emphasis on the humanities, including early and fine printing press books, and English and American literature and philosophy." A recent catalogue had a 1668 first edition of Milton's *Paradise Lost* for $3,500. Payment by check or money order. Delivery by Postal Service in Texas and outside the U.S., by United Parcel in the other states. Books are returnable for refund or credit within 10 days of receipt.

See also *Out-of-Print and Used Books and Modern First Editions,* above.

Art and Illustrated Books

AUDUBON BOOKS AND PRINTS. *See listing under* Paintings, Prints, Posters, Maps, and Decorative Printed Material.

†**DOVER PUBLICATIONS,** *31 E. Second St., Mineola, N.Y. 11501. Tel. (516) 294-7000 or (800) 231-2302 (except in New York). Free 50-page sale catalogue issued twice a year.*

Reduced-price paperback books, mostly nonfiction. Many art books offered, including *Leonardo on the Human Body*, with 215 plates, plus books on animals, music, and needle-craft. Also available are posters, cards, paper dolls, and toy books. Payment by check or money order. Refunds in cash or credit for anything returned for any reason.

HACKER ART BOOKS, *54 W. 57th St., New York, N.Y. 10019. Tel. (212) 757-1450.*

A PHOTOGRAPHER'S PLACE, *P.O. Box 274, Prince St., New York, N.Y. 10012. Tel. (212) 431-9358. Free 16- to 24-page catalogue issued 3 or 4 times a year.*

Books on photography, including history, criticism, photo-journalism, technical aspects, the nude, out-of-print titles.

PRINTED MATTER, *7 Lispenard St., New York, N.Y. 10013. Tel. (212) 925-0325. Annual 170-page catalogue costs $4, plus free Christmas catalogue and spring flyers.*

This company publishes inexpensive, mass-produced works of art in book form. "Artists' books take art and ideas into places where there are no other facilities for the housing of those ideas. They are direct communication between artists and audience, and they make it possible for ideas in art to exist in the hands of all people."

C. J. SHIENER, BOOKS. *Antiquarian and modern pornography and sex books. See listing under* Erotica and Far-Out Amusements.

E. WEYHE INC., *749 Lexington Ave., New York, N.Y. 10022. Tel. (212) 838-5466 or 838-5478.*

Art books and old prints.

W. HENBORN ART BOOKS, *1081 Madison Ave., New York, N.Y. 10021. Tel. (212) 288-1558.*

A large selection of books on art and architecture.

See also *Museum, Botanic Garden, and Public Radio Gift Catalogues.*

Poetry, Literature, Mysteries

*****WALTER J. BLACK,***1075 Northern Blvd., Roslyn, N.Y. 11576. Tel. (516) 627-4920.*

This firm owns the following book clubs and series: Detective Book Club, Zane Grey Library Series, Golden Giants Library Series, Classics Club, and Gardner Mystery Library. All of these follow the "negative-option" rule in which the member (customer) is given a preview of forthcoming selections and has the opportunity to decline receiving them. There are substantial discounts off list prices.

GOTHAM BOOK MART, *41 W. 47th St., New York, N.Y. 10036. Tel. (212) 719-4448.*

Poetry, literary history and criticism, film history, plus jewelry (this shop being in the center of New York's diamond district). They sell new and old books and literary magazines.

Books on Business and Technology

ENTERPRISE PUBLISHING CO., *725 Market St., Wilmington, Del. 19801. Tel. (302) 654-0110. Free catalogue.*

Books dealing with small businesses, how to incorporate, save on taxes, etc.

INTERMEDIATE TECHNOLOGY BOOKS BY POST, *9 King St., London, WC2E 8HN, England. Tel. (01) 836-9434. Free 36-page catalogue issued twice a year.*

This organization was formed by the late E. F. Schumacher, who held that rural poverty could be overcome by simple farming technologies requiring modest capital investments. The books available address economics, agriculture and fish culture, cooperatives, and the generation of energy, among other subjects. Payment by check or money order. Shipment by Postal Service. No returns unless authorized.

LITERARY MARKETS, *725 S. Beach Rd., Suite 105, Point Roberts, Wash. 98281. Tel. (604) 277-4829. Brochure price list.*

A small company trying to build up a stock of books that show writers of prose and poetry where they may sell their works.

MAXWELL SROGE PUBLISHING, *731 N. Cascade Ave., Colorado Springs, Colo. 80903. Tel. (303) 633-5556.*

This is an appropriate entry for a book that lists catalogues, since Sroge sells a large line of newsletters, books, and reports used by individuals and companies in the mail-order business or considering entering it. Some of the topics available include food, books, ready-to-wear clothes, sporting goods, and crafts.

WRITER'S DIGEST BOOKS/NORTH LIGHT, *9933 Alliance Rd., Cincinnati, Ohio 45242. Tel. (513) 984-0717 or (800) 543-4644 (except in Ohio, Alaska, and Hawaii). Free 12- to 20-page catalogue issued twice a year.*

Where to sell books, photographs, songs, even computer programs. Also, books with tips on writing and art. Payment by check, money order, Visa, or Mastercard. Delivery by Postal Service or, if requested, by United Parcel. Refund or credit on books returned within 15 days.

Selected University, Scholarly, and Small Presses

ACADEMIC PRESS, *111 Fifth Ave., New York, N.Y. 10003. Tel. (212) 741-6800. Free 68-page catalogue.*

Books in the biological, physical, and social sciences.

ANTIOCH PUBLISHING CO., *Box 28 RM 7, Yellow Springs, Ohio 45387. Tel. (513) 767-7379 or (800) 543-2397 (except in Alaska, Hawaii, and Ohio). Free 12-page catalogue issued once a year.*

Bookplates, children's books, calendars.

CAMBRIDGE UNIVERSITY PRESS, *American Branch, 32 E. 57th St., New York, N.Y. 10022. Tel. (212) 688-8885 or (800) 431-1580 (except in New York).*

A wide range of scholarly publications.

COLUMBIA BOOKS, *1350 New York Ave., N.W., Suite 207, Washington, D.C. 20005. Tel. (202) 737-3777.*

Books to help you get along in Washington—directories of trade and professional associations, lobbyists, public relations agents, and sporting and hobby groups.

*COLUMBIA UNIVERSITY PRESS/NEW YORK UNIVERSITY PRESS, *136 S. Broadway, Irvington, N.J. 10533. Free annual 32-page joint sale catalogue.*

A recent catalogue had 800 titles, all of them offered at a discount. There is a heavy emphasis on literature, with biographies and studies of Shakespeare, Yeats, Forster, Joyce, Chekhov, Mann, Ibsen, Dostoevsky, Pushkin, Sartre, Proust, Nabokov, Gorky, Sand, Wordsworth, Conrad, Milton, et al. Also, lots of other areas of the arts and humanities, with the sciences seemingly tacked on at the end.

CONGRESSIONAL QUARTERLY, *1414 22nd St., N.W., Washington, D.C. 20037.*

Government, politics, and public issues in paperback books from the publisher of one of Washington's most respected fact-gatherers, plus hardcover reference books on government for desk top use.

*CORNELL UNIVERSITY PRESS, *124 Roberts Place, Ithaca, N.Y. 14850. Tel. (607) 257-7000. Free 64-page catalogue issued twice a year.*

Almost 600 titles in the sciences, education, arts, and humanities. Cornell has Carl Sagan on its faculty, so it is not surprising that one of the astronomy books, *UFO's—A Scientific Debate*, was co-edited by him (with Thornton Page); it lists for $18.50 but is offered here at $12.95. Similar discounts on other books as well. In literature, there are big discounts on Cornell's studies of Wordsworth; in history, there is an ambitious series called "Aspects of Greek and Roman Life." Separately, the press publishes a smaller catalogue devoted to woman's studies.

CRANE, RUSSAK & CO., *3 E. 44th St., New York, N.Y. 10017. Tel. (212) 867-1490. Free annual 18-page catalogue.*

Books concerning professional and academic research in international affairs, public policy, energy, earth and marine sciences, management, and social sciences.

CREATIVE ARTS BOOK CO., *833 Bancroft Way, Berkeley, Calif. 94710. Tel. (415) 848-4777. Free 30-page catalogue issued twice a year.*

This company publishes general nonfiction, how-to books, biographies, and juveniles. Their recent catalogue featured a book by one of my favorite people, Raymond Sokolov, about one of my favorite subjects, A. J. Liebling. Payment by check or money order. Shipment by Postal Service. Purchase may be returned within 5 days for refund.

DUKE UNIVERSITY PRESS, *6697 College Station, Durham, N.C. 27708. Tel. (919) 684-2173. Free 24-page catalogues issued twice a year.*

A current project is a series of studies under the heading "Living With the Shore." Recent books have included works about the South Shore of Long Island, the Atlantic coast of South Carolina, and the Gulf coast of Louisiana, so it is clear that the inquiry is to range widely. Some discounts are available from time to time.

GENERAL HALL, INC., *23-45 Corporal Kennedy St., Bayside, N.Y. 11360. Tel. (718) 423-9397. Free 16-page catalogue issued 2 or 3 times a year.*

A small company with an interesting list of scholarly books mainly in the social sciences. A recent catalogue included books on crime, the violence in Northern Ireland, blacks in the professions, research into the problems of aging, and women under communism in the Soviet Union and China.

HAWORTH PRESS, *28 E. 22nd St., New York, N.Y. 10010. Tel. (212) 228-2800. Free 8-page catalogue.*

Books in the social and behavioral sciences, including a large line of books concerning women's issues—history, health, employment, sexuality, politics, family. Payment by check.

HEINEMANN, *4 Front St., Exeter, N.H. 03833. Free brochure.*

Titles in women's studies. Payment by check.

INDIANA UNIVERSITY PRESS, *10th & Morton Sts., Bloomington, Ind. 47405. Tel. (812) 335-6804. Free 20-page catalogue issued twice a year.*

*LOUISIANA STATE UNIVERSITY PRESS, *Baton Rouge, La. 70803. Free 16-page catalogue.*

A lot of attention to Louisiana, the South, and the Civil War, plus some ventures into European and American history and literature. More than 400 books offered at discounts, some of them substantial.

McGILL-QUEEN'S UNIVERSITY PRESS, *849 Sherbrooke St. West, Montreal, Que., Canada, H3A 2T5. Tel. (514) 392-4421. Free 8- to 32-page catalogue issued 2 or 3 times a year.*

Many titles in the social sciences, the arts, and the humanities, with an emphasis on Canada, although not to the exclusion of other cultures. Payment by check, money order, Visa, Mastercard, Barclaycard, Bank-Americard, Access, and Interbank. Shipment by Postal Service. Refund or credit on books returned within year of invoice date.

*MERRIMACK PUBLISHERS' CIRCLE, *Box 817, 47 Pelham Rd., Salem, N.H. 03079. Free 20-page catalogue.*

The catalogue I received offered 55 paperbacks in women's studies from Virago Press and the Women's Press. They were offered at a 20 percent discount.

*M.I.T. PRESS, *28 Carleton St., Cambridge, Mass. 02142. Tel. (617) 253-2884. Free 40-page catalogue issued twice a year.*

Architecture, urban planning, engineering, business, physical sciences. Special sales catalogue.

NEW DIRECTIONS PUBLISHING CO., *80 Eighth Ave., New York, N.Y. 10011. Tel (212) 255-0230. Free 16-page catalogue issued each year.*

Modern literature, poetry, criticism, and belles lettres.

NEW WORLD BOOKS, *2 Cains Rd., Suffern, N.Y. 10901. Tel. (914) 354-2600. No catalogue.*

People who read about this company's books in articles or advertisements may order direct.

NORTHERN ILLINOIS UNIVERSITY PRESS, *DeKalb, Ill. 60115. Tel. (815) 753-1075.*

Scholarly books in history, literature, political science, and science.

*OHIO UNIVERSITY PRESS/SWALLOW PRESS, *Scott Quad, Athens, Ohio 45701. Tel. (614) 594-5505. Free 24-page catalogue issued twice a year.*

Regional studies, poetry, fiction, literature of the 20th century, the Renaissance, and the Victorian era. A recent catalogue included *Children's Literature in Hitler's Germany* by Christa Kamenetsky. A special sales catalogue offers discounts of 20 to 80 percent. Payment by check, money order, American Express, Visa, or Mastercard. Delivery by Postal Service.

OXFORD UNIVERSITY PRESS, *P.O. Box 900, 200 Madison Ave., New York, N.Y. 10016. Tel. (212) 679-7300. Free 100-page catalogue issued twice a year.*

There are many very British Oxford University Press books, like *The Oxford Illustrated History of Britain,* and also many decidedly un-British works, such as a biography of Ty Cobb. This is a particularly rich listing of books, many of which are available in general book stores. Payment by check, money order, Visa, or Mastercard. Shipment by Postal Service. Books may be returned within 2 weeks.

ROUTLEDGE & KEGAN PAUL, *9 Park St., Boston, Mass. 02108. Tel. (617) 742-5867. Free catalogue.*

Many titles in the arts, humanities, and social sciences. There is a separate catalogue on women's studies. This is the American branch of an old London publishing firm.

RUTGERS UNIVERSITY PRESS, *Distribution Center, P.O. Box 4869, Hampden Station, Baltimore, Md., 21211. Tel. (201) 932-7037.*

Rutgers University Press is the largest publisher of books about New Jersey. The cover of a recent catalogue had an illustration from a book being offered, a reprint of Mrs. Henry Wood's *East Lynne,* one of the best-selling novels of the 19th-century, "the melodramatic saga of a woman who leaves her virtuous husband to run off with a scoundrel and lives to regret it." Don't laugh; it sold nearly a million copies by the end of the century.

SAGE PUBLICATIONS, *275 S. Beverly Dr., Beverly Hills, Calif. 90212. Tel. (213) 274-8003. Free 16-page catalogue issued 12 times a year.*

Many titles in the social sciences. Payment by check, money order, Visa, or Mastercard. Delivery by Postal Service. Books may be returned for credit within 180 days.

SCHOCKEN BOOKS, *200 Madison Ave., New York, N.Y. 10016. Tel. (212) 685-6500. Free 48-page catalogues issued twice a year.*

This is the publisher of the works of Franz Kafka and S. Y. Agnon. It also issues books in the fields of Jewish studies, women's studies, the social sciences, and history.

THE SHOE STRING PRESS, *995 Sherman Ave., P.O. Box 4327, Hamden, Conn. 06514. Tel. (203) 248-6307. Subject catalogues.*

This is a scholarly publisher of nonfiction—literature, history, military history, and international policy studies, reference books, and books for the continuing education of professional library staff. Most of their books are sold through wholesalers.

*SLAVICA PUBLISHERS, *P.O. Box 14388, Columbus, Ohio 43214. Tel. (614) 268-4002. Free catalogue.*

Books on the folklore, history, literature, and linguistics of Slavic cultures. Discounts for direct purchases. Payment by check, money order, Visa, or Mastercard. Delivery by Postal Service or United Parcel. No returns except in case of incorrect or defective books.

*SMITHSONIAN INSTITUTION PRESS, *1111 N. Capitol St., Washington, D.C. 20560. Tel. (800) 247-5072 (except in Iowa) or (800) 532-1526 (in Iowa). Free 28-page catalogue.*

Members of the Smithsonian Associates, a support organization, get these catalogues automatically, but nonmembers may also write and request them. The books are of excellent quality and deal mainly with the natural sciences and the vast collections of the Smithsonian, among which are comics (an area of great interest these days). Recent Smithsonian books that I have enjoyed include *The Smithsonian Collection of Newspaper Comics,* edited by Bill Blackbeard and Martin Williams, and *Washington on Foot,* edited by John T. Protopappas and Lin Brown, which would make an excellent guidebook for a first-time visit. The Smithsonian Press also

produces phonograph records. I especially enjoyed a 3-record album of Bach's 6 Brandenburg concertos performed by the Aston Magna Festival Orchestra led by Albert Fuller. To avoid jamming them onto 2 disks, they were recorded on 5 sides, which resulted in one side that might have been used to record, say, a Bach suite, being left blank, for reasons of interest mostly to audiophiles. Discounts to members. Payment by check, money order, American Express, Visa, or Mastercard. Complete satisfaction or full refund, replacement, or exchange, with the Smithsonian paying return postage.

SOUTHERN ILLINOIS UNIVERSITY PRESS, *P.O. Box 3697, Carbondale, Ill. 62901. Tel. (618) 453-2281.*

History, education, music, literature, and social sciences predominate.

TEMPLE UNIVERSITY PRESS, *Broad & Oxford Sts., Philadelphia, Pa. 19122. Tel. (215) 787-8787. Free 28- to 32-page catalogue issued twice a year.*

This press publishes "books that speak boldly and informatively to the condition of American society" in the fields of American history, women's studies, medical sociology, labor history, social policy, and ethnic studies.

TEXAS A. & M. UNIVERSITY PRESS, *Drawer C, College Station, Tex. 77843. Tel. (409) 845-1436. Free 28-page catalogue issued twice a year.*

The catalogue of books on the history and lore of Texas also includes titles from Rice University, Texas Christian University Press, and the Texas Historical Association.

TRANSACTION, *Rutgers University, New Brunswick, N.J. 08903. Tel. (201) 932-2280. Free 48- and 72-page catalogues: book catalogue is issued twice a year and journals catalogue is annual.*

Books and periodicals in the social sciences.

UNIVERSITY OF ALABAMA PRESS, *P.O. Box 2877, University, Ala. 35486. Tel. (205) 348-5180. Free catalogue issued twice a year.*

Political science, history, biography, literary history, philosophy and religion, Southern studies and folklore.

UNIVERSITY OF BRITISH COLUMBIA PRESS, *303-6344 Memorial Rd., Vancouver, B.C., Canada V6T 1W5. Tel. (604) 228-3259 or 228-5959. Free 16-page catalogue issued twice a year.*

Biography, history, architecture, anthropology, and other scholarly studies of Canada. Payment by check or money order. Delivery by Postal Service. Credit for returns made within a year, but they must be in mint condition.

*UNIVERSITY OF CALIFORNIA PRESS, *2120 Berkeley Way, Berkeley, Calif., 94720. Free 50-page catalogue.*

A recent sales catalogue offered 900 titles, at reduced prices. Some examples: The $16.95 *White Tribe of Africa*, David Harrison's examination of South Africa, at $10; the $150 facsimile edition of D. H. Lawrence's *Sons and Lovers* for $73.50; the $125 facsimile edition of Shakespeare's plays in quarto for $98.75.

UNIVERSITY OF CHICAGO PRESS, *5801 S. Ellis Ave., Chicago, Ill. 60637. Tel. (312) 962-7733. Two free annual catalogues—one on paperbacks and the other on books in the natural sciences.*

The paperback catalogue lists the books published by the press during the past year plus some from its backlist. A recent catalogue had Jacques Barzun's *Berlioz and His Century*, and the critical writings of Oscar Wilde, *The Artist as Critic*, edited by Walter Allen. The press's books in natural science are described in a catalogue called *The Diversity of Life*; some of the titles are very technical, but others are appropriate for nonexperts interested in the environment. From time to time the press also issues separate catalogues of books in political science, philosophy, women's studies, sociology of sports, art and architecture, homosexuality, medieval and renaissance studies, economics, and American studies.

UNIVERSITY OF GEORGIA PRESS, *Athens, Ga. 30602. Tel. (404) 542-2830. Free 16- to 31-page catalogue issued 2 or 3 times a year.*

There is a holiday flyer with books on Georgia and the South, but the main catalogue ranges more widely, mostly into literature and history. My attention was drawn to Edward A. Martin's *H. L. Mencken and the Debunkers*.

UNIVERSITY OF HAWAII PRESS, *2840 Kolowalu St., Honolulu, Hawaii 96822. Tel. (808) 948-8697. Free 15-page catalogue issued twice a year.*

Books about Asia and the Pacific, with emphasis on Hawaii and Japan.

UNIVERSITY OF ILLINOIS PRESS, *54 E. Gregory Dr., Champaign, Ill. 61820 (send orders to Box 1650, Hagerstown, Md. 21741). Tel. (301) 733-2700 or (800) 638-3030 (except in Maryland). Free subject catalogues.*

One recent catalogue dealt with books on Appalachia, another on the Civil War (Illinois does have an affinity to Lincoln) and music, mostly American (with an emphasis on country, western, and jazz), but also had a cassette of songs recorded by the New Hutchinson Family Singers that included 25 of the 1,500 songs referred to in Joyce's *Ulysses* and *Finnegans Wake*, which sounds like a marvelous idea, since one of them is the punning "There Is a Flower That Bloometh."

UNIVERSITY OF MICHIGAN PRESS, *839 Greene St., Ann Arbor, Mich. 48106. Tel. (313) 764-4392. Free 32-page catalogue.*

Unlike most other university presses, Michigan has not gone over to a flashy catalogue with photographs and copies of dust jackets to attract attention. Instead, there is simply a long list of the available scholarly books.

UNIVERSITY OF MISSOURI PRESS, *P.O. Box 7088, Columbia, Mo. 65205. Tel. (314) 882-7641 or (800) 638-3030. Free 20-page catalogue issued twice a year.*

Payment by check, money order, American Express, Visa, or Mastercard. Shipment by Postal Service or United Parcel. Refund or credit for returned books in good condition.

UNIVERSITY OF NEBRASKA PRESS, *901 N. 17th St., Lincoln, Neb. 68588. Tel. (402) 472-3581. Free semiannual general catalogue; also 6 to 10 subject catalogues, some as long as 30 pages, issued each year.*

A recent catalogue featured *Dust Bowl Descent* by Bill Ganzel with excellent photographs taken in the 1930's and 1970's. There is a lot about the Middle West, Indians, cowboys, and Nebraska. Payment by check, money order, Visa, or Mastercard. Shipment by Postal Service or United Parcel. Refund or credit on returned books.

UNIVERSITY OF NEW MEXICO PRESS, *220 Journalism Building, Albuquerque, N.M. 87131. Tel. (505) 277-4810. Free catalogues of up to 28 pages issued 3 times a year.*

Books on the Southwest. Payment by check, money order, Visa, or Mastercard. Shipment by Postal Service, United Parcel or, at extra cost, Federal Express. Refunds in cash or credit.

*UNIVERSITY OF NORTH CAROLINA PRESS, *P.O. Box 2288, Chapel Hill, N.C. 27414.*

Regional studies.

*UNIVERSITY OF NOTRE DAME PRESS, *Notre Dame, Ind. 46556. Tel. (219) 239-6346. Free 24-page catalogue issued twice a year.*

This is the largest Catholic university press in the world. The emphasis here is on religion, ethics, philosophy, the arts, and the humanities. One catalogue offers 20 percent discounts plus some specials. Payment by check, money order, Visa, or Mastercard. Delivery by Postal Service or United Parcel. Refunds for books returned in saleable condition with invoice.

UNIVERSITY OF PITTSBURGH PRESS, *127 N. Bellefield Ave., Pittsburgh, Pa. 15260. Tel. (412) 624-4110. Free 20-page catalogue issued twice a year.*

This press "exists to publish fine scholarly books that cannot make money, but it also publishes many popular books, especially about Pennsylvania," among them *A Guide to Historic Western Pennsylvania* and *Pickles and Pretzels: Pennsylvania's World of Food.*

UNIVERSITY OF SOUTH CAROLINA PRESS, *University of South Carolina, Columbia, S.C. 29208. Tel. (803) 777-5243. Free 30-page catalogue issued twice a year.*

Art, history, and the humanities, with special attention to South Carolina and the South. Some books—such as *Correct Mispronunciations of Some South Carolina Names* by Claude and Irene Neuffer—seem a bit too local for non-Carolinians, but others—like *Gone With The Wind as Book and Film* edited by Richard Harwell—have broader appeal. Payment by check, money order, Visa, or Mastercard. Delivery by Postal Service or United Parcel. Refunds for returned books.

UNIVERSITY OF TEXAS PRESS, *P.O. Box 7819, Austin, Tex. 78712. Tel. (512) 471-7233 or (800) 252-3206 (except in Texas). Free 36-page catalogue issued twice a year.*

This is the publisher of *Vision in Spring,* the collection of 14 love poems by William Faulkner that a reader is invited to study as a precursor of the works of fiction that followed. There is a wide selection in natural history, American history and biography, and the arts.

*UNIVERSITY OF WASHINGTON PRESS, *P.O. Box 85569, Seattle, Wash. 98145. Tel. (206) 543-8870. Free 20-page catalogue.*

Books in art, humanities, history, politics, social sciences, Asian studies and sciences, with special attention to the Pacific Northwest. Many museums are covered in the art books. A recent sale catalogue with 500 titles offered discounts of up to 90 percent.

UNIVERSITY OF WISCONSIN PRESS, *114 N. Murray St., Madison, Wis. 53715. Tel. (608) 262-4922 or 262-8782. Free 30- to 40-page catalogue issued twice a year.*

UNIVERSITY PRESS OF AMERICA, *4720 Boston Way, Lanham, Md. 20706. Tel. (301) 459-3366. Free subject catalogues in 17 areas issued each year.*

Catalogues issued in religion, psychology, philosphy, history, government, sociology, anthropology, cosmology, education, literature, language and linguistics, music, journalism and speech, economics, classics, Judaic studies, business, math, science, and minority and women's rights. Texts and scholarly works.

UNIVERSITY PRESS OF KENTUCKY, *102 Lafferty Hall, University of Kentucky, Lexington, Ky. 40506. Tel. (606) 257-2951. Free 16-page catalogue issued twice a year.*

Lots of attention to Appalachia and to Kentucky. One homegrown subject is discussed in *The Social History of Bourbon: an Unhurried Account of Our Star-Spangled American Drink* by Gerald Carson. Nonregional subjects of books from this press include Emily Dickinson, satires on women in Restoration England, Edmund Wilson, and iconography in medieval Spanish literature.

*YALE UNIVERSITY PRESS, *92A Yale Station, New Haven, Conn. 06520. Tel. (203) 432-4969. Free 40- to 50-page catalogue issued twice a year.*

Books in the arts, humanities, archaeology, history, political science, law, economics, psychology/psychiatry, science, and medicine. An additional catalogue I received offered discounts on more than 200 titles. Payment by check, money order, Visa, or Mastercard. Delivery by Postal Service or United Parcel. Refund or credit for returned books.

YANKEE PUBLISHING, *Main St., Dublin, N.H. 03444. Tel. (603) 563-8111, (800) 258-5466, or (800) 542-5405 (in New Hampshire). Free catalogue issued twice a year.*

Books related to New England. Payment by check, money order, Visa, or Mastercard. Delivery by Postal Service or United Parcel. Refunds for returned books.

Government Publications

CONSUMER INFORMATION CENTER, *Pueblo, Colo. 81009. Free 16-page catalogue issued 4 times a year.*

The General Services Administration, a U.S. Government agency, publishes books and pamphlets of such matters of interest to consumers as cars, children, employment, education, food, gardening, health, and housing. Payment by check or money order.

NATIONAL TECHNICAL INFORMATION SERVICE, *U.S. Department of Commerce, 5285 Port Royal Rd., Springfield, Va. 22161. Tel. (703) 487-4600. Free 20- to 42-page catalogue.*

This service gathers the specialized business, economic, scientific, and social information originated by federal agencies.

UNITED STATES GOVERNMENT PRINTING OFFICE, *New Books Catalogue, Superintendent of Documents, Washington, D.C. 20402. Tel. (202) 783-3238. Free 24-page catalogue issued 6 times a year.*

Some of the titles are very technical and of limited interest—like *Managing the Family Forest in the South* and *AC Voltage Calibrations for the .1 HZ to 10 HZ Frequency Range*—but there obviously is a need for such research, and this is perhaps the only way the research can get to the people. There is also lots of real government stuff—like census reports, court decisions, federal regulations. Payment by check, money order, Visa, or Mastercard. Delivery by Postal Service or United Parcel.

UNITED STATES GOVERNMENT PRINTING OFFICE, *New Catalogue, P.O. Box 37000, Washington, D.C. Free catalogue.*

This is a catalogue of the Government's 1,000 "best sellers," including *The Space Shuttle at Work, Starting a Business, U.S. Postage Stamps,* and *National Parks Guide and Map.* I would imagine that the same purchase and shipment rules as above apply.

Foreign Books, Foreign Language and Culture, Travel Guides

BIRKHAUSER BOSTON, *P.O. Box 2007, 380 Green St., Cambridge, Mass. 02139. Tel. (617) 876-2335 (for inquiries) or (617) 576-6638 (for orders). Free 40-page catalogue issued twice a year.*

This is the American affiliate of the German-language publisher Birkhauser Basel. The principal offerings are English-language books on science, mathematics, computer science, engineering, architecture, and the like. A catalogue is to be issued combining the English and German books. Birkhauser Boston also offers a catalogue for the German publisher Suhrkamp/Insel, which has books in the arts and humanities. Finally, in something unrelated to German, the firm has a new catalogue offering books and software for computers.

BRITISH BOOK SOURCE, *P.O. Box 6493, New York, N.Y. 10128. Tel. (212) 410-0448. Free catalogue issued twice a year.*

This is a specialist in books from and about Britain. There are novels, biography, travel, art, children's, reference, and cook books.

FRENCH & SPANISH BOOK CORP., *115 Fifth Ave., New York, N.Y. 10003. Tel. (212) 673-7400. Catalogues costs $2.95.*

The company, also known as the Dictionary Store and the Librairie de France, issues catalogues on French and Spanish books and a catalogue on dictionaries in all languages and subjects.

THE GOOD BOOK GUIDE, *91 Great Russell St., London WC1V 3PS, England. Tel. (01) 580-8466. The 40-page catalogues issued 5 times a year costs $15 for all 5 issues.*

The guide independently selects and recommends books published throughout Britain. It has received the Queen's Award for Export Achievement for having made British books available worldwide. Payment by check, money order, American Express, Visa, Mastercard, Diners Club, or Access. Delivery by Postal Service, United Parcel, or airmail. Returns accepted only if goods are damaged or faulty; refund, credit, or replacement.

ISBS INC. *(International Specialized Book Services), P.O. Box 1632, Beaverton, Ore. 97075. Tel. (503) 292-2606 or (800) 547-7734 (except in Oregon). Free 4- to 8-page catalogue issued 4 or 5 times a year.*

Foreign books, mainly from Australia, New Zealand, and the Orient, on a variety of subjects including science, medicine, and fishing. One recent catalogue was on gardening and another, more specialized, on books dealing with horticulture. Payment by check, money order, Visa, or Mastercard. Delivery by United Parcel. Refund or credit for books returned within 30 days.

HUGH MACPHERSON (SCOTLAND) LTD. *Books on Scotland and its people. See listing under* Men's Clothing.

DAVID MORGAN. *Books on Wales, in Welsh and in English. See listing under* Men's and Women's Clothing.

MOTILAL BOOKS (U.K.) LTD., *52 Crown Rd., Wheatley, Oxford, OX9 1UL, England. Tel. Wheatley 3478. Free 6- to 30- page catalogue issued 6 times a year.*

This is a mail-order distributor of books on Indology, Indian history, yoga, and philosophy. Payment by check or money order. Delivery by Postal Service, air freight, or accelerated surface post. No returns.

NOMADIC BOOKS, *P.O. Box 454, Athens, Ga. 30603. Tel. (404) 546-1353. Free 24-page catalogue issued twice a year.*

This concern offers "perhaps the widest selection of unusual and budget guidebooks for the whole world, a variety that exceeds even most large-city bookstores." How's this for a descriptive title: *Africa on the Cheap?* Or *West Asia on a Shoestring?* Also available is the excellent Harvard Student Agencies' series of "Let's Go" books. Payment by check or money order. Delivery by Postal Service. Refund or credit on returns within 15 days.

OLD COUNTRY IMPORTS, *Irish books. See listing under* Fine and Unusual Gifts.

RASHID SALES COMPANY. *Arabic books and dictionaries. See listing under* Records, Audio Tapes, and Compact Disks.

SPEEDIMPEX USA, *45-45 39th St., Long Island City, N.Y. 11104. Tel. (718) 392-7477. Free annual catalogue.*

This is a catalogue of Italian books. The 220-page issue I received has hundreds of books, most of them in Italian, on literature, humor, history, biography, music, travel, photography, cooking, and lots more. Also available are video cassettes of Italian movies with some not-bad actors: Claudia Cardinale, Sophia Loren, Marcello Mastroianni, Anna Magnani. Payment by check or money order. Delivery by Postal Service or United Parcel. Books not returnable unless defective or damaged in shipment.

Magazines

*AMERICAN EDUCATIONAL SERVICE, *419 Lentz Court, Lansing, Mich. 48917. Tel. (517) 371-4618. Free 12-page catalogue issued twice a year.*

Sharp discounts are offered on 200 magazines. This service is open only to students and educators.

PUBLISHERS CENTRAL BUREAU, *1 Champion Avenue, Avenel, N.J. 07001. Tel. (201) 382-7600. (See also this listing under* General Booksellers).

From time to time, this company issues free catalogues offering subscriptions to popular magazines (including some specialty magazines), some at discount. Catalogue listings vary each time. In the recent past, Publishers Central Bureau has offered subscriptions to such magazines as *American Health, Cuisine, Field & Stream, Fortune, Home Viewer, Organic Gardening, Parents, Popular Science, Prevention, Time, World Press Review,* and *Young Miss,* among others.

Comics

BUD PLANT INC., *P.O. Box 1886, Grass Valley, Calif. 95945. Tel. (916) 273-9588 or (800) 824-8532 (except in California, Hawaii, and Alaska). Quarterly 52-page catalogue costs $1.*

Comic books to recall a youth misspent with Superman hidden inside geography books in school. Payment by check, money order, Visa, or Mastercard. Shipment by Postal Service, United Parcel, or Federal Express. Refund or credit for purchases damaged in shipment, but contact company first.

*COMIC COLLECTOR SHOP, *73 E. San Fernando, San Jose, Calif. 95113. Tel. (408) 287-2254. Free brochure issued 6 to 12 times a year, but send self-addressed stamped envelope.*

Old and new, underground and, presumably, above-ground, comics. Ten percent discount on orders over $30. No returns unless wrong comics sent, in which case refund or credit given.

EDUCOMICS, *Box 40246, San Francisco, Calif. 94140. Tel. (415) 647-6423. Brochure.*

This company publishes comic books with social-awareness themes, such as the dangers of nuclear war, and was the first American company to reprint *I Saw It*, a comic book by a survivor of the atomic attack on Hiroshima, Keiji Nakazawa. Payment by check or money order. Shipment by Postal Service or United Parcel. Purchases may be returned at any time, if in resaleable condition, for refund or credit, less a 10 percent reshelving fee.

GRAND BOOK INC., *659 Grand St., Brooklyn, N.Y. 11211. Tel. (718) 384-4089. The 16-page catalogue costs $1.*

This is a catalogue for the aficionado: no drawings, but column after column of tiny print (smaller than phone book type) of available comic books and their prices (*Babe Ruth Sports*, Nos. 4, 5 and 7, are $10 each). I think I threw away a fortune as a child.

KRUPP DISTRIBUTION CO., *Kitchen Sink Comix, 2 Swamp Rd., Princeton, Wis. 54968. Tel. (414) 295-6922. Free catalogue.*

The comic book art of Will Eisner, plus other books such as *Gay Comix*, *Bizarre Sex*, and Milton Caniff's *Steve Canyon*. Payment by check, money order, Visa, Mastercard, Eurocard, or foreign bank draft. Shipment by Postal Service, United Parcel, or sea or air freight. Defective copies can be returned for credit or replacement.

RIP OFF PRESS, *P.O. Box 14158, San Francisco, Calif. 94114. Tel. (415) 863-5359. The 32-page catalogue issued 2 to 4 times a year, 50 cents.*

This supplier of comics or, as they put it, "comix," has been "serving a distinguished reading public with the finest in underground humor since 1969." The dirty comic books are clearly labeled (*Bizarre Sex*, *Young Lust*) as are those on homosexuals. Payment by check, money order, Visa, or Mastercard. Delivery by Postal Service or United Parcel. Refund or credit on comix (oops, comics) returned within 5 days of receipt.

SMITHSONIAN INSTITUTION PRESS, *Books about comics. See listing under Selected University, Scholarly, and Small Presses, above.*

❖ 21 Gifts

Quite clearly, just about anything in this book could make a nice gift, so the existence of this chapter should not deter consideration of gift purchases from catalogues found elsewhere. For example, the Jewelry section and the Food chapter obviously would provide good gift ideas, and the reader ought to consider gifts of books, art, antiques and other items that can be found by dipping into one chapter or another.

A few specialists in gifts deserve special attention—Fortunoff's and Horchows. Also included here are museums and botanical gardens, which are another source of especially nice gifts.

Fine and Unusual Gifts

ACCENTS, *P.O. Box 683, Springfield, Va. 22153. Tel. (703) 455-1140. Free annual catalogue.*

"Gifts of Distinction." Imported jewelry, like a Yemenite necklace and earrings set, a Russian tea urn, and a Turkish coffee set.

ARTISAN GALLERIES, *4120 Main St., Dallas, Tex. 75226. Tel. (214) 827-2191. Free 32- to 40-page catalogue issued twice a year.*

This company is a source of unusual gift and collectors items. The backbone of its line consists of Panel Thistle glass pieces made from molds 80 to 100 years old. Payment by check, money order, American Express, Visa, or Mastercard. Shipment by Postal Service or United Parcel. Purchases may be returned for refund or credit.

H. L. BARNETT, *Brunswick House, Torridge Hill, Bideford, Devon, EX39 2BB, England. Free annual 72-page catalogue.*

My family has been using this company for several years to send Christmas gifts to friends in England. It saves on shipping costs, and you don't have to worry about the gifts getting there on time. We send mostly wine, but there are also gifts of glassware, china, crystal, leather, perfume, clothing, and the like and there is a large selection of things for children. Payment by check, money order, American Express, Visa, Mastercard, Diners Club, Access, Barclaycard, Eurocard, or Chargex.

BOKRA TRADING CO., *P.O. Box 467428, Atlanta, Ga. 30346. Tel. (404) 992-9212. Free annual 20-page catalogue.*

Imported items from Egypt, primarily silver charms and cartouches and 18-karat gold charms, cartouches, and rings.

BOLIND INC., *P.O. Box 9751, Boulder, Colo. 80301. Tel. (303) 443-3142. Semiannual 80-page catalogue costs $1.*

The specialty here is personalized gifts, such as a set of brown bags that say whose lunch is inside. There are also personalized coffee mugs, children's clothes racks, and even dollar bills with your face instead of George Washington's. Payment by check, money order, Visa, or Mastercard. Shipment by Postal Service or United Parcel. If any mistakes are made on personalized items, they may be returned for exchange. Nonpersonalized items may be returned within 10 days for refund.

HARRIET CARTER GIFTS, *North Wales, Pa. 19455. Tel. (215) 368-3367. Free 112- to 120-page catalogue issued 5 times a year.*

A large assortment of gift suggestions, including a personalized umbrella that folds up so small that it will fit in a purse or pocket.

CASH & CO. LTD., *P.O. Box 47, St. Patricks St., Cork, Ireland. Tel. 353-21-964411. Semiannual 48- to 60-page catalogue costs $2.*

Sweaters, shawls, capes, jackets, skirts, and other woolen goods, plus jewelry, porcelain, dinnerware by Royal Worcester and Wedgwood, and crystal by Waterford. Prices are said to be ⅓ below normal American retail levels. Payment by check, money order, American Express, Visa, or Mastercard. Delivery by Special Air Lift from Ireland. Purchases may be returned for refund within 30 days.

†*CHASE COLLECTION, *1120 Mayberry Lane, State College, Pa. 16801. Tel. (814) 238-6332. Semiannual 12-page catalogue costs $1.*

Solid wood cooking and serving accessories, including cutting boards, lazy Susans, trays and giftware, plus such contemporary furniture as chairs, tables, and magazine racks, and lamps. The company says its prices are discounted. Payment by check, money order, American Express, Visa, or Mastercard. Shipment by Postal Service, United Parcel, or freight. Refunds for purchases returned within 1 month.

*CHERING SERVICES INC. & CHERING METALS CLUB INC., *5799 Yonge St., Suite 1103, Willowdale, Ont., Canada M2M 3V3. Tel. (416) 222-4499. Brochure.*

"The world's only nonprofit dealer in gold and silver." This discount company says no other dealer can match its prices. Payment by check, money order, Visa, or Mastercard. There are no returns.

GAYLE CHASIN'S PERSONALIZED GIFTS, *12853 Castleton, St. Louis, Mo. 63141. Tel. (314) 576-5866. Free annual 26-page catalogue.*

Payment by check or money order. Shipment by Postal Service or United Parcel. No returns on items unless damaged in shipment.

CLYMER'S OF BUCKS COUNTY, *Canal St., Nashua, N.H. 03061. Tel. (800) 258-1791 (except in New Hampshire) or (603) 882-9530 (in New Hampshire). Free 48-page catalogue.*

I always think of Bucks County, Pennsylvania, when I see the words "Bucks County." In any event, this company says it ranges wide to find gift items made by craftspeople in all parts of the country. One item I liked in a recent catalogue is an 11 ½" casting of a lovestruck frog. Payment by check, money order, American Express, Visa, or Mastercard. Except for personalized items, purchases may be returned within 15 days for refund, credit, or exchange.

*DEEPAK'S ROKJEMPERL PRODUCTS, *61 10th Khetwadi Lane, Bombay 400 004, India. Tel. 388031. Annual catalogue costs $1.*

Discount prices on precious and semi-precious gemstones and bead necklaces. Also available are handicrafts in bone, sandalwood, rosewood, buffalo horn, brass, and silver filigree. Payment by money order, cashier's check, or certified check. Shipment by Postal Service or air/sea parcel post. Purchases may be returned, if unaltered, within a month of receipt for exchange.

WALTER DRAKE & SONS, *Drake Building, Colorado Springs, Colo. 80940. Tel. (303) 596-3854. Free 96-page catalogue.*

Hundreds of items for gifts and personal use.

THE EBURY COLLECTION, *115 Powdermill Rd., P.O. Box 65, Maynard, Mass. 01754. Tel. (617) 897-8010. Free 24- to 32-page catalogue issued 4 times a year.*

Here are gifts from a London-based company that has suppliers in both Britain and on the Continent. There is a nice reproduction of a 12th-century chess set from the Isle of Lewis, the original of which was discovered in 1831. Many of the originals on which the copies are based are in the British

Museum. (The London address is 36 Ebury St., Belgravia, London, SW1, England.)

ELIZABETH EDGE STUDIOS, *5060 W. Lake Rd., Canandaigua, N.Y. 14424. Tel. (716) 396-2656. Free 8-page catalogue.*

Here are modern-day reproductions of century-old objects, such as cast iron toys (animals, war scenes, the 1892 World's Fair) and banks that are activated when a coin is deposited. Payment by check, money order, Visa, or Mastercard. Shipment by Postal Service or United Parcel. Purchases may be returned within 10 days for refund.

FALLERS, *Mervue, Galway, Ireland. Tel. 091-61226. The 56-page catalogue costs $2.*

This company, founded in 1879, offers crystal, silver, china, porcelain, linen, and Aran sweaters, among other things. Payment by check, American Express, Visa, or Mastercard. Delivery by Special Air Lift Service. Purchases may be returned, after writing to Fallers, for refund.

FAVORITE THINGS, *102 Cleaveland Rd., Pleasant Hill, Calif. 94523. No catalogue.*

This company has a small line of high-quality gifts, such as a curious square teapot of the kind formerly used on the liner Queen Mary. Payment by check or money order. Shipment by United Parcel. Purchases may be returned for refund.

*FORTUNOFF, *P.O. Box 1550, Westbury, N.Y. 11590. Tel. (516) 294-3300, (212) 343-8787, or (800) 223-2326 (except in New York State). Semiannual 12- to 24-page catalogue costs $1.*

While this company does not describe itself as a discount store, it offers fine jewelry, silverware, leather goods, and table linens at lower than regular retail prices. Payment by check, money order, American Express, Visa, Mastercard, Diners Club, or Fortunoff charge. Delivery by Postal Service or United Parcel. Purchases may be returned within 10 days for refund or exchange, but special order and customized merchandise are not returnable.

†GEARY'S, *351 N. Beverly Dr., Beverly Hills, Calif. 90210. Tel. (213) 273-4741, (800) 252-0013 (in California outside the 213 area code) or (800) 421-0566 (except in California, Alaska, and Hawaii). Quarterly 8-page catalogue costs $1.*

Crystal from Lalique and Baccarat, sterling silver by Georg Jensen and Gorham, dinnerware by Wedgwood, plus many other items for the dining room and gifts for just about every place. Payment by check, money order, American Express, Visa, or Mastercard. Shipment by Postal Service or United Parcel. Refunds and credits granted.

GIGGLETREE, *Winterbrook Way, Meredith, N.H. 03253. Tel. (603) 279-7081. Free 80- to 100-page catalogue issued twice a year.*

This catalogue is subtitled "A Catalogue of Delights," and some of the things do have that air about them, like a terra cotta rabbit on the cover of a recent issue. The cookware section is called "Gigglegourmet," the gardening section "Giggleblooms," and so on.

GIMBEL & SONS COUNTRY STORE, *P.O. Box 57, 36 Commercial St., Boothbay Harbor, Me. 04538. Tel. (207) 633-5088. Free annual 32-page catalogue.*

You may have read about the lawsuit in which the Gimbels department store tried to keep this store from using the Gimbel name. The settlement has resulted in this catalogue noting on the cover that it is not associated with the department store. The store sells what it calls "general merchandise" but specializes in thimbles (with a catalogue listing 500!) and dolls.

†**GUMPS,** *250 Post St., San Francisco, Calif. 94108. Tel. (800) 227-4512 (except in California, Alaska, and Hawaii); (800) 652-1662 (in California); 982-1616, ext. 420 (in San Francisco); or (800) 227-3062 (in Alaska and Hawaii). Free 36-page catalogue.*

This company has a very nice line of merchandise. There are paintings on silk panels, ancient porcelain, jade jewelry, such modern pieces as crystal decanters and wine glasses, Wedgwood, and silver-plated flatware.

HAMPSHIRE PEWTER CO., *P.O. Box 1570, Wolfeboro, N.H. 03894. Tel. (603) 569-4944. Semiannual 14-page catalogue costs $2.*

The medium is an old one and some of the products here are reproductions, but some of the designs of this company have an up-to-date look about them, particularly a handsome bud vase. Payment by check, money order, Visa, or Mastercard. Shipment by United Parcel. Purchases may be returned within 20 days for refund or credit.

THE HORCHOW COLLECTION, *P.O. Box 819066, Dallas, Tex. 75381. Tel. (214) 980-4040 (in Dallas),*

(800) 527-0303 (elsewhere except in Texas), or (800) 442-5806 (in Texas). The 32-page catalogue issued 9 times a year costs $3.

Splendid merchandise. Clothing, accessories, fine porcelain objects.

HOUSE OF TYROL, *P.O. Box 909, Gateway Plaza, Cleveland, Ga. 30528. Tel. (404) 865-5115 or (800) 241-5404 (except in Georgia). Quarterly 40-page catalogue costs $1.*

"Shop the Alps from Your Home," this catalogue suggests. There are lots of things here that I would call doodads—a Munich spoon, an Oktoberfest thimble, a beer glass in the shape of a shoe, and a lot of porcelain objects that might be appreciated by collectors. Payment by check, money order, American Express, Visa, Mastercard, Diners Club, or Carte Blanche. Shipment by Postal Service or United Parcel. Purchases may be returned within 14 days for refund or credit.

†**KAPLAN'S-BEN HUR,** *P.O. Box 7989, Houston, Tex. 77270. Tel. (713) 861-2121. Semiannual 48-page catalogue costs $1.*

This company maintains a bridal registry and offers many wedding gifts, such as Haviland china, porcelain, and crystal. Payment by check, money order, American Express, Visa, or Mastercard. Shipment by United Parcel. Purchases may be returned within a "reasonable" time for refund or credit.

CHARLES KEATH LIMITED, *4030 Pleasantville Rd., NE, Atlanta, Ga. 30340. Tel. (404) 449-3100 or (800) 241-1122 (except in Georgia). Free 36-page catalogue issued 12 times a year.*

Among the unusual items here are a foot-long wood and brass cricket, a set of bronze steak knives, silk flowers, wooden carved cattails in an Italian terracotta vase, a brass mailbox, and a cast iron duck to be used as a doorstop. Among the less esoteric things are women's clothing, rugs, lamps, and clocks.

†LITTLE SWITZERLAND, *P.O. Box 887, Charlotte Amalie, St. Thomas, U. S. Virgin Islands 00801. Free 32-page catalogue.*

There are jewelry, watches (including Rolex), china (including Royal Copenhagen), crystal (including Baccarat and Rosenthal), and other objects. Payment by check, American Express, Visa, Mastercard, or Diners Club. Delivery by Postal Service.

*LONG ISLAND GIFT CENTER, *945 Hempstead Turnpike, Franklin Square, N.Y. 11010. Tel. (516) 354-3232. Brochure costs 50 cents.*

This company says it offers a 25 percent discount on all items. Among the main products are desk pen sets.

CAROLE MARTIN, *49 Westmore Dr., Rexdale, Ont., Canada M9V 4M3. Tel. (514) 687-5505. Free 48- to 64-page catalogue issued twice a year.*

Nice gifts for the kitchen, dining room, bath, and the home generally. Payment by check, money order, Visa, or Mastercard. Shipment by Postal Service. Purchases may be returned within a year for refund.

NASCO'S COUNTRY COLLECTION, *901 Janesville Ave., Fort Atkinson, Wis. 53538. Tel. (800) 558-9595. The 32-page catalogue costs $1.*

How about a full-size fiberglass Holstein cow standing on your lawn? This company has it. It also has some charming prints of a long-gone agricultural America that will never return except in pictures like these. There are many other delightful things for gifts or personal use. Payment by check, money order, American Express, Visa, or Mastercard. Shipment by Postal Service or United Parcel. Purchases may be returned for refund within 30 days.

OLD COUNTRY IMPORTS, *P.O. Box 35030, Chicago, Ill. 60635. Tel. (312) 889-7533 or (800) 621-7442. Free 24-page catalogue.*

The old country to which reference is made is Ireland, and the imports include Aran sweaters, china, glassware, and Irish books and records. Payment by check, money order, Visa, or Mastercard. Shipment by United Parcel. Purchases may be returned for refund.

*THE OLD HOUSE, *298 Head of the Bay Rd., Buzzards Bay, Mass. 02532. Tel. (617) 759-4942. Annual 16-page catalogue costs 50 cents.*

Discount prices on such things as note paper, linen towels, and ceramic tile. Payment by check, money order, Visa, or Mastercard. Shipment by Postal Service. Purchases may be returned within 10 days for refund.

THE PADDLE WHEEL SHIP, *P.O. Box 12429, St. Louis, Mo. 63132. Tel. (314) 993-9068 or (800) 325-4268 (except in Missouri). The 40-page catalogue issued twice a year costs $1.*

"Gifts Inspired by the Classic South." More specifically, the gifts are intended to recall the riverboats of the Old South. There are copies of brass lamps, watches, plantation owners' hats for men and camisole tops for women.

THE PARAGON GIFTS, *Tom Harvey Rd., Westerly, R.I. 02891. Tel. (401) 596-0134. Free 68-page catalogue issued 4 times a year.*

Among the many gift items are several with an ocean motif. including shells printed on pillows and a nice handbag with a scallop shell quilted onto it.

POTPOURRI, *204 Worcester St., Wellesley, Mass. 02181. Tel. (617) 237-7755 or (800) 225-4127 (except in Massachusetts). Free 64-page catalogue.*

Here is a wide range of gifts, with one catalogue listing a book on the art of Claude Monet, a silk dress, and a tea kettle. Payment by check, money order, American Express, Visa, or Mastercard. Purchases, if not used and if not personalized, may be returned within 2 weeks for refund.

*ROSS-SIMONS OF WARWICK, *136 Lambert Lind Highway, Warwick, R.I. 02886. Tel. (401) 738-6700 or (800) 556-7376 (except in Rhode Island). Semiannual 40-page catalogue costs $1.*

Discounts of 20 to 40 percent on jewelry, 30 to 70 percent on Gorham sterling, and 25 to 40 percent on Royal Doulton china. Payment by check, money order, American Express, Visa, Mastercard, Diners Club, or Carte Blanche. Shipment by Postal Service or United Parcel. Purchases may be returned within 3 weeks for refund or credit.

*SAMARTH GEM STONES, *P.O. Box 6057, Colaba, Bombay, 400 005, India. Tel. 234339. Annual price list costs $1.*

Precious and semi-precious gemstones from India and elsewhere, fashioned into necklaces, carvings, and cabochons. Discounts of 10 to 40 percent. Payment by bank draft, international money order, certified check, or letter of credit. Shipment by Postal Service. Purchases may be returned within 15 days of receipt for credit.

SAXKJAERS, *53, Kobmagergade, 1150 Copenhagen K, Denmark. Tel. 1-110777. Free 4-page catalogue issued twice a year.*

The emphasis here is on gifts made of porcelain, pottery, and glass. There are dolls, crystal paperweights, and fine porcelain dinnerware. Payment by check or money order. Shipment by Postal Service. Purchases may be returned at any time for refund.

*NAT SCHWARTZ & CO., *549 Broadway, Bayonne, N.J. 07002. Tel. (201) 437-4443 or (800) 526-1440 (except in New Jersey). Free annual 48-page catalogue.*

The company offers large discounts on sterling silver, china, crystal, and gifts; for example, 12 five-piece place settings of Wedgwood Runnymede Blue for $1,404, compared with the $2,540 list price. Payment by check, money order, Visa, Mastercard, or wire transfer. Shipment by United Parcel. Purchases may be returned, if unused, within 30 days for refund.

SHANNON MAIL ORDER, *Shannon Free Airport, Ireland. Tel. (061) 62610. Semiannual 56-page catalogue costs $1.*

China, Irish crystal (including Waterford), pottery, Royal Doulton figurines, Wedgwood, and Limoge. Other products available include lace and Irish linen, jewelry, Aran sweaters and skirts, and perfume. Payment by check, money order, American Express, Visa, or Mastercard. Shipment by Postal Service. Purchases may be returned within one month of receipt for refund or credit.

*THE SHOPPERS' PARADISE, *Candlelight Associates, 61 Kimberley Rd., 6th Floor, Tsimshatsui, Hong Kong. Free 72-page catalogue.*

The prices are "much lower than from other countries" for cloisonné and lacquerware, hand-painted porcelain, Oriental rugs, bedding, table linens, decorated furniture, teak clocks and furniture, jade and ivory carvings, decorated women's handbags, and gold jewelry. Payment by check, international money order, or bank draft. Shipment by Postal Service or ocean freight. Purchases may be returned for refund or exchange.

THE SILVERS, *1201 Boston Post Rd., Milford, Conn. 06460. Tel. (203) 874-3881 or (800) 243-9280. Free 32-page catalogue costs $2.*

Many fine gifts, including a tea cart, framed reproductions of manuscripts by Beethoven, Bach, Chopin and Mozart, electronic gadgets, and things for children (which is not to suggest that the foregoing aren't o.k. for children, too).

*ALBERT S. SMYTH CO., *25 W. Aykesbury Rd., Timonium, Md. 21093. Tel. (301) 561-2416 or (800) 638-3333 (except in Baltimore). The 24-page catalogue issued 2 to 4 times a year costs $1.*

This company offers discounts of 20 to 45 percent off the price of jewelry, giftware, clocks, watches, china, and crystal. Payment by check, money order, American Express, Visa, Mastercard, Diners Club, Carte Blanche, or Choice. Shipment by United Parcel. Purchases may be returned within 30 days for refund or credit.

SPENCER GIFTS, *433 Spencer Building, Atlantic City, N.J. 08411. Tel. (609) 645-3300. Free 96-page catalogue.*

Novelty items.

*STECHER'S LIMITED, *27 Frederick St., Port of Spain, Trinidad, West Indies. Tel. (62) 32585. Brochures.*

This company offers goods at prices 25 to 40 percent below U.S. prices. The products include watches from Switzerland; china and porcelain from England, Denmark, Germany, and France; and crystal, leatherware, and jewelry from around the world. Payment by check or money order. Shipment by Postal Service or air freight. Refund or replacement of goods if Stecher's is at fault.

TREVOR THOMAS OF NEW ZEALAND, *Box 250 Moab, Utah 84532. Tel. (800) 321-2413 (except in Utah) or (800) 321-3251 (in Utah). Brochure.*

All manner of things from New Zealand. There are wool jerseys, cardigans and comforters, fruit, books, assorted foods, and stamps. Payment by check, money order, American Express, Visa, or Mastercard. Purchases may be returned for refund at any time, although there is a 30-day limit on the return of tapes.

TRIFLES, *P.O. Box 344432, Dallas, Tex. 75234. Tel. (800) 527-0277 (except in Texas), (800) 442-5801 (in Texas), or 233-0643 (in Dallas). Free 32-page catalogue.*

Attractive dresses for lounging or partying, casual clothing for men, plus housewares and other items. Payment by check, money order, American Express, Visa, or Mastercard. Purchases, other than personalized or custom orders, may be returned within 30 days for refund.

VALERIE'S CHOICE, *Linwood Square, Linwood, N.J. 08221. Tel. (800) 222-0053 (except in New Jersey) or (800) 222-0252 (in New Jersey). Free 80-page catalogue.*

Lots of doodads and other gift items.

LILLIAN VERNON, *510 S. Fulton Ave., Mount Vernon, N.Y. 10550. Tel. (914) 576-6300. The 152-page catalogue issued 7 times a year, costs $1.*

This is one of those catalogues that seems to have 1 or 2 items in every conceivable category, which makes it a good candidate for this section because you can probably solve any gift problem here. Pay-ment by check, American Express, Visa, Mastercard, Diners Club, or Carte Blanche. Shipment by Postal Service or United Parcel. Refund or credit on unsatisfactory merchandise.

*WINDSOR GIFT SHOP, *233 Main St., Madison, N.J. 07940. Tel. (201) 377-7273 or (800) 631-9393. Free 8-page catalogue.*

This shop has a bridal registry for silver, china, and crystal and offers discount prices.

See also *Crafts to Buy*.

Gifts for Nature Lovers

THE NATURE CO., *P.O. Box 7137, Berkeley, Calif. 94707. Tel. (415) 524-8340 or (800) 227-1114. Free 36-page catalogue issued twice a year.*

Very nice gifts with a nature theme: a fossil in a sandstone block, an Ansel Adams book of photographs, stuffed penguins made out of synthetic "fur." Payment by check, American Express, Visa, or Mastercard. Shipment by Postal Service or United Parcel. Purchases may be returned for refund within 90 days.

WILD ANIMAL TRACKS, *Campbell Lake, Box 45, Little Fort, B.C., Canada V0E 2C0. Tel. (604) 677-4308. Brochure.*

Joan Winter, a naturalist, searches out wild animal tracks and then reproduces casts of them and sells them as ornamentation. Payment by money order. Shipment by

Postal Service. Purchases may be returned for refund.

WILD WINGS, *Lake City, Minn. 55041. Tel. (612) 345-5355. Semiannual 64-page catalogue costs $2.*

Birds in wood, china, and crystal, on plates and lamps, as stuffed toys, carvings and decoys. There are bird and other wildlife prints, pictures of cowboys in action, and Indian portraits, and also a list of books on similar subjects. This is a large, colorful catalogue of gifts for people who like the outdoors.

WILD WOOD GALLERY, *P.O. Box 300, 4001 S. Salina St., Syracuse, N.Y. 13205. Tel. (315) 469-5078 or (800) 535-6600 (except in New York State). The 16- or 32-page catalogue issued 3 times a year costs $1.*

This company offers a large selection of decorating accessories and gifts, a lot of them with wildlife themes, such as wildflower prints, hand-carved duck decoys, and ceramic pieces. Payment by check, money order, American Express, Visa, or Mastercard. Shipment by Postal Service or United Parcel. Purchases may be returned within 60 days for refund.

Museum, Botanic Garden, and Public Radio Gift Catalogues

---

*AMERICAN MUSEUM OF NATURAL HISTORY, *Central Park West at 79th St., New York, N.Y. 10024. Tel. (212) 873-1300 or (800) 247-5470 (except in Iowa). Free 16-page book catalogue issued 2 or 3 times a year.*

Forty titles in anthropology, archae-ology, evolution, ecology, wildlife art and photography, and paleontology. Discounts range from 10 to 50 percent off publishers' prices.

BRITISH MUSEUM, *Publications Dept., 46 Bloomsbury St., London, WC1B 3QQ, England. Tel. (01) 323-1234. Free 24-page gift shop catalogue issued approximately every 2 years.*

This is one of the 3 or 4 leading museums in the world, and it sells reproductions of sculpture and jewelry in its collections. "When a British Museum replica is created, it is either molded or modeled from the original under stringent museum supervision." The sculptures include the heads of Sophocles and Socrates, and the jewelry includes copies of ancient Greek, Egyptian, Persian, and Byzantine necklaces, rings, pendants, and bracelets. Payment by check, money order, American Express, Visa, Mastercard, Access, or Eurocard. Shipment by Postal Service.

CENTER FOR ENVIRONMENTAL EDUCATION, *624 Ninth St., N.W., Washington, D.C. 20001. Tel. (202) 737-3600 or (800) 972-1000 (except in the District of Columbia metropolitan area). Free 32-page Whale Gifts Catalogue issued 4 times a year.*

This catalogue offer gifts intended to raise funds and increase support for the center's activities, which are devoted to the protection of the marine environment and its inhabitants—whales, seals, and sea turtles being among the species most threatened these days. The items available include calendars, jewelry, ersatz scrimshaw, and T-shirts.

COLONIAL WILLIAMSBURG FOUNDATION, *P.O. Box CH, Williamsburg, Va. 23187. Tel. (804) 229-1000 (ext. 5493) or (800) 446-9240 (except in Virginia, Alaska, and Hawaii). The 40-page fall catalogue and the 24-page spring issue cost $2.*

This is a marvelous place that recreates life in Colonial times. My family once spent a Thanksgiving here. Many of the products made by the craftspeople who work in the village are available for sale; it's top quality stuff. Payment by check, American Express, Visa, or Mastercard. Shipment by United Parcel. Purchases may be returned within 60 days for refund.

FOLGER SHAKESPEARE LIBRARY, *201 E. Capitol St., S.E., Washington, D.C. 20003. Tel. (202) 546-2626. Semiannual 16- to 48-page catalogue costs $2.*

As noted above, this is one of my favorite places in Washington. We enjoy the plays in the Folger Shakespeare Theater; my family once bought me a tour of the innards of the Library itself as a birthday present, and we have bought many items in the gift shop to give to friends. There are, of course, numerous books by and about Shakespeare, histories and biographies relating to the Folger's specialty—the Elizabethan and renaissance ages—and music, drama, costumes, and novelties. Here's a T-shirt inscription for your running friends: "Jog On, Jog On," from *The Winter's Tale.*

HISTORIC CHARLESTON REPRODUCTIONS, *P.O. Box 622, 105 Broad St., Charleston, S.C. 29402. Tel. (803) 723-8392. The 80-page catalogue issued every 3 years, costs $6.50.*

If you tour the historic houses of Charleston, some of the furniture in this cata-

logue will be familiar to you. The catalogue offers reproductions of the furniture in the houses, and royalties from their sales go toward maintaining the houses. There are chairs, sofas, tables, desks, secretaries, bookcases, china, lamps, and a lot more.

LIBRARY OF CONGRESS, *Information Office, Box A, Washington, D.C. 20540. Free 36-page catalogue.*

This repository of the nation's intellectual heritage has a much broader than a lot of people realize. There is, for example, a series reproducing humorous cat drawings from 1926, suggesting that the current popularity of such caricatures is not unique, but rather a recollection. There are exceptional photographs tracing America's heritage, reproductions of antique maps, cowboy posters, and lots more. (For those planning a visit to Washington, here is a tourist tip: The Library of Congress and the Folger Shakespeare Library, which is just around the corner, are 2 of the most interesting places in Washington.)

METROPOLITAN MUSEUM OF ART, *Fifth Ave. & 82nd St., New York, N.Y. 10028 (the mail-order address is Metropolitan Museum of Art, Special Services Office, Middle Village, N.Y. 11381). Tel. (212) 879-5000 (for the museum) or (718) 758-8991 (for mail order). Catalogue issued 4 times a year costs $1; there is a 116-page Christmas catalogue and smaller spring and special subject (poster, children) catalogues.*

This is another of the world's leading museums, and it is a lot more accessible than the British Museum in London. The gift shop of America's greatest museum has quite a bit to offer, including some excellent books and posters; the art reproductions used for

Christmas cards are marvelous, and there are copies of other things in the Metropolitan's collection—sculpture, jewelry, silver, glass, and porcelain. Payment by check, money order, American Express, Visa, or Mastercard. Shipment by United Parcel, but Postal Service is used if customer specifies. Purchases may be returned within 45 days of shipment for refund or credit.

MINNESOTA PUBLIC RADIO, *45 E. Eighth St., St. Paul, Minn. 55101. Tel. (612) 221-1510. Free 16- to 24-page catalogue issued twice a year.*

The catalogue is called *Wireless,* and a lot of the pages feature gifts relating to Garrison Keillor and his program, "A Prairie Home Companion," that originates at Minnesota Public Radio and is broadcast throughout the country by the National Public Radio network. Revenues from catalogue sales go toward programming on Minnesota Public Radio. The gifts available feature items both related and unrelated to the radio program, one of the things in the latter category being Russell Baker's marvelous autobiography, *Growing Up.* Payment by check, money order, Visa or Mastercard. Shipment usually by United Parcel. Purchases may be returned for refund or credit.

MUSEUM OF FINE ARTS, BOSTON, *479 Huntington Ave., Boston, Mass. 02115. Tel. (617) 427-1111 or (800) 225-5592 (except in Massachusetts). Catalogue issued 2 or 3 times a year costs $1.*

Here are reproductions from one of America's oldest museums. There are silk scarves, jewelry, silver tea and coffee services, books, records, and posters.

MUSEUM OF MODERN ART, *11 W. 53rd St., New York, N.Y. 10102. Tel. (212) 956-7262. Free catalogue issued several times a year.*

Modern designs based on objects in the museum, including coffee and tea pots designed by Mori, tables, chairs, and flatware, plus posters, Christmas cards, books, toys, and games.

MYSTIC SEAPORT MUSEUM STORES, *Mystic, Conn. 06355. Tel. (203) 536-9688. Annual 36-page catalogue costs $1.*

Gifts and things with a nautical flavor.

NATIONAL GALLERY OF ART, *Publications Service, Washington, D.C. 20565. Brochure.*

Prints, posters, calendars, and books. Payment by check, money order, American Express, Visa, or Mastercard.

NATIONAL TRUST FOR HISTORIC PRESERVATION, *Preservation Shops, 1600 H St., N.W., Washington, D.C. 20006. Tel. (202) 673-4200. Brochure costs 50 cents.*

Gifts, ornaments, china services, and toys based on reproductions of early American articles. Payment by check, money order, American Express, Visa, or Mastercard. Shipment by United Parcel. Purchases may be returned within 30 days for refund.

NEW YORK BOTANICAL GARDEN, *Bronx, N.Y. 10458. Tel. (212) 220-8720. Free 24-page catalogue.*

Posters, tableware, gardening equipment, calendars, and books. Payment by check, money order, Visa, or Mastercard. Purchases may be returned for refund or credit as long as undamaged and unsoiled.

B. & O. RAILROAD MUSEUM, *Nostalgia Station, 901 W. Pratt St., Baltimore, Md. 21223. Tel. (301) 837-3625. The 24-page catalogue costs $1.50.*

"All aboard for a trip to yesterday." Authentic dining car china and flatware, and lots of things with the symbol of the Chessie system—the napping kitten.

SMITHSONIAN INSTITUTION, *P.O. Box 2456, Washington, D.C. 20013. Tel. (202) 357-1826 or (703) 455-1700. Several free gift catalogues issued each year.*

This is our nation's attic, and among the gifts available from the attic are copies of sculpture, prints, tablecloths, toy reproductions, books, and posters. There is also a separate marvelous catalogue of books and recordings published by the Smithsonian (see listing under *Selected University, Scholarly, and Small Presses*).

TEXTILE MUSEUM SHOP, *2320 S St., N.W., Washington, D.C. 20008. Tel. (202) 667-0441. Annual 30-page catalogue costs $1.*

There are books on the art of textiles and also some textiles themselves, including scarves, ties, T-shirts, and sweatshirts.

WINTERTHUR MUSEUM, *Winterthur, Del. 19735. Tel. (302) 656-8591. The 24- to 32-page fall catalogue on gifts and spring catalogue on gardens cost $1 each.*

The gifts are reproductions of the best of early American decorative art—dinnerware, Paul Revere tankards, brass sconces and candlesticks, blue-and-white porcelain, jewelry, textiles, and flatware. The garden catalogue includes plants grafted from the splendid specimens at Winterthur. Payment by check, money order, American Express, Visa, Mastercard, Diners Club, or Carte Blanche. Shipment by Postal Service or United Parcel. Refund or credit for purchases returned within 30 days.